IMPOSSIBLE EXODUS

Stanford Studies in Middle Eastern and Islamic Societies and Cultures

IMPOSSIBLE EXODUS

Iraqi Jews in Israel

ORIT BASHKIN

STANFORD UNIVERSITY PRESS
STANFORD, CALIFORNIA

Stanford University Press
Stanford, California

©2017 by the Board of Trustees of the Leland Stanford Junior University.
All rights reserved.

No part of this book may be reproduced or transmitted in any form or by any means, electronic or mechanical, including photocopying and recording, or in any information storage or retrieval system without the prior written permission of Stanford University Press.

Printed in the United States of America on acid-free, archival-quality paper

Library of Congress Cataloging-in-Publication Data

Names: Bashkin, Orit, author.

Title: Impossible exodus : Iraqi Jews in Israel / Orit Bashkin.
Description: Stanford, California : Stanford University Press, 2017. | Series: Stanford studies in Middle Eastern and Islamic societies and cultures | Includes bibliographical references and index.
Identifiers: LCCN 2017011528 (print) | LCCN 2017013518 (ebook) | ISBN 9781503602816 (e-book) | ISBN 9780804795852 (cloth : alk. paper) | ISBN 9781503602656 (pbk. : alk. paper)
Subjects: LCSH: Jews, Iraqi--Israel--Social conditions--20th century. | Jews, Iraqi--Civil rights--Israel--History--20th century. | Jews, Iraqi--Israel--Government relations--History--20th century. | Immigrants--Cultural assimilation--Israel--History--20th century. | Israel--History--1948-1967.
Classification: LCC DS113.8.I72 (ebook) | LCC DS113.8.I72 B37 2017 (print) | DDC 304.8/56940567--dc23
LC record available at https://lccn.loc.gov/2017011528

Cover design: Angela Moody
Cover photo: Ovadia Ezra, and his brother, late 1960s, Kibbutz Sdeh Nahum
Typeset by Bruce Lundquist in 10/14 Minion Pro

TABLE OF CONTENTS

	Acknowledgments	vii
	Prologue: Suham–Drora–Sparrow	1
	Introduction: The Death of an Arab Jew	3
1.	Human Material	21
2.	Children of Iraq, Children of Israel	67
3.	The Only Democracy in the Middle East	103
4.	Elements of Resistance	151
5.	Israeli Babylonians	181
	Conclusion: The Death of Arab Jewishness	221
	Appendix: Main Transit Camps	231
	List of Abbreviations	233
	Notes	235
	Bibliography	281
	Index	291

ACKNOWLEDGMENTS

I am indebted to the many friends and colleagues who helped me, guided me, and stood by me, while I was writing this book. I am very privileged that Joel Beinin read this work. I have been influenced by his scholarship on Israel and Palestine. His insights, incredibly helpful comments on the manuscript, and advice significantly shaped the text. I am particularly proud, and thankful, that two brilliant scholars, Roger Owen and Abbas Shiblak, read the text. I have admired them both for many years. I am extremely proud to be publishing this work in the series edited by Kate Wahl. Not only because of the excellence of the series, which by now has shaped Middle Eastern Studies in the United States, but also because of Kate's careful attention to the manuscript and her invaluable guidance. She is the best editor one could hope for. I am thankful to Shira Robinson's kindness and collegiality; Shira was willing to share, and allowed me to quote from, a very important paper she wrote while she was studying for her doctorate at Stanford University; the paper deals with Iraqi-Jewish teachers in Arab schools in Israel, and its data and bold conclusions were important to Chapter 5 of this book.

I started working on this project during a sabbatical year I spent at the Herbert D. Katz Center for Advanced Judaic studies at the University of Pennsylvania. I thank the director of the center, David Ruderman, for his support and encouragement. I was extremely fortunate to work with a brilliant group of scholars in the center, especially the scholars of Middle East Jewry, Vered Madar, Martin Jacobs, Miriam Frenkel, and Julia Phillips Cohen, and especially, my two champions, Chaim Noy and Eitan Bar-Yosef. Etty Hileli facilitated my research at the center, and also spent many hours with me talking about the experiences of her Algerian father in Israel of the 1950s and 1960s. The historians at Penn were likewise extremely supportive, especially Heather Sharkey, Vanessa Ogle, and my dear Eve Troutt Powell.

I thank the librarians and the staff at the libraries and archives I worked at: the Central Zionist Archive, Israel State Archives (Ginzach ha-Medina),

JDC (American Jewish Joint Distribution Committee archive), Lavon Institute, Metzudat Ze'ev, Yad Ya'ari, and Yad Tabenkin. I thank the Central Zionist Archives for allowing me to use images taken from their archives in this book. I also thank Michael Dunn and Jacob Pascal of the *Middle East Journal* which published my paper on elements of spatial resistance for the comments readers of the journal provided for this article from which small sections in Chapter 4 are drawn. Finally I wish to express my gratitude to Daniel McNaughton, who meticulously read the manuscript, to the brilliant Andrew Frisardi of Stanford University Press, and to the ever so patient Emily Smith.

Complicating my view of Mizrahi history in Israel were the many conversations I held with Israeli writers, historians, and intellectuals: Amos Noy, Zvi Ben-Dor Benite, Orly Noy, Gadi Algazi, Haya Bambaji-Sasportas, Menashe Anzi, and Almog Behar. I am also deeply indebted to Lev Luis Grinberg, who helped me understand a maze called the Histadrut. Dan Diner helpfully suggested I discuss the concept of "social engineering" in my book. Israel Gershoni, my friend and mentor, was gracious enough to share with me his recollections on his youth in a kibbutz in the 1950s and 1960s. I also wish to express my gratitude to friends and colleagues who invited me to lectures, workshops, roundtables, and conferences to discuss my work on this book: Amal Ghazzal, Elliott Colla, Peter Wien, Kimberly Katz, Zainab Saleh, Jens Hanssen, Max Weiss, Ussama Makdisi, Emily Gottreich, Asad Ahmed, Christine Philliou, Adam Sabra, Sherene Seikaly, Rami Ginat, Lior Sternfeld, Harith Al-Qarawee, Shachar Pinsker, and Andreas Wiese. I discussed some of this book's themes in a conference dedicated to the works of Sami Michael at Northwestern University during the fall of 2015, where I got to meet Michael, one of the heroes of this book (and a personal hero of mine), and to hear Nancy Berg, Ktzia Alon, and Ella Shohat on issues related to my project. These conversations were very insightful. Keith Watenpaugh inspired me to work on the history of children. I hope he likes Chapter 2.

I thank my amazing friends at the University of Chicago, Kay Heikkinen, Franklin Lewis, Fred Donner, Persis Berlekamp, Hakan Karateke, Lucy Pick, Hala Abdel Mobdy, Martha Roth, James Chandler, Na'ama Rokem, Noha Aboulmagd Forster, McGuire Gibson, Ghenwa Hayek, Tahera Qutbuddin, and Holly Shissler. Liran Yadgar, my teaching assistant in my classes on Israeli history, kindly shared with me his perceptions on Iraqi and Egyptian history in Israel.

I am grateful to Uri Horesh, with whom I traveled to the museum in Kafar Qassem where we discovered an important document that ended up in Chapter 4, and who is always a model of courage and dedication. My friend Youval Rotman, and his remarkable mother, Drora (Suham) Rotman (from Beit Shakarchi), provided me with indispensable insights. Drora spoke to me on her experiences as an Iraqi child at the transit camp of David, explaining, with great patience, the educational, dietary, and psychological aspects of being a transit-camp child. A poem about Baghdad that she wrote was truly inspirational; she also wrote the text which became the prologue to this book. Drora's brother, Ovad, an Iraqi Black Panther, clarified some issues relating to Iraqi resistance, and Kobi Auslander was helpful by simply being there in Israel.

Finally, I thank my wonderful parents, Yossi and Rachel Bashkin, for their help, support, and encouragement. Our own family owes a great deal to labor Zionism and its settlement movement during the 1930s and 1940s. Golda Meir, whom I critique in this book, literally saved my grandfather's life. And yet, despite my deep criticisms, my parents always stood by me.

This book is dedicated to the two Iraqi Jews I love most in this world, Ovadia Ezra and Sasson Somekh. Ironically, I did not to get to see them much while finishing the manuscript, but they were constantly on my mind. Ovadia's mother was born in Basra. She came with her children to Israel in 1950 and was settled in a transit camp. Her husband who previously worked in the airport could not find occupation in Israel and died a few years later; she sent three of her children to kibbutzim; while she, and her other children, including Ovadia, survived in poverty, living on a diet where meat was a rarity. Like many Mizrahim, Ovadia was sent to a vocational school. He later lived in a kibbutz, and then moved to Tel Aviv where he completed his Ph.D. in philosophy at Tel Aviv University (while working as a porter at the airport to finance his study), becoming one of the most original thinkers in Israeli philosophy, and writing about rights, affirmative action, and political philosophy. He was, and still is, a committed leftist, having served three times in Israeli military jails for refusing to serve in the Lebanon and the occupied West Bank. Sasson Somekh was my professor of Arabic literature. We often discussed Iraqi and Arabic literature and reflected on his youth in Baghdad, his friendship with Nagib Mahfuz, and his activities in the literary and academic field. During the early stages of this research, I learned another, more silenced history, of Sasson's youth in Israel: his arrival from Baghdad at a transit camp in Ra'anana, where his family resided in a shack by a public bathroom, his parents' fall from grace, his father's death a few years after migration, his mother's attempts to rebuild a modest life in Israel, his struggles to master Hebrew better than the the native Israelis, the *sabras*, (which he did), and his activities in the cultural venues of the communist party. I have known Ovadia and Sasson since I was twenty years old. I hope this book does justice to their struggles and brilliance, their Iraqi Jewish community, and the lessons they have taught me over the years.

IMPOSSIBLE EXODUS

PROLOGUE
Suham–Drora–Sparrow

AUTUMN 1951: she was eight years old when she heard her name for the first time, her new name, her Hebrew name.

It was the year of the mass migration from Iraq to Israel, and the family moved from a newcomers' camp to a permanent settlement: a transit camp. The camp stretched between Mount Carmel to the east, the Carmel shore to the west, and the cemetery to the south—the military cemetery, where children used to go and watch the funerary rites of soldiers.

The transit camp's name was Camp David, but everybody called it "Winds Camp" because of the strong winds that blew there in the winter. In their first winter the wind blew off all the tents they were living in, exposing them and their belongings to the heavy rains. Later they would get permanent housing: canvas and wooden shacks, clustered together haphazardly all around the camp's grounds.

In her first week of school, the school nurse asked for a girl's name: *Suham*? What does that mean? Is it some sort of a bird? We will call you, then, *Drora* ("sparrow" in Hebrew, and it also means "freedom"). Thus blessed with the sweet and satisfying smile of the school nurse, the girl was reborn. Her parents were not asked for their view of the matter.

It was a beautiful autumn day, cloudy and chilly. She felt the raindrops in the air pleasantly clinging to her cheeks. She inhaled the humid air. It filled her lungs and washed her entire body with a special freshness that will never return. A soft and white fog embraced the nurse and the group of children standing around her in the schoolyard, and distanced them from the searing sight of naked shacks, the ever-blazing sun, and the emptiness that filled the bare spaces between everything.

The nurse was tall and beautiful. She wore a tight blue gown and a snowy starched cap that crowned her head, with a thick bulb of her black hair tightened on top. Amid the children of the transit camp with their baggy gray cloths, amid the wooden shacks used as classrooms and the trodden faded soil, the nurse was the most colorful and spectacular thing the girl saw in those days.

The old name that was tossed away as a useless object reemerged fifty years later, when she opened her son's ID card, looking under "mother's name." A little girl in an old childhood photo instantly surfaced, staring at her with endless sadness. And she was back at the moment her name was lost, starting all over again.

Drora Rotman, 30 October 2012
translated by Orit Bashkin and Youval Rotman

INTRODUCTION
The Death of an Arab Jew

IN 1958, 'Ezra Susu, a sixty-five-year-old disabled goldsmith and father of a disabled child, went into one of the many welfare bureaus in Israel. He drank sodium acid from a bottle, collapsed, and died on his way to the hospital. In the Knesset discussions that followed his death, the deputy welfare minister tried very hard to argue that 'Ezra did not commit suicide: "One should not assume that there is any connection between his being in the welfare bureau at that day and his drinking sodium acid. I very much doubt if he wanted to kill himself." Knesset members learned more details about this man from the deputy minister: he was generally depressed and his wife was blind, but his two daughters and his son were married and his family had recently moved to a nicer neighborhood. In fact, 'Ezra was happy that day; he had come to pay a debt in the welfare bureau and was pleasantly surprised to discover that the debt was only three and a half Israeli liras, and not more, as he had originally thought. He took a sip from the bottle, which, so he thought, contained something to drink; unfortunately, he paid with his life for his mistake.[1] It is very doubtful that a goldsmith would have mistaken acid for water. Thus to understand 'Ezra's story, we need to read beyond the depictions of the welfare bureau and think about why 'Ezra might have been unhappy; whether his ethnicity had anything to do with his situation; and most importantly, why the state was so insistent in arguing that he was truly happy in the land to which he had immigrated.

This book tells the story of the many Jews who, like 'Ezra, immigrated to Israel from Middle Eastern countries, as the state doubled its population in less than a decade after its establishment in 1948. Among these were Iraqi Jews; during the years 1950–51, 123,000 Iraqi Jews made their way to Israel; over the next decade they became Israeli citizens and eventually adopted Hebrew as their spoken and written language.[2] These Jews, however, were not native sons returning to their homeland, but rather immigrants arriving at a new location, where they encountered prejudice and discrimination. The Iraqi-Jewish experience in Israel challenges the notion that Israel served as a melting pot for various global Jewish communities. The adoption of Israeli citizenship was a painful, violent, and traumatic transformation, and the rupture between Iraqi Jews and their Iraqi and Arab cultures did not occur overnight. In Israel, Iraqi Jews had to negotiate their most basic needs with a state, whose officials were unable, and often unwilling, to attend to their wishes and understand their pains and sufferings. In this process of becoming Israelis, however, Iraqi Jews resisted many state politics in both their public activities and in their everyday actions. This book, then, looks at the Iraqi migration to Israel to shed light on the dual processes of dehumanization and rehumanization, the latter being the victories in the daily and public battles to maintain human dignity the Iraqis managed to win.

Migration was an important part of the leading ideology of the Israeli state, Zionism. Created in the late nineteenth century, this European movement called for the establishment of a Jewish homeland in Palestine. The Zionist concept that Iraqi Jews had to grapple with most was that of Exile. During the Ottoman period (which ended in 1917) and under the British mandate (which ended in 1948), Zionist activists tried to increase Jewish migration to Palestine and negotiated extensively with the British as well as other world powers concerning the quotas of Jews who were allowed to settle the area, in an attempt to establish a Jewish majority in the land. The act of migration itself came to acquire ideological, almost mystical, elements. In Zionism, "exile" signified a space of Jewish humiliation, weakness, and loss of identity. In the premodern era diasporic Jews had been wanderers dependent on the grace of kings and aristocrats, and in the modern era of emancipation their newfound status as citizens further encouraged anti-Semitism on the part of non-Jews, who resented their entry into the labor market and public life. Therefore, the Jewish inability to be identified, and to identify, with one national space, could only change in the Jewish homeland in Israel. There, the new Jew would become everything the Jew in exile was not: confident, brave, strong, independent, and most importantly, connected to the land. Thus migration to Palestine was marked by the word

Aliyah, literally, "ascent," but also a term with the essential connotation of the Jewish pilgrimage to the Temple in Jerusalem (*'aliyah la-regel*).[3]

This ideal of Aliyah contrasted sharply with the realities in Mandatory Palestine and Israel. As Aziza Khazzoom has shown, each wave of Jewish migrants to Palestine and Israel othered and orientalized the next generation of migrants.[4] However, the Jews who had lived in Palestine before 1948 (the *yishuv*), namely the members of the old Sephardic community and especially European Zionists, shared certain formative experiences. The insightful scholarship of Michelle Campos and Abigail Jacobson has underlined the differences between the Ashkenazi and Sephardi communities in Ottoman and Mandatory Palestine.[5] However, for both communities, the years of the national Palestinian revolt (1936–39), the years of the Holocaust, in which many Ashkenazi Zionists lost their entire families in Europe, and during which many Jews denied entry to Palestine by the British perished in Europe, and the 1948 War, in which one percent of the Jewish population in Mandatory Palestine was killed, were crucial in shaping their collective mentality and their ideological commitments. The members of the *yishuv* thus looked differently at the new waves of migrants who arrived in the state of Israel after 1948, who included Holocaust survivors (labeled *plitim*, "refugees," in state discourse), Jews from Romania and Bulgaria, and Jews from Middle Eastern countries. Despite the property taken from the Palestinian population during the 1948 War, support from international Jewish organizations, and financial compensation from Germany, the state of Israel, which demanded that each and every Jew make his or her way to the Jewish homeland, did not have sufficient financial resources to absorb such masses of people and provide them with housing, employment, instruction in Hebrew, and basic social services. Although many members of the *yishuv* helped the newcomers in important ways (often by volunteering), the former also felt superior to the latter, who, the former felt, did not come to Israel out of ideological commitment, as had the previous Zionist migrants, but rather out of necessity.[6]

While the idea of migration has specific meanings in Zionist history, mass migrations are an important part of global modern history, especially as we seek to understand the dual process of movement of people and capital, alongside the fragmentations into nations, ethnicities, and distinct cultural regions.[7] In the Middle Eastern context, the movement of refugees in the post–World War I era had generated new ideas about borders, citizenship, and minority rights.[8] The view of refugees and migrants as changing the landscape of the

Middle East is also true in the period after World War II. The displacement of the native Palestinian population during the creation of the State of Israel in 1948 changed the landscape of Syria, Jordan, Lebanon, and Gaza under Egyptian control, states that faced the mass arrival of Palestinian refugees who could not return to their homeland. Concurrently, the waves of newcomers to Israel, of Jewish refugees from Europe who survived the Holocaust, as well as of Jewish Middle Eastern migrants, created new realities in Israel. These migration waves birthed a new Israel; they inspired new demographic discourses, formed a new ethnic labor class, and generated new racial politics in cities and towns.[9]

Interest in Middle Eastern communities and the potential of new settlers arose in Zionist circles especially after the Holocaust. After the establishment of the state, the state elites genuinely feared that Jews in the Muslim world would be persecuted because of their Jewish identity and their presumed affiliation with Israel. More crucially, the state needed migrants to populate territories conquered in 1948, and required manpower to enlist in its military and new industries. Concurrently, however, state elites knew that resources were scant and many officials and bureaucrats succumbed to utter panic when faced with these migration waves. Moreover, as with other migrants, refugees, and immigrant communities across the globe, state officials and members of the *yishuv* were concerned about the newcomers' foreignness and questioned their ability to assimilate.[10] The Arab culture of Iraqi Jews, as well as that of Jews from other Middle Eastern countries, was perceived as primitive and degenerate. In addition, it was racialized: these Jews were sometimes called *kushim*, *shhorim*, and *schwartzes* (derogatory terms meaning "black") to signify their foreign and non-European racial identity.[11]

Iraqi Jews, then, arrived to a state whose elites had very conflicting notions about migration and very poor means to absorb them. Some Iraqi Jews had come to Israel in small numbers prior to the establishment of the state in 1948. Some came out for religious reasons and others with ideological motivations. The establishment of the State of Israel and the escalation of the Arab-Israeli conflict considerably worsened the position of Jews in Iraq. After 1948, the State of Israel increased the activities of Zionist emissaries and the local Zionist underground in Iraq in order to convince more Jews to leave. Starting in the 1950s, it also negotiated with the Iraqi government about the fate of Iraqi Jews, whose property, mobility, and dwelling place suddenly became a part of the Arab-Israeli conflict. Many of the matters relating to Iraqi-Jewish life were decided in clandestine negotiations between the Iraqi and the Israeli governments, negotiations that Iraqi Jews had no control over. Within Iraq, right-wing nationalists argued that the pro-Palestinian Iraqi position ought to be translated into a policy of treating Jewish citizens as Israel had treated the Palestinians. The community was trapped, and it left.

In Israel, Iraqi Jews, who had hoped for a better life away from persecution, found themselves struggling with segregation and poverty in a landscape shaped by decisions over which they had little control.[12] In their first years in Israel, Iraqi Jews, as well as other migrants from Arab countries, lived like refugees: they had no property; they could not find work, feed their children and themselves, or get access to water without the support of the Israeli state; and they resided in shacks and tents. The state elites, however, assumed that the community's pains were the normal, necessary course of migration. Nationwide considerations regarding settlement and demography guided these elites, rather than the Iraqis' interests and desires. This made the newcomers particularly vulnerable, as an urban and educated community was suddenly voiceless and poor. Although Ashkenazi soldiers, doctors, nurses, teachers, social workers, and officials protested the horrid conditions in which the newcomers lived, Iraqi Jews felt disrespected, humiliated, and abused. Nonetheless, their alienation from Israeli society has gradually shifted into a unique form of Israeli patriotism, which enable Iraqis to deal with being outcasts and strangers in their new homeland.[13]

The living conditions of the Israeli Iraqis in the 1950s were similar to those of the Palestinian community; Iraqi Jews shared much with both the Palestinian refugees and the Palestinians who became Israeli citizens, who now lived under a strict military regime that strongly inhibited their civil rights, as Shira Robinson showed in an important recent book.[14] The Palestinian refugees and the Iraqi Jews in Israel suffered displacement and dealt with horrendous poverty and loss of social status. In Israel, both Iraqi Jews and Palestinians were third-class citizens: the Palestinians' civil rights were crushed by a military regime, and Iraqi Jews suffered from the state's neglect and from police brutality. This is not to say, however, that these populations were the same. Whereas the Palestinian refugees wanted to return to their land, and were denied citizenship rights in their new countries of residence, Israel did grant citizenship to the Jewish migrants. In public discourse, they were Jews returning to their homeland after long years in exile, not refugees yearning to return home. The state's perception of the Iraqi Jews as returnees rather than refugees created a different situation from that of the Palestinian refugees in Arab states: while many Arab states washed their hands of the Palestinian refugees and called for international bodies to take care of them, Israel insisted on absorbing them by relying on the state's poor economic resources, American support, global Jewish donations, and later reparations from Germany.

The most apt term for how the state interacted with the Iraqi-Jewish community is *social engineering*. State elites believed that all immigrants, especially Middle Eastern Jews, needed to become Hebrew speaking, socialist Zionists. The existence of poor communities of Jewish migrants in Israel gave the state's elites the power to decide where these migrants would be settled, what jobs they might and might not hold, their degree of education, and the level of their salaries. In fact, many of the people in charge of the management of the newcomers' lives would later on assume the highest leadership positions in Israel. These include the man who initiated the foundation of the transit camps to settle the migrants, Levy Eshkol; the charismatic young officer working in the transit camps during difficult winters, Yitzhak Rabin; and especially the diva of labor Zionism, Golda Meir, who was the minister of labor during the 1950s. Within this framework, the name *Hasbara* (literally "explaining"), a term that is now synonymous with Israel's diplomatic efforts abroad to explain Israel's cause and buttress its positive image, was also used internally. It marked the effort to explain to the newcomers themselves the logics behind, and the great benefits embodied in, the state politics which governed their lives. Despite the great pretensions of the social engineers, however, their project was run poorly, because the state had very limited economic resources. Moreover, the Israeli state during the 1950s was a bureaucratic maze. Many Zionist institutions created under Ottoman and British rule continued functioning while the state created its own apparatus. Thus different institutions carried out the same tasks and functions, and many state-within-a-state mechanisms existed. Implementations of official state policies were thus partial and often unsuccessful. The newcomers found this bureaucracy impossible to negotiate, but on the other hand, certain loopholes allowed them to challenge state decisions.

During the 1950s, Iraqi Jews, as well as other Middle Eastern Jews and European migrants, were settled in transit camps, known as Ma'abarot (singular: Ma'abara). In 1951, close to eighty thousand Iraqi Jews resided in a hundred transit camps.[15] American Jews who visited these camps depicted them as "shanty towns," "slums," or "miserable collections of tin, wood and canvas huts."[16] The term *ma'abara* means a place of transition, and it is translated throughout the book as a "transit camp." Indeed, these camps were originally perceived as sites in which Jewish migrants would stay for a brief period of time. Tragically, however, many Jews remained in these camps for much longer periods (between one to seven years). Initially, residents lived in tents which were later replaced by huts and shacks. The transit camps suffered from poor sanitary and hygiene conditions, poverty, and neglect. They were the first site Iraqi Jews encountered and where they saw state officials and met other European and Middle Eastern Jews. While Iraqi Jews hated these camps, and longed to return to their homes in Iraq, for the Israeli state and society, the Iraqi-Jewish identity became closely connected to their residence in the transit camps. The important challenge for all Iraqi Jews at that time had to with acquiring the social mobility that would allow them to leave the transit camps.

The transit camps were liminal ethnic spaces which, in many ways, challenged the very essence of the nation-state. The Israeli elites did not see, and did not want to see, Iraqi Jews, as well as other residents of these camps in their midst. Concurrently, however, the blame for the hunger, disorder, and malaise typical of the lives of Iraqi Jews in these camps was not placed on the state's policies, but rather these problems were seen as a reflection of the primitive Iraqi culture of the migrants. In the mainstream media, the image of the transit camps was that of an exilic, exotic, and un-Israeli space, where people refused to assimilate and preferred living in poverty rather than contributing to the Israeli economy. The transit camps, however, were also spaces that preserved the cherished memories of Iraq and the Arab culture of its people.[17] Iraqi Jews writing today about their experiences in the transit camps highlight, not only the trauma of migration and dislocation, but also the nostalgia for simpler times, typified by modesty, communal solidarity, and friendship.[18] This book challenges both the nostalgic image of the transit camps and the state's attempts to pathologize and stereotype their residents, and looks at everyday lives in these camps.

Historian Thomas C. Holt underlined the significance of everyday experiences of black men and women and their recollections of their relations to their families, neighbors, and friends. Holt demonstrated how these silenced histories of everyday acts of petty exclusions were connected to historical processes and structures, which sustained racism on a much larger scale.[19] Previous scholarship on migration to Israel has tended to focus exclusively on the state itself and its actions toward, and representations of, Middle Eastern Jews;

it focused less on individuals. During the 1950s and the 1960s, Israeli sociologists, anthropologists, and historians celebrated the mass migration to Israel as a great achievement of the Israeli melting pot policy. In the State of Israel, so it was argued, occurred a "merger of exiles," in which different Jewish cultures and identities were merged into the Israeli national culture.[20] In the 1980s and 1990s, scholars challenged these perspectives, pointing out that the marginalization of Middle Eastern Jews enabled the state to benefit from an underprivileged and cheap labor force whose lower social status was determined by its ethnicity. During the 1990s and 2000s, post-Zionist scholarship in the Israeli academy, a scholarship that was critical of both Zionist ideology and its implementation, have studied the state's mechanisms of discrimination in different fields: education (notably, the placement of Middle Eastern children in vocational schools) and the state's settlement policies (notably, the settlement of Middle Eastern Jewish families in border regions), as well as the state's labor, land, and housing policies. Pointing to the state's violence embodied in the melting pot ideology, scholars bemoaned the erasure of the Arab, Turkish, Persian, and Eastern cultures of the Jewish migrants. These scholars have also highlighted the potential of the hybrid and hyphenated identities of Middle Eastern Jews to challenge the state's relationships with its Arab neighbors and Palestinian citizens and subjects.[21]

As much of the scholarship on ethnic relations in Israel has directed its attention to the state, the voice of the individual (especially that of women and children), as well as his or her daily experiences, were often lost. While it is important to analyze politics and major bureaucratic institutions, this book examines how Iraqi Jews themselves dealt with the traumas of migration and discrimination: how family life took shape when families lived in crowded tents and wooden shacks; how Iraqi men attempted to support their families in an unfair labor market; and how Iraqi women raised children in the most horrendous conditions, when just procuring a necessity as basic as drinking water required a long journey outside the transit camp. Children were among the victims of these conditions. They went to bad elementary schools; some were used as extremely cheap workers; still others had a diet that was far from nutritious, one that was based on a food stamps regime in which dairy and meat products were quite rare under severe austerity measures. This book is inspired by the important studies of Esther Meir-Glitzenstein, Deborah S. Bernstein, and Orit Rozin on this topic, while it focuses on the political meanings of everyday race relations, survival, and mobility in these contexts.[22]

The focus on the Iraqis themselves is linked to two important themes in Israeli history, resistance and agency.[23] Bryan Roby's recent study uncovered dozens of cases in which newcomers from Middle Eastern countries protested and rejected state politics from 1949 to 1967. Roby has labeled this a struggle for civil rights and has drawn intriguing parallels between this struggle and the African-American civil rights movement, which happened at the same time.[24] Iraqi Jews were part of this culture of resistance and organized dozens of protests. They participated in strikes and held meetings in cities and demonstrated in the camps where they lived.[25] Resistance, moreover, came in many manners and forms. In my opinion, Iraqi mothers in transit camps who managed to get their children out of the cycle of poverty by working several jobs; teachers who organized classes and schools, without state permission; and Iraqi children who critiqued the lifestyle of the kibbutzim that hosted them, were no less heroic than those of the more organized groups of the Israeli Black Panthers in the 1970s. Perhaps they were even more so. And I hope my book will do justice to their heroism and their struggles.

Living in Israel and fighting discrimination there changed the Iraqi-Jewish community's identity. As they became part of Israeli society, Iraqi Jews were transformed from being Iraqi citizens into Mizrahi (Hebrew for "Eastern") Jews and Iraqi Israelis. In Iraq, the Jewish intelligentsia had self-identified as Eastern (in Arabic: *sharqi*) Jews. This Eastern identity signified many things: beyond a geographical location, it suggested that the majority of the state's citizens were Arabs and Muslims; that the Iraqi-Arab culture of the state shared common elements (from food to music to cinema) with other Muslim and Arab countries, such as Iran, India, Turkey, and Egypt; and that, like many other countries in the East, Iraq was struggling with colonialism, imperialism, and Western representations of the Orient. As Ella Shohat has shown, in Israel being an Eastern Jew, or in Hebrew a Mizrahi Jew (plural: *Mizrahim*), meant something completely different. It was an identity juxtaposed with the European and Ashkenazi identity of the state's founders.[26] Being a Jew whose culture was Arab, Turkish, Iranian, or Indian was perceived as problematic by the state's Jewish and European elites, who considered themselves the representatives of European civilization in the East, and who identified Arab culture with the debased culture of its Palestinian and Arab enemies. For their part, Iraqi Jews in Israel did not cast off their Mizrahi heritage, referring to themselves as Mizrahim and *sharqiyyun*. They claimed that they were discriminated against because they came from Eastern countries, and they felt that they had much in common with their fellow Middle Eastern Jewish immigrants to Israel.

Iraqi Jews used the term *sectarianism* (Arabic: *ta'ifiyya*; Hebrew: *'adatiyut*) to describe how the state enforced a separation between Mizrahi and Ashkenazi Jews. Although the term was used in Iraq to describe religious differences between Sunnis, Shi'is, Jews, and Christians, Iraqi Jews used it to mark the difference in Israel between different ethnic groups of Jews. They came from a sectarian state (Iraq) that had engaged in "divide and rule" politics between various religious and ethnic communities, and they recognized the same politics in their new state with respect to Jewish ethnicities. Communist Iraqi Jews also evoked the term to depict the Israeli division between Jews, Muslims, and Christians, and between Arabic-speaking Jews and Arabic-speaking Christians and Muslims. Indeed, while the term sectarianism is often reserved for Lebanon, Iraq, and Syria, it could also be used productively to depict Israel of the 1950s and early 1960s, a place where one's housing, political affiliations, and employment were often determined by one's ethnic and religious identity. To paraphrase historian Ussama Makdisi's observations about Lebanon, Arab, Mizrahi and Eastern identities in Israel were politicized as part of an obvious struggle for resources in the context of mass migration, yet naturalized as reflecting age-old religious and cultural feuds between East and West.[27] Moreover, as Max Weiss has observed with respect to Lebanon, these politics of difference in Israel were modified into durable national institutions, inextricably bound up with the complex process of state formation.[28]

Despite the significance of their Mizrahi Israeli identity, Jews who came to Israel from Iraq also considered themselves Iraqis, even in the Jewish state. In Iraq, calling oneself an Iraqi was an act of patriotism, bespeaking identification with Iraq as a homeland rather than with the East in its entirety. In Israel, Iraq became a symbolic locus of nostalgia. Iraq was connected to memories of wealth, social capital, childhood, and warmth. In a way, it became a lost paradise to which many yearned to return. Indeed, the distinctions between the various kinds of Mizrahim (who were as diverse as the differences between rabbis from Bukhara and communist Jewish atheists from Cairo), and the linguistic differences between Mizrahi communities (whose members spoke Persian, Turkish, Arabic, Kurdish, Ladino, Aramaic, and Hebrew), became especially salient in the Israel of the 1950s, when Iraqi Jews encountered other Middle Eastern communities. Iraqi Jews sometimes collaborated with such groups, but at other times highlighted their specific Iraqi culture. Their Arabic was different from the Arabic spoken by North African Jews; they could not initially communicate with Jews from Turkey and Iran; and they were highly critical of the Palestinian-Sephardi elites who had been living in the country since before 1948. Furthermore, the state itself and its mainstream media engaged in taxonomies, which distinguished between different kinds of Mizrahi Jews.[29]

There are also noticeable differences between various Mizrahi communities with respect to the process of leaving one's birthplace. While Yemenite Jews came to Israel after long and deadly journeys, and prolonged stays in transit camps in Yemen, Iraqi Jews arrived in Israel after a short flight. In the Iraqi case, the Israeli state could not select the candidates for migration, and entire families came, including the sick and the elderly. In the case of North African Jews, however, a selection process that prevented the sick and needy from leaving was put into place, and medical aid was already provided to potential newcomers in Morocco. Jewish newcomers from North Africa in the 1960s were sent directly to border regions rather than transit camps in central Israel. More broadly, just as scholars of Jewish communities in the Middle East have moved beyond such categories as "the Jews of Islam," or "Oriental Jews," when discussing the multiplicity of categories and historical experiences related to Middle Eastern Jewish identities, it is vital to break the more general category of "Mizrahim," in order to explore the histories and identities of specific Middle Eastern countries in Israel.[30]

Esther Meir's fascinating study of Iraqi-Jewish history in Israel has done much to underscore the uniquely Iraqi features of this community. Meir's insightful study, the first to focus on the history of Iraqi Israelis, uncovered Iraqi-Jewish attempts both to engage in and to challenge Israeli politics. Meir examined sites inhabited by Iraqi-Jewish migrants, especially the transit camps, the kibbutzim, and new Iraqi urban spaces (such as the cities of Beersheba, Ramat Gan, and Or Yehuda). Indeed, as she illustrates, the efforts of Iraqi men and women to support their families had everything to do with their Iraqi background.[31] Iraqi Jews came from a sociopolitical system where corruption was prevalent; where Jews were barred from universities after 1948; where social mobility was closely linked one's religion and place of birth; and where sectarianism was a determining factor in the class system. That said, for most of their lives—especially before 1948—Iraqi Jews could choose where they lived and worked, and they operated within a society that had witnessed great upward mobility during the interwar period, when Iraqi Jews moved to better suburbs in Baghdad and used their education to progress up the socioeconomic ladder.[32] This experience contrasted sharply with what they found in Israel, where the state's elites believed they knew better than the citizens themselves where people should settle and what they should do for a living. In this sense, the Iraqi Jews were far more liberal than the state's elites, who purported to educate them in the ways of freedom and democracy and to liberate them from what they assumed to be the primitive tradition of their Iraqi homeland. In their petitions, practices, and protests, Iraqi Jews offered one of the first critiques of the politics of the Israeli state.

Iraqi-Jewish communities were one of the most Arabized groups in the Middle East; members of the community spoke Arabic and the Jewish graduates of high schools and universities were well versed in the Arabic language and Arab culture. The first generation of Iraqi migrants in Israel continued speaking in Arabic, in defiance of state ideology. Motivated by its melting pot ideology, the state promoted Hebrew as the national language, and the other languages spoken by Jews, such as Russian, German, Yiddish, Ladino, and especially Arabic, were seen as belonging to the exilic realm. Arabic was particularly threatening, since it was the language of the exiled Palestinian population, the language of Christian and Muslim citizens of the Jewish state, and the language of the Arab states with which Israel was at war. Despite the fact that Arabic was officially a state language, many of the Arabic place names in the new state were replaced with their Hebrew equivalents, in order to create an ancient geography that would erase the Palestinian past and at the same time link the Jews to their birthplace. Mizrahi Jews in particular were encouraged to abandon their Arabic mother tongue. After the establishment of the state, a significant push was made to teach Hebrew to immigrants. Consistent with this effort, state officials had to change their European surnames to Hebrew surnames, and public performances in Yiddish were outlawed. Speaking, reading, and especially writing in one's mother tongue thus acquired subversive and unpatriotic meanings in the new state.[33]

Recent scholarship on Zionist language politics, however, paints a more complex picture, arguing that Hebrew monolingualism among Israel's Jewish population was more fantasy than reality under the mandate, in the first decades of the state's existence, and even later on. Lital Levy has demonstrated how Arabic has deeply affected modern Hebrew literature;[34] Liora Halperin has accentuated the fact that Mandatory Palestine was a multilingual society in which Hebrew, Arabic, English, Yiddish, Ladino, French, German, and Russian were spoken and read;[35] and Na'ama Rokem and Amir Eshel have pointed out the existence of German–Hebrew bilingualism in Hebrew literature.[36] These scholars have underscored how the languages of the diasporic past never disappeared in Israel; they do not speak of the "triumph" of Hebrew, but rather of Hebrew's relations to the other languages that are spoken and written in Israel. The persistence of bilingualism in Israel was certainly true in the case of the Iraqi Jews.

During the 1950s, Arabic was alive and well as a language spoken by the Jewish populations of Israel. The fact that many Iraqi Jews lived together in isolated transit camps and villages did much to preserve the Iraqi dialect.[37] Many Israeli accounts from this period complain that Arabic was spoken in cafés in transit camps and in cities where Jews from Arab lands resided, and that Jews still continued to listen to music played on Egyptian and Lebanese radio stations rather than to Israeli music. Furthermore, despite the state ideology that privileged Hebrew, the state communicated with Iraqi Jews in Arabic. Because all political parties wanted to reach out to the newcomers, political leaflets circulating in the transit camps were written in Arabic for the Iraqi and other Mizrahi Jews, and meetings of various political parties in the transit camps were held in Arabic. Within this multilingual context, a modest, albeit important, print market in Arabic emerged, to which Iraqi Jews were active contributors. As Reuven Snir has shown, Iraqi Jews published essays, poems, short stories, and novels in Arabic during the first decades of the state.[38]

The migrants' Arabic language and Arab culture complicated their relationships with Israel's Palestinian citizens. Connections between the Iraqi population and the Palestinian population existed in liminal spaces, such as trade between the people of the transit camps and the residents of nearby Arab villages, and in the political activities of opposition parties. In most cases, however, the struggles of the Iraqis and the Mizrahim, on the one hand, and the Palestinians, on the other, were disconnected; Iraqi Jews underlined their Jewish identity as the foundation of their patriotism, which the state elites ignored as they battled for their civil rights. They demanded rights, in other words, as Jews in the Jewish state. Moreover, both the state and Iraqi Jews used the Arab culture of Iraqi Jews for the state's needs. Iraqi Jews used their Arabic language skills as a way of gaining employment with state institutions and underscored their loyalty to Israel. They marketed their skills as individuals who knew Arab culture and Arab politics and therefore could be useful to the state's strategic interests. Iraqi Jews were able to find positions in the state's security services, its Arabic propaganda machinery, and its institutions whose purpose was to defuse the resistance of the Palestinian Israelis and ensure their acceptance of the state.

Iraqi Jews, moreover, had to learn quickly how to deal with the maze of parties and institutions in the Israeli political scene. The ruling labor Zionist party at the time was MAPAI (Mifleget Po'aley Eretz Yisra'el; the Party of the Workers of the Land of Israel). Established in 1930, MAPAI in a short time achieved dominance in the Jewish political scene of Mandatory Palestine. It ran a kibbutzim movement that was based on the party's socialist principles; controlled the labor unions and the factories through the Histadrut, the state's chief organization of trade unions; and supervised the Aliyah through a pre-state Zionist immigration organization called the Jewish Agency. It was led by David Ben Gurion, who became Israel's first prime minister. The party's ideology combined Zionism and settlement. Although Ben Gurion chose not to side with the Soviet Bloc, MAPAI's self-image, which was projected to the Israeli public, was that of a socialist and democratic party. This self-perception, however, was to a large extent belied by its major actions. Its policy toward the Palestinians, who lived under a military regime and whose land was subjected to confiscation, meant that ethnic and racial politics trumped its commitment to equality. MAPAI's foreign policy was driven less by diplomacy and took on a belligerent stance, as well as being very costly (in particular the expensive unsuccessful 1956 campaign against Egypt).[39]

MAPAI had an immense impact on Iraqi-Jewish life in Israel; the Jewish Agency governed the transit camps, the Histadrut controlled the labor market in which Iraqi Jews operated, and the public image of the migrants was shaped in the party's newspapers, *Davar* (Word) and *Ha-Dor* (The Era), which were widely read in Israel. MAPAI's leadership treated the newcomers as potential voters who should be thankful to the party for its efforts on their behalf. Many were forced to join its ranks, while others joined it willingly, believing they could make use of its institutions for the benefit of their community. They found niches for themselves working within the MAPAI's institutions, like the Histadrut, and in institutions within the transit camps themselves.

Opposition to MAPAI, whether communist, rightist, or socialist, underlined the fact that newcomers to Israel suffered from an extremely low standard of living. Partly motivated by the desire to win the votes of the newcomers, and partly by a strong sense of injustice, opposition parties in Israel were crystal clear about what their representatives had seen in the transit camps and the state's new slums. To the left of MAPAI stood MAPAM (Mifleget Po'alim Me'uhedet; the United Workers Party). Established in 1948 as a merger of several socialist parties, it combined a socialist, pro-Soviet, and internationalist group and a more nationalist and rightist faction. MAPAM was the second-largest party in the first Knesset and the third-largest in the third Knesset. By 1954, a split had emerged, as many members were dismayed at the leadership's stance on the Soviet Union. A faction called Ahdut ha-'Avoda (The Unity of Labor), identified with the more rightist group, left the party. MAPAM was a Zionist party, having its own pre-state youth movement (Ha-Shomer ha-Tza'ir; The Young Guard), its newspapers 'Al ha-Mishmar (On Guard), and its publishing houses. Led by Meir Ya'ari, the party was nonetheless more to the left than MAPAI on questions relating to Israel's relations with Arab states and to the rights of Arabs, especially the ending of the military rule of Israel's Palestinian population.[40] As this book will show, MAPAM, and its Iraqi-Jewish members, played a leading role in exposing MAPAI's mistreatment of newcomers from Arab states, although it failed to offer any alternative solution to the Iraqis' plight.

The ostracized communist party, MAKI (Miflaga Komunistit Yisra'elit, Al-Hizb al-Shuyu'i al-Isra'ili) also tried to court the Iraqis. Emerging from pre-state Jewish and Arab communist parties in 1948, the party was led by Jewish and Palestinian communists. It was loyal to the USSR, and supported the two-state solution (a position that allowed its members to sign the Israeli Declaration of Independence). During the 1950s, the party was active in defending Palestinian rights and objected to the 1956 war with Egypt. In 1954 it was strengthened when Moshe Sneh, a member of the Mifleget ha-Smol Ha Sotzialistit (The Socialist Left Party) joined its ranks after leaving MAPAM. In 1955, the party gained electoral successes, and received strong support in the transit camps (reaching about 20%). In 1965 MAKI was split into two different parties, but at this point many of its Iraqi intellectuals had left the party. I therefore focus on the party's activities until this point.[41]

It is surprising, perhaps, that middle-class Iraqi Jews would vote for a pariah communist party, detested by all major bodies in Israel, especially MAPAI. And yet, MAKI appealed to the Iraqis, particularly because of its respect to their Arab culture, its critique of MAPAI's corruption, and the role its Iraqi activists played in organizing protests and rallies in the transit camps on behalf of the newcomers.[42] Being a prominent cultural hub, which counted many Palestinian writers and poets among its members, it attracted educated Iraqi Jews and former Iraqi-Jewish communists. MAKI's Iraqi intellectuals addressed Palestinian issues in their writings and discussed themes common to all other Arab writers, such as the Arab struggle against colonialism, while also deliberating their problems as poor Jewish newcomers from Arab states.[43]

Right-wing parties also attracted Iraqi Jews who were less drawn to socialist and communist ideas. Herut (Liberty) was founded in the summer of 1948 under the leadership of Menachem Begin and absorbed the members of rightist underground militias that were active in Mandatory Palestine, Irgun Tzva'i Le'umi (Nationalist Military Organization; or ETZEL), and some members of the Stern Gangs, Lohamey Herut Yisra'el (Fighters for the Freedom of Israel; or LEHI). Herut's leaders looked to the rightist ideology of Ze'ev Jabotinsky for inspiration, and supported a liberal economy and a free market. Concurrently, it believed in a tough position toward the Arabs. Herut's foreign policy goals seemed absolutely insane in the realities of the 1950s; continuing to advocate the policies it had developed during the mandate years, the party still spoke of a greater Israel on both banks of the Jordan River, and promised its voters that with a strong Israeli military, the Jordanian king could be toppled. Party leaders also expressed the desire that more newcomers come to Israel, despite the fact that the country severely lacked the resources for their absorption and that the newcomers who were already in Israel lived under extremely difficult conditions.[44] Herut, and as well Ha-Tziyonim ha-Klaliyim (The General Zionists), a party which likewise promoted Zionism and economic and political liberalism, attracted Iraqis. Herut, however, unlike the General Zionists, was an ostracized body. Seemingly, it made little sense for Jews who came from an Arab country to vote such an anti-Arab party. And yet, because of its critique of MAPAI and willingness to work in the transit camps, it attracted many.

Finally, a political party called Ha-Sephardim raised concerns regarding Iraqi Jews, and newcomers from Muslim lands, and their racial discrimination in Israel. The party's small size, however, allowed MAPAI to manipulate its leadership. It had its roots in the Ottoman and mandatory periods, and included many members of the Palestinian Sephardim.[45] While Iraqis always came second to the party's Sephardi leadership, and while this party was small to make an actual political difference, it still raised sectarian issues vigorously and consistently.

Despite this maze of political parties, and the near impossibility for destitute immigrants to challenge MAPAI, Iraqi Jews made use of this situation, joining Israeli political parties and trying to influence their leadership. By writing petitions to the ministers and politicians, and especially by participating in electoral campaigns, they found important avenues for effecting change and managed to engage in the new politics of the state. However, Iraqi Jews failed to find a party that met their needs; Iraqi members in all parties repeatedly complained about discrimination against them and neglect of their plight, and that the parties' Eastern European leadership did not understand their concerns.

As part of their socialization into Israeli politics, Iraqi Jews worked in the propaganda and publications machinery of political parties. Almost every political party in Israel had a journal in Arabic, which was addressed to the newcomers from Arab states and the Palestinian Israelis. MAPAI published the newspapers *Al-Akhbar* (The News), *Al-Yawm* (The Day) and *Al-Watan* (The Homeland);[46] Herut circulated *Al-Huriya* (Liberty); MAPAM made sure its chief newspaper addressed to the Palestinians, *Al-Mirsad* (The Observer), also included stories about the Iraqis and printed two Arabic newspapers, *Sawt al-Ma'abir* (Voice of the Transit Camps) and *Ila al-Amam* (Onward), designated especially to Arabic-speaking Jews;[47] and MAKI's publications, which dominated the Arabic printed press, *Al-Ittihad* (The Unity) and *Al-Jadid* (The Innovative), featured stories and items by and about Iraqi Jews.[48] The information in these newspapers was often biased; all parties used their publications to present a rosy image of their achievements and to smear their rivals, and most misrepresented Arab politics so that they would fit a Zionist framework (Herut being most creative in this domain). Nonetheless, these newspapers provided Jewish intellectuals, who had written in Arabic in Iraq, a crucial platform. In their stories, news items, and articles, Iraqi writers, especially the communists, wrote about the sufferings and aspirations of their community, and discussed the concerns and troubles of other Mizrahi and Arab groups.

. . .

The story of Iraqi Jews in Israel, then, is connected to many other stories—those of the Mizrahi, Jewish, Palestinian, and Arab communities. Their experience parallels that of other Jews—Yemenite, Egyptian, Romanian, Moroccan, Tunisian, Turkish, and Polish—who were settled in transit camps and shared the suffering and humiliation that Iraqi Jews endured, and exhibited the humanism, fortitude, and heroism that Iraqi Jews showed in overcoming these difficult circumstances. Around the same time when Iraqi Jews were rotting in transit camps, Palestinian refugees in Lebanon, Jordan, Syria, and Egyptian-controlled

Gaza lived through the same conditions; all of these communities dealt with harsh winters, the loss of social status, and the ongoing struggle to maintain human dignity. The story of these refugees and migrants should make us think differently about the history of the entire region. Liberal Zionist discourse emphasizes that Israel before 1967 was an ethical society, attempting to meet the challenges of survival and migration. In Middle Eastern national discourses, the 1950s are often represented as a golden age of politics and culture. In Egypt and Iraq, postcolonial revolutions led to land reforms and the diminishment of colonial influence, and ignited processes of mass education and social justice. Intellectuals in Beirut, Damascus, Baghdad, and Cairo were writing exciting works in poetry and prose, works that contemplated resistance, commitment, and revolution. But for Middle Eastern refugees the period from 1948 to 1967 was one of the most horrific eras in the region's history. This is the period during which they dealt with the shock of losing their homes, livelihoods, and, essentially, everything that they had, amid the indifference of the people living around them. Across Israeli borders sat vast Palestinian communities longing to return to Jaffa, Haifa, Acre, the Galilee, and the many other places they were forced to leave behind. And within Israel sat vast Jewish communities longing for Baghdad, Basra, Amara, Hilla, and Mosul. This book tells their story.

1 HUMAN MATERIAL

IN 1951, an Israeli medical doctor wrote a letter to Prime Minister David Ben Gurion, calling attention to the miserable living conditions in the transit camps. The health of the residents was deteriorating because of the circumstances—the overcrowding and inadequate housing—and compounding the problem was the failure of the camps' administrations to provide basic medical care. Children, newborns in particular, were sick and there were not enough antibiotics to treat them. Yet hospitals outside the camps turned away these children when their parents brought them for treatment. Ninety-nine percent of the children suffered from lice or from insect bites. Malnutrition was not a rarity. The doctor described a case of a child with typhoid fever who was actually treated at a hospital. After his recovery, however, the authorities in a transit camp refused to give him additional food: "How can you deny soup to a [sick] child?" wondered the doctor. He wanted the prime minister to act. "Despite the low cultural level, despite the wild instincts, they should be treated with patience, tolerance and love," he contended, adding that, sadly, the children are treated with much contempt. He continued: "Here they are, and they should be accepted. The name 'blacks [*Schwartzes*]' does not fit them. We are not American Yankees, and they are not Negros. Moreover, do we really accept and support how the Americans treat the Negros?"[1] The situation, he concluded, would have long-term effects; this was a case of "historical injustice."[2]

This doctor, not knowing much about Jews from Arab lands, assumes the worst: that they are essentially uncivilized. Nonetheless, he blames the state—

its authorities, its callous administration of the transit camps, and its inadequate medical system—for the newcomers' sufferings. And he observes that Israel is becoming Americanized in its racial relations; Middle Eastern Jews are categorized as "black Jews" and are subject to the kind of discrimination experienced by African Americans in the United States. Many similar condemnations of the horrendous situation in the transit camps were voiced in the 1950s, by the mostly Ashkenazi nurses, sanitary workers, doctors, and social workers; unfortunately, these complaints often fell on deaf ears.

Iraqi Jews arrived in Israel as one group among mass waves of migration that transformed the economic, political, and social life of Israel and altered its ethnic makeup; 102,000 Jews arrived in Israel in 1948, 240,000 in 1949, 170,000 in 1950, and 175,000 in 1951.[3] Many Jews came from Muslim states: 123,300 Jews from Iraq; 48,300 from Yemen; 45,400 from Morocco, Algeria, and Tunisia; 34,500 from Turkey; 8,800 from Egypt; 31,000 from Libya; and 21,900 from Iran. European newcomers flocked the state as well: 118,000 Jews came from Romania; 106,400 from Poland; 37,300 from Bulgaria; 18,800 from Czechoslovakia; 14,300 from Hungary; 10,800 from Germany and Austria; 8,200 from the USSR; and 7,700 from Yugoslavia. While these waves of migration ensured a Jewish majority in the new state and the spread of Jewish settlement across the country, it was unclear how the state, established only in 1948, and recovering from a bloody civil war, could provide housing, education, and food to these Jews. Moreover, the power relations between various Jewish ethnic groups in Israel changed, because many of European and Middle Eastern Jews were settled in the same locations and competed for the same resources, and because now mostly Eastern European Jews, who arrived to Mandatory and Ottoman Palestine before 1948, were charged with managing the lives of many Middle Eastern Jews.[4]

Upon their arrival to Israel, Iraqi Jews, like other newcomers, were placed in transit camps; in many camps they formed the majority of the inhabitants. They were referred to by the state as newcomers, or 'olim. This chapter suggests, however, that the Iraqis were migrant-citizens. On the one hand, they had been granted citizenship rights upon their arrival, so that they could vote in general elections and receive welfare benefits and social services. On the other hand, because the authorities believed they came from a primitive country and were thus in need of instruction and discipline, and because the state did not have resources to attend to their most basic needs, Iraqi Jews were treated as migrants-citizens, who should be thankful for the little they got, and, especially, although by no means exclusively, in the case of women, who were undeserving of full citizenship rights.

In tandem with the view that Iraqi Jews had the potential to become Israeli citizens was the state's cold-eyed evaluation of them as nothing more than "human material" (*homer enoshi*). This classification was common at the time: different groups of migrants were referred to variously as "good human material," "bad human material," "problematic human material"—or even "human dust" (an expression used by Israel's first prime minister to characterize Holocaust survivors). The word *material* reflects the complete dependency of the Iraqi migrants on the state, due to their utter lack of economic resources. But the word also reflects their dehumanization as a result of the process of migration.

The Israel that took in the Iraqi Jews between 1950 and 1951 was, in a sense, finding its own way just like the immigrants, having come into existence just two years earlier. It was a state on the verge of an economic collapse and that nevertheless undertook to absorb a huge number of immigrants. Moreover, many Zionist organizations that facilitated the settlement of legal and illegal immigrants in Ottoman and Mandatory Palestine remained in existence, since their influential leaders were reluctant to relinquish their power to the new state and its newly founded ministries. However, these organizations had worked on a small scale and had very little experience in absorbing mass waves of migration. The state thus lacked both the capital and the administrative capacity to handle the waves of immigrants in the 1950s. This chapter depicts the experience of the Iraqis in this new state, where they expected to be able to build a new life, but encountered countless difficulties in the simplest of tasks: eating the food they used to love, getting married, raising children, earning a living, and having a roof over their heads proved more challenging than they had ever imagined.

LEAVING IRAQ

The Jewish community in Iraq for the most part was urban: ninety thousand lived in Baghdad, and many others resided in the cities of Basra and Mosul. A minority known as the "Kurdish Jews," who spoke Aramaic, lived in towns and villages in northern Iraq. During the twentieth century the community became more integrated in Iraqi life; many of its members belonged to the Iraqi upper and middle classes and influenced Iraqi literature and culture. The community had access to a flourishing system of private and public education, which eased their entrance into the elite classes.

Very few Iraqi Jews in the interwar period imagined themselves leaving Iraq. Their emigration from Iraq was a result of the Arab-Israeli conflict. Although Iraqi Jews were not part of this conflict, they paid the price for the deterioration of the relations between Jews and Arabs, in Mandatory Palestine, in Israel, and in the entire region. The Jewish community began to come under pressure in the mid-1930s as profascist and pro-German forces gained influence in the Iraqi public sphere. The massacre of over 170 Iraqi Jews in a series of urban riots after a failed pro-German military coup (known as the Farhud, "violent dispossession") was the low point in the history of this community. However, between the years 1942 and 1948 Iraqi Jews rebuilt their lives and pursued integration into the cultural, economic, and political spheres of Iraqi with renewed vigor. The years 1948–51 saw an abrupt reversal of this trend. In May 1948, the State of Israel was created and the Iraqi government promptly declared war on Israel, announcing a state of emergency. Over the next three years Jews employed at governmental ministries were let go, Jewish bankers and businessmen could not conduct business as freely as before, and students found it difficult to enter universities. The right-wing press worsen this situation by publishing articles on the treasonous Zionist character of the Iraqi-Jewish community; some articles called to treat them in the same fashion that Israel treated the Palestinians—namely, to let them go. In September 1948, Shafiq 'Adas, a wealthy businessman, was publicly executed in Basra for selling military supplies to Israel, to the accompaniment of an anti-Semitic demonstration. Elements within Iraq's pro-British ruling elites, whom the Jews trusted, especially during the days of World War II, now turned their backs on the Jewish minority; some even called for a population transfer. Officially, this antidemocratic campaign was seen as a way of deterring Iraqi Jews from supporting Zionism. Nonetheless, these modes of collective punishment and intimidation alienated those Iraqi Jews who enjoyed a very comfortable life in Iraq and did not want to leave their country.[5]

The State of Israel contributed to the escalation of the already explosive situation in Iraq. With the realization of the dimensions of the Holocaust, the Zionist movement began to look at the 750,000 Jews who lived in the Muslim world, 135,000 of whom lived in Iraq, as potential migrants and settlers.[6] Zionist emissaries sent to Arab countries established the basis for youth movements. They hoped to capitalize on the love many Iraqi Jews felt toward the land of Israel to bolster their movement. The Jewish elites in Iraq, however, were not Zionist; the Arabized middle classes, the politicians, the journalists, the writers, and the chief rabbi feared that affiliation with Zionism would endanger the Jews of Iraq, cast a heavy doubt on their patriotism, and connect them to the conflict in Palestine.

Starting from 1945, nonetheless, the Iraqi Zionist movement, as well as the Iraqi Communist Party (both of which were illegal), attracted young Iraqi Jews with their promises of an equitable socialist society and a remedy for anti-Semitism. The Zionist movement nonetheless remained a minority movement, counting some two thousand members, most of whom belonged to youth groups. The communists were mostly anti-Zionists, seeing Zionism as a colonialist movement in the Middle East. However, what started as a membership in a relatively harmless Zionist youth movement became a viable political option after 1948. As the Iraqi state became more oppressive, more and more Jews considered the option of migration, and the Zionist movement assumed more leadership roles in the community. At this point, the movement became militant and its members identified with the new State of Israel. The connections the Iraqi Zionists cultivated with Israel allowed them to negotiate the departure of the Iraqi Jews from Iraq, the speed of that departure, the future of Iraqi Jews' property, and their citizenship status.

In October 1949, the Iraqi police targeted the Zionist underground; one hundred Jews were jailed and seven hundred arrested. This crackdown served to alienate the wider community, however, as many were arrested who had nothing to do with either Zionism or communism. On April 8, 1950; and January 14, March 14, May 10, and June 5–6, 1951, bombings occurred at Jewish institutions in Baghdad, with five killed in an attack on the Mas'uda Shemtov Synagogue. In the summer of 1951, the Iraqi police claimed to have discovered a Zionist spy ring. More arrests were made; two Zionists, Saleh Shalom and Yusuf Basri, were executed for their alleged involvement in the bombings; and twenty more were sentenced to prison sentences. Some scholars support the claims made by the Iraqi authorities, and argue that either local Iraqi Zionist organizations or the State of Israel itself bore responsibility for the bombing as a way to persuade Jews to emigrate, while the official line in Israel is that anti-Jewish Iraqi radicals were behind the bombings. There are more circumstantial evidence against either Israel or the local Zionist underground; the former wanted to frighten Jews into signing up for migration, while the latter wanted to show to the Israeli authorities the grave danger awaiting Iraqi Jews, and increase the entry quotas of Iraqis, who already declared their desire to be resettled in Israel, to this country. Nonetheless, the Iraqi state itself had its share of anti-Jewish elements, especially the toxic anti-Jewish incitement in the right-wing press, which might also have wanted to repel the Jews from their country.[7]

This increasingly hostile climate pushed Jews to emigrate, and in the years 1949–50 hundreds left Iraqi illegally, taking their property with them. In an attempt to gain some control over migration, the Iraqi government passed a law in March 1950, to be effective for a year, giving Jews the option of registering for legal emigration to Israel provided they renounce their Iraqi citizenship. This law was passed after bitter debates in the Iraqi parliament. Despite the tense situation, many Iraqi Muslims and Christians did not want to see Iraqi Jews leave their homeland and feared their living conditions would be much worse in Israel. Moreover, Iraqi politicians hoped that only poor Jews and radicals (communists and Zionists) would leave the state and that the majority would stay in Iraq. At this point, however, the community was too intimidated. On March 10, 1951, the government passed a law freezing the assets of all Jews who emigrated. From that point on Iraqi Jews who migrated to Israel lost all their financial resources.[8] The combination of these two laws put Iraqi Jews in a horrible position; they became landless and penniless.

Zionist officials interpreted the experiences of Iraqi Jews in the years 1948–51 and the Farhud as indicating that the Jewish community was in peril and needed to be saved by the Jewish state. The state migration agencies considered the Iraqi case to be "a termination of diaspora" (*hisul galut*), meaning a case in which the community in its entirety was to be brought to Israel. This was different than the situations in Morocco, Turkey, or Iran, where groups of Jews were allowed to emigrate but had the option of returning. Indeed, Zionist leaders like David Ben Gurion and Golda Meir held that all Jews should be brought to Israel, even if the state had no means of absorbing them. To many Zionists, a key lesson from the Holocaust was that it was better for Jews to endure a materially poor existence in Israel than to live elsewhere under the threat of annihilation.[9]

One unexpected outcome of the arrival of the Iraqi Jews in Israel was that their lot became connected to that of the Palestinians. During the course of the 1948 War between Israel and the Palestinians, between half a million and a million Palestinians were made to leave, and their property was confiscated by the Israeli state. Iraqi Jews, as well as other immigrants, were seen as potential settlers in the depopulated Palestinian territories and as a demographic tool that would ensure a Jewish majority in the state. The frozen Iraqi-Jewish property was linked to the Palestinian property; Yehouda Shenhav has intimated that these ideas were raised in the negotiations with the Iraqi state before Jews left Iraq.[10]

From 1951 on, the State of Israel officially insisted that the issues of the Palestinian refugees and their property were to be resolved in tandem with the issue of the confiscated property of Jewish communities in Arab countries, and refused to negotiate separately about the property of Iraqi Jews.[11]

On the other hand, not all in the State of Israel were eager to welcome Iraqi Jews, even prior to their arrival. Zionist officials were concerned that Jews from Muslim lands would come to form a significant portion of the population and stoked fears about the large number of communist Jews from Iraq. It was also a fact that the poor state had very little in the way of resources to provide to immigrants. It had lost one percent of its population during the 1948 War; the Jews who came from Europe and from other Arab states also lost their property, and donations from American Jewry, which peaked sharply in 1948, declined during the following decade. Until the Reparation Agreement with Germany, which provided for the return of Jewish property confiscated and looted during the Holocaust, the economic prospects of the state seemed particularly dim.[12] Moreover, concerns about all the newcomers circulated in the public sphere. Religious parties, for example, objected to the arrival of certain Holocaust survivors; they did not want the country to take in uncircumcised children or men who had married non-Jewish women. It was also thought that immigrants in poor health would burden the state.[13] Dr. Yosef Meir, a key health official in the Zionist movement, had voiced his contention as early in 1943 that only the healthiest should be granted entry, and he held to this position through the 1950s.[14]

Moreover, the commitment of Jews from Muslim lands to the Zionist project was considered questionable at best. Pinhas Lavon, the chair of the Histadrut, and later Israel's minister of defense, believed that bringing into Israel a large number of immigrants lacking in Zionist zeal would destroy the Zionist project from within.[15] The view that Mizrahi Jews should have stayed behind was articulated publicly in Israel after their arrival, especially during times of sectarian riots. Officials likewise complained that the sick, the needy, the old, and the widowed burdened the state's budgets. In fact, with respect to North African Jews, the state adopted a selection procedure that left out the old and the disabled.[16]

The major fear, however, was that the state could not attend to the economic needs of the Iraqis. Shlomo Hillel, an Iraqi Zionist who led negotiations about the departure of Iraqi Jews with the Iraqi government on behalf of the State of Israel, recalls a conversation with Levy Eshkol, who was to care for the settlement of immigrants in the new state. Eshkol, according to Hillel, told him in

1950: "I heard 60,000 [Iraqi Jews] will come within a year.... Now listen to what I tell you.... Tell these good Jews of yours, that we will be very happy if they all came, but let them take their time. We do not have at the moment any possibility to absorb them. We do not even have tents. If they come, they will have to live in the street."[17] The Israel Defense Forces (IDF) General Moshe Carmel explained to Hillel that Eshkol should be taken seriously: Yemenite Jews, Holocaust survivors, and Iranian Jews filled the available camps; the state was facing "an army of the unemployed men" (*tzva muvtalim*); and the police had their hands full with unemployed Arabs and communists.[18] Indeed, given the poor state of the Israeli economy and the masses of people arriving, mostly without property or means of support, it was irresponsible to push for the immigration of Iraqi Jews. The state, moreover, could barely manage the large waves of migrants that arrived in the years 1948–51. Although Iraqi Jews endured great indignities in Iraq, the quality of life for those who stayed in that country during the years 1951–63 was much better than that for Iraqi Jews in Israel. Given the economic conditions in Israel, the fate of the Iraqi Jews was sealed even before they set foot in Israel. But neither the state nor the Iraqi migrants knew the extent of the colossal challenges ahead of them.

THE GATE OF TEARS

The route to Israel from Iraq went through Cyprus, about a three-hour trip, and from there it was about another hour or so. The Israeli government paid the Iraqi government twelve dinars for each passenger, but charged each family member who could afford it fourteen dinars in order to cover the poorer travelers. Iraqi Jews were allowed to take three summer and three winter suits, one pair of shoes, a blanket, six pairs of underwear, socks, and sheets. They were also permitted to bring fifty dinars in the form of a check, which was worthless in Israel since the Israeli government refused to make up the lost sum. The rest was left behind, and eventually lost.[19] A humiliating inspection at the Baghdad airport, during which every single item Jews took with them was carefully inspected, began the journey. Those who managed to ship goods to Israel discovered they arrived much later; it was not easy to track down the shipments in Israel. And in some cases there were entry tariffs, which made it extremely difficult to get property released from Israeli ports and storehouses.[20]

One of the most powerful bodies responsible for the absorption of Iraqi Jews was the Jewish Agency for the Land of Israel (Ha-Sokhnut ha-Yehudit le-Aretz Yisra'el; hereafter Jewish Agency), which was established in 1929 as a liaison between the authorities of the British Mandate and the Jewish community. In this era, the Jewish Agency was a leading player in the bringing in and settling of newcomers (both legally and illegally) and the organizing of fundraising efforts abroad to support these efforts. Its activities were scaled back after the establishment of the state, but its Absorption Division remained the main organizational entity responsible for the settlement of newcomers.[21]

When Iraqi immigrants landed, they were sprayed in the airport with DDT. The precedent for this was the British authorities having sprayed Holocaust survivors and Jewish illegal immigrants from Europe with DDT before they were shipped to camps in Cyprus. Only those who arrived on private flights and American Jews were spared. Spraying was done in a shack, in groups of four, although some children resisted being sprayed. The Iraqis were then given their initial identification papers, among them the newcomer's certificate (*t'udat 'oleh*), documenting their arrival in Israel. The contents of their baggage were inspected as well.[22]

Iraqi writer Rahamim Rejwan's short story "On the Road to the Transit Camp" ("Ba-derech la-ma'abara") narrates how Iraqis experienced this moment. The story opens with a scene of a group of Iraqis, in their fine dress, anticipating a warm welcome, possibly with flowers, in the new state. When they land, three men arrive from the airport and approach them, ordering them to stand in parallel rows. Some still believe they are about to receive flowers, cigarettes, and food. The men are told to untie their ties, open their collars, and unbutton their shirts. The women find this request particularly bizarre. Then the men spray a white powder all over the Iraqi men and on the hair and breasts of the Iraqi women. The story records the conversations between the newcomers:

> "Ha ha," the sound of the laughter of one dressed-up lady from Abu Sifin was heard,[23] "they are cleaning my husband's little one. Does it have to be cleansed as well?" . . .
>
> "What does it matter, give me a break, they are used to cleanliness here. We must be like them," someone commented.
>
> "This powder doesn't smell right!" said one woman all of a sudden.
>
> "I don't think it's a regular powder." . . .
>
> One man refused to be sprayed with powder . . .
>
> "You must," the sprayer said. "Otherwise you can't get food."[24]

Jokes and questions flit about; the three men spraying the group turn away embarrassed, failing to realize whether the group is protesting or joking; they therefore yell at them to remain calm. Finally, one of the Iraqi Jews, a pharmacist, realizes what the material is. The laughter ends.

After being sprayed, they wait for hours in the airport for an official to arrive. There are no beds available for small children. One woman who is lactating and nursing volunteers to breastfeed other children. The men of the Zionist underground who had depicted the migration in rosy tints are now silent. When a clerk finally shows up, they stand in front of a small window to meet him. He is rude and standoffish, no different than the condescending Iraqi bureaucrats.[25]

This story by Rejwan reflects many of the experiences of those coming to Israel. The description of men and women wearing their finest clothes to celebrate their arrival in Israel is echoed in other testimonies of the time.[26] Many Iraqis would have no use for these fine clothes later on in the transit camps, since they would be employed in agriculture and forestry. The story is constructed as a tale of dashed hopes. Told from the immigrants' perspective, it narrates their discovery that Israel is as bad as Iraq, if not worse. At the same time, the story also exposes the mechanisms that allow the migrants to face the situation, especially mutual help; they talk to one another, calm one another, and help each other. They also employ one of the oldest mechanisms in the Jewish historical arsenal for dealing with difficult and absurd situations: their sense of humor.

From the airport, most Iraqis boarded crowded trucks which began a long journey, lasting between three to ten hours, to a classification and absorption camp called Sha'ar ha-Aliyah, or the Gate of Aliyah. Those who did not spend the night at the airport were still covered with the white DDT powder, and were tearful, red-faced, and coughing. Many of the trucks did not even have improvised seats and passengers had nothing to hold on to.[27] Fu'ad Amir (later Elie Amir), who had come from Baghdad with his family, all of them dressed in their finest clothes, recalls how his father was afraid that their luggage would be stolen, which was a common occurrence. Fu'ad jumped on the truck and, surrounded by other people's luggage, made his way to the camp on his own. Upon his arrival, he jumped down from the truck and began walking in the camp, where "a horrible stench caught me: atrocious smells coming from the sewage water, flowing between the tents and from the bathroom. A wave of unpleasant smells came from the dining-room as well."[28]

Iraqi Jews gave Sha'ar ha-Aliyah a new name, the "Gate of Tears." A former British military camp near Haifa, it had been taken over by the Israeli government in March 1949 to serve as the main processing center for immigrants. A smaller camp in Atlith was another facility for documentation, classification, and medical exams. The Absorption Division of the Jewish Agency was in charge of maintaining the camp; at a cost of half a million dollars per month, it used up a third of the division's budget. At the peak of activity, a thousand people were processed per day, with twelve thousand to fifteen thousand people staying in the camp. The operation of the camp employed a total of four hundred workers, cooks, drivers, porters, sanitation workers, kosher inspectors, and social workers. The immigrants in the camp underwent a series of medical examinations and vaccinations. The camp functioned to quarantine newcomers, from Europe and the Middle East alike, whom officials feared would spread leprosy, STDs, TB, and skin diseases. The sanitation and hygiene conditions were horrendous, and people had to wait in line for many hours for food and the various offices.[29]

A barbed-wire fence of three kilometers surrounded the camp, because the authorities saw the immigrants as potential vectors for disease and as threats to the social order, and took steps to confine and control them. Three months after the camp opened a police station (*notrim*) was added. The primary duties of the six policemen assigned to the camp were maintaining order in the food lines, breaking up demonstrations, and looking into complaints of stolen baggage. But grievances about policemen who took bribes, stole food from the public kitchen, and used force too often to keep order circulated in the camp. Two young women accused the camp guards of humiliating them; the guards were also blamed for giving favors to women out of indecent intentions. In theory, people were not allowed to leave the camp, but it was impossible to stop the movement in out and out, which was enabled by the bribing of the guards and the policemen.[30]

The expectation was that people would stay in the camp for five days, but most Iraqis stayed for ten, sleeping in tents. Ashkenazi cooks prepared the food, which the Iraqis threw out because they found it tasteless. The mashed potatoes and peas with spinach the Iraqis considered children's food, and they were disgusted by the herring they were served. Initially, they preferred to go hungry, but eventually it was either starve or eat the Ashkenazi food. Families also resented their being served dinner in the overcrowded common dining room. In the maze of tents and people from different communities, they wanted something to remind them of the intimacy of a household, and began to take food to their tents.[31]

In the camp, Iraqis started looking for relatives to help them out, searched for jobs on their own, and gleaned information about the places they were about to be sent to. The veterans in the camp explained to them what they knew about the regime in Israel. Victor Muʻallim, an educator from Iraq, arrived at Shaʻar ha-Aliyah in March 1951 and stayed there for sixteen days. A worker for the Jewish Agency took an oil lamp to show him and his family their tents. The family had many challenges: finding a bucket to get water, finding utensils to eat with, locating the bathroom, and then getting used to a public shower and the poor sanitary conditions. Their sense of the intrusive Israeli governmental presence was reinforced by their encounter with the IDF's recruiters. Local Iraqi networks helped Muʻallim: he was told the chances of working in his profession (a teacher) were nil, and that he should insist on being sent to a place close to Tel Aviv. He was also approached by Iraqis who worked for MAPAM's newspaper, *Al-Mirsad*, and by the Iraqi communist Yaʻaqub Qujman, who attempted to convince him to join their parties.[32] Rahamin Rejwan, the author of the short story quoted above, sums up how he and his countrymen felt in the Gate of Tears:

> They cursed the day when they thought of making Aliyah. . . . They knew the country was in great difficulties, and food was not ample. But they were unwilling to forgive the indifference, the injury to their feelings and traditions, the contempt they felt, and the . . . humiliation they encountered every step of the way. They cursed it all. Here in Shaʻar ha-Aliyah the Second Israel was born.[33]

"Second Israel" is a term that refers to the world of transit camps and development towns in which Jews, mostly from the Middle East, lived. To Rejwan it was born in Shaʻar ha-ʻAliyah. Not surprisingly, the conditions he describes led to protests. Riots broke out in 1949 when a local policeman beat a newcomer to death. In August 1951 riots flared up again as Iraqi Jews resisted being moved to other transit camps. In April 1951, Shaʻar ha-ʻAliyah was full, and consequently the many Iraqis who were still coming were sent directly to the transit camps. It reopened after a while. The camp was finally shut down in 1962.[34]

A NEW STATE: PERMANENT AND TEMPORARY SPACES

From Shaʻar ha-ʻAliyah, Iraqi Jews were sent to transit camps, the Maʻabarot. The decision to build these transit camps in 1950 marked a shift from the previous solution to the problem of how to house migrants from Europe and the Middle East, including the ones who already migrated from Iraq, who arrived in the years 1949–50. Those resided in "newcomers' camps" (*mahanot ʻolim*), which were jointly run by the state and the Jewish Agency. The immigrants lived in tents and deserted British barracks, did not work, and received state support. As the stays in these camps unavoidably lengthened, the authorities realized the cost of supporting the immigrants was mounting. These camps suffered from the same problems of Sha'ar ha-'Aliyah: dreadful sanitary conditions, overcrowding, and unpalatable (to Iraqis) Ashkenazi food. In April 1950, the state made the decision to shut down these camps. To encourage people to move, the administration of the camps closed the kitchens, with the result that infant mortality increased. The authorities made some accommodation for those facing greater hardship: the old and the sick were provided with extra financial support, and the physically disabled and the chronically sick were allowed to stay in a camp in Pardes Hannah.[35]

Levy Eshkol was credited with developing the concept of the transit camp. Newcomers would continue to live there in tents and shacks, but would be able to find jobs and thus feed themselves and take care of their children. The stay in the transit camp was intended to be temporary, with residents eventually to be moved to permanent housing and new settlements. The Jewish Agency was in charge of building the camps and was supposed to fund the positions of sanitary workers and a nurse, and the state supported other public services that the camps' denizens needed. Each camp was to have a labor bureau; and the local municipalities were to take care of providing water, garbage collection, and health issues. Eshkol's original idea was that most of the inhabitants of the camps would be employed in forestry and agriculture, but actually many of the camps were built on the outskirts of major towns and cities, with the assumption that the newcomers would find jobs nearby. By May 1950, 4 transit camps with seventeen thousand souls were operating; by December 1951 Israel had 123 camps.[36]

Most of the Iraqis were sent to the transit camps from Sha'ar ha-Aliyah. Some depopulated Palestinian villages and territories that were not annexed to a kibbutz, a *moshav* (a cooperative agricultural settlement; plural: *moshavim*), or a *moshava* (a small township or community whose members engaged in agriculture; plural: *moshavot*), were still available; on their ruins these camps were built. The building of the transit camps was thus a part of a larger project of Israelizing former Palestinian territories. Initially, many of the transit camps took the names of the Palestinian villages on which they stood, such as Zarnuga, Kubeiba, Shobaki, Zakiyya, and Ijlil; eventually, they were renamed in Hebrew and annexed by moshavot and larger cities. This process paralleled the annexation of depopulated Palestinian villages and their lands by Israeli cities and townships. The municipalities, especially in central Israel, were eager to enlarge their territories. Concurrently, however, their leaders were terrified by the possibility that transit camps would be built nearby; they wanted the land, not the people.[37]

Iraqis arrived at the transit camps from Sha'ar ha-'Aliyah in flatbed trucks. Nurses in the camps complained about this form of transportation, depicting the suffering of women, old people, and children.[38] The Ministry of Interior reported that certain camps were entirely populated by Iraqis; other transit camps were flooded with Iraqis as well. The densest concentration of camps, populated by hundreds of Iraqis, was built on the ruins of three Palestinian villages in south-central Israel: Khayriyya, Sakiyya, and Kfar 'Ana. Each village had a cluster of camps built around it.[39]

The majority of the transit camps were run by the Jewish Agency. This institution appointed the director of the camp, decided which migrants would be sent to which camp, and determined the pace of the evacuation of their residents to permanent housing. Most camps included the following institutions: the director's office, a labor bureau, a welfare bureau, and a shack used as a clinic. Most migrants lived initially in tents, but later the tents were replaced by shacks made of tin and wood. In the 1951–52, the large transit camps included between five thousand and eight thousand people, and were divided into two or three subcamps. The incompetent bureaucracy led to the transferring of people from camp to camp without justification.[40] A hierarchy of the transit camps was soon created. Those in central Israel, which were located within a walking distance of an existing moshava, like the transit camp of Ramat ha-Sharon, were considered better than the more isolated transit camps of the north and the south, or those next to Jerusalem.[41]

In many camps, Iraqi met Ashkenazi migrants and migrants from other Muslim states. The ethnic makeup of the camp transit was diverse. A survey of residents in 1953 showed that 79,157 arrived from Iraq; 16,455 from Iran; 12,214 from Yemen; 12,745 from Algeria, Morocco, and Tunis; 17,463 from Libya and Tangier; 6,878 from Egypt; 7421 from other Asian countries; 8,205 from Poland; 34,424 from Romania; 54 from North and South America; 4,337 from other European countries; and 11,673 from unidentified countries.[42] Although friendships, and joint battles for the provision of services, united European and Mizrahi residents, many Iraqis complained that the Ashkenazi directors of camps and other officials favored Ashkenazi Jews, especially in job and housing placements. The Ashkenazim stayed in the transit camps for shorter periods of time, while the Mizrahi migrants could stay there for as long as seven years.[43]

The camps were built quickly and without much planning. Many of the sites were not fit for construction, for example because the soil was too sandy or the area was prone to floods in the winters. Some camps were built without the Ministry of Interior's formal approval, and as a result the local municipalities refused to provide services to these camps.[44] The most unfortunate Iraqis were sent to Khayriyya, a transit camp next to Israel's biggest landfill, serving Tel Aviv and its neighboring cities and towns. The Khayriyya camp was an ecological disaster. The smells were horrible; animals were attracted to the garbage; the rotting of organic materials endangered the health of residents; and fires from the burning of garbage threatened the camp's wooden shacks. Even the school was located too close to the landfill. Israeli health specialists asked that a special burning facility be built to prevent health problems, but it was too expensive. The people of the camp petitioned to have the landfill shut down as a health hazard.[45] Tel Aviv's mayor dismissed the petition on the grounds that the landfill had existed prior to the transit camp, and that the residents were only at risk on hot summer days and when garbage was burned.[46] In 1957, 120 doctors put forth their own petition that the mountainous landfill of Khayriyya be closed. The minister of health Israel Barzilai admitted that the Jewish Agency had not consulted with the Ministry of Health regarding the siting of the camp, and that the residents were the victims of lack of cooperation between different arms of the government. However, it was simply too expensive to build a special facility. The case was transferred to the Knesset's Committee on Public Services.[47]

When the Iraqis saw the camps for the first time, they were shocked. They had been told many tales by the Jewish Agency in order to convince them to leave Sha'ar ha-Aliyah: in the new place, they were told, they would get new houses and employment would be available in the vicinity. None of these tales was true. Some residents even had to construct their own tents.[48] The writer and educator 'Ezra Murad (born 1933, 'Amara) describes a group of traumatized Iraqis, seeing the long line of tents awaiting them in the southern transit camp in depopulated Arab village of Qastina (today the city of Kiryat Malachi):

> "Tents? We will live in tents?" "Could it be?" "Who needs tents?" Our hands lost their strength, our faces, darkened, and the objects we put on the truck seemed seven times heavier. . . .
>
> "Maybe just for a few days," an old man calmed us down. . . .

We settled in one tent. The drivers left and we stayed in the darkness. Our mothers began lamenting and mourning, as our fathers stared at the ground . . . and were silent as if unable to speak. It was a sleepless night. And we, the older ones, lit a fire and sat down to tell stories of the lost paradise.[49]

The tents were bought from a variety of places, such as American companies which sold military supplies, and even this source became harder to come by after the outbreak of the Korean War. Lucky immigrants then moved into *badon*s, larger tents that consisted of a tarpaulin built on a frame of wood, or into *pahon*s, shacks made of tin. The most fortunate moved into wooden shacks. However, these were the most expensive to build, due to wood prices,

FIGURE 1. Tents in the winter. Source: Central Zionist Archive (CZA), NKH\403259. Reprinted with permission.

and the Jewish Agency did not want to invest in them. The tents and the hybrid shelters made of canvas and tin were too flimsy to withstand winter weather, and had to be rebuilt every year. Eventually, most of a camp's residents made the transition from a tent to a *badon* or from a *pahon* to a wooden shack. Newcomers paid rent for the wooden shacks. Many, however, could not even afford the down-payment to move into a shack, thus staying longer in tents and in constructions made of tin and canvas. As could be expected, all these forms of temporary housing had serious shortcomings. It was very hot in the constructions made of canvas and tin in the summer. Since many camps had no electricity, the residents used lanterns and candles for lighting, and as a result tents caught fire.[50] The most acute problem was population density; families blessed with many children would be assigned only one tent or a shack. Families with four or five children sometimes managed to get two tents. In the transit camp in Ness Ziona, five to eight people would live in a single room.[51]

The furnishings of the tents and shacks were, unsurprisingly, as substandard as the dwellings themselves. In 'Ezra Murad's words,

> Tnuva boxes dragged
> To serve as closets,
> A darkened lantern
> Not fit to use,
> A patched military coat,
> A shivering baby
> Lying on a rusty bed
> With a straw mattress,
> His eyes peeping as the wind blows,
> And piles of wood
> To heat,
> To warm the heart![52]

Showers and toilets were public, few in number (sometimes there were only four or five showers for a camp of hundreds), and were poorly maintained, if at all. The toilets were often flooded and the drainage trashcans and septic tanks were cleaned out infrequently; in general the camps endangered the health of the citizens.[53] The water available for showering and drinking was sometimes unsuitable, being drawn from abandoned wells in depopulated villages turned into transit camps. Moreover, access to water was not a right: when residents could not afford water services, they were cut off.[54] In the clusters of camps in

Sakiyya the water was brown. The Health Ministry replied that "although the water tastes bad," it is potable.[55] In camps lacking a connection to the water system, individuals had to walk to get water in nearby camps. Moshe (Morris) Huri, a child of an Iraqi family growing up in the transit camp of Kiryat Ono, narrates his daily routine:

> It was usually the chore (or the game) of the children. I remember that the trip to the water was one of my favorite, if tiring, chores. . . . To walk in the sand dunes; your legs sinking in; you fall over; the bucket is half-empty, and then [you start] over. . . . The public baths were made of tin. . . . They involved the loss of privacy, to which we were unaccustomed. We, like most children, did not like taking showers, but under these conditions it was important to maintain a decent level of hygiene, and hence another chore was placed on the parents.[56]

Indeed, people in the camp had to wait until partitions were built between stools and showers to give them some sense of privacy. Women who wanted privacy and were concerned about the proximity of their showers to the men's showers preferred to wash their children and themselves in their tents and shacks, using buckets and faucets.[57]

Officials with the Ministry of Health sporadically inspected the water sources, the showers, the garbage-collection practices, and the protection of camps from pests and wild animals around the camp, and their findings confirmed the dismal picture the residents described. Health experts were worried about vermin, such as lice, cockroaches, mice, and rats.[58] The possible outbreak of typhoid fever caused by rats was another concern mentioned in the reports.[59] The Ministry of Health trained sanitary workers to work in the transit camps, but the municipalities were not always willing to pay for it.[60] The use of DDT to combat vermin revealed to Iraqi immigrants that the substance with which they had been sprayed on their arrival was now used to combat vermin.[61] The process of dehumanization was now completed.

THE ROAD TO NOWHERE

Some transit camps were close to towns and urban centers, while others were built in remote and isolated places. Although the state did establish labor and welfare offices and sent specialists and guides, many camps remained neglected, receiving little in the way of services from the state. This was in part due to the impossible bureaucratic maze that the newcomers encountered. The Iraqis, as other newcomers, relied on the Jewish Agency for most services, and consequently suffered due to the battles of that agency with the Ministry of Interior, which had its own Absorption Division (established in December 1949), the Ha-Mahlaka le-Ma'abarot u-le-Yishuvey 'Olim (Division of Transit Camps and Settlement of Newcomers). Originally, the ministry was tasked with providing cleaning services to the camps, and taking care of various issues of housing and security, relying on help from local municipalities.

Dov Rozen, the head of the Ministry of Interior's Absorption Division, wanted to have more authority over the transit camps, but the Jewish Agency was unwilling to cede any degree of control. Many of the fights appear to have been driven by the political affiliations of Rozen and Giora Yoseftal, the head of the Jewish Agency's Absorption Division. Yoseftal was close to Ben Gurion and was naturally identified with the ruling political party, MAPAI, the party most associated with the agency. Rozen, for his part, belonged to Ha-Po'el ha-Mizrahi (The Worker of the East), the major religious Zionist party. The Jewish Agency's prominent presence in the transit camps meant more power to MAPAI. Yoseftal and the government desired this; Rozen wanted to thwart them. The ensuing power struggle unnecessarily slowed the process of improving life in the transit camps.[62]

To limit the power of the Jewish Agency, Rozen proposed that the Ministry of Interior Affairs provide services through the local municipalities in whose vicinities the camps were built, in those cases where the camp would not be eventually abandoned, but rather would be granted municipal status, often as part of the adjacent city or moshava.[63] From the vantage point of state management and governmental jurisdiction, Rozen's position made sense: it signaled the transition from a pre-state institution (the Jewish Agency) to a post-state normalcy. It faced only one significant obstacle: the last thing the local municipalities wanted was to incorporate the transit camps to their territories. As Deborah ha-Kohen explains, the authorities panicked at the possibility of having to spend their tax revenue to provide services to the unemployed and those with low incomes. The thought that the latter group might vote was even more frightening. Rozen dismissed their concerns, arguing that the taxes paid by the newcomers would cover the services they would receive, and continued his campaign to have more camps placed under his ministry's authority. In the meantime, Yoseftal kept sending Iraqis to camps, ignoring the municipalities, thinking the camps were still under the agency's control. The struggle between the two heads was replicated in the camps in the contention between officials with their organizations.[64] For example, in the transit camp in Tira (near Haifa) the workers of the Jewish

Agency tried to push out the Ministry of Interior's staff, while at other places the Ministry of Interior people rejected the agency's men.[65]

An additional complicating factor was that local municipalities would refuse to provide basic services to the camps. The city of Holon contended that it was not obligated to provide water to the nearby transit camp on the grounds that the camp was temporary.[66] The division of the responsibility for making water, education, jobs, and welfare services available in the camps meant that in some cases the administration of a camp fell through the cracks.[67] Rozen's capitalist fantasies that the unemployed residents and those with low-paying jobs could somehow save up enough capital to invest in some kind of housing and pay municipal taxes were wildly unrealistic, and electricity was being cut off in the camps because of unpaid bills.[68] Some camps, especially those in central Israel, were built outside the municipal boundaries of any village or city.[69] If two municipalities were adjacent to a camp, they would fight to force the other to provide the services. Municipal officials were not afraid of defying the Jewish Agency in preventing the construction of a camp in their territory. For its part, the Jewish Agency took advantage of the joint responsibility for the camps to withhold fiscal support. In May 1950, the agency declared that until the migration of Iraqi Jews was completed, it could not give any more funding to transit camps.[70] The Iraqi activist Ishaq 'Abbudi reflected on the sad state of affairs in MAKI's Hebrew newspaper *Kol ha-'Am*:

> We [a delegation from the transit camp of Ramat ha-Sharon] were invited to help the Ministry of Interior in collecting water fees from the people of the camp, since they intend to reduce the amount of water supplied to the camp. The Ministry of Interior has suddenly remembered that there is a place on the map of the country called the transit camp of Ramat ha-Sharon only because it needs taxes. When for three years the people of the transit camp demanded their rights to jobs and humane housing . . . the site of the transit camp could not be found on the map.[71]

The camps were isolated, not only because cities and municipalities refused to recognize them, but because the roads that connected the transit camps to cities and towns were of poor quality and the transportation system was inadequate. During the winter of 1950–51, the Ministry of Labor established a bus service to some transit camps whose costs were sponsored by different ministries. Roads were not paved in most transit camps, and it was difficult for cars to circulate in them and to reach the camps themselves.[72] Bus stations were few and far between, and workers had to wake up very early and walk long distances to catch the bus.[73]

Being isolated meant that the dwellers of the transit camps had to rely on the medical services within the camps. Orit Rozin carefully documented the lack of health and sanitary conditions in the transit camps and the appalling neglect of those perceived by the state as naturally unhygienic.[74] In the early 1950s thousands of Iraqis lived with no medical services in their camps.[75] The welfare bureau in the camps,[76] rather than the doctors and the nurses, often determined who had the right to be hospitalized for free (although the Iraqis were mostly insured, the little they had to pay was a financial burden to some). The state focused on preventative medicine, particularly for mothers and children, through the Histadrut health providers and the Health Ministry. Female guides with the Histadrut's women's organizations and the Ministry of Welfare arranged for the provision of these services. Medical doctors and nurses did not go the camps enthusiastically. Officials toyed with the idea of drafting doctors, as part of their military service, and some were indeed assigned to newcomers' villages and remote places.[77] To address this urgent need, some nurses established Yad la-Ma'abara (A Hand for the Transit Camp), an organization which collected funds and whose nurses volunteered as providers of child care and preventative medicine in the camps.[78]

As in other cases, the state bureaucracy was an obstacle, as the Health Ministry and Kupat Holim (the Histadrut's health provider) struggled over spheres of influence and power, on the one hand, and charged each other for services they could not afford, on the other. Often clashes occurred between the health and welfare ministries as to which cover the cost of medical treatment. The clinics that did exist in the camps did not always have the necessary medicine, and getting test results was also quite difficult. In fact, when Iraqis could find a way to send a child to the hospital, and could afford the care, the child would be better off, because parents and doctors at the camps could request and receive an extra allowance of food for a sick child.[79]

The combination of poor transportation and nonexistent medical services created hellish situations for the sick, especially for pregnant women and children. Children suffered both physically and psychologically, and even died, due to the lack of access to medical care. Iraqi writer Yosef Za'rur, a resident of the transit camp of Tel Mond, wrote in Arabic to the Ministry of Health that on May 7, 1952, a woman from his camp had gone with her sick one-year-old baby to seek help from the director of the camp. The baby's condition was worsening and the doctor on call was away. The woman then walked six kilometers to the nearby camp but no doctor was on call. She walked to still another moshav, Kfar Hess, where she found a doctor, but he refused to take care of her and her child. He told her to walk to Netanya, a city quite far from Kfar Hass, and in the morning, the baby died.[80]

Danny Dvir (né Salih) depicts in his memoirs what it meant to be a sick child under these conditions. When he became ill, a doctor was called to take care of him. His mother went to the neighbors who collected money to pay for the doctor's house visit. The doctor said the boy needed to be hospitalized and the family waited for the father, who worked long hours, to return from his job. The father carried Danny on his back to the bus station, which was located a few hundred meters from their home. Danny knew that hospitalization was a financial burden the father could not afford, but they waited for a long time for the bus, nonetheless. The father went to flag a ride, but no cars were to be seen: "He returned to the bus station, hugged me and asked again: 'Son, how do you feel now?' I felt that there was one answer he wanted to hear. I mustered all my powers and said: 'Dad, I feel better.' . . . Father rose in relief. He continued hugging me to his heart and in a calmer voice said: 'Son, let's go home.'"[81]

Contributing to the isolation of the camps was the scarcity of phones. It took a year or more for some transit camps to get a phone.[82] Where there was a phone, it was likely to be disconnected because people could not afford the payments and they were used only for emergency calls to for ambulances and to the fire department and the police.[83] Postal service was also irregular; in the first years of their existence the camps at Khayriyya, Kfar 'Ana, and Sakiyya had neither phone nor postal service for the Iraqi immigrant residents.[84]

The poor roads made it difficult for trucks to bring goods to the camps, and what they did bring were often of poor quality or were overpriced. In the case of food, what could be brought in was limited by the lack of means for refrigerating perishables.[85] Initially food was to be provided by the Ministry of Trade and Industry, and later the Ministry of Agriculture took on this responsibility.[86] A complicating factor was that, beginning in April 1949, the government instituted austerity measures. The daily rations for all Israelis were set by an American expert and included an unlimited ration of bread, and varying rations of corn, sugar, flour, and dairy products; the immigrants, like other citizens, were given documents with which they could get food. Individuals had notebooks in which the food they took was recorded and stamped each time (*pinkas mazon*). Moshe Huri describes what a transit camp kitchen looked like: "[With food it] was not a question of taste. The idea was to get what was needed and in sufficient quantity.... The kitchen corner was shelves of jars because everything was 'powders': milk powder, eggs powder ... and so on. And all for food stamps, and in modest portions."[87] Another source of dissatisfaction was that grocery stores in the transit camps did not price products fairly and lacked many ingredients. Not only was food hard to come by; the transit camps needed urgently shoes, clothing, kitchenwares, and furniture.[88] For some people, the only beautiful or festive pieces of clothing they had were the garments they brought from Iraq.[89] A Histadrut cooperative, the state's largest supplier and merchandise body, called Ha-Mashbir ha-Merkazi, provided goods to ninety camps, through a subbranch called Ha-Mashbir la-'Oleh, while the Hita'hadut ha-Soharim (Association of Merchants) did so for twenty-four. Ha-Mashbir, however, did

FIGURE 2. A woman cooking in a transit camp. Source: CZA, NKH\404367. Reprinted with permission.

a poor job of getting goods to faraway transit camps, and complaints mounted regarding the suppliers' tardiness and prices. A typical problem was that merchandise needed during wintertime would arrive during the spring and summer.[90] In some camps, on the eve of a holiday when Iraqis actually had money (given as a special bonus) to buy meat, suppliers did not show up.[91] Ironically, a daunting task in the Jewish states was to commemorate the Jewish holidays in faraway transit camps in the Galilee and near Jerusalem.

THE NEW CLASS: IRAQI-JEWISH MEN AND THE QUESTION OF LABOR

Iraqi-Jewish men struggled in the first few years to find their place in the alien society of Israel; they not speak Hebrew and could not comprehend the socialist ideology that framed Israeli society. Middle- and upper-class men now found themselves living alongside people whom they remembered as the urban poor in Iraq; poverty flattened all social differences from the past. Most men were willing to work in any occupation, but the system created by the state was convoluted and unfair.

The Iraqis who were able to survive economically can be categorized into three main groups. The first were those with relatives who had come to Israel before 1949 and could offer some help; this group had a support network, and therefore they did not need to rely on the Jewish Agency. The second were those who managed to have some capital transferred to Israel, either by legal or illegal means, before the denationalization and asset-freezing laws went into effect in Iraq. The third group consisted of Iraqis who were familiar with the British bureaucratic and regulatory apparatus in Iraq, which naturally had much in common with the administrative structure of Mandatory Palestine inherited by the young State of Israel. Eventually, they were able to find work with pharmacies, banks, the government's revenue division, and accounting companies, as well as those who could serve in the state's Arabic propaganda and security arms. But many Iraqis with transferable capital and mobility skills spent a year or two in the transit camps before moving to cities like Ramat Gan; some could not find employment even at this stage.[92] Moreover, many of the former merchants and owners of shops and small businesses could not so easily reconstruct their occupations and thus stayed much longer in the camps and the city's new slums. These men became a part of the new working class in Israel. As shown in the studies of Swirski and Lissak, the Israeli economy benefited from the cheap Mizrahi labor force, who powered the construction projects, industries, and agricultural sector.[93] For the Iraqis, however, they were thrust by necessity into a humiliating and terrifying experience.

Several studies of the occupation and employment of Iraqi Jews reflect the professional decline of Iraqi men and their shift to agriculture, construction, and unskilled labor in their first decade in Israel.[94] Tikva Darvish, who looked at the differences between the professions of Iraqi Jews in Iraq and in Israel, discovered that in the immediate decade after coming to Israel some Iraqis managed to retain their professional occupations. Provision of services remained almost the same (25.2 percent in Iraq and 27.2 percent in Israel) while employment in trade and industry declined (33.8 percent in Iraq and 12.8 percent in Israel). However, she also demonstrates that the numbers of Iraqis employed in agriculture rose from 2.5 percent in Iraq to 17.3 percent in Israel and that the number of those engaged in construction rose from 1.5 percent in Iraq to 13.0 percent in Israel.[95] Yaʻaqov Nahon, who studied the characteristics of the Israeli economy over two decades (1961–81), further argues that Mizrahim occupied lower-status professions in the Israeli labor market. In 1961, he showed, Iraqis still found positions as directors and free professionals in Israel based on their education and professional training in Iraq, although the percentage of European Jews in these occupations was much higher. In 1972, the number of Iraqi Jews working as free professionals, academics, and in technical services declined. This generation paid the price for the poor education system in the transit camps and could not recover their parents' status.[96]

Let us now turn to the transit camp economy, namely to the structures and job opportunities Iraqis faced in their first decades in Israel, while living in these camps. In the transit camp, employment was typically not continuous and did not allow the Iraqis to support their families. The minister of labor offered training courses in eighty-two camps in construction, clerical work, nursing, and other professions; some required a fee, a hardship for the newcomers. The Histadrut paid for the training of policemen and stenographers, and also of Iraqi Jews in agricultural labor in kibbutzim.[97] Yet Iraqis came to feel that connections, rather than skills, were required to get a job. In their view, work placements were based on sectarian and political considerations; Ashkenazim and government supporters always came first.[98] Initially, the majority of Iraqi men were not given jobs in the professions they knew, being assigned instead to low-paying public works jobs. This system, called ʻavodat dahak (literally: "adversity labor") was a type of daily workfare in which the Iraqis performed agricultural labor, paved roads, and did forestry tasks. Work assignment in these state-funded public works was based on issuing work permits at the labor bureau located in each camp. Some traded them in for more food or other benefits.[99]

Many members of the state socialist elite worked in agriculture after immigrating to Ottoman and Mandatory Palestine. Labor Zionism produced an extensive literature explaining the importance of working the land as a means of creating a new and productive Jew. The state leadership saw the communities in agricultural settlements that existed prior to the establishment of Israel, the moshavim and especially the kibbutzim, as the nation's revolutionary vanguard. Predictably, then, the leaders believed that working the land was a way of turning Iraqi Jews, and Mizrahi Jews more generally, into productive Zionists. For their part, middle- and upper-class Iraqis associated this type of work with the peasants and tribesmen they had known in Iraq and consequently found it deeply humiliating. More troubling than the psychological aspect was the fact that the wages which were not enough to support a family. Even men who worked a few days a week—seventeen days a month was the cut off—were categorized as working men and were not eligible for state unemployment assistance.[100]

Iraqi workers did find work in the factories near the camps. The arrival of so many people to Israel, in fact, allowed the state to develop its industries and populate them with the newcomers. In the years 1949–57 the number of workers in the Israeli market grew from 60,000 in 1949 to 162,000 in 1957. This manpower, coupled with money received from Germany and the United States, supported the poor state's large industrialization efforts. Working in factories, however, was not as reliable an income source as one might expect: manufacturing was sensitive to fluctuations in the Israeli economy and the whims of its bureaucracy and was moved from place to place, as the state pushed them to relocate to border and depopulated regions.[101] Vacation days were not guaranteed, and the widespread use of unskilled labor made for an increase in work-related accidents.[102] Factories which were connected to the state's military industry were more stable.[103] In larger factories, trucks would come early to pick the workers to their place of work and bring them back at the end of the day.[104]

Some men worked illegally in the cities and villages around the camps. This occurred frequently when a transit camp was located next to a moshava, with farmers being eager to take advantage of the situation by paying very low wages and workers who were unable to complain to the authorities. The state retained some laws from the previous mandatory administration, but enacted the bulk of its labor laws which regulated labor rights, protected benefits and minimum wages, and defended women's rights in the labor market in the mid-1950s, as the Iraqis were already working, with the Histadrut itself objecting to laws regulating minimum wages.[105] Therefore, many of the workers operated in a legal system that had many loopholes and which did not protect them from having their wages withheld or from being fired without just cause. Other men offered their professional skills as craftsmen illegally. Shoemakers, for example, would walk between homes in nearby cities trying to sell their skill, or to get used shoes, fix them, and then resell the shoes in the transit camps themselves.[106]

The Ministry of Labor established a total of fifty-three labor bureaus in the camps, but transit-camp residents also visited those in nearby moshavot and cities, which were opened more frequently and connected directly to Histadrut workers councils. The Histadrut pushed for having all the labor of the newcomers supervised through its labor bureaus and workers' councils, so that it could ensure its control over the labor market (a goal that was very important to MAPAI).[107] Undercutting its own effort to provide employment, however, the Ministry of Labor dictated that some offices were only open two days a week, despite the great demand for work. The bureau in the transit camp would usually have a window protected by iron bars from behind which the clerk would call out the names of those who were fortunate enough to be assigned work, and then he would hand them their work permits. Dozens would gather in line, old and young. Work assignments were based on the size of the family. In some camps, a head of household who had more than three children got three to four days of work; a head of household of two, two days; and families with no children got a day or two every other week. The Ministry of Welfare worked closely with the Ministry of Labor, staffing offices in some transit camps to help families in need. A family would fill out forms and wait for a visit by an inspector from the ministry. If the family was found to be in need, it would get more support. The evaluation process, however, was long, taking three to five months.[108]

Because the roads to the camps were bad, and buses and other forms of transportation infrequent, Iraqi workers had to get up early and return very late at night. Some worked in places outside the camps and returned for the weekend. That meant, in addition to being forced to work in low-paying jobs, parents were separated from their children. Kochava, who lived in the transit camp of Talpiot (near Jerusalem), describes what her father experienced: "[My parents'] economic condition in Iraq had been very good. Here my father worked as a construction worker, and not just a construction worker, but one who worked for daily wages, a man whose neck was placed under the sword of being fired. I remember how he would put pocket money under our pillows, especially on rainy days, saying, 'Pray that they do not send me home today,' because on rainy days they would send the workers home without any pay."[109]

Another difficulty faced by Iraqi men who worked in government projects and in factories was the withholding of wages, which happened because of the ongoing economic crisis and also the Israeli bureaucracy. Conflicts between the ministries of labor, welfare, finance, and the local municipalities—the bodies responsible for distributing pay—created these delays. The factory managers withheld salaries as well.[110] Those Iraqis who worked in agriculture had to cope with the seasonality of that type of employment and times when no money was coming in. At other times, workers refused to go to the seasonal work, demanding a permanent job.[111] However, refusing to take a job assigned by the state meant denial of food, housing, and future job assignments. The authorities also attempted to exercise control over the transit-camp workforce by punishing those who worked a second job in addition to their assigned job.[112] Behavior in the camp often influenced one's chances of employment; troublemakers were sent to the end of the line.[113]

Even under these conditions, unemployment was still high. The Histadrut Workers Councils, an organization that had representatives in the labor and welfare bureaus, complained about the enormous difficulty of finding positions for immigrant workers.[114] Jerusalem and Tel Aviv attracted large numbers of the unemployed. Sometimes it was a long walk just to get to a labor bureau: despite the large number of labor bureaus in the country, transit camps were not always located near to one.[115] Those who could not work eight hours a day because of their age or their physical conditions were deemed ineligible by the labor bureau in Jerusalem and were automatically directed to the welfare bureau.

The old and the disabled—the most vulnerable—were typically not allowed to work and were assigned immediately to the welfare bureau. A man over the age of fifty-five (and in some cases forty) was considered "old" and often denied a work assignment.[116] The father of Iraqi novelist Sami Michael, for example, was fifty when he came to Israel and thus "was considered an old man." Having formerly been a wealthy cloth merchant, he was reduced to working as a gardener at the Ministry of Defense building.[117] The Jewish Agency sent individuals who could not support themselves to relatives outside the camps or to transit camps closer to urban centers. Others were fortunate enough to be assigned jobs that did not involve physical labor, through the coordination of the ministries of interior, labor, and welfare; those included running a kiosk or collecting taxes in the transit camps. The welfare bureaus in the camps had lists of cases prioritized for each such position. However, the office could be closed for months, if funding did not come through.[118] Welfare, as anything else, was connected to proper conduct in the camp. The welfare bureau in Kfar Nahman, for example, stopped helping families in need because they were late paying their rent.[119]

A 1959 survey conducted by the American Jewish Joint Distribution Committee (JDC), a Zionist relief organization based in New York that funded relief in the transit camps, found the most difficult welfare cases in the transit camp of Amisav (Petach Tikva), which was populated mostly by Iraqis, as well as Iranians and Yemenites. Predictably perhaps, they characterized the Mizrahi people of the camp as fatalistic and superstitious, and as coming from cultures where the demands of society from individuals were minimal and manual labor was considered humiliating. Immigration, accordingly, brought them from a medieval society to a progressive, industrial Western culture. Out of the 172 "social cases" they surveyed, 157 individuals were deemed unhealthy; 28 individuals suffered from problems in spine and disk; and 34 were diagnosed with mental diseases (such as mental deficiency, neurosis, and anxiety). Sixty-seven percent of these individuals did not understand Hebrew, 48 percent were illiterate, and 62 percent were unemployed, in part because of limited work capacities.[120] While some of the difficulties these men encountered could be attributed to illiteracy and lack of professional training, migration itself was also a factor in turning them into "social cases." Migration created their poor living conditions, the injuries they suffered because of their manual labor, the fact they had to study a new language at a later age, and the challenge of coping with the Israeli and American-Jewish assumptions about Arab and Persian societies.

An example of what happened to a man whose professional skills were useless in Israel is that of Shim'on Mu'allim Nissim (known in Baghdad as Shim'on Effendi), who had been the director of a famous Jewish school in Baghdad, Rachael Shahmon. Despite having held one of the most influential positions in the Jewish education system in Iraq, Shim'on ended up in a transit camp. His former student Sha'ul Haddad described his living conditions:

> He lived by himself, old and tired, filled with anger and bitterness. Only God knows what he ate and drank. My friend, David Halutz, who lived in this transit camp, told me that the man must have lost his sanity. More than once, he left his tent without his clothes on, and the children of the camp would bother him. David Halutz would chase them and get Shim'on Effendi to his camp.... It is possible that had they known his past they would not have abused him. I, in any case, cried when I heard ... about the difficult turn in the life of the great Shim'on Effendi.[121]

A man whose training, social status, and even name (most people referred to him as Shim'on Effendi and not by his family name) bespoke the recognition of his talent by the majority Iraqi society was essentially cast onto the dust heap in Israel.

Unemployment and low wages stunted the professional and educational development of the second generation. Teenagers had to leave high school to help support their families. Iraqi students who managed to get into a university in Jerusalem could not find financial aid or part-time employment and had to abandon their studies as well.[122] Many also had to deal with the difficult psychological trauma of seeing their fathers, and their fathers' generation, suffer as a result of the migration to Israel.

Men responded to these harsh conditions by striking and protesting. The demonstrations and the long lines in the labor bureaus gave birth to a character that was a common feature in many camps, the local "thug" (*biryon*). The thugs were sometimes criminals with connections to individuals outside the camp, but more often they were unemployed young men who were hired to keep order in the welfare and labor bureaus, break up strikes and suspicious gatherings, and disrupt political rallies of parties not favored by the authorities of the transit camps.[123] One such thug was Sha'ul, whose father, Nahum, ran a company in Baghdad but upon his immigration to Israel at the age of forty-five could not find his desired work at an office or a bank. Sha'ul dropped out of high school because of difficult conditions at home. As his father spiraled downward in a transit camp, Sha'ul was drafted by the IDF, and when he returned to the camp he became an alcoholic. He was hired by MAPAI for five liras per month to break up illegal meetings and demonstrations, but ended up quitting this job because he could not stand against his fellow Iraqis who were demanding bread and work. He later became a thief and served time in jail, but after being released he was able to put his life back together.[124]

Under such difficult living and labor conditions Iraqi men came up with their own solutions and relied on the mutual-help systems that came into being in the transit camps. When families moved into wooden shacks, they planted vegetable gardens next to them to supplement the meagre rations they were given. The state provided loans in support.[125] There was intense competition for becoming a proprietor of one of the grocery stores that opened in the camps. These were the most coveted positions because men from cities in Iraq knew this work and preferred it to manual labor; men over fifty-five were allowed to apply for them as well.[126] The minister of the interior had to negotiate with the

Health Ministry concerning the opening of stores, whose employees were appointed by a local committee in the camps and approved by the Welfare Ministry and the Jewish Agency.[127]

Constructing the stores took a while, especially in the years 1950–51 when the camps' dysfunctionality was most keenly felt.[128] The completion of the stores marked the beginning of small-scale commercial development in the camps, as Iraqis subsequently opened kiosks, bakeries, and other shops. In Khayriyya a newcomer taught a course in accounting,[129] while a former accountant opened a dancing hall. Small markets came into being in transit camps and in slums where people bought animals such as pigeons, goats, chickens, ducks, and geese. The transit camp in Ramat ha-Sharon, for example, included food stores whose owners sold (at times illegally) meat, fish, and vegetables, and also offered the services of a dentist and a barber.[130] Later, itinerant peddlers using donkeys and horses to move their wares, everything from oil to groceries to cloth, became fixtures in the transit camps.

Iraqis also applied for licenses to build synagogues, and in some camps there were to be more than one.[131] The synagogues did not always have rabbis; some people used them as a haven for personal contemplation. Other Iraqis got licenses to operate local cafés, which became the social hubs of the camps. In such places Arabic music was played. Since some cafés had electricity and thus could have radios, they attracted men; alcohol was another draw.[132] The men would gather there at end of the workday, listen to stories, tell jokes, and play cards.[133] In some camps the cafés turned into small clubs. Once such club, for example, featured the shows of a popular belly dancer identified by the somewhat exotic name Mary Conga.[134] Although the synagogues and cafés were very different types of venues, they offered Iraqi men a space away from their families and from their workplaces. In both, Iraqis tried to re-create their activities in their former homes, and create a religious or leisurely routine not controlled by the state. In such difficult times, this sort of thing mattered a great deal.

A HOUSEHOLD WITH NO HOUSE: GENDERED CONCERNS

Like the men, Iraqi women in the transit camps faced a new set of challenges. Their husbands, who often had been white-collar workers in Iraq, struggled in the face of poverty. The men who could not regain their former status sometimes grew depressed and did not know how to deal with the new circumstances. Many Iraqi women rose to the occasion and did whatever it took to provide for their families and create some sense of normalcy in their lives. These women, who once had had servants, or at least a roof over their heads, now found themselves struggling for their daily bread and doing work they associated with the poorest women in Iraq.

Most Iraqi women did not know any Hebrew, so there was keen interest in the study of this language. Educationally, the social order in Iraq turned things upside down. Illiterate women and young girls had more opportunities to learn to read and write, while educated teenagers, who had gone to middle schools and high schools in Iraq, now dropped out to help support their families. The state organization most visible in the women's lives was the Histadrut's Irgun Imahot 'Ovdot (Organization of Working Mothers), which offered night classes, lessons in Hebrew, and professional training. Iraqi women took part in these activities both to pass the time and in hopes of improving their situations.[135] Sociologists note that the level of literacy among Iraqi women increased after their migration to Israel.[136] The records of transit camps around Jerusalem (Talpiot and Makor Haim) show that all of their events, such as Hanukah parties, language and Bible classes, lectures on Israeli history, and sewing classes were attended by Iraqi women in 1950–51. Over time, Iraqi women from within the camps even led such courses.[137] The Ministry of Labor also provided classes for women in sewing, rug making, and child rearing.[138]

Women found it extremely difficult to maintain family life in the transit camps. Planning a wedding party, and later celebrating the birth of a child, proved a challenge. It was hard to finance these family parties, and empty spaces in the overcrowded transit camps were hard to come by. Brides and grooms improvised, getting married in the local café in the transit camp, the shack of the youth movement, or available empty shacks; some marched to the nearby agricultural town to use their halls or restaurants, if they could afford it. But the memory lingered of weddings in the past, when the finest food was offered to the guests.[139] One former bride recalls her sad wedding story; being poor she had to be married with no food to offer to the guests, with neither a bride dress nor a wedding photo. Years later, when she was older, she and her husband borrowed the appropriate attire and took a wedding photo instead of the one they desired so many years earlier.[140]

Delivering and raising babies in the transit camps was likewise very challenging due to the poor transportation and medical services. In the Sakiyya transit camp, Iraqi immigrants waited long hours for ambulances to take women in labor to hospitals. In one case, they called an ambulance at six in the morning, the baby was born at eight o'clock, and then died in the camp. The mother was hospitalized, severely ill, after the ambulance picked her up.[141] A woman in the north delivered her baby in the transit camp and suffered severe bleeding with no ambulance in sight.[142] In another case, when the ambulance came, the family of the pregnant woman could not afford the fee for the ambulance fare. Her husband, upset, asked if the cost of the fare equaled that of his wife's life. Their baby eventually died.[143]

The extreme difficulties that women encountered when seeking hospital care to give birth are illustrated by the story of Madeline, who lived in Sakiyya. When Madeline was about to give birth, it took her family hours to find a means of transportation. Finally, they managed to have her driven to the hospital after negotiating with the officer in the military camp nearby, who secured a truck for them. The nurse in the hospital, unaware of what the family had gone through to bring Madeline there, castigated family members for not bringing Madeline earlier to the hospital. She explained to them that Madeline was not a goat or a cow, and they needed to adapt to the new norms in the country. When Madeleine heard one of the nurses saying that the patient was probably a primitive woman, who was accustomed to giving birth with the help of old midwives or witches, she promptly informed them she had been a teacher in Iraq who spoke Arabic, English, and French. The nurses fell silent.[144]

Babies disappeared in Israeli hospitals and some were given up for adoption without parental consent. The vast majority of these babies were Yemenite. There is a gap between what the state was willing to acknowledge until very recently—sixty-nine unsolved cases of babies who mysteriously disappeared, and accounts by activists who claim that the number is actually in the hundreds.[145] However, even official accounts corroborate that babies were hospitalized without nametags and that babies whose parents did not visit them for a few months were given up for adoption.[146] An NGO called AMRAM (Amutat Amram–Hatifat Yaldey Teyman, Mizrah u-Balkan), dedicated to the problem of kidnapped babies from Yemen, the East, and the Balkans, has documented dozens of parents who believed their presumed-to-be-dead children were still alive. Their online archive includes forty testimonies of Iraqi and Kurdish families who immigrated to Israel in the years 1949–51 and never saw the bodies of their children after their presumed deaths. In their testimonies to AMRAM these women narrate stories that seem to suggest a pattern. A mother gives birth to a child or hospitalizes her child when he or she is sick. The baby later disappears and no death certificate and no burial site is shown to the parents.

In some cases of children of Yemenite parents, eighteen years after the birth of the child, conscription orders reached the homes of the children presumed to be dead; in other cases, parents find the children alive in the hospital.[147] In one such case an Iraqi brother and sister were offered candy, taken to a kibbutz, and told that they had new parents. Their father struggled to find them; after he finally located them at the kibbutz, he was convinced it was better for the children to remain with their new parents. However, the son's own resistance and stubbornness resulted in him being returned to his parents.[148]

The space of the transit camp and the paucity of services that it offered made women's lives miserable. As noted above, many camps lacked drinking water, so women had to trudge long distances to faucets and wells. The Iraqi writer Esperance Cohen recalls that after getting some dishes and kitchen utensils, she would wait until midnight to wash them. At that time the line was shorter than during the day, and her husband could stay with their small children. And sleeping was far from restful. Family members were kept awake by howling jackals. Their narrow beds, like all other beds provided by the Jewish Agency, were made of iron, with hard mattresses, and they sunk into the mud and sand.[149]

Feeding a family was no easy task. Women often took care of the vegetable gardens next to their shacks and tents in order to provide more food for their families. In defiance of statewide austerity measures, residents illegally bought chickens and goats to be used as a source of eggs and milk.[150] Cooking was dangerous because women used portable paraffin cooking stoves (primus); if it fell over, the tent and shacks in which they lived could catch fire. Food products were delivered to people based on quantities specified by the austerity measure laws; pregnant women and young children merited more food. Many Israelis were able to supplement the rations fixed by the austerity rules: those who had farms or lived in moshavim and kibbutzim, or who had relatives in such places, could get milk, eggs, and meat, while urban Israelis often bought such products on the black market. In the transit camps, in contrast, the local stores suffered from a chronic shortage of food. Meat was a rarity, and often was delivered only for major holidays, and sometimes not even then. As Orit Rozin has shown, women who wanted to smuggle meat and eggs from relatives in kibbutzim and moshavim had to evade, like all other Israelis, inspectors who would go on buses and cabs and search for unauthorized goods. The welfare bureau, the women's organizations, and the institute for nutritional guidance were at odds over the question of rations. But the debate resulted in no improvement.[151]

Two accounts by children who lived in the Talpiot transit camp convey the challenges of maintaining a household without a proper house. Kochava Sagi (then Yosef) relates about her mother:

> I remember how my mother used to go to the secretariat in the camp every day to find out when we [were] moving [from the transit camp]. We lived in a shack made of aluminum. We built a little kitchen outside the shack and tried to improve our conditions. . . . The toilets and showers were a hundred meters away, and I always needed someone to escort me to the bathroom because of the danger. The fear was that a child would fall into a hole; the toilets then were made of tin placed over holes.[152]

Amalia Juna (then Shemesh) provides this depiction of her mother:

> In Iraq, my parents [had] lived well. They had a big house . . . ; my father was a teacher and our economic situation was really good. My parents had a shop where my uncle worked and my mother sewed. And . . . here [we] were crammed into a shack made of canvas. I remember my mother carrying water, and working a tough job in a restaurant, washing dishes there until midnight. . . . The quarrels [in the camp] arose because of the overcrowding and the shortages. For example, who gets to hang their laundry today?[153]

In addition to regular chores, then, mothers now dealt with an entirely new set of problems: the taking of children to the bathroom, leaking roofs, and fights with their neighbors over pails for washing dishes or ropes for hanging laundry. The long lines for services, the competition for jobs and for tin shacks and wooden shacks when they became available, created friction between women. At the same time, there were many cases of mutual help: men and women lent one other money for food or to pay for a visit to the doctor, and mothers babysat their neighbors' children when mothers had to work, thus creating a network that provided the things the state could not.

The state, for its part, saw Iraqi women as desperately in need of education and discipline. As Sahlav Stoler-Lis and Shifra Schwartz have illustrated, the nurses and female social workers sent to the camps did not think that the blame for the hunger, disorder, and malaise in the transit camps lay with the state, but rather with Iraqi mothers, because of their primitive background.[154] In other words, Iraqi women who were impoverished and dependent on the state, which could not provide them with potable water, kitchen utensils to cook and eat with, and decent living spaces in which they could raise and feed their children, were characterized as being unhygienic and incapable of taking care of their children. Nurses were therefore sent to the camps to demonstrate to mothers how to use diapers, cook, and take care of their children, and their achievements in guiding the Iraqis were recounted triumphantly in the press. One of the ways of disciplining Iraqi mothers was the distribution of the contents of the "Care" packages. Manufactured in the United States and donated to the Ministry of Health, a Care package consisted of diapers, sheets for a baby's bed, and baby clothing. The nurses opened the packages, and each mother would get an item from them. As Stoler-Lis and Schwartz note, "the size of the gift, its giving or denial, were the sole prerogative of the nurse."[155] Sometimes nurses rewarded mothers who collaborated with them and punished others. Mothers were also made to pay for these items, "to learn that you don't get things for free."[156]

Not all husbands agreed that their wives would work outside the home, but the difficult economic conditions pushed women to the Israeli labor market. Many women found positions in in agricultural work, although married women disdained agricultural employment, such as picking cotton and collecting potatoes, nuts, and peanuts, and preferred to work in factories.[157] Women also worked illegally in farms.[158] In the transit camp of Ramat ha-Sharon women would board trucks that drove them to the nearby fields where they worked. Lucky ones were employed in cooking and cleaning in the nearby agricultural boarding school of Ha-Kfar ha-Yarok.[159] One Iraqi migrant recalls that she ceased working because it was difficult for her father to see his beautiful young girl returning burned and exhausted from the hard work in the fields.[160] In camps near agricultural towns and cities, some women and young girls cleaned houses, mostly illegally.

Other women worked in factories, although they were often the first to be fired when factories suffered financial difficulties.[161] Women who needed work, especially widows who relied on the state, and who had lost their network of support (uncles, fathers, brothers who were able to provide for them in Iraq), turned to the workers councils and to labor bureaus in the cities. Shoshanna Arbeli Almozlino (née Fahima Irbili),[162] who immigrated to Israel in 1947, worked at the labor bureau at Ramat Gan in its female section, where she met hundreds of women from Sakiyya, Khayriyya, and Kfar 'Ana. One of the few Mizrahi women in the bureau, she attempted to help fellow Mizrahi women but could only offer six or seven positions to the hundreds of women who were begging for employment; as a young woman she had to choose whether the widow or the wife with the sick husband would be among the lucky ones placed in a factory. Her role, however, could save lives, as the following episode indicates:

> In 1955, an unemployed Iraqi woman, a widow with three orphans from the transit camp of Petach Tikva, arrived again . . . at the labor bureau. All her pleas to the male clerks, who were not from her land, who did not speak her language, and were unable to speak French and English as she was, had failed. She and her three orphans now faced the peril of hunger. . . . One day, a young female clerk arrived at the bureau. . . . The widow understood that she was from her community, started crying, took the hands of the Iraqi woman and kissed them, saying to her in Arabic: "You must help me! By my children's eyes, I am a widow and I have no way to feed my children. Give me work, any work. I will work harder than men. You will see! You will not be sorry!" The young woman started crying as well, and told the other woman, in Iraqi Arabic, that she could work at Elite (a chocolate factory). She worked shifts, night times as well, harder than any man, for long decades. The Iraqi widow is my grandmother and the Iraqi clerk was Mrs. Shoshanna Arbeli Almozlino.[163]

Some educated women used their language skills and worked as telephone operators, handling international phone calls. Other educated women worked within the camp as teachers in schools (once they had mastered Hebrew) and in the Histadrut women's organizations. Working married women and widows would leave their children at home in the care of older brothers and sisters or friendly neighbors. Young women had to struggle to get an education and professional training, often because they were expected to sacrifice their opportunity to do so for a male family member. Those who entered the higher education system recalled the discrimination they faced from professors and the condescension of fellow students or professors.[164]

Younger women also faced sociological and psychological challenges. According to press reports, the economic conditions prevented many young women from marrying.[165] The anthropologist Phyllis Shalgi and the psychologists Miriam Goldwasser and Hannah Goldman wrote about their work in a mental health and psychology clinic (then called "the station for psychological hygiene") in Jaffa. In an article on "disturbed Iraqi women," published in 1955, they diagnosed the features of fifteen Iraqi women who had visited clinics in Jerusalem and Jaffa, and ten additional Iraqi women. The young women were all diagnosed as suffering from depression, which was manifested in crying, self-pity, and suicidal thoughts. According to the report, all the girls had a high level of intelligence and aspired to having a career (their first goal) and to marriage (which came second). They had difficulty integrating into the new schools, and felt that their jobs were unsatisfactory. The experts argued that the deterioration of their fathers' images and their lack of experience in sublimated heterosexual relations led to many problems. One girl they studied, a twenty-three-year-old woman who suffered from depression, had a problematic relationship with her forty-five-year-old father, formerly a successful merchant who was now unemployed. Her sister, to whom she was close, had died. Another sister worked outside their home. She did not want to marry an Iraqi man, but rather an Ashkenazi, but found that Ashkenazi men disrespected her Iraqi culture and only wanted to engage in sex. The experts argued that her unwillingness to engage in sexual relations led to her inferiority conflict and that she was rigid and unable to communicate her emotions, which caused her to overestimate her own intellectual capacities. They nonetheless depicted her as warm and sensitive.[166]

Read even slightly against the grain of the patronizing assumptions of the three experts, we sense the pain of these girls categorized as "disturbed." Suffering from the loss of social status, unable to attend Israeli educational institutions because they did not speak Hebrew or were too poor, and overqualified for manual labor or work in a factory, these girls were trapped in the jobs they eventually succeeded in finding. It was not easy watching their fathers have their dignity stripped from them. Dating was a challenge: they came from more socially conservative households and found themselves in a society where sexual relations before marriage were permissible, but the Ashkenazi men they met, like everybody else outside of the boundaries of the Iraqi community, disrespected their culture. Where other women threw everything they had into the efforts to survive, to engage in relationships, to build families, these young women did not have the strength. I do not know how widespread depression was at the time, among both Iraqi men and women, but anecdotal reports such as this one, autobiographies in which the authors complain about lack of interest in them as children by their mothers, or items in the press about fathers becoming disengaged alcoholics suggest a recurring pattern. Furthermore, young women were among the most vulnerable elements in the transit camps. The press reported that women were subjected to rape and a few autobiographies also mention cases of sexual harassment and attempted rape.[167] In other cases, Iraqi men protected women who were sexually harassed; they did not bother waiting for the police and handled the criminals themselves.[168]

The most desperate women, like men, also turned to criminality. There were reports in the press about prostitution in the transit camps. Officials confirmed these reports, acknowledging the existence of brothels in the transit camp of Talpiot and babies born to single mothers. The state, instead of sending these and other girls who turned to criminality to educational institutions, often jailed them.[169] Bechor Sheetrit, the minister of police, depicted the women in jail as "difficult human material; prostitutes, psychopaths, much wilder and more untamed than male prisoners."[170] The jails were crowded and children were sometimes jailed with their mothers.

THE PROMISED LAND: WOODEN SHACKS, SHIKUNIM, AND THE KURDISH SOLUTION

From the mid-1950s on, Iraqis slowly moved into neighborhoods in cities. The move out of a transit camp was not always one to a modern apartment. Some Iraqis moved to poor neighborhoods and slums in Jaffa, southern Tel Aviv, Haifa, and Jerusalem. Some moved to neighborhoods not too far from the original camps into wooden shacks that were only a slight improvement over what they had known, often on the same lands of the Arab village on which the transit camp was built. The poor neighborhoods of some cities and towns in Israel came into existence in this manner. Typically, a moshava would annex these poor neighborhoods, thus increasing its territory and population, eventually becoming a city. The members of the middle classes, however, especially those with capital accumulated through professional employment, managed to move to better places.

By the mid-1950s the Israeli government, having come to the conclusion that the transit camps had outlived their usefulness, drafted a plan to close them and move residents elsewhere. Implementation of this plan was slow because although the government wanted Iraqis, as well as other newcomers, to settle in border regions, many refused. By 1955 the number of people living in the transit camps had been reduced from 157,140 to 88,116. This trend continued as most residents had moved to permanent residences by the years 1957–60. By the end of 1963 only 15,300 remained in these camps.[171] Most of the construction was done by a Histadrut company, Solel Boneh, which built 113,000 permanent units for newcomers, as well as 58,000 shacks of different kinds in the transit camps during the 1950s. A housing company belonging to the Histadrut, Shikun 'Ovdim, managed the selling of units in new neighborhoods for newcomers and more established citizens in cities and moshavot. The limited ability of tenants in Israeli public housing to eventually buy such apartments and the state's control over them created many problems for the tenants, their children, and their grandchildren, as is still the case to this day.

A government company called Amidar carried the housing projects. Ten years after Amidar's construction, two hundred thousand units had been built as public housing for individuals who could not afford to buy or rent homes.[172] Amidar was in charge of public housing both in and outside the transit camps and therefore its decisions about the cost of rent, the location of housing it built, and movement to neighborhoods had a significant impact on the lives of Iraqi Jews in Israel. Amidar not only had charged rent for the wooden shacks in the transit camps, but also had demanded a move-in fee, which most families could not afford initially. Within the camps, Amidar raised the rent it charged from people who lived in wooden shacks by 85 percent according to some accounts, although a discount of 25 to 50 percent was given to heads of household who had low-paying jobs, to parents who had lost their children in war, and to tenants whose social conditions were even below the poverty typical of the transit camps.[173]

The reality was that for Iraqis and for other immigrants saving enough for key money payments to move to a wooden shack and later to an apartment seemed like an impossible task. The system of "key money," exported from 1940s England under the British mandate, expected a tenant to pay the state (at times half of the value of the property) for the right to rent a property for an unlimited time, with the understanding that rents would be much lower than what would normally be the case.[174] Most Iraqis could not afford key payments—either for the wooden shacks in the transit camps or for permanent housing. Another complicating factor with respect to the housing policy in Israel was the astonishing gap between investments in the Iraqis (and for that matter any newcomer in the 1950s) and the Aliyah from America. In 1953, half a million Israeli liras (IL) were invented in a project aimed to bring newcomers from the United States to Israel, with each American family getting four thousand ILs for housing. The scope of the state's financial help was kept in secret because of the fear that it would create a nation-wide scandal.[175] In comparison, in 1951, the budget given from the Ministry of Interior directly to the transit camps was three thousand IL in Zarnuga, fifteen hundred IL in Kfar 'Ana, and six thousand IL in Ramat ha-Sharon.[176]

The housing projects suffered from an ongoing shortage of raw materials and a lack of skilled workers. In the early 1950s, construction companies could not even build houses for people who wanted to buy for investment purposes.[177] In addition, the national building companies had to fight with the Keren Kayemet le-Yisra'el (Israeli National Fund; or KKL), an entity established in 1901 to buy and develop lands, which controlled vast territories whose officials were unwilling to relinquish for public construction.[178] The quality of public housing was far from satisfactory. Some of the apartments built for the newcomers were small (twenty meters by thirty-one meters was the size of a unit given in some places).[179] Complaints were voiced in the Knesset about apartments and houses built by Amidar from the north to the south; some were built without wiring for electricity, doors, baths, or stairwells.[180] In 1954, a group of newcomers moved into wooden shacks that turned out to lack kitchens.[181]

A sense of the state of housing can be drawn from the memos of Zelig Lavon, the CEO of Shikon 'Ovdim, some of which were written to his brother, Pinhas, the chair of the Histadrut. Shikun 'Ovdim was established by the Histadrut under the mandate and remained in operation after the founding of the State of Israel. While it should be noted that in the years 1948–52 the construction field experienced a deep crisis, his letters reflect certain priorities, which did not, to say the least, favor the Iraqis. In 1950, Shikun 'Ovdim built eight thousand units for veteran members of the Histadrut and IDF staff. Some got apartments for free, and some even made a profit when they sold their previous apartments. Despite the great deals they had received, the Histadrut members were unhappy about the quality of the apartments.[182]

As part of his housing plans, Zelig Lavon came up with what he deemed to be the brilliant idea of the "the growing home" (*ha-bayit ha-gadel*), a basic unit to which new rooms could be added later.[183] He targeted the former transit-camp members as the market for the "growing homes," and suggested that his company be designated to build permanent homes for them because of security concerns: "I am certain that the Minister of Defense did not overlook the military dangers. We might fear that in the slightest conflict, those who live in temporary housing would be the first to abandon their houses, block the roads, and create a state of panic."[184]

Another factor that slowed the closing of the camps was that doing so was an intensely politicized process. It had racial dimensions, as the Ashkenazim were the first to leave; in some moshavot Mizrahi residents populated one neighborhood, while Ashkenazi another.[185] When the state initiated the process of closing a particular camp, water and other services were cut off. In order to push out the residents in the transit camp of Beit Lid, for example, the municipality cut off the electricity. The residents responded by demonstrating, and organized a strike in protest.[186] That Amidar had built the shacks in the transit camps gave it the power to evict those living in them when a camp was closed down or when the land could be used for other reasons. However, many people already left (or escaped) the transit camps at the times of their official closure or evacuation. The shifts in population and in municipal boundaries created by the closure of the transit camps had political consequences.[187]

The most violent evacuation of a transit camp happened in February 1953, in the transit camp of Kfar Saba, where five thousand to six thousand newcomers from Iraq, Iran, and North Africa resided. On February 18, 1953, the mayor of Kfar Saba was instructed by the deputy prime minister to evacuate the camp within twenty-four hours for security reasons. The explanations given were that there were rumors that forty Arab infiltrators had hidden in the camp, and that the camp's Jewish communists were in touch with communists across the border. Trade relations between families in the transit camp and the Palestinians also caused fears. Soldiers and policemen thus arrived to the camp at nighttime and boarded its people on military trucks. They gathered the frightened people of the camp and pushed them to the empty trucks without allowing them to take their belongings. Those who resisted were told that they would be arrested and jailed if they refused the orders to leave. The petrified people of the camp were scattered all over Israel.[188]

The closure of the transit camp of Amisav (near Petach Tikva), whose population was 85 percent Iraqi, illustrates the political nature of the process. At the beginning of 1955, 7,500 people lived in the camp; in 1960 the number had declined to 875. Officials in the JDC, the Israeli Welfare Ministry, and Petach Tikva's own municipality described the chaos involved in the movement to permanent housing. Individuals signed housing contracts without understanding the financial commitment they were undertaking; they were unclear about their future rents or their obligations as property owners; and a culture of what these officials called "sign now, think later" typified the state's interactions with them.[189] To further complicate the shift to permanent housing, political parties worried that having the camp's residents as voters in Petach Tikva would weaken their position, and therefore its annexation to the city was delayed. As late as 1962, two hundred families, mostly Iranians, were still living in shacks. People with ties to MAPAI were able to leave the camp earlier than others.[190]

As Esther Meir has shown, there were two dominant models for Iraqi urban settlement in Israel: one typified by Or Yehuda, a municipality created from transit camps, and one typified by Ramat Gan, a city whose social fabric changed because of migration of Iraqis. The city of Or Yehuda represented the consolidation of the transit camps of Kfar 'Ana, Khayriyya, and Sakiyya into one municipality. When these camps were about to be cleared, both Tel Aviv and Ramat Gan fought for the territory around the camps. The Ministry of Interior tried to cut their services attempting to push people out of the region, but the residents demanded that the camp be recognized as an independent municipal region and finally, in 1960, the region of the three transit camps was recognized as an independent municipal unit. MAPAI made sure that Mordechai Ben Porat, a leading Zionist since his time in Iraq and a MAPAI member, would lead the new municipal region.[191] Or Yehuda, in a way, was the city of those left behind, of those who could not move to the big cities and escape poverty. Out of 2,225 families living in Or Yehuda, 616 lived in public housing, 223 in deserted Arab homes, and 1,368 individuals lived in wooden shacks. Most people in the city did not own their own businesses, and one-third lived on state benefits.[192]

Immigrants with more resources or those who were able to find employment within their professional training left for neighborhoods in cities and moshavot in central Israel. Ramat Gan was the major hub. Twenty thousand Iraqi Jews settled there, mostly members of the upper and middle classes. Once young men became more established, or went into the military and gained some form of social standing, they began looking for their old friends. Graduates of the Alliance School in Baghdad reconnected and formed a group of roughly fifty, who met in Ramat Gan and organized lectures, trips, and dances.[193] In the same city, another group of Iraqi Jews met regularly and published a journal. Iraqi writers such as Sasson Somekh and David Semah formed a literary circle that gathered together authors from Iraq. The group was a crucible of cultural creativity, while the others served as a way to remember the past and cope with the present. Being in a city made for a little more opportunity for relaxation, as the struggles of daily life eased somewhat.[194]

The other solution to the housing problem of Iraqi Jews, especially those from northern Iraq, was newcomers' moshavim in the north and in the south of Israel. The kibbutzim, for their part, refused to accept Iraqi adults who wanted to engage in agriculture. The moshavim movement did not want to absorb newcomers in its own communities but was willing to build villages for them in other parts of the land, and send young instructors to live with the new residents and guide them in agricultural work. This settlement pattern was part of a larger project to spread all newcomers throughout Israel. During the 1950s, the state constructed 39 moshavim for newcomers from Iran and Iraq, 84 for North African Jews, 31 for Yemenite Jews, 6 for Egyptians, 4 for Indian Jews, 91 for European Jews, 14 for Israelis, and 13 for other groups, out of a total of 282 moshavim. Not all of these communities survived.[195]

These moshavim were built in the vicinity of Jerusalem, in order to create a buffer zone of Jewish inhabitants around the city, and in border regions, where security conditions were poor. Some were built on the ruins of Palestinian villages in order to prevent the original inhabitants from coming back.[196] The idea of settling Jews from Iraqi Kurdistan in villages was driven by the Zionist evaluation of the Iraqi "human material" that I referred to earlier. When Zionist emissaries toured northern Iraq in the 1940s and early 1950s they were enthusiastic about the Kurdish Jews. Less educated than the Baghdadis, they appeared to be strong, healthy, and fit for agricultural work. Thus, while some Kurdish Jews were sent to transit camps, many were sent to this form of agricultural settlement in the moshavim. This policy, however, made little sense, especially in southern Israel. The Kurdish Jews had lived in and farmed in the fertile and mountainous regions of northern Iraq, and the desert of southern Israel presented an entirely different environment. Moreover, while the effort was made to populate individual villages with Jews from one country or of one minority group, this did not always occur. In some villages, the communities learned to live with one another in varying degrees of harmony. In others, tensions mounted; the Yemenites of the village of Lifta, for example, sent a letter complaining about the Kurds who terrorized them.[197]

The isolation of these agricultural communities was unbearable at times. The chronic shortage of supplies, especially food, the lack of potable water, and the absence of any medical services, most critical when a sick person required hospitalization, were felt acutely in these moshavim. Compounding the villagers' sense of isolation was the remedy implemented for the lack of services: the villagers were to be trained to provide the services themselves. In some cases, residents were directed to build their homes (for minimal wages), roads, and buildings for public services themselves, which meant that it took a very long time for these villages to get essential services. In addition, it took time for the farms to be productive. Some villages were eventually entirely deserted. The Ashkenazi guides and the instructors the moshavim movement sent to this region, who suffered with the Kurds and the Iraqis, constantly complained about the need to provide better services to these communities and were fearful that infiltration of guerilla groups from across the borders would endanger the residents' safety. In general, many tried to escape these communities; in fact the migration from the moshavim was much more profound than those who left the transit camps. In both the transit camps and the villages, however, the state fought to have the residents stay put.

CONCLUSIONS

In July 1952, the Israeli citizenship law, based on the law of return, was passed, according to which any Jew who migrated to Israel automatically became a citizen. At this moment, as Esther Meir notes, hundreds of Iraqis wanted to give up their Israeli citizenship because they were afraid it would dash their dreams of retrieving their property and put an end to their hopes of leaving Israel and reconstructing their lives in Iraq.[198] Given the realities described in this chapter, this should come as no surprise.

The leadership and institutions of Israel felt they had been successful in accommodating the newcomers. From the state's vantage point, many of the Iraqi men and women found work and served the state well as clerks, bureaucrats, and particularly as cheap laborers. They populated deserted villages, thus preventing their original inhabitants from returning. Some were settled in border regions, creating a tighter Jewish hold on zones of which other Arab states claimed ownership. Jerusalem's Jewish character was bolstered by their presence in the transit camps of Talpiot and Makor Haim. The human material, turned into Israeli dust, fulfilled its duty.

For the human material, however, the experience was entirely different. They arrived in a country where the simplest of chores, for both men and women, became a daily challenge. When they arrived in Israel, they found themselves utterly dependent on the state, which controlled many aspects of their daily lives: food, housing, work, and health care. In this sense, their arrival in Israel was not an "ascent"—the meaning of the word Aliyah—but rather a "descent." Iraqi men and women suffered from a particular state of subalternity, in that they had memories of different times and places in which they belonged to the upper and middle classes, to times when they had homes and permanent jobs. On the one hand, these memories were debilitating, because Iraqis were almost paralyzed by the grave loss they had experienced. On the other hand, they used the social capital they brought from Iraq, and a great deal of ingenuity and entrepreneurship, to maintain their human dignity under very difficult conditions.

Finally, Iraqi Jews were quite isolated from the Israeli state apparatus. In the years 1949–54, Israel was not much of a state; it was extremely poor; its key laws regarding labor and citizenship were yet to be written; and its pre- and post-state institutions clashed with one another. The transit camps were far from cities, from the main roads, and from Hebrew-speaking society. The meager salaries of most Iraqis meant they were unable to participate in Israel's leisure and cultural life. The face of the Israeli state they encountered in their camps was comprised of bureaucrats and representatives who managed their lives, often arrogantly and unsuccessfully, and clashed with one another. These were their first encounters with the state. And they gave them a horrible first impression.

2 CHILDREN OF IRAQ, CHILDREN OF ISRAEL

GE'ULA SEHAYEK AL-'ANI's autobiographical novel, *Ganevet ha-tarnegol* (The Rooster Thief) narrates the childhood of Amalia, a young Iraqi-Jewish girl in the transit camp of Hartuv. One scene describes the interaction between the transit camp's children and the state-provided youth counselor (*madrich*). An important ceremony in the camp was the raising of the Israeli flag: "In one of these ceremonies, one girl innocently asked the counselor: 'Why do we need to stand every day for the sake of this rag?' I shall never forget the face of the counselor. It turned red in anger, and he found it difficult to control himself; within a split second he slapped her powerfully on the face."[1] The counselor then explained to the children about the soldiers who had died in Israel's wars, about the struggle of the Jews against the Arabs and the British, about the history of Zionism, and about the great achievements of the State of Israel. Amalia remained unconvinced: "At this stage, I became impatient and raised my hand. The counselor signaled me to talk. I asked: 'Where is this Land of Israel that everybody is talking about, and why do people admire it? All I see here are wooden shacks, unpaved paths, and public bathrooms. This is not a nice place. Tell me: is this the land of Israel you know?'"[2] Amalia is a child, and not a grownup dependent on the state for a livelihood; she is able therefore to ask difficult questions and wonder why she had come to Israel in the first place. Her life of poverty and misery causes her and her friend to question the symbols of the state and challenge its representative.

This chapter tells the story of Iraqi-Jewish children like Amalia, who grew up in transit camps, in the new neighborhoods in Israel, and on kibbutzim.

On one hand, children were quicker to adjust to the new living conditions in Israel. As they grew older, their memories of Baghdad faded; they learned Hebrew more quickly; and for those without the memory of homes and schools in Iraq, the space of the transit camp was at times one of pleasure. Running between the wooden shacks and the tents and playing with friends, they did not understand the gravity of the situation. The state was willing to invest in their primary education because children were perceived as the future generation; unlike their parents, whose culture was looked down upon by the state's elites, the children were vessels for hope for a better future as new citizens of the state. On the other hand, children were the most vulnerable group among the newcomers. Those who could remember Baghdad, Basra, Hilla, and Amara did not understand what they were doing in Israel. They suffered from malnutrition; their parents could not always deal with the pain of displacement and sometime took out their anger on their children; they attended poor-quality schools; and they often had to leave school to work to support their families. And yet, Iraqi-Jewish children were resourceful, adept, and creative. They learned how to adjust to the new conditions, and just like their parents, they found ways to challenge and resist the state. They, too, had complicated relationships with the land they left behind and the nation they became citizens of. Throughout this chapter I will return to al-'Ani's *Rooster Thief*: we will check up on Ge'ula's fictional character, Amalia, and see how she experienced certain events that were described by real-life teachers, workers, fathers, mothers, and the children of the transit camps.

RAISED IN A TRANSIT CAMP

The transit camps were dangerous spaces for children. As noted, the camps were distant from major Israeli cities, and there were no ambulances in their proximity, a situation which jeopardized newborns, infants, and sick children. Mice, rats, and insects likewise threatened the children's health.[3] As a result, children and infant mortality were greater in these years than during the pre-state years.[4] Israel, like other countries in the 1950s, suffered from the spread of polio. In 1950 alone, 1,621 cases were diagnosed; 30 to 40 percent of the children infected remained paralyzed as adults, with vaccination becoming available only in 1954.[5] Prime Minister David Ben Gurion was aware that infant and child morality was a grave issue in the new state. In 1950, he noted that it had increased after the great Aliyah. After the Holocaust, he declared, Jewish people should not lose a single child. He bemoaned the fact that children were perishing due to substandard housing, but said he preferred that families not be broken up and that children be kept with their families.[6]

The scarcity of food was especially devastating for children in the transit camps. Doctors warned about malnutrition and hunger, as in the poorest camps, children went through the garbage for food. Even the poor-quality bread that was available was too expensive for some fathers.[7] A long battle was waged in the Knesset to guarantee that children would receive a glass of milk per day in school. Local committees in the transit camps were instructed to give the Ministry of Education a list of schools and kindergartens, so that the ministry could provide milk powder, sugar, and cacao once a month to a center specified by the committee. Parents were required to pay the government for this food: in many cases, they were given credit.[8]

Other supplies were sorely needed. Nurses reported that there were no clothes to dress little children; babies went home not in diapers but in rags or pieces of cloth.[9] It was also difficult to find beds for small children. Parents were usually given only two or three beds, which meant small children and babies went lacking. Parents improvised, making wooden boxes (previously used for oranges or other packages) that they had scavenged into small beds or cradles, and using other materials they could find or steal.[10] Reports from the transit camps in Talpiot and Makor Haim (near Jerusalem) noted the children had very few clothes to wear; no raincoats for the winter, and that boots and shoes were very scarce. This was to be anticipated in a camp in which three hundred families had no breadwinners. The Histadrut Organization of Working Mothers provided some aid to some of these children.[11]

On the one hand, children who grew up in transit camps describe how they enjoyed playing outside with their friends, conversing with them, and running about. Unaware of their parents' sufferings, they played with objects they found. As is well known around the globe, the creativity and imagination of children can alleviate the most difficult circumstances. Later, living in their enclaves in the city, they maintained these practices to some extent. Along these lines, the twins Herzl and Balfour Hakak have described their life in a Jerusalem neighborhood whose residents were mostly Mizrahi. Born in 1948 to Zionist parents (as their names clearly suggest!), they migrated to Israel in 1950. First they lived in a transit camp, before moving to the neighborhood in Jerusalem. The twins were considered the poster children of Iraqi migration. In 1965, Balfour won the national and international Bible competition (where young adults were tested on their knowledge of the Bible), with his brother coming in second. After participating in this prestigious event, which was attended by the prime minister, the children became household names in Israel. But their stories about life in their neighborhood paint a modest picture: they gathered children around them and established a secret youth group. They and their friends drew imaginative pictures; and they used everything in their neighborhood in their play, from tree branches to empty cans, since real toys were very scarce. Because of their talents, their short stories were published in the state's major children's newspaper, *Davar li-Yeladim* (Davar for Children), and in other venues, and were even read on the radio.[12]

But not all children were as lucky as Herzl and Balfour. Some remained in the camps for as many as three, five, and six years, and a few did not make it out of the camps at all. The space inside and outside of the transit camps was extremely unsafe for children to play in since some camps were close to borders or located in deserted places. Herut Knesset members complained that there were still land mines in Talpiyot transit camp in the vicinity of Jerusalem.[13] In 1954, a child living in the transit camp at Holon was killed when he was playing by a dunghill and an old shell exploded. An eighteen-year-old teenager lost her eye in this event.[14]

Children paid the most horrific price for the fact that they and their families were living in tents and shacks and that lighting was mainly in the form of oil lanterns and candles. A nine-year-old girl rescued from a tent that caught fire during the winter of 1951 suffered burns all over her body. She arrived at the clinic wearing a filthy coat.[15] A two-year-old baby was burned alive when her shack, made of cloth, caught fire; there was no water in tanks to put out the fire, and no phone with which to call the fire department.[16] Iraqi communist Elihau Shviro noted that had social services been provided to the camps, the tragedy would not have happened.[17] Even burial was a complicated matter. In 1951 a child died in the transit camp of Petach Tikva, whom Hevre Kadisha (the company in charge of burial services in the Israeli Jewish sector) refused to bury for financial reasons. The father, the men of the camp, and two workers, thus saw to the burial.[18] Near Haifa, three children were burned alive when their tent caught fire. They had been raised by their widowed father, who tried to commit suicide twice after the tragedy.[19]

Let us now return to Amalia to see how she deals with living in the camp. The first thing that troubles her is the memory of the other home, in Iraq: "I want to sit in the beautiful garden [in Amara] and eat pomegranates. Why are we here in this tent anyway? What happened to our house in Iraq?" As a child with no stake in the narratives of either the state or her parents, she continues: "The memories of the past, of the house in Amara, intertwined with those of the present. The longing for the good life was sharpened against the misery of the present. During the days . . . my memories carried me back to our Arab neighbors who loved us very much and the tranquil atmosphere at home."[20] Amalia's family is forced to live in two shacks without furniture. Everything is difficult—her parents have to cut off the tips of the children's shoes when the children outgrow them, because they cannot afford to buy new ones, and only when clothes donations arrive from the United States do the children wear relatively new clothes. Children yearn for the meat delivered to them during the holidays, and Amalia is often hungry. For Iraqi children like Amalia, cut off from the world, the camp was the only world they knew. She describes how she befriends people from all over the world—Iraqis, Romanians, Poles, Russians, Persians, Yemenites, and Tunisian. Her interaction with the outside world, then, is through other migrants. The world outside of Hartuv remained a distant universe for the children of the camp.

FAMILY TIES, FAMILY LIVES

The poverty and the pressures of everyday life in the camps complicated relationships between children and their parents. We cannot, of course, provide statistics of children's emotions in the camps, but from memoirs, notes written at the time by parents and teachers, we can point to a few trends. Some children idolized their parents, and greatly appreciated the efforts the parents made on their behalf. Other children, acculturated by an education system that treasured Hebrew and disrespected their parents' heritage, grew distant from their parents. Children have also written about the guilt they felt years later, after their parents had died, for not having understood their parents' depression and suffering.

The economic hardship of transit camp life took a harsh toll on families. Writing in *Al-Mirsad*, Sasson Hesqel argued that children suffered from their fathers' frustration over unemployment and hard labor. Some fathers got drunk or spent their time playing cards and gambled instead of returning to the shacks where they lived. The government, wrote Hesqel, betrayed and neglected the new generation of Jews.[21] Some desperate fathers ceremoniously abandoned their children at government facilities, especially in the welfare bureaus, to protest poverty and mistreatment. Eliyahu Rahamim worked as a construction worker and had to leave his job because of an illness. He wanted to open a grocery store in a transit camp but his request was turned down. In protest, he left his children in the labor bureau. The children were returned to the mother. The teenagers in the family were already working: the seventeen-year-old daughter worked in a grocery store, while her sister cleaned houses for a living. The other children, who seemed to have attended school occasionally and been fed, were left in the charge of the welfare bureau.[22] In another incident, a father who was denied a license to open a store in a transit camp threatened to send his children to the mission in Nazareth. Jewish children had attended Christian missionary schools in Iraq, especially in Mosul, but this was unacceptable in the Jewish state. The police prevented him from doing so.[23]

To cover the expenses of day-to-day life and of schooling, some fathers worked away from home, and children only saw them on weekends. Other children learned to appreciate their parents' heroic battles. Shim'on Ballas's short story from *Al-Ittihad* in 1953 focuses on a young family from Iraq and their son, Sabbah. Sabbah's father had been a shoemaker in Iraq. Unemployed in Israel, he protests, together with other unemployed workers, and is arrested as a result. His mother is arrested after trying to sell labor permits illegally to get food. The son's shock increases at seeing his mother dragged into court and his father beaten by the police. Sabbah then realizes that he should be angry at the state, not because of his hunger, but because of the ways in which "those in uniforms" mistreated his parents and their fellow immigrants.[24]

When parents could not deal with poverty and misery, their children assumed leadership roles. Children, once they were able to make a living and speak Hebrew, were sometimes better at handling the realities of the new country. Iraqi writer Rahamim Rejwan authored a short story called *Yeled shovav* (A Naughty Boy), about the relationship between a child and his father. The father, Ya'aqov, is blind; his illness could be cured, but the family cannot afford the treatment. Ya'aqov had once led a very different life: he had studied in the Midrash in Baghdad, and had made a living by selling vegetables. Now the family lives in the transit camp in Sakiyya. Being blind, he cannot work; when he is assigned to agricultural labor, he is injured by the plow; the best he can do is grow vegetables in his yard. His wife, Mariam, finds a job cleaning schools; the humiliation of being supported by his wife is hard on him. His daughter, Samira, is in third grade, and his son, Sami, is in first.

During the course of the story, Sami's relations with his father change. The son begins to steal things from school. Expelled several times, it is only the intervention of social workers that allows him to go back to school. Sami's life improves when his father seems to find a livelihood in Tel Aviv, selling matches, making two liras a day. The situation in the family improves; the father even gives Sami two liras so that he can go on a school field trip. Students at Sami's school, however, tell Sami that his father might not be telling the truth. Sami goes to the city and discovers his father is indeed deceiving him. He is a beggar. Sami then takes the money his father has given him for the field trip, and put it in his father's hands. The beggar is happy.[25]

This short story includes many familiar motifs found in other stories about blindness and poverty. The father, blind and unable to function in the new state, is completely at the mercy of society. Nevertheless, it is significant that the son's assumption of power over his father is depicted as neither natural nor empowering. On the contrary, the loss of patriarchal authority is painful; it leads to the son's misbehavior in school, petty theft, and worse yet, a horrible sense of the son's humiliation at seeing his father's helplessness.

Back to Amalia in the Hartuv transit camp: perhaps the most devastating aspect of Amalia's life is that she grows to hate her mother and her father. Amalia describes how her parents are completely indifferent to her when she is very sick and in need of warmth and compassion. Her mother, who had led a middle-class existence back in Iraq, cannot cope with her new situation. She prevents her daughter from studying so that she can help with the domestic chores, causing Amalia to feel that she is a slave to her mother. She becomes upset when her mother gets pregnant because there will be yet another mouth to feed and another baby to wash and diaper. Her father, a former merchant, has trouble finding work. When he finally lands a job at the factory in Beit Shemesh, he stays away from her. When he returns, he takes out his frustration on Amalia, beating her up.[26] Amalia's story demonstrates how poverty tears families apart and underlines the effects of growing up with a constant sense of disappointment. Amalia remembers when the family was functional, but neither she nor her parents can return to this state of functionality and Amalia records her inability to relate to, not to mention love, her father and her mother.

BEING SCHOOLED AND UNSCHOOLED: EDUCATION IN THE TRANSIT CAMPS

Transit-camp children attended the elementary schools opened for them, but often did not go farther in school, as parents did not have enough money to send children elsewhere or enable their elder children to obtain higher degrees, especially before 1957. The quality of the transit-camp schools was very bad.

As was the case with the transit camps more generally, bureaucracy played a part; local municipalities, the Jewish Agency, and the Ministry of Education quarreled about who should fund what. The local transit-camp committees and the state's authorities were in charge of organizing education, building playgrounds, and arranging cultural activities.[27] The implementation of educational policies, because of the state's bureaucratic maze, was far from satisfactory. In Ness Ziona, the municipality refused to pay its share for the teachers' salaries. In Rehovot, the city refused to pay anything for the schools in the transit camps. Consequently, women affiliated with organizations of the Histadrut came to work with young children in the place of professional teachers.[28]

The Israeli Compulsory Education Law took effect in 1949, but was implemented differently in the transit camps. The creation of the education system itself was a convoluted process. Before 1953, Jewish schools were associated with different ideological factions (such as Haredi, labor Zionist, and Zionist-religious).[29] Initially, the intention was to have three schools in each transit camp, one for each of the factions. In reality, most transit camps struggled to open a single school. After all branches of the schools that belonged to different political parties were united under one education system (1953), the main division between schools in Israeli society at large was between the Arab, Haredi-religious, and public sectors. Most of the schools built in the camps were public schools. Registration of students in transit-camp schools all over the country proceeded slowly, most notably in the southern transit camps of Kubeiba and Zarnuga and the transit camp of Rehovot.[30] Parents sometimes did not want their children to attend a particular school, such as a religious one.[31]

Wooden shacks were used as school buildings. Some had no lights and lacked proper toilets.[32] They did not have the most basic elements, such as tables, chairs, cleaning materials for the classrooms, chalks, pens, and papers.[33] The lack of drinking water (as we saw in Chapter 1) was a problem in a more than a few transit camps. In Khayriyya, the janitor had to bring water to the school because there were no water taps for the children.[34] In Sakiyya, the circumstances faced by teachers were especially difficult: 80 percent of the children were registered for school, which had no lighting other than oil lanterns, nor chairs, so that children sat on the floor.[35] The tables were dirty and the camp's residents took advantage of the school not having doors to steal what little the school had. The director of the school in Sakiyya decried the fact that the Jewish Agency did not fix the wooden shacks used for the school, and that he had to spend long hours in the offices of the Jewish Agency asking for tap water for his school, so that the students would not have to leave to get a drink of water.[36] Complaints such as these, as well as other grievances of the school's administrators, were met with indifference.[37] Children studied in big groups and in shifts.[38] In Khayriyya, forty students attended six classes, studying in shifts of four and a half hours each.[39] The regime of shifts allowed working children to attend school, but in some camps the night and afternoon classes were irregular.[40]

Educational supervisors also complained that the students looked poor, especially female students.[41] In the transit camp of Nahlat Yehuda, children did not go to elementary school because the parents could not pay the registration and lunch fees. The children in the lower classes studied in shifts and walked twenty minutes just to get to school.[42] Many girls did not attend school because they needed to help their parents.[43] Girls did receive some vocational training, although in many camps girls studied with boys. The transit camp of Khayriyya received sewing machines for vocational instruction and the Ministry of Education opened there a class for fifteen illiterate girls, which operated for just six hours a day.[44]

Due to the continual shortage of staff, teachers were transferred from place to place. For example, teachers from Kfar Saba were sent to the Kubeiba transit camp, which lacked instructors.[45] The teachers, such as the ones in Be'er Ya'aqov, had difficulties even getting to the schools, using buses and driving or walking on unpaved roads. Teachers experienced difficulty and delays in getting paid.[46] In Sakiyya, the teachers, as well as the janitor and the secretary, worked for four months with no pay. Some teachers worked two jobs (the Histadrut organizations proposed they could work for a half-day in agriculture).[47] The IDF draft reduced the pool of young individuals willing to teach in elementary schools. For example, the teachers union of the Histadrut asked that a certain comrade 'Ovadia, about to be drafted, be allowed to start his military service later, as his services as a teacher were badly needed.[48] The Histadrut also considered the candidacy of a soldier, who supported a family of five, as a teacher of night classes in Hebrew for older people in Sakiyya, which were held in a wooden shack.[49] The Histadrut trained teachers who had minimal qualifications: to work in a kindergarten one had to be between the ages of seventeen and a half and twenty-five and have a high school education of at least ten years. The other skills required were knowledge of Hebrew, crafts, singing, and drawing.[50] Some teachers exhibited a condescending approach to the children and their parents, while others were more sympathetic, making house visits and cooking for children when their mothers were sick.[51] But even the most dedicated teachers faced difficulties. Elisheba, the kindergarten teacher in Ramat ha-Sharon transit camp, and the parents of the children in the camp, created toys for the small children. However, as she went to the warehouse to bring wool to fill the dolls, she found mice and rats in the boxes that stored the wool. When she organized parties for the children during the holidays, the shack for the kindergarten was too small, and she saw the parents' faces peeping through windows.[52]

Educational supervisors were sent to the transit camps to oversee the state of instruction. This was done under the auspices of the teachers' union of the Histadrut and the Ministry of Education. Often the supervisors had to fill out questionnaires as to the pedagogy methods, dyadic games, and the development of creativity in the camps. These give us a sense of what transpired in the classroom and the approaches of the supervisors themselves. Some reports were optimistic. Reports to Ben Gurion, for example, indicated that the situation in transit camps such as David was "good"; children were feeling good and the level of education was satisfactory.[53] Other reports presented a gloomier picture. Miriam Blumberg noted in her visit to Sakiyya that forty children needed help in their studies. An Ashkenazi kindergarten teacher taught in a small, dark, dirty classroom located in a wooden shack. A long corridor was used for food preparation, washing dishes, and storage. The children kept their coats on in the classroom while working and playing. Some children were neglected, playing outside with no supervision. The teacher in kindergarten showed them objects and asked the students to identify them, and later all sang Hannukah songs. The inspector's advice was to make sure the children take off their coats (not stating how they would stay warm), that each child has a towel and handkerchief to blow his or her nose (making no mention of the meager budget), and that different objects, like photo books, be introduced to the class. She also asked the local council not throw their garbage into the kindergarten's grounds.[54]

The state, and various political parties, sent counselors (*madrich*) (often associated with the youth movements) to the transit camps to work and play with the youth. On the one hand, the fact that the counselors spoke Hebrew, a language the children did not initially understand, distanced the former from the latter. On the other hand, because parents were poor, troubled with the burdens of daily life, and at times resentful of girls' education, the counselors emerged as key mentors for young children and teenagers. Lea Na'or, as a young teenager was an instructor in the youth movement, Ha No'ar Ha 'Oved, attracted a group of a hundred children who awaited her and a fellow teenager instructor every week, in one of the transit camps near Herzliya. Na'or recalls that "groups of children were climbing on us, holding us, and dragging us."[55] They two sang and danced with the children, walked with them between the orchards and the tulips fields, and hosted them in Lea's family yard where they ate fruits. They also played with the children. The latter activity was important since the press complained that poor transit camps children played sadistic and unhealthy games.[56]

It was crucial for the state to make the schools laboratories of Zionism. Students were to learn Hebrew and about the principles of their new state. The counselors and the teachers both attempted to emphasize the children's Israeli identity. Hebrew films and plays such as *Kazablan*, the story of a Moroccan Jewish IDF war hero who was later relegated to the margins of society, were shown in the transit camps.[57] Holidays were of the utmost importance, from celebrations of Hannukah to the commemoration of the heritage of Chaim Weizmann.[58] With very limited resources, the Ministry of Interior provided food and extra funds for such occasions.

In 1952 the Ministry of Interior instructed all youth counselors, schools directors, and other public officials in the transit camps to commemorate the holiday of Tu Bi-Shvat. The holiday (on the fifteenth day of Shvat) was the state's tree holiday. Although having Biblical and Talmudic roots, Tu Bi-Shvat was revived by religious Zionists in Ottoman Palestine and was adopted by the new state as an official holiday commemorating love of the land, the planting of trees, and the rejuvenation of nature. It was doubtful whether grownups in the camp felt like rejoicing at the beautiful nature of Israel, but based on discussions held in Jerusalem, the minister of interior suggested that Solel Boneh, the Jewish Agency, and private construction companies build platforms in honor of the holiday, and decorate them with flags and photos.[59] Films, performances by children for their teachers, and special pay for ushers were included in the plans, as well as the distribution of posters in Hebrew for the purposes of propaganda (*ta'amula*) and the teaching of Hebrew.[60] During these celebrations, each child was to be given a fruit bag, presented as a gift from the local committee of the camp.[61] Two goals were achieved in one holiday—the transit camps' committees were presented as responsible for indoctrinating the children with the ideology of the state, and a new national holiday was now associated with something the children valued very much: food.

Independence Day celebrations were likewise imperative and planned meticulously. In January 1952, the planning for the celebration started and culminated in the month of May, on the actual holiday. Each of the transit camps was given a flag, and the Ministry of Interior pushed to have regional celebrations where the flags would be raised to impart a sense of honor in the hearts of the residents.[62] The fact that the flags were sent from Jerusalem to each camp would create a psychological and patriotic fervor among the newcomers, the Ministry of Interior officials hoped, as it would give them a chance to "unite with eternal Jerusalem," even though many did not have the privilege of seeing it yet.[63] Children benefited from the celebrations. Some got to watch movies or puppet shows; others listened to speeches on the radio, which were broadcast in the camps via loudspeakers furnished especially for the celebration; and some marched in parades.[64]

As Shira Robinson noted, the state felt it crucial to celebrate Israel's Independence Day in Arab villages and cities and forced citizens to participate in these celebrations as a way of indoctrination and Israelization.[65] While the Iraqi residents of the transit camps in 1952 might have wanted to renew their ties with Baghdad, Basra, and Mosul, rather than create new ones with Jerusalem, the Ministry of Interior thought that they, and their children, needed to celebrate, even when there was precious little to celebrate. For the transit-camp children, however, a free day, accompanied with special plays, indicated that new national calendar had to be taken into consideration.

The state at times underused the most important resource it had in the transit camps, Iraqi men and women who had been teachers in Baghdad. The Jewish community in Iraq had enjoyed a flourishing educational system and many of its employees found themselves in the transit camps. Other Iraqis were writers and intellectuals who were now willing to work as teachers. Many knew very little Hebrew, but they realized what future awaited their children, and the children of their friends and family, if the education system in the transit camps was not run by and for Iraqis. Once the schools were established in the transit camps, the state did employ Iraqi teachers, among them Eliyahu Yig'al, Yosef Sha'ul, Shalom Kattav, Elisheva Gurji, Carmela Levy, and Esther 'Amari.[66] The model of an educated Baghdadi turned teacher was in fact quite common.[67] In the transit camp of Rehovot, where 104 students attended school in 6 learning groups, the key teachers were Baghdadis: a social worker, Sadiq 'Ezra, who had graduated from a gymnasium in Amara, and Naji Mashiah, a graduate of a gymnasium in Baghdad.[68] These were activist teachers who wrote to the ministry complaining about lack of essential teaching materials and food for their students.[69]

Out of all the teachers, Victor Muʻallim was the most active. Muʻallim had been a prominent educator in Baghdad; a socialist, he had run a successful night school for workers and students. After immigrating, he was sent to the transit camps in the Or Yehuda region. Most alarming to him was the sight of children running between the tents and in the orchards with no guidance. He thus summoned three friends who had been teachers in Baghdad and the four pleaded with the authorities to open a school. They explained that these children were used to studying in fine schools, with first-class facilities and laboratories; that they themselves were quality teachers from Baghdad; and that Iraqi teenagers typically attended high schools. Muʻallim said he was willing to teach students under a nearby tree, which provided some shade; all he needed were chairs and tables. The group was told the state had no funds available, and that their stories about the education system in Baghdad were mere propaganda. Undaunted, the Iraqi teachers took boxes (originally meant for oranges) and used them as chairs and tables; they even created blackboards out of them. This was the origin of the school in Sakiyya, where Muʻallim and his friends were employed as teachers.[70]

When the camps were united under the administration of the city of Or Yehuda, Muʻallim served as the head of the educational bureau in the local council in the years 1969–84. His first battle was to ensure the children got a daily meal in school for free or very cheaply. He fought the ministry for this, because he knew it would increase the chance that children would be sent to school rather then put out to work by their parents. During the 1960s, twelve female soldiers who worked as teachers also aided him. While Muʻallim was teaching in a very poor region, he did his best to make sure that "his children," attending elementary schools and the city's only public high school, were being taken care of. In this case, this did not mean making sure they would get into college, but simply that the schools would shelter them from child labor, poverty, and their surroundings.[71]

Tikva Agasi (née Amal Salih) was another teacher of transit-camp children. She had graduated from the law college in Baghdad and had worked in Jewish schools in that city, so that it was natural for her to become a teacher in the transit camp of Ramat ha-Sharon. Tikva was one of the most experienced teachers, but she did not know Hebrew. She recalled how the feeling of solidarity between her and her Iraqi compatriots, notably David Khalachi and Sami Muʻallim, saved her. To help her overcome her lack of knowledge in Hebrew, David taught her to memorize the lessons, and explained how to pronounce words so that her students could understand her. By contrast, she considered her Histadrut teachers union supervisor, Y. Geffen, an intruder, rather than a helpful colleague. He suspected, after observing a very fine lesson, that she was merely repeating the same material from the class the day before; she simply looked to him overprepared. In another incident, when she momentarily left the class in search of chalk, a colleague had to testify that she did not skip class that day.[72] And yet, despite her lack of knowledge of Hebrew, Tikva felt she had something native Israeli teachers might not have had: a bond with the Iraqi students. She was given the "disturbed" class in the transit camp, but she very much liked the students. When a group of social workers came to the class, she mentioned that the children came from troubled households. As a result, she was summoned to the principal's office and told that members of the committee suspected her of being a communist. Upset, Tikva retorted, "Get yourself over to their shacks, as I do from time to time, and look at the situation closely rather than accusing me in a threatening tone . . . of being a communist."[73]

Shalom Kattav (al-Katib) had been a writer in Baghdad whose work was published in Arabic before coming to Israel. He initially was sent to work in road construction and in the vineyards of Zichron Ya'aqov, and then, at the age of twenty, found himself teaching in the Or Yehuda transit camps and then directing a night school.[74] Kattav dedicated poems to his students. He contrasted his love of his students, their blessed faces (often depicted as dark) with the characterization of them by the state, which saw these students as problematic social cases. Most importantly, in his poetry it is clear that working under these impossible conditions gave him a sense of mission and endowed him with a sense of satisfaction knowing that children were saved through his guidance, or as he puts it:

> From the hearts of my students
> I have always collected
> Corals
>
> *
>
> From their silenced mouths
> I have always fathered
> Flowers[75]

Some children were able to overcome the difficulties in the elementary schools in the transit camps and the new neighborhoods formed from the transit camps, and moved on to high schools in the cities and the moshavot. They were quick to discover that their elementary schools, even if they excelled in their studies, did not provide them with the tools to succeed in a good high school. Many Mizrahi children, Iraqis included, were sent to vocational schools, rather than high schools, as schools built in poor neighborhoods, which absorbed the inhabitants of the transit camps, were often vocational.[76] Some Iraqis were able to complete their high school or professional education at the IDF schooling facilities. The IDF also instructed illiterate men in writing and reading skills.[77]

The most unfortunate children, defined as young criminals, were placed in institutions outside their homes. Three hundred and ninety young adults were in such institutions in 1958, and many more were yet to be placed. MALBEN (Mosadot le-Tipul be-'Olim Nechshalim; Institutions for the Care of Backward Immigrants), an organization founded in 1949 and run by the Jewish Agency and the American Jewish Joint Distribution Committee (JDC) to provide care to the aged, infirm, and disabled, offered services to young adults defined as psychologically "defective," outside of the education system. Many of these children were neither criminal nor defective, having simply been pushed toward crime or remained illiterate because of the poor conditions in the camps.[78]

It was simply inevitable that transit-camp teenagers, to a lesser or greater extent, would be marginal to mainstream Israeli society, by virtue of their isolation. Teenagers desired to expand their horizons, but had little opportunities to do so; those who lived in transit camps when public libraries were constructed, or resided close to towns where a public library was available to them, used this resource to their benefit; a Herut activist depicted how they devoured the books they could find there.[79] Stories in communist and socialist newspapers focused on other aspects of lives of the youth at the transit camps. Reporters observed that the teenagers grew up too quickly; boys dressed as grownups, gelled their hair, smoked, and read cheap novels rather than literature. Girls used lipstick, dressed in the latest fashions, even in shorts; none of them were drafted into the IDF. Those who had earned some pocket money traveled to Tel Aviv; every trip, though, showed them what the city people had and what they lacked.[80] Music was a significant outlet for the youth in the transit camps and poor neighborhoods. While the kibbutzim and people who identified with the labor Zionist movement listened mostly to Hebrew songs, often performed by military bands, or to Hebrew versions of Russian, German, and Yiddish songs, Iraqi youth who gathered in the local cafés in the transit camps and in run-down clubs in the new neighborhoods, listened to Arab, American, and European music, which was deemed corrupting by the state's socialist elites.[81]

In Khayriyya, a man who had been an accountant in Iraq opened a dance hall where he taught teenagers how to dance. To the socialist press of the 1950s and 1960s, the values adopted by these teenagers represented social and cultural degradation. Reading the reports today, we see how teenagers forced to assume the responsibilities of adulthood sought some forms of amusement.

Returning to Amalia, it is the case that despite her critiques of the state's education system, she realizes that education was her way out of the camp. She likes studying. Her school, though a wooden shack and ill-equipped to educate the wide range of students it served, was nevertheless a refuge and an entry point into mainstream Israeli society. On her first field trip to Jerusalem, organized by the school, she is aware of her pride at being an Israeli. The ceremonies that the state organizes and the trips appeal to her, because they show that there is some community beyond the circle of poverty she knows too well.[82] Amalia is not a native admirer of the state, even as a child. But she realizes what Victor Muʻallim, Shalom Kattav, and many other Iraqis realized at the time—that education was something worth fighting for, even if the conditions were impossible and even if it meant clashing with parents and the authorities.

LABOR ZIONISM:
CHILD AND TEENAGE LABOR

When they became old enough to attend high school, many Iraqi teenagers were forced to help support their families by going to work. Some children worked at even a younger age; some left their schools, while others continued with their primary education, yet since they studied in shifts, and since some agricultural labor was seasonal, they could still participate in the labor market. The Knesset discussed the fact that children could not go to high school for economic reasons. An organization called the Sephardi Federation helped with fellowships, but this was not enough.[83] Going to work as a teenager was particularly difficult for those who had belonged to the middle and upper classes in Iraq, for whom high school had always been an option. Girls were more likely than boys to be denied the opportunity, as some parents chose to sacrifice the education of several sisters in Israel so that at least one member of the family would get an education. In families where the father died, the young male adult in the family, even if a teenager, would often become the breadwinner.[84] As child and teenage labor was not always documented and was often a matter of temporary arrangements, it is difficult to estimate the actual number of Iraqi children and teenager workers, their ages, and their places of dwelling. However, public discussions, reports in the press and the Knesset, and the protests of Knesset members present a bleak picture of the young laborers who were often completely at the mercy of employers when it came to rights, benefits, and pay.

In the moshavot of central Israel, children were employed in agricultural labor. The children who resided in the Kfar Saba transit camp worked with their parents in agricultural seasonal labor, especially picking peanuts. After finishing with their daily labor, the children would then raid the territory where they worked to pick up the leftovers which were not collected by the farmers to bring to their families.[85] Stories from the transit camp of Ramat ha-Sharon indicate the dangers involved in child and teenage labor. Some of the children and teenagers in this camp worked with their parents in the nearby farms. They too brought the leftover vegetables to their homes; some girls also worked in housekeeping and cleaning.[86] Not all cases ended well for these young laborers. The police arrested a ten-year-old child; the policemen who found him in the fields thought he was thief; they refused to believe a ten-year-old boy would actually be employed in this profession. After the parents found the child, he was released. The parents did not send him to work anymore.[87] At times, parents convinced their children to go to work, at others, parents and family members refused to do so. An eight-year-old child was offered a lira a day, to work for a farmer, but her brother refused to let her do so.[88]

The communist newspaper *Kol ha-'Am* reported that children from the transit camp of Karkur worked for ridiculously low wages in the nearby villages. They children went to the communities and shouted: "Work, work." People from the farms in Kfar Pinnes and Gan Shomron paid a lira or less per day or simply with food.[89] The law of guardianship (*hok ha-hanichut*), securing the labor rights of young adults, was not put in place until 1954. Four years after the law was enacted, Knesset member Ruth Hektin reported to Minister of Labor Mordechai Namir that many children were still working in professions for which they were too young. Namir denied the accusations.[90] In 1951, Knesset member Moshe Sneh raised the issue of child and teenage labor, mentioning that in the transit camp of Kfar Nahman children were employed picking peanuts. The director of the elementary school had sent the fourth- and fifth-grade students to work to pay for books and supplies that the parents could not afford.[91] Other educators, however, protested child and teenager labor. Local education officials complained that children in transit camps of Khayriyya and Sakiyya did not attend school because they worked in shifts.[92] Likewise, the director of the school in Sakiyya noted that the classes were empty because the parents sent their children to work.[93]

In 1953, S. Ben Ishaq described his encounters with the children he had met on the way to the transit camp of Tira (near Haifa) in the newspaper *Al-Mirsad*. These children were coming back from work, some having gone considerable distances. "We work for one lira a day," said Malka, a thirteen-year-old from Baghdad. "Father does not work, so what can we do?" Ben Ishaq asked a couple of children how they had heard about the village close to their transit camp where they worked. "A woman came to the camp and asked who wanted to work. Our mother said we did." A twelve-year-old said that he had studied agriculture in the momshav Nahalal, but that his father needed his help. The father, a merchant, did not want his son to be an agricultural worker. Malka also shared with the reporter stories about her life. She had gone to school in Baghdad for four years, and was continuing her studies in the transit camp of Ijlil (near Herzliya). However, her father, at the age of forty-two, was too old to work, so he sent her out to earn money. She was working ten hours a day for a lady. When Ben Ishaq asked her if she wanted to study, she merely replied that the work was not so hard, but admitted that the high school student, the son of the lady for whom she was working, mistreated her.[94]

Victor Muʻallim relates that students who graduated from elementary schools in Or Yehuda went on to work temporary jobs. On his way to his work as a teacher, he used to see them in the morning hours waiting at the bus station or riding old bikes to the nearby cities to deliver newspapers, milk, or bread to stores. Muʻallim's short story "Neft be-Ramat Gan" (Oil in Ramat Gan), depicts the cry of the young workers to their employer, Master (*adon*) Shaykeh, for whom they dug pits and holes under very difficult conditions: "'Sir, Master Shaykeh, tell us—do you want us to die? Do you want to kill us because we are newcomers? Aren't you Jewish? Have you no mercy? Don't you fear God? We are suffocating in here. . . . You need to call the police! We are calling the police!'"[95] The story centers on Ephraim and Yehuda, two teenagers who used to attend high school in Baghdad; now in Israel they avoid the draft, and work a few days a week, digging pits for Shaykeh:

> If master Shaykeh had two workers from the transit camp, it is a sign of a great grace and incomparable goodness. He used to stand in front of his worker-slaves, preaching to them about ethics, industriousness, loyalty, and speed, and did not forget to mention to them, at every moment, that they were newcomers;

they were nothing more than poor dwellers of transit camps, primitive, uneducated, and penniless. Ephraim and Judah were silent, for who would dare disobey the master?[96]

They do feel that the bread they earn is mixed with "cancerous poison," and decide to punish Shaykeh. They get gasoline and pour it in the pit; Shaykeh believes that oil is about to spring from the land, and pays them a month's salary so that they will not inform the authorities and he can keep the profit for himself.

The story reflects the reality that young adults, close to draft age, could not get permanent jobs, because employers feared they would be drafted any day. The Iraqi teenagers, familiar with stories about the discovery of oil in their homeland, here use oil to get money. Most significant, however, is the use of language in the story. The word "slaves" (*'avadim*, instead of workers) that appears in the text and the evocation of the Hebrew word *adon* to construct the image of Shaykeh as a callous slave owner reflect the great anger of the teens at their employers.

Muʻallim's fellow teacher, Shalom Kattav, dedicated poems to children who were forced to work. His poems depict the mothers who were being blamed for their children's poverty and the contractors making money through the labor of children. In another poem, "Be-shuq ha-Tikva" (In ha-Tikva Market), the speaker represents a young child forced to sell dill in the market:

> Dill for ten!
> The voice of
> The thin boy lashed out
> While Bible and Hebrew
> And God knows what else
> Are being studied by his friends
> Now[97]

The speaker depicts his mother hugging the child on the way to the market, "Between the rods of her dark tent," thinking that this son could one day be an officer in the nation's army, if only given a chance. The poem ends with the same lines with which it opened:

> Dill for ten
> The compacted voice
> Of the dark boy
> Cried
> In spite the free education system[98]

To Kattav, the free public education system was merely an empty slogan. Ben Gurion gave speeches about his desire to see the newcomers integrated into the new army and wished for a Yemenite chief of staff. In reality, however, these promises were meaningless. A child was still selling dill at the market, to the distress of his mother.

Amalia's life story is very much about child labor. When her father gets some pistachios and peanuts from relatives, he makes his children go out to sell the nuts. Assuming a role of peddler is extremely humiliating for a young child who remembers her life in Amara; she and her brother hate appearing to their neighbors and friends as poor children in need of money. More troubling is the labor she had to do at home. When her father gets sick, she must leave school. She is ten years old: "I faded away. At times I cried and tried to convince mother to let me go back to school, to release me from the arduous labor of being a housewife. But mother was insistent: this is impossible."[99] She is finally allowed to return to school, but must work: she earns some more money by cleaning the dining room after school. Amalia's "career" sums up the challenges involved in child labor. Everybody used these children: their employers, and at times, even their own parents. Working sometimes had a very negative psychological effect, as children like Amalia remembered when they had been in school and wanted to return.

RAIN: THE CHILDREN'S ENEMY

One can argue that the greatest enemy of the young State of Israel during the years 1951–56 was not Egypt, radical ideologies, or terrorism. It was the weather. During the months of November and December 1949, newcomers felt the cold Israeli winter; in January 1950 snow covered the state. For many Israelis, this was reason to rejoice; snow was rare in the coastal region. It was quite the opposite for people who lived in tents and shacks and suffered from the floods and the cold weather. The greatest fear was for the children; how would they survive the harsh weather? The situation was repeated in the winter of 1950–51. The latter winter was more significant for Iraqi children and their parents, as most of the community was now in Israel. The winters, however, broke the spatial boundaries between various communities in Israel: children were sent to cities, soldiers and volunteers came to the camps, and government officials made a strong effort to alleviate the hardships of life in the transit camps.

In the winters of 1949–50 and 1950–51 many children were moved from their "homes" in the transit camps, mostly tents and shacks, which collapsed, and housed with families across Israel, including in the cities.¹⁰⁰ This was done under the auspices of Operation Rooftop (Korat Gag). While many organizations were involved in Operation Rooftop, the Jewish Agency handled most of the coordination until January 1951, when management of the operation was assumed by the Ministry of Welfare.¹⁰¹ Most children (those aged six to twelve) were first taken to stations or quarantines where they were classified, washed, examined medically (to make sure the hosts will not take in children with diseases), and dressed in new clothes before being sent to the city on buses. Others were treated in the camps of the IDF. Host families were given extra food stamps so that the children could be fed. According to a report to the Knesset regarding the winter of 1950–51, 1,057 children were placed with families; 782 were placed on moshavim and kibbutzim; the IDF took care of an additional 495; 609 were hosted in public places; and organizations affiliated with the Jewish Agency took 264 more. In total, out of six thousand children in need of immediate evacuation in the winter of 1950–51, about four thousand were housed outside the camps.¹⁰² Some children did not want to leave their parents and were taken against their will. A reporter for *Kol ha-'Am* depicted the children crying as they were put on trucks.¹⁰³ Some parents did not even know where their children were housed.¹⁰⁴

The Jewish Agency drafted thirty buses from the IDF to transfer the children and paid for their clothing. Children were divided into three groups: babies, children of kindergarten age, and school-age children. The agency decided that babies would not be separated from their mothers, despite the miserable living conditions. Children given shelter in the cities were to remain there until night and then be returned to their families, but in the case of hard rains, they could stay all night.¹⁰⁵ Any public building with a roof could serve to host the children, as well as private facilities, such as synagogues, theaters, and cinema halls. The Jewish Agency used two hundred buildings. Bridge clubs, despite having no kitchens in which food could be prepared for the children, were used as shelters. The city of Tel Aviv, in whose close vicinity there were no transit camps, refused to allow the use of the city's synagogues.¹⁰⁶

This was very humiliating for Iraqi children: all of a sudden they were in new homes where children slept in beds, where they had toys and properly fed—where they were sheltered from the life in the transit camp. The fact that children were separated from parents was not a mere coincidence. The state did not want grownups to leave the camps for fear they would not return; as a result, only children were evacuated. Some parents ended up being evacuated as well because of

FIGURE 3. Children in the Or Yehuda transit camps; a flooded *pachon*. Source: CZA, PHKH\1281919. Reprinted with permission.

deaths, but typically families were split up. Representatives of the Iraqi-Jewish religious community protested the placement of their youth in secular places.[107]

During these winters, the state put out a call for volunteers; at times not all were willing to lend a hand. All major state bodies were involved: the Histadrut, the Jewish Agency, and the Ministries of Labor (which coordinated the operations), Transportation, Health, and Interior. The purpose of Operation Cover for the Winter (Ksut la-Horef) was the collection of warm clothes and shoes for the winter; women's organizations distributed them, as they took care of the children. Jewish organizations outside of the country collected funds and donations of goods as well. Collections from organizations, both abroad and in Israel, as well as donations from individuals gathered clothes, toys, and supplies to the children of the transit camps. Within the camps, the Ministry of Interior ordered the building of tin shacks for the children because the tents were collapsing.[108] During the winter of 1950–51 the state ran a propaganda campaign with posters, ads in the newspapers, editorials, and radio announcements, calling on Israelis who were better off to participate in Operation Rooftop and host at least one child from among the ten thousand aged from five to twelve who were living in transit camps.[109]

People responded to the call. Lea Na'or, who lived in Herzliya, recalls that she and her sister went to the city hall "to take a boy from the transit camp." These children were on the second floor of the building: "There were some volunteer women and two or three kids that nobody took. We were given the child who cried in the corner."[110] They took him to the wooden shack where they lived and bought him candy, but he kept crying. He did not understand Hebrew. They tried to get him home, but his parents and other family members, who were suffering from the cold, convinced him to stay with the family from Herzliya. After the rains were over, they looked for the child in the transit camp, but they never found him again.[111]

While many families opened their hearts and doors unconditionally, others tainted their generosity with racism. Approximately 2,811 families wanted to know the age, gender, community (eda), and the language of the child before they committed to taking him or her in.[112] Host families had genuine fears of the spread of polio, but other considerations were of a different nature: some Ashkenazi families would only take Ashkenazi children and sent children back to the stations from which they came if they belonged to the "wrong" community.[113] Giora Yoseftal, of the Jewish Agency, remembered bitterly those who did not want to help him, like the religious kibbutzim whose members refused to give diapers for babies from the transit camps, fearing that theirs would run out. The Iraqi child, so they explained to him, went naked in the summer, and so his mother needed at most two diapers for him. However, once this baby was placed in state care, the parents were demanding six diapers.[114] *Kol ha-'Am* reported that in Herzliya four Mizrahi children were taken away from their host families because the Ministry of Welfare, which was run by religious parties, objected to their being sent to secular homes, although both the host families and the children's parents wanted them to stay.[115]

The IDF played a leading role in these operations. The transit camps were integrated into military operations planned by the state before the first winter. In November 1950 the chief of staff, Yigal Yadin, was put in charge on the transit camps under Mivtza' Ma'arabot (Operation Transit Camps). For four months, 37 transit camps out of the total of 108—6 in the north, 16 in the center, and 15 in the south—were under his command. The IDF was in charge of their internal organization, sanitation, and medicine, and whatever else the camps' residents might need. The soldiers of the IDF stayed in the camps through the winter and into the spring and did everything from digging ditches to supplying shaving knifes. During the winters, the IDF provided the children with basic medical care, sending female soldiers to take care of babies. It was also involved in providing ringworm treatment.[116] The paramilitary organization GADNA took care of five hundred children.[117] The work of the IDF provoked some less-than-generous comments on the part of politicians. One Knesset member, Y. Gil, noted his fear that the IDF was "accustom[ing] these people not to work." Minister of Labor Golda Meir, on the other hand, was delighted with the IDF's participation, which she saw as a national success: "As citizens, we can only be jealous of an army possessing such a form of organization, which allows it to do things much more rapidly than other citizen."[118]

The relief campaign did not go entirely according to Golda's depiction. Anarchy prevailed and riots broke in many camps. In the winter of 1950–51, the directors of the transit camps of Rishon le-Zion, Holon, and Khayriyya resigned. Hungry parents in the latter camp invaded the food storehouses and looted them. In the transit camp of Kfar Ono parents robbed the local grocery store, as the directors of the camps made their escape. Thousands of newcomers protested at the Jewish Agency, asking for roofs for themselves and then their children.[119] A frightened but determined Yoseftal wrote in his diary on 14 January 1951 that order in the camps had collapsed. He was convinced that the people in the transit camps around Tel Aviv, Lod, Petach Tikva, "mostly newcomers from Iraq and other difficult elements," were miserable, passive, and easily incited "by all sorts of elements from outside."[120]

A similar pattern unfolded in the winter of 1951–52. Here, too, the IDF was involved. As during the previous winters, children suffered tremendously; supplies, such as blankets, went missing; over a thousand people volunteered, some endangering themselves trying to save people in the Ha-Tikva neighborhood in Tel Aviv and in other camps. The IDF, high school students, and ordinary citizens were involved in these efforts.[121] This time, however, children were no longer sent to homes but rather to public institutions. During the month of December the city of Petach Tikva needed financial help as the transit-camp people arrived in the city, and its Histadrut building was packed with the refugees. One hundred and twenty families were evacuated from the camp in Sakiyya; 240 were rescued from the transit camp in Petach Tikva, and the Zarngua camp was evacuated as well.[122] Municipal administrations again came to the rescue, among them those of Nahariyya, Haifa, Pardes Hannah, Hadera, Aven Yehuda, Herzliya, Kfar-Sava, Bat-Yam, Holon, Ness Ziona, Ramla, Migdal-Ashkelon, and in the cities in the north. In Ramat Gan, the mayor went in a truck and assisted children himself.[123]

Many children were sheltered in public spaces, as tents and wooden shacks collapsed.[124] In the Haifa region 350 grownups were evacuated as well. The municipality of Haifa wanted to evacuate whole families and sent buses for this purpose, but no family remained united because the children were evacuated under different operations.[125] In Migdal Gad, policewomen took care of the children who remained. In total, during this winter, seventeen hundred families were evacuated and twelve hundred children sent away. Some were evacuated at night, so people fell into ditches and hurt themselves. In one transit camp, one hundred abandoned children were found in tents.[126]

Bureaucracy was again an issue: officials would not send cars to evacuate the children in the transit camp of Ramat ha-Sharon until they were promised the city would take the children. *Kol ha-'Am* praised the communist women organizations that took part in the providing of food, clothing, and toys. However, in Ramat Gan, according to *Kol ha-'Am*, it took the municipal authorities a whole week to find housing for the children from Khayriyya and Sakiyya. *Kol ha-'Am* added, "The city of Ramat Gan obliged itself to house the children and found for this purpose a place distant from the city, lest the aesthetic sentiments of the city's bourgeoisie be offended." The children stayed in an old slaughterhouse, sleeping on its cement floor. The people of Ramat Gan, the communists among them, contributed clothes and food, and finally the city placed children in a more appropriate location, a school.[127] In Petach Tikva MAPAM and the residents of the camp addressed the city's mayor, asking that synagogues, schools, and clubs be appropriated for the housing of newcomers, a demand that was only partially met.[128]

Even with the transit-camp residents suffering from harsh conditions, the Ministry of Interior worried about settlement policies. The state, as before, feared that people who were evacuated from the tents and wooden shacks might refuse to return, as the following memo shows:

> When evacuation is needed . . . evacuate only those who were hurt most by the floods or are in danger if they stay put. Naturally, preference should be given to children, the ill, and the women, but do not help with the evacuation of those who want to take advantage of this opportunity and leave a camp or the transit camp. Remember: it is easy to get people out of camps and transit camps but it is difficult to put them back there![129]

The repeat of the same disasters year after year underlined the fact that the state could not take care of its citizens living in shacks and tents, and especially of its children. The Jewish Agency bore the brunt of public criticism because of its sloppy building practices and the poor housing conditions.[130] The repeated calamities inspired increased demonstrations in the transit camps of Khayriyya, Rishon le-Zion, and Ramat ha-Sharon. Parents who lived in tents said that unless they were transferred to wooden shacks their children would get sick again. Yoseftal himself was beaten up in Rehovot. The communists increased their activities and gave the Jewish Agency a reason not to meet with demonstrators under the pretense that radicals incited the protesters, although Yoseftal noted that while some demonstrators were communists, others saw demonstrating as a mere pastime.[131] The immigrants threatened sabotage, namely, that they would cut apart the shacks made of cloth, unless they were given wooden housing. Yoseftal felt that since it was impossible to replace twenty thousand cloth shacks with wooden ones there was no point in talking to the protesters.[132]

The demonstrations and protests, usually orchestrated by Iraqis, were not seen by Yoseftal as merely the cries of desperate parents whose children were being taken away from them. The protests were linked to their Iraqiness. In 1951, Yoseftal noted in his diary:

> The Iraqi newcomers exhibited an *unconscionable* inability to help themselves. We are used to indifferent Yemenites, who accept everything as decided by the

Heavens. I saw that the newcomers from Iraq could not pick up a tool and do something [to help themselves]. I visited one transit camp and saw shocking things. The newcomers broke through a door of one institution and went inside.[133]

Yoseftal neglected to note the contradiction in his own words: when Iraqis let others work, they were blamed for indifference. Where they broke into empty shacks to take shelter from the rains, they were seen as burglars. Moreover, he blamed Iraqi parents for not taking care of their children:

> The lack of care for the children is the most shocking thing in the whole situation. I do not say it is only with the Iraqis. You find a thing like that with the Persians and the Kurds, but in no way with the Yemenites. In most cases, the newcomers exhibited a horrible indifference. . . . It is an apathy [that is] also expressed in the lack of organization of family and individual life. . . . I think the Yishuv has shown in these days an ability to act. But after the volunteers saw the apathy of the newcomers, they cannot put their heart into volunteering for long. We hear this not only from the boys in the youth movement, but also from soldiers. It is unreasonable to ask a soldier to dig a ditch around someone's tent, while three boys are sitting inside playing with dice.[134]

Another example he gave was that when Kibbutz Giva'at Brener (near Rehovot) took in the children of the transit camps, they gave them clothes. When they came the second time, they were again barefoot and barely dressed; at this time the kibbutz members felt that the parents of the children were trying to get free clothing out of them, and so they refused.[135]

Yoseftal's reflections classify behavior according to ethnicity; Yemenite Jews act in one way, while Kurds, Iraqis, and Persians (all of them) behave in another. The report leaves out the Iraqis who did act to save their children, and links the inability to provide a decent family life to race and character. While many Iraqis invaded shacks, stole food to have something for their children, and separated from their children to save the lives of the latter, their apathy was the only detail stressed in the diary. Yet this apathy was a form of resistance and despair. In refusing the efforts against the floods, the Iraqi newcomers indicated to the state that, given the fact that it had done so little on their behalf, they themselves would refuse to do anything that would not substantially improve things for themselves and their families. The Iraqis themselves were less shocked than Yoseftal. The chief of staff asked an Iraqi soldier about his mood as he was digging a ditch in a transit camp, while inside the tent nearby three boys slept on the beds and did nothing to help him. The soldier replied that he was happy to work; his family, he said, in the transit camp of Rehovot, was probably sitting inside the tent while another soldier was digging a ditch for them. He did not mind.[136]

Not all officials were as harsh as Yoseftal. More nuanced comments were offered by the well-respected Lieutenant Colonel Yitzhak Rabin, who was stationed in the transit camps during October 1951. Rabin distinguished the class differences between Iraqi Jews: some were educated urbanites from Baghdad and Basra, whereas the Kurdish Jews had not had as much exposure to Western ideas and culture. The prior social status of the newcomers from Iraq was higher than those from Yemen and Iran, however, although Iraqis were more reluctant to engage in physical labor. For Rabin, too, the primary reason for their conflicts with the agency was that the Iraqis lacked knowledge of Jewish life and Zionism. For Rabin, however, the Iraqi behavior was attributed to issues of the migrant's class and ideology, and not to their Oriental character.[137]

The harsh winters continued through 1956, although their impact diminished as more people left the camps, and more wooden shacks were built. The period 1952–53 was still a challenge.[138] In 1953, the IDF took care of twenty-four transit camps and was in charge of placing children.[139] From the mid-1950s on, the new neighborhoods in Tel Aviv and Jerusalem were the scenes of destruction because of the rains. In 1955, neighborhoods in southern Tel Aviv suffered tremendously, and one hundred families were evacuated. Y. Ben Yehuda, Minister of Interior Affairs, dismissed the events by saying that this was not the sort of disaster for which the state could be expected to plan and budget. In his opinion, depictions of the effects of the floods were greatly exaggerated.[140]

SOCIALIZED INTO SOCIALISM: EXPERIENCES ON KIBBUTZIM

Some parents, because of the difficult living conditions, opted to send their children to kibbutzim. The kibbutzim's youth organizations were originally intended for children and young adults, initially taking in teenagers who had fled Nazi Germany and Nazi-occupied Europe, but they also open their communities to teenagers from the Arab world, including Iraq. After 1948, the kibbutzim absorbed mainly youth who were newcomers. Groups of Iraqi teens and children (called "Babylonians," *Bavlim*) were scattered in the kibbutzim across Israel.[141] Some forty kibbutzim, identified with all political branches of labor Zionism, took in groups of children. The smallest group comprised eight children, the largest, sixty-two; most groups ranged from twenty to thirty-five. The children were organized in groups of young teenagers (*hevrot no'ar*) and children (*hevrot yeladim*). Some were established in the most well-respected kibbutzim of Israel, including Yagur (fifty teenagers; forty children), Ginosar (thirty teenagers), Sdeh Nahum (thirty teenagers), Kfar Gil'adi (forty-five teenagers; twenty-eight children), Kfar Menachem (twenty-five teenagers), Gan Shmu'el (fifty teenagers), Dgania A (thirty teenagers), and Dgania B (thirty-eight teenagers). In total, about seventeen hundred Iraqi children and teenagers resided there.[142]

It was very difficult for parents to send their children away. Iraqi Jews had rarely sent their children to the few boarding schools that existed in Iraq (mainly agricultural colleges). It was preferred that children live at home, attend school during the day, and spend time with their parents during the afternoons. Dinners, lunches, and the holidays together were key moments in family life. Parents also resented the kibbutzim's socialist outlook, and their secularism. But now, living in poverty and often being unable to provide for their children, many Iraqi parents believed that the kibbutzim offered a way out for their children, where they would be fed and educated.[143]

The experiences in the kibbutzim were diverse. Like all members of the kibbutz teenagers and children worked in agricultural and domestic labor. They worked half the day and studied the other half. A teenager who later grew to love the life in the kibbutz wrote: "I have never worked in my life and I did not speak Hebrew. When it was explained to me how to work, I could not even understand (the counselor). Every time I came to my work placement, I said: 'This is hard work.' Even the less difficult tasks looked difficult to me. I thought life in the kibbutz was like a jail."[144] Iraqi children also found it difficult to adjust to the new practices of the kibbutz. Ashkenazi food was initially unpalatable to them. While they had come from a Westernized Iraqi society, they found the secularism of the kibbutz baffling and disconcerting. They failed to fathom why members of the kibbutz were called comrades (*haver*); why the kibbutz was perceived as a big family; and why holidays were not celebrated in the intimate space of the home but rather commemorated in nationalized public ceremonies that memorialized the victories of the Hebrews over their enemies. Passover, for example, no longer celebrated the exodus, but was transformed into a holiday of liberty and spring, in which kibbutz members ate bread (something that is absolutely forbidden according to Jewish law). Some kibbutzim initiated practices that were particularly strange to Iraqi-Jewish children, like abolishing the celebrations of bar mitzva and bat mitzva and instead celebrating the entry of the child into the youth movement Ha-No'ar ha-'Oved.[145]

Some Iraqi children wanted to study more hours than were allotted to them for this purpose by the kibbutz. However, in general the kibbutzim did not encourage their own children, and the Iraqis as well, to take the nationwide matriculation exams; they ought to be socialist farmers, not "intellectuals." Iraqi teenagers who had attended high schools in Iraq were accustomed to regarding the teacher as a figure of authority, who was referred to as "Mister So-and-so." Now they had to get used to the fact that teachers were called by their first names, sometimes with the word "comrade" (*haver*) beforehand. Moreover, because of the legacy of the kibbutzim's having fought the British during the mandate period and because of their socialism, the studying and speaking of English was looked down upon, whereas in Iraq it had been greatly valued.[146]

The teenagers were exposed to socialist indoctrination and joined a Zionist socialist youth movement. But for many, the socialist ideology, practiced at every signal moment in kibbutz life, and discussed at length in meetings with teachers and instructors and in the kibbutzim's gatherings, was off-putting. David Ben Baruch, who wrote an important book on the experiences of Iraqis in the kibbutzim,[147] describes in an autobiographical short story what happened to Iraqi children when they arrived at the Kibbutz Merhavia. Four-five boys and girls were welcomed to the kibbutz and were given a counselor. The room in which they slept had a surprise for them:

> When we got to our shacks made into dormitories, we saw a big picture hanging above the northern window, so that when you entered the wooden shack the photo was immediately obvious; it was of a large man with a thick moustache, looking like a great leader. One of the children said, "This must be the father of the kibbutz," for in Iraq, it was common to hang the photo of the grandfather or the father in the living room. We accepted his opinion and decided this was the father of the kibbutz.[148]

It was later explained that they were mistaken. It was Stalin.

The dress code in the kibbutz was also a challenge. The boys and girls each received a package, which included Sabbath clothes and work clothes. The girls found it sometimes difficult to wear shorts. Some girls and boys had much nicer clothes that they had brought with them from Baghdad and Basra, but were discouraged from wearing them. European skirts, ties, or anything that did not conform to the kibbutz dress code, were frowned upon. For the children who came from more religious households, the fact that girl wore shorts was also problematic.[149]

The teenagers initially spoke Arabic among themselves, but gradually shifted to Hebrew. The counselors, who instructed them in both agricultural and educational matters, did not know Arabic and they needed to understand what they were saying. In other kibbutzim the Iraqi children were paired with children from many countries, such as Iran, Czechoslovakia, Romania, and Turkey, and Hebrew served as the language of communication. All the Arab names of the children and the young adults were changed to Hebrew names.[150]

As Esther Meir has shown, the teenagers and the children had conflicting feelings toward the kibbutz: many saw it as a very positive experience, others did not. On the one hand, they loved the new opportunities that the kibbutz opened up for them. They befriended members of the kibbutz, including people they met in kitchens and while doing their daily chores in fields and houses; they spoke to them; and they interacted with them as they learned to speak Hebrew. Instead of being mistreated by corrupt Ashkenazi directors of labor and housing bureaus, they were hearing firsthand accounts of Ashkenazi life in Europe and mandatory Palestine from people they respected. Some very much enjoyed being with older individuals on the kibbutz, with their counselors whom they respected and loved, and with those who talked to them about their socialist ideals and their struggles. Others also report about their infatuation with nature, and the beautiful scenery around them.[151]

On the other hand, the Iraqi teenagers resented the fact that their parents, whom they witnessed decline in status from respectability to poverty, were rejected by the kibbutzim. They likewise sensed that they were discriminated against because they were not born on the kibbutz and because they were of the wrong race and color.[152] A teenager who lived in Kibbutz Ramat Yohanan, for example, was deeply insulted when he was given a toothbrush and was told that this instrument was not meant for cleaning his shoes.[153] Another young teenager wrote about the ways in which he was treated in Kibbutz Ma'oz Haim; he and his friends were called "Arabs," "ignorant," and "blacks" by fellow kibbutz members who also wondered whether they knew how to eat with a fork; his account underlined the feelings of discrimination on the part of the Iraqi newcomer, and the sense that kibbutz members connected Iraqi Jews to other groups marked as nonwhite.[154] In Yagur, kibbutz members shouted at the Iraqi youth, "You are worse than the Arabs."[155] We note, importantly, that *Arab* is a derogatory word; certainly in the eyes of the kibbutz members, but also in the eyes of the youth. Shoshanna Arbeli Almozlino also recalls that the young Iraqis were shocked by the level of ignorance displayed by kibbutz members with respect to the Middle East. Shoshana came to Kibbutz Sdeh Nahum as a teenager in 1947, and recalls:

> They were certain that we came from a backward, primitive place, and that we lacked any knowledge or education and were completely ignorant of all the achievements in technology and the progress of the modern world. In the first days we were often insulted by the astonishing questions of the kibbutz members.... They wanted to find out, sometimes with some hesitation, whether we had heard in Iraq about electricity and the radio and whether there were universities or cinemas there. After we overcame the initial shock, we sometimes repaid them with practical jokes: we told them, for example, that in certain regions in Iraq, one could find small tribes of cannibals and would burst into laughter when some kibbutz members asked us if we ourselves had met these creatures.[156]

It was only later that the kibbutz members realized the Iraqis were high school graduates.

The teenagers' grievances about the ignorance they encountered are corroborated by reports that were written by kibbutz members. In these reports, kibbutz members reflect on what they saw as the primitive background from which the Iraqi youth came. Lea Grinstein, from Kibbutz Gan Shmu'el, was to give a sex education class to young Iraqis residing in her kibbutz. She told them to ask her anything that came to their mind and so they did: "When do you begin to have sexual relations? Can you live without sex? Does homosexuality cause disease? Does masturbation cause paralysis?" In her account, which later became the guide for all such sex education classes in the youth movement associated with the kibbutzim, Lea did not wish to give them too much sexual freedom because of their "hot Oriental temperament." On the other hand, she wanted to demystify wrong information and destroy the superstitions and the approach of the "household of the East with its enslavement and fears."[157] When she finally replied to the children's inquires, she talked about sublimation (which they did not understand); she told the girls not to have sex before the age of nineteen; she mentioned that "among us" (meaning "among kibbutz members") one does not go to prostitutes; and that masturbation is not a sin "but one should not overdo this, for it causes weakness." The issue of homosexuality was not addressed.[158] Lea's own conservatism aside, we note that the main guiding principles for her dealing with the boys are her misguided assumptions about their homes and their Middle Eastern culture, contrasted with what happens among "us," the kibbutz members, which was sexually and culturally normative.

One of the best novels written on Iraqi youth in Israel is Elie Amir's *Tarnegol kaparot* (Scapegoat; 1983), which depicts the lives of a group of Iraqi teenagers in a fictional kibbutz called Kiryat Oranim. The novel is based on its author's autobiography. Amir (né Fu'ad Elias Khalaschi) arrived to Kibbutz Mishmar ha-'Emek at the age of thirteen after his family migrated to Israel from Baghdad. The novel depicts positive aspects of the youth in the kibbutz; it shows how the young teenagers rejoice in the discovery that they would live, once more, in actual rooms rather than in shacks and tents, and receive food beyond the meager portions at the transit camps. The teens also meet Ashkenazim whom they befriend, including kind kibbutz members, and especially teens who come from Poland and Romania and reside in the kibbutz with them. But the novel also tells a gloomier story about their difficulties in the kibbutz; how certain members refer to them as animals and cavemen and how teenagers in the kibbutz refuse to interact with them. Some kibbutz members even anticipate that they would walk around in the pajamas they brought from Iraq.[159]

Most importantly, the novel uncovers, with great sensitivity and nuance, the psychological and emotional effects that the shift to the kibbutz had on their identity and their relationship with their parents. The Iraqi teenagers have to fight for vacations to see their parents, and sense that the new society in which they reside belittles their parents' practices and cultural mores and seeks to transform them. The teenagers are asked to change their names into Hebrew; 'Abd al-'Aziz becomes Avner, Fa'uziyya, Ilana, and Jamil, Yoram. The protagonist, Nuri, insists on keeping his Arabic name, not changing it into Nimrod. Their love for Arabic music is likewise frowned upon as being a mere attraction to wailing and yelling, and they are encouraged to listen to Mozart and Beethoven instead. Exposing their bodies in the public baths of the kibbutz (something they were not accustomed to in their homes) seems humiliating and unnatural. Secularization is mandatory and harsh: Nuri lies that his father is not religious to get into the kibbutz. To adapt to the kibbutz's ethos, they forsake their cultural and religious traditions, yet this process of abandoning the memories of their homes is excruciating and painful. Their problematic relationships to their families' past, and especially their parents' degrading present, are encapsulated in a scene where Nuri reflects on the transit camp near Kiryat

Oranim. Although the transit camp is close to the kibbutz, and although their own Iraqi parents lived in similar camps, the Iraqi teenagers try to avoid it. This was because the transit camp represents

> the dark side of our lives. The nightmares we escaped. The dirt, the hunger, and whatnot. When we approached the transit camp while running . . . , we would turn our backs to it. Going back, very quickly, to the kibbutz. Just not to smell its odor, just not to know. But the transit camp was in our souls. Observing us from the back, running on the road, it took its vengeance upon us by its mere existence, breathing down our necks, unrelenting, so distant and yet so powerful, pulling us to it again and again. Something more powerful than us stopped us, preventing us from crossing the in-between domain between it and Kiryat Oranim, the borderline.[160]

This novel is taught today in many Israeli schools, and has appeared in forty editions thus far. Indeed, it captures an important moment in Israeli history. In the end, many of the young teenagers left the kibbutzim. While residing in the Kibbutzim, Iraqi teenagers underlined the hypocrisy of the kibbutzim members who talked loftily of brotherly love and socialism but had stereotypes and strange opinions about Jews from Middle Eastern lands. But the kibbutzim gave a great deal to these children. They provided the children with food, clothing, and an education, which was no small matter. They literally saved hundreds from hunger and poverty. And they also taught the children how to speak the language of the state: not just Hebrew, but also the language of socialism, of labor Zionism, and of Israeli patriotism. Whenever Iraqi teens formulated their demands, they knew how to use the language of the state to articulate those demands and their own visions.

CONCLUSION

Many of the experiences depicted in this chapter were not unique to Iraqi children, and were shared by Polish, Romanian, Hungarian, Egyptian, Turkish, Bulgarian, and North African children. Iraqi children were spared, relatively speaking, from the horrors that befell other Mizrahi children. Some twenty-five thousand immigrant children and thirty-seven hundred Palestinian children underwent dangerous radiation treatment for ringworm disease. Iraqi children were treated as well, but it seems that the process was accelerated after 1952, and that the children treated were mostly Yemenite and North African.[161] The majority of the babies believed to be kidnapped were Yemenite.

However, these Iraqi children also had uniquely Iraqi experiences: they were living with Iraqi parents, among Iraqi migrants, in transit camps populated by Iraqi Jews; and they mostly played with Iraqi children. Moreover, the strategies with which they and their parents dealt with the situation were shaped by their Iraqi identity. The high percentage of Iraqi teachers and educated men and women among the newcomers created a push for a better education system. The memories of cities in Iraq that these children shared were another factor that brought them together.

Families were greatly impacted by the circumstances of life in the transit camps. They were broken apart when sons and daughters left for kibbutzim; fathers lived far away in order to make a living and visited their children over the weekends. But in the most profound ways, families were torn apart internally; as children watched their fathers and mothers suffer a decline in social status, they shared the parents' pain and they suffered as a result.

The Israeli state did have an effect on the lives of these children, although the children saw only a few of the state's representatives, notably teachers, guides, and nurses. Since the state elites were socialist, they invested in measures to make sure that Iraqi children were educated and fed. In truth, it was very difficult to find the resources to support children under the difficult austerity measures of the 1950s. But the state would have been much more successful in its approach to the children if its officials had fewer stereotypes about the nature of Iraqi families. It could have helped more if its officials had paid heed to the parents, to the talented teachers who wanted to teach, and to the high school students who found difficulties adjusting to the new system; and if officials had not been so quick to dismiss just complaints about the situation as nothing more than reflections of the primitive nature of the children and their families. The great emphasis on flags, the celebrations of Independence Day, and the state's glorious trees (which the children only rarely saw) might indicate that the state's officials doubted the children's patriotism. It was in this area that the state invested a great deal, so that at least on the surface these children would appreciate these national developments.

Israeli society was also divided on how to treat Iraqi children. On the one hand, large segments of society did help the children. Families that were themselves dealing with austerity measures took children in, and volunteers and women's organizations from across the political spectrum assisted the children and their families, especially during the harsh winters. But the presence of a large number of poor immigrants also exposed the darkest side of Israeli society: the employers who used child labor and paid scant wages; the Ashkenazi families who sent Mizrahi children back to collapsing tents in the depths of a harsh winter because they were not of the right sect and color; and the many state officials who claimed that the problems of hunger, neglect, and child labor stemmed, not from poverty and failed state policies, but rather from their "primitive" parents.

Children, even in the most challenging circumstances, tried to come to terms and cope with the situation. At times, they resisted the state's attempts at disciplining them. Even in the kibbutzim, teenagers and children did not forget their heritage that easily. The resistance of these children and teenagers cannot be quantified, but we can sense it, in the Iraqi youths' fooling of the members of Kibbutz Sdeh Nahum with stories of Iraqi cannibals, in the children's kindness to their Iraqi teachers, and in their pranks and jokes. For us, it might seem little. For them, it sometimes meant the world.

3 THE ONLY DEMOCRACY IN THE MIDDLE EAST

IN 1951, Golda Meir, the Israeli minister of labor, responded to accusations concerning the dreadful living conditions endured by newcomers to Israel, especially those from Iraq. She replied:

> Despite my awareness of the sufferings of people who dwell in the tents, and the inequality between those who dwell in houses and those who dwell in tents—and giving a speech about inequality does not bring about equality—still, if I have to choose between stopping immigration until we can settle each and every one of them in the future, or continuing with the immigration, and that many thousands would dwell in camps, I choose the latter. And I am certain the newcomers would choose this with me. *A tent in Khayriyya is more important than a house in Iraq, for the newcomers and for the state.*[1]

Golda's words reflect the MAPAI's arrogant position. Golda (not the Iraqis themselves) knows what is best for the Iraqis; their interests, unsurprisingly, correlate to those of the State of Israel. Using the first-person singular ("I"), Golda designates herself as the authority to chart the course of the Aliyah, which involved thousands of people. Most importantly, however, Golda's speech underscores the unlikelihood that the living conditions of the Iraqi men and women of Khayriyya will be improved: how could they expect anything from a state whose minister of labor, who is supposed to look out for their concerns, believes that it is better for them to rot in their tents than live in houses? Part of the answer is actually found in Golda's own words. Read only slightly against the grain, Golda's dismissal of "those who give speeches" actually highlights the important institution of the Knesset as a public platform for the delivery of speeches, or, more broadly, for discussing the Iraqi migration, Ashkenazi-Mizrahi relations, racism, and inequality, within the Israeli political system. It also pushed the Iraqis, in Golda's party, and in other parties, to look for venues that can represent their concerns.

Golda's assumption about the incapacity of Iraqis to become informed participants in the Israeli political system was current in the Israeli public sphere. Seemingly, this argument made sense. Distant from the main cities, being unable to speak Hebrew, and beset with unemployment and poverty, these people faced significant obstacles to their becoming actors in political life. Moreover, neither the state nor the mainstream media were interested in the concerns of the "human material" populating the newcomers' camps and transit camps, lest the immigrants find the means to resist their assigned roles of laborers and settlers. And yet, the Iraqi newcomers were active in the Israeli political sphere of the 1950s because they, like other newcomers, were given the right to vote for the Knesset. MAPAI, the ruling party, anticipated being the beneficiary of the gratitude of the newcomers, who were seen as a reservoir of votes. At the same time, the other Israeli parties hoped to attract Iraqis; given their profound hatred for the regime under which they lived, Iraqis seemed ripe for recruitment by opposition parties. The national elections of 1951, just as the Iraqi Jews were arriving in Israel, served as the catalyst for the politicization of these immigrants, by themselves and through the efforts of the preexisting parties. Nonetheless, engaging in politics was no simple undertaking. In Israel of the 1950s and 1960s, a clear separation between party politics, employment, recreation, and education was impossible. Almost everything, from sports groups to youth movements to factories, was politicized, and access to employment and housing, as well as the Jewish Agency itself, was under the control of the governing party, MAPAI. Challenging it was therefore a formidable task.

This chapter proposes that the Israeli political system, despite being only partially democratic, offered venues in which Iraqi Jews could voice their complaints. I do not analyze actual voting patterns, because the elections were corrupt and one cannot assume that the results reflect the actual choices of voters. Instead, I look at the parties with prominent Iraqi involvement and those that had Iraqi members who were active in the transit camps and published in the Arabic newspapers of the parties. The chapter explores how the parties' leaders conceptualized Israel's sectarian problem and their relationship to the Iraqi community in particular. It focuses mainly on the parties in which Iraqis had significant representation or on parties whose leaders affected the immigrants' politics. Despite their efforts at outreach, however, none of the political organizations in Israel offered a comprehensive solution to the Iraqi problem. At each and every step of the way, the parties' refusal either to critique Zionist ideology or to recognize the racism of their own members curtailed the possibility of providing a genuine solution.

GOLDA'S COMPLAINT: MAPAI AND THE IRAQI IMMIGRANTS

MAPAI was the major political party in Israel which orchestrated, and thus controlled, anything to do with the Aliyah; from the number of migrants, to the places where they settled, to their employment. Tending to the needs of migrants and conceptualizing their status in the new state during this period engaged many of MAPAI's officials and employees, who ran the operation of bringing masses of people to the poor state of Israel and were identified with the successes and failures of this project. MAPAI was concerned with the socialization, health, and education of the migrants, and these topics occupied its ministers, Knesset members, instructors, guides, and social workers. They knew that these migration processes would change their state and many realized the enormity of the task, given the meager economic resources, and it occupied the party's elite.

The vision of the state of MAPAI's leader, Prime Minister David Ben Gurion, was close to etatism or statism, namely, the belief that the state should govern both economic and societal matters.[2] While he believed that the state should have political parties, and that citizens (including newcomers) should vote, he also saw MAPAI as the guiding force of the state. The kibbutzim, in this framework, were the avant-garde, leading society to socialism and Zionism.[3] In this context, the Iraqis, being less advanced in their political development, were not on an equal footing as citizens. MAPAI used its power over employment and housing to ensure that the Iraqis would vote for it. The Jewish Agency, which ran most of the transit camps, and decided on transfers from tents to shacks, and from transit-camp housing to permanent housing, was under MAPAI's control, thus making its power acutely felt in many camps. The structure of the transit camps tied the Iraqi Jews to the Histadrut, which was ruled by MAPAI, alongside representations of other parties identified with leftist causes. The expectation was that Iraqis, along with all the other newcomers, would become Histadrut members, and most were given membership cards in Sha'ar ha-'Aliyah. The Histadrut had officials in the transit camps and it was virtually impossible for a newcomer to survive in the Israeli labor market without belonging to some of its many suborganizations.

As was the case in other socialist countries, the Histadrut represented both the major companies that belonged to the state and the labor unions. Its labor unions were crucial; the local workers' councils (*mo'atzot po'alim*), which acted on the municipal level in matters concerning employment and pay, were to help Iraqis in their job placement and workplace; the Histadrut's teachers' union (from 1950 on) shaped education in the transit camps; and its women organizations were active in managing Iraqi women's affairs. The Histadrut's institution Hevrat ha-'Ovdim (literally: the Workers Cooperative; established 1923) united all the Histadrut's industrial, financial, and commercial bodies, and thus molded daily lives at the transit camps, from funding, to construction, to health, and cemented MAPAI's influence in these sites. Some of the important bodies related to Hevrat ha-'Ovdim included Kupat Holim, the main health provider in most of the transit camps; the building and construction cooperative, Solel Boneh, which built apartments and shacks in the transit camps and in many of the new neighborhoods; Ha-Mashbir ha-Merkazi, the state major supplies corporative, which provided supplies to many transit camps and newcomers' moshavim (from clothing items to grain and agricultural equipment), through its subcompany, Ha-Mashbir la-'Oleh; Tnuva, the cooperative marketing dairy and agricultural products which was effective in the newcomers' moshavim; and its housing companies, Shikun 'Ovdim, which managed many neighborhood housing solutions for the newcomers. In 1952 Shikun 'Ovdim teamed up with the Histadrut's Bank Po'alim (Workers Bank) to form a mortgage bank, Bank le-Mashkanta'ot, which was the biggest in the country.[4] While the Histadrut chair, Pinhas Lavon, pushed for decentralization of its many organizations, Ben Gurion preferred centralization and control over the market.[5]

As economist Yitzhak Greenberg explains, this structure helped the newcomers in the sense that all services were connected, and one major organization handled their enormous needs. On the other hand, this maze of bodies and unions left Iraqi Jews at the mercy of one party, regardless of their actual political choices. Iraqis therefore feared that articulating the wrong political opinion could cost them their jobs or their houses. Their concerns were not unfounded. The court in Petach Tikva, for example, that heard the case of an unemployed worker accused of disorderly conduct at the labor bureau, condemned the fact that in the transit camp, work placement was based on party affiliations.[6] In their autobiographies, Iraqis explain that they joined the Histadrut and MAPAI because that was the unwritten law of the time. Indeed, the number of the Histadrut's members rose from 181,000 in 1948 to 640,000 in 1958.[7]

The formative experiences of MAPAI's leaders, who were mostly Eastern European Zionists, took place in Ottoman and mandatory Palestine. Settlement under the Ottoman and British regimes and the Aliyah were the essential principles of the party, and were very meaningful to the party members themselves. Many therefore dismissed the complaints of the Iraqis by recalling that when they had come to the land of Israel, they, too, had lived in shacks and had endured great hardship, which they painted as decisive moments in their biographies.

With regard to the Iraqis, party members undertook a kind of essentializing ethnography, in order to classify them vis-à-vis other groups of Mizrahi Jews, as well as vis-à-vis Ashkenazi migrants. The willingness to settle, commitment to Zionist ideology, and loyalty to MAPAI were the important litmus tests. Thus, David Teneh, with the Jewish Agency, noted that among the newcomers, the Yugoslavs, Czechoslovakians, and Bulgarians were the most civil and productive, but that some of them might be communists. The "loud and bitter" Romanians and Hungarians, who hated the Jewish Agency, lacked commitment to

TABLE 1. Centralization and Control: The Four MAPAI Officials Who Managed the Employment and Housing of the Iraqis, 1948–63.

Levy Eshkol	Golda Meir	Giora Yoseftal	Mordechai Namir
1948–49: The Jewish Agency (chair of settlement division); 1949–52: The Jewish Agency (general treasurer)	1948–56: Minister of Labor (MAPAI)	1947–56: The Jewish Agency (head of the absorption division), 1952: The Jewish Agency (general treasurer)	1950–56: chairman of the Histadrut
1951–52: minister of agriculture and development (MAPAI)	1955–56: chairwoman of the board of Amidar	1953–55; 1960–62: chairman of the board of Amidar	1956–59: chairmen of the board of Amidar
1952–63: minister of finance (MAPAI)	1956–66: minister of foreign affairs	1960–61: minister of labor (MAPAI); 1961: minister of housing and development (MAPAI)	1956–59: minister of labor

the ideal of settlement and wanted to settle in the cities. Having less potential to become useful citizens, for the most part, were the Jews of the Orient: the Yemenites were noteworthy for their love of Israel, but were poor and afflicted with diseases; North Africans were hot-tempered and suffered from an inferiority complex, tending to assume they were being discriminated against. The Turks were good human material: they were clean, healthy, and committed to their families. The Iraqis were lumped together with the Syrians, Iranians, and Libyans: they knew some Hebrew, there was some support for Zionism, and they wanted to settle.[8] Such categorizations were common in this period and offered diverse taxonomies: in comparison to certain groups of immigrants, Iraqis were insubordinate, but in comparison to others, like the North Africans, they were closer to achieving integration into Israeli society.

Ben Gurion wanted the Iraqis to be integrated into Israeli society, and resisted the idea that this was not possible. But he did categorize Iraqi Jews as Jews of Islam—Jews from backward countries—and thus in need of guidance. In 1951 Ben Gurion regretted the immigration to Israel of the criminal and the infirm, but noted that all other Iraqis should have come; the country was founded for the salvation of Jews, and Iraqi Jews had lived in hell before immigrating. True, they did not come because of ideology; they had not immigrated in the days of Ezra and Nehemiah (when the two led Babylonian Jewry back to the land of Israel), nor after the Balfour Declaration of 1917 (in which the British government recognized a Jewish homeland in Palestine). And yet, Ben Gurion argued, "I do not find a major difference between a Jew who came from Russia—supposedly the Jewish intelligentsia—and a Jew who came from Babylon. It is the same human material. However, the Jews of Europe had better educational possibilities than those of the Jews of Islam. Therefore, the new immigration wave [from Iraq] suffers, and because of its suffering, the state suffers, [especially] from the lack of professional capabilities."[9]

Initiatives that actually helped the Iraqis a great deal, like sending children to kibbutzim, and sending volunteers to the transit camps and the newcomers' villages, stemmed from the conviction that Iraqis needed to be guided into socialism and Zionism. The kibbutzim movement and the Histadrut sent many guides and counselors to the transit camps: youth counselors, agricultural guides, social workers, and nurses to instruct the newcomers whether they needed such instruction or not. Ben Gurion even hoped that IDF would be part of such educational ventures, and that drafting more Mizrahi Jews would encourage integration. In this context, the word *Hasbara* (propaganda) denoted the education of the newcomers in both the ways of the modern world and the principles of Zionism (via Hebrew classes, national holidays, Hebrew films and so on).[10] It also meant indoctrinating Iraqis so that they would vote for the right party, MAPAI. The Hasbara policies manifested themselves in MAPAI rallies in the camps, requests for broadcasts in colloquial Iraqi for Iraqi Jews for fifteen-twenty minutes a day (one hundred radios had been provided to the transit camps, in order to connect the isolated Iraqis with the Israeli public sphere),[11] and Hasbara campaigns run by the Histadrut and the Jewish Agency in places like Kfar 'Ana.[12]

The electoral campaigns that MAPAI ran were not the most democratic, to say the least; they were corrupt and violent and as a result almost always successful. As Orit Rozin has shown in a seminal study of the second Israeli national elections, MAPAI used very dirty techniques to ensure its victory; the lack of privacy in the ballots tarnished the electoral process. Where the U.S. electoral system had its Watergate, the Israeli electoral campaigns during the 1950s had their MAPAM-gate, General Zionists-gate, and naturally MAKI-gate—the phones of political figures in these parties being tapped.[13] Before the elections MAPAI divided all the transit camps between different political parties so that their different bodies could exercise control there; MAPAI got the majority of the camps under its control. Officials in these camps saw themselves not as the representatives of public order, but rather as committed to ensuring that the people in the transit camps under their administration would vote for the right party. Paid thugs broke up meetings of opposing political parties, and MAPAI officials warned the Iraqis in the transit camps not to attend rallies or meetings of—let alone vote for—other parties if they did not want to jeopardize their livelihoods, housing, and educational opportunities for their children. Although other socialist parties were also part of the Histadrut, MAPAI used Histadrut funds for its electoral campaigns and claimed all of the Histadrut achievements as its own.[14] Other public funds were also used for propaganda aims. Herut member M. Olmert wondered, for instance, why the local committee in the poor region of Or Yehuda used public money to produce a brochure about the achievements of the council, when the region clearly had much higher spending priorities.[15]

Typically, MAPAI or the Histadrut had an office in the form of a wooden shack in the transit camps. Even in the very poor camp of Sakiyya the Histadrut was given a structure as a space for cultural activities.[16] The Histadrut office in each camp was to handle matters relating to labor initially; within a short time these offices extended their influence in other spheres. In one transit camp, the clerk of Amidar, the company tasked with housing placement, received people in the MAPAI club—not in his office. Requests for electricity and water connections were made in the MAPAI club as well.[17] The directorship of the camps, in fact, would not grant permission for activities that were seen as not recognizing the hegemony of MAPAI. Thirty residents of camp of Khayriyya wanted to open a cultural club, which would meet weekly in a public space. However, since the twenty-three residents of this group were not Histadrut members, their request was denied by the transit-camp directorship.[18] In the nearby transit camp of Kfar 'Ana, a man offered Herut his own shack, if the party loaned him money to build a house, knowing full well how difficult it was for opposition parties to operate in his camp.[19]

The apparent contradiction between the ostensibly socialist MAPAI government, on the one hand, and the inability of the very same socialist government to attend to the socioeconomic needs of its poor Iraqi citizens, on the other, was manifested in the stance of MAPAI members toward the newcomers. MAPAI members refused to acknowledge that that the Iraqis were steered toward undesirable, low-paying jobs in the agricultural and public-works sectors. In many cases, there was no financial need to send people to workfare projects, as the money could be given to them as benefits. But the notion that the benefits might instill in the Iraqis a sense of laziness and accustom them to relying too much on the state was very prominent in their thinking. Golda Meir argued that it was wrong, from the standpoint of personal discipline, to have the unemployed live off the state, and thus they ought to be assigned to whatever work was available: "Also for the sake of my own children, I cannot allow unemployment."[20]

The way for MAPAI's leadership to justify its inability to support the unemployed was to argue that the Iraqis were exaggerating their need for help. The problem was not that they could not integrate into Israeli society and find work because of the structure of the Israeli economy and the absence of nationwide resources; it was that they simply did not want to. To refute the claim that the newcomers were too poor to make even a modest downpayment for renting a wooden shack, Ben Gurion told his fellow ministers about a man from whom five thousand liras had been stolen to evidence that people in the transit camps had cash. His minister of finance, Dov Yosef, mentioned a newcomer from Iraq "who has money, yet is still homeless and lives in a camp." Fellow ministers from religious parties provided narratives of their own. Minister Moshe

Shapira reported that after one resident passed away, thirty-one thousand liras were discovered hidden in his tent.[21] MAPAI's minister of police, a Mizrahi Jew himself, admitted that the newcomers had savings but chose to live in squalor.[22] The party's discourse, then, attempted to shift the blame for the miserable state of the camps onto the newcomers' lack of talent and professional training. When Hannan Rubin (MAPAM) argued that the state had no valid insurance policy for employees in case of work accidents, Mordechai Namir, MAPAI's minister of labor, replied, "It might be the case that the main reason for the high rate of work-related accidents in the country is the large number of newcomer workers [*ovdim 'olim*] who lack experience."[23] Zelig Lavon, the chair of Shikun 'Ovdim, argued that the quality of the building in the country was deteriorating because of unskilled workers.[24]

It was crucial for MAPAI officials to control the representations of transit-camp life for the purposes of domestic social engineering and the solicitation of donations from abroad. While its own employees at the transit camps complained about the harsh living conditions, with some being sympathetic to the plight of their residents, when it came to publish discussions, such sympathies quickly vanished. Golda Meir proposed that it was better not to talk of the newcomers as miserable or in need of mercy, "because by doing so we educate them to be a passive element."[25] MAPAI Knesset members likewise engaged in Hasbara themselves: Eliyahu Carmeli drew the parallel between the experience of the people of Israel, who had lived for a long time in the Sinai Desert before coming to the Promised Land, and that of the residents of the transit camps, enduring a modern Sinai of sorts. When he visited a transit camp, though his "impression was harsh," he was nonetheless happy to find not only youth but also the elderly supporting the Zionist project, despite the difficult conditions:

> Those who were peddlers, shop owners, and craftsmen in the small towns of their exiles in Iraq, Yemen, Persia, and North Africa now settle in transit camps on mountaintops, in order to revive the desert of the land, to work it, guard it, and solidify its borders.[26]

This speech highlights the ways in which MAPAI's Ashkenazi leadership misunderstood and misrepresented the lives of Iraqi Jews. Out of ignorance, Carmeli superimposes his understanding of Jewish life in Eastern Europe on the realities in Iraq in order to celebrate the Aliyah. In point of fact, the majority of Iraqi Jews had lived in the capital city, Baghdad, but also in the cities

Basra and Mosul. It was in Russia, Carmeli's homeland, where Jews faced legislation that limited their settlement to confined regions. Carmeli assumes Iraqi Jews must have been peddlers and merchants, yet many had worked for the state as clerks, teachers, and lawyers, and also been middle-class professionals. This lack of knowledge on the part of the MAPAI leaders of the conditions in Iraq gave rise to deeply entrenched misrepresentations of the lives of the Iraqis, before and after the arrival of the latter in Israel.

The most effective tool of MAPAI's Hasbara was its daily press. Party officials and bureaucrats, especially those belonging to Histadrut, were described as responsible educators who helped the uninformed newcomers become acclimated to the Israeli way of life.[27] Writing on the transit camp in Petach Tivka, *Ha-Dor* noted that the director appointed for the camp "took care of its residents like a compassionate father" to whom the representatives of the residents could express their demands so they could jointly strive to solve the problems.[28] Another article in *Ha-Dor* said of the camp in Talipot that the only bright spots in the camp's general darkness were the building of the Histadrut, the clinic of Kupat Holim, and the guides who taught the children.[29] A reporter for *Davar* described the children in Sakiyya going to kindergarten to celebrate the holiday of Hannukah and eating biscuits and chocolates while being supervised by female soldiers.[30] In another report in *Davar* about the breaking up of a demonstration of Iraqis from Mosul and Akra in Tiberias, the writer commended the fine behavior of the police, who did not use dogs (!), and the chief of police's ability to bring order to the camp.[31]

If anything was wrong in the transit camps, it was the fault of their denizens, according to the letters from officials in the camps that *Davar* printed. A representative of the Or Yehuda municipality pointed out that the transit camp of Sakiyya owed money to the municipality, since it was populated by "social cases" who enjoyed tax reductions. When residents refused to move from their tents into wooden shacks in new camps far from their jobs or in remote areas of Israel, these demands were labeled irrational. *Davar* noted that it was impossible to explain to some forty-two hundred residents of a transit camp who refused to leave that newcomers could not decide for themselves where they would live and how much tax they would pay.[32] An article in *Davar* criticized the residents of the transit camp near Tiberias, who claimed they had no money and therefore refused to leave: "As long as they lived in the transit-camp they were absolved from paying rent and taxes. But if they move to permanent housing in Tiberias they would have to rent monthly and suffer the burden of taxes!"[33] The question of whether the newcomers could afford the permanent housing was not discussed.

These reports were not a mere exercise in public relations. For many people in the Israel, who had little or no contact with the residents of the transit camps, *Davar*, the most popular newspaper in the country, was an essential source of information. This paper, which reached most of the MAPAI's kibbutzim and moshavim, as well as many in the cities, told the *yishuv* what it wanted to hear: the government was doing all that it could do; that the harsh conditions in the camps were the newcomers' fault, as Iraq was a backward Middle Eastern country; and that punitive measures and police force were a justified reaction to the violence of the Iraqis.

When it came to addressing the Iraqis, however, the language of the party changed. In its electoral campaigns, the party tried to underscore Ben Gurion's image as caring for the Jews of the Middle East. During the 1951 elections it circulated, in Arabic, David Ben-Gurion's plans for the next four years. Ben Gurion was quoted as saying that the party's activities in the domains of finance, bureaucracy, and settlement on a nationwide scale reflected the party's responsibilities toward both the state and each individual "whether a worker, a clerk, an intellectual, an industrialist, or a merchant, so that each person feels as if he is standing on a firm economic base."[34] Here, wisely, the emphasis is placed, not on agriculture and settlement, but rather on a wide-ranging list of occupations, to indicate to the newcomers that the state's plans will enable them to reconstruct their lives in Iraq.

MAPAI, which by the early 1950s has already printed two Arabic newspapers, was so concerned about the unique grievances of Iraqi Jews that it printed Arabic publications specifically for addressing their apprehensions and fears. An important venue was *Al-Watan* ("the homeland"), which printed twenty-seven issues between April 1952 and November 1952, and was edited by an Iraqi-Jewish intellectual, 'Ezra Haddad. *Al-Watan* did publish many petitions written by Iraqi Jews, and gave voice to their sufferings and their pains in the transit camps. In that, it faithfully served as a mediator between the state's ruling party and the newcomers. And yet, *Al-Watan* called its Iraqi readers to merge with the new Western society in Israel and not to criticize the state.[35] As Ya'aqov Yehoshu'a, a prominent scholar of the Arabic press in Palestine and Israel, noted in 1956, "Every joyous occasion the life of the kibbutz was accentuated, and every event that indicated the merger of Iraqi Jews into Israel was underscored."[36] An Arabic literary journal which MAPAI published during 1955 printed short stories written in Arabic by Iraqi Jews, as well as praises to the Histadrut and the state. All of MAPAI's publications vehemently attacked the opposition parties to the left and right of MAPAI.[37]

Iraqis responded to MAPAI's hegemony in Israeli society by becoming politically active. Many in the camps joined MAPAI, and that party won all the elections in which Iraqis voted. Some were motivated by their genuine appreciation of Ben Gurion, whose image remained positive in contrast to those of the Jewish Agency and members of his own party; some remembered helpful guides and social workers; and many feared the repercussions of not voting for MAPAI. Others revolted. Not all protests were necessarily directed against MAPAI, but some riots did flare up in locations associated with the party, such as the Kupat Holim shack or the shack of the Histadrut.[38]

The Iraqis who joined the party wanted to bring about change from within. MAPAI had a special section in the party and in the Histadrut called the Department for Eastern Communities (Ha-Mahlaka le-'Edot ha-Mizrah), which was to attend to the newcomers' needs and a special Babylonian division led by David Fattal (from 1952), gathered Iraqis within the party, to ensure that they would not create a separate party.[39] MAPAI needed Iraqis to staff its Arabic-language newspapers, which were marketed to both Middle Eastern Jews and the Palestinian citizens. MAPAI employed Iraqis to deliver votes in the transit camps and ensure control in the municipalities that emerged from the transit camps, like in Or Yehuda. In fact, MAPAI was the only party that paid activists during electoral campaigns. Finally, MAPAI used Iraqis, who spoke Arabic very well, to connect with the Palestinian population of Israel through the Histadrut.

Joining MAPAI meant, of course, accepting the governing ideology and MAPAI's very specific understandings of Zionism and socialism. It would be wrong, however, to assume that Iraqis joined MAPAI solely out of opportunism. In a context where community members were unemployed and dependent on the state, Iraqis who worked for the Histadrut and MAPAI's administrative arms possessed much power as mediators with valuable connections, and many used them to help fellow Iraqis get a job, a housing solution, and education for their children. Many of the leading Iraqis in MAPAI had immigrated to Israel before the 1950s. Some were Zionists who arrived in Mandatory Palestine in the 1930s, like Mordechai Ben Porat and Shlomo Hillel, who later returned to Iraq as Zionist emissaries. Others were Zionist teenagers in Iraq, who had arrived in the 1940s and entered Mandatory Palestine illegally to settle in kibbutzim and moshavim. As the Zionist negotiators with the Iraqi government, Hillel and Ben

Porat were responsible for the spread of Zionism in Iraq and for the negotiations over the Iraqi-Jewish property. While both should be held accountable for the fact that Iraqi Jews arrived in Israel without any capital, none of the Iraqi activists anticipated the degree of poverty Iraqis would encounter in Israel.

The biography of Shlomo Hillel indicates what a parliament member working for MAPAI could and could not do, on behalf of his community. Hillel immigrated to Mandatory Palestine in 1934 when he was eleven years old. In the 1951 elections MAPAI decided that the party needed an Iraqi representative in the Knesset. Hillel hesitated; in May 1953 he relented and became the first Iraqi member of Knesset. Where the welfare of his community was concerned, he did not vote with his party, though in matters of security and foreign relations he was mostly loyal to MAPAI.[40] In an interview with the newspaper *Davar*, Hillel spoke about the difficulties of positioning himself between sectarian politics (*'askanut 'adatit*) and the rule of the party. He admitted that although he knew many Iraqis well, he did not understand the gravity of the community's unique problems. He insisted that he did not want to be a sectarian politician, although he had been elected as such, and wanted to be active in many other domains as well.[41]

Hillel, however, did work on behalf of Iraqis, and spoke for them about their concerns, among which was police violence, as well as the poverty and neglect the Mizrahim faced. After a demonstration of Iraqi Jews was brutally crushed by the police in Ramat Gan, Hillel defended the unemployed demonstrators in the Knesset. Assuming the role of the Iraqi voice, he contended that the Ramat Gan police were wrong. The demonstrators wanted to be moved from transit camps to a new neighborhood they were promised, and were therefore justified in protesting. Hillel revealed that he knew some of the demonstrators who had been arrested from the days of the Zionist underground in Iraq. He asked why fourteen- and fifteen-year-old youth were beaten by the police, and connected police violence to issues of race, pointing out that some children were sent to a psychiatrist, while others were beaten. The minister of police, Bechor Sheetrit, replied that Hillel should not rely on the reports of people he knew. The demonstrators were bitter; the police merely arrested five people after negotiations with the protestors failed, and the young boys in question started to break the order. The Knesset could not settle its differences regarding the incident and responsibility for resolution of the case was shifted to the minister of labor.[42]

In a way, the situation in the Knesset mirrored the one in many camps. Mizrahi policemen (here represented by the minister) clashed with Mizrahi men (here represented by Hillel). But Hillel's voice here and his connections to the community were crucial. He knew them, he represented them as Zionist patriots in the Knesset, and he raised the issue of age and race to counter Sheetrit's narrative. Hillel also devoted attention to the issue of education. When the Ministry of Education wanted to terminate the tuition reductions granted to Iraqi students, Hillel spoke in the Knesset against it, opining that if problems were not solved at the present time, they were not likely to be solved in the future. Also driving his concern with education was his belief that MAPAI needed to prepare its future leadership by educating the Iraqis. Hillel's being in the Knesset was crucial, as someone who could speak for silenced populations. Iraqi Jews were also savvy in how they used Hillel; many trusted him, others did not. Nonetheless, when he left the Knesset for a diplomatic post, Hillel felt that the party regime had all the power, and Knesset members were powerless.

Trying to bring about change from inside, however, came with a price, since criticism was frowned upon. Iraqis writing for MAPAI's Arabic press were required to sing the praises of that party by underscoring the need for a strong military and lauding the achievements of the Jewish Agency and the state's settlement policies. Nissim Rejwan, an Iraqi intellectual who held a central position in MAPAI's journal, *Al-Yawm*, chose to speak his mind. He wrote about the difficulties of Iraqi Jews not only in the Arabic press but also in English newspaper the *Jerusalem Post*, which had the potential of damaging Hasbara efforts abroad. He was fired from *Al-Yawm* as a result.[43]

LEFT OF CENTER: MAPAM AND THE COMMUNISTS

The leftist parties in Israel criticized MAPAI for its poor treatment of the newcomers from Arab countries and frequently expressed pro-Iraqi and pro-Mizrahi positions. These parties raised the issues of racial and ethnic discrimination in the Knesset and in their publications, in hopes of attracting the newcomers to their parties. The lot of the immigrants also served as an opportunity to show that MAPAI was not really a socialist party. Leftist politicians used the old communist slogan "bread and labor" as the socialist standard by which to best measure MAPAI's policies. Joel Beinin's insights on the Israeli left's approach to the Palestinians hold very true in the Mizrahi case as well: the Israeli left did not mount a formidable challenge to the problems of racism and inequality and failed to offer alternative solutions to the newcomers' needs.[44] In all the leftist parties, Iraqi activists protested the discrimination they faced, as Mizrahim, from the Ashkenazi leadership. However, because of its willingness to discuss racism within the Jewish community and to draw parallels between the problems of the Mizrahi Jews to the Palestinians, the Israeli left complicated the discussion about ethnicity in Israel and brought to the surface issues MAPAI tried to silence.

Shades of Red: MAPAM

MAPAM was a very important party in Israel of the 1950s, although its political power was weakened in 1954. Nonetheless, the space MAPAM could offer Iraqi Jews was rather limited, for cultural and social reasons. As was the case with MAPAI, party members were for the most part Eastern European Zionists who had migrated to Ottoman and Mandatory Palestine. Both parties promoted the vision of Israel as a melting pot; characterized Jewish life in exile as a spiritual, political, and social failure; and held the perception that Mizrahi Jewish culture reflected the reactionary and feudalist order in the Arab states from which they came.[45] The kibbutzim associated with MAPAM, whose members, like MAPAI's members, appropriated lands confiscated from Palestinian villages after 1948, were no different than those of MAPAI and were willing to take Iraqi teenagers, but not families who arrived in the 1950s. As with MAPAI, MAPAM's solution to the problem of housing was settlement in the periphery and vocational training for the youth. In its 1951 election poster, MAPAM promised its voters that a strong MAPAM was the only power capable of breaking "the obscene pact between MAPAI and the bourgeoisie." A strong party in power would "eliminate the transit camps and unemployment, renew mass migration, expand the settlement in the borders, and raise the level of life of the working people."[46] This view, however, sharply contrasted with what most Iraqi Jews wanted: to belong to the bourgeoisie (rather than being agricultural and industrial laborers), and they refused to settle in towns and villages across the border.

Unlike MAPAI, however, MAPAM was willing to connect the Mizrahi question to the Palestinian question, noting that the two populations did experience racial discrimination. MAPAM officials enlisted Iraqis who were communists, socialists, or former kibbutz members so that MAPAM officials could communicate with both Arabs and Arabic-speaking Jews in Israel. The party printed pamphlets by Iraqis, as well as the newspaper *Ila al-Amam*, and a nationwide Arabic newspaper aimed for both Palestinians and Arabic-speaking Jews, *Al-Mirsad*, for which many Iraqis wrote.[47] Away from the oversight of MAPAM's Ashkenazi officialdom, these Iraqis wrote frankly about problems relating to racial and ethnic discrimination. MAPAM's Arabic election notices promised Iraqi Jews that MAPAM would eliminate the rule of MAPAI's minority and its regime of marketeering and intimidation.[48]

MAPAM used a term which gained currency in the Israeli public sphere, "Second Israel," to refer to the universe of development towns, transit camps, and slums where immigrants lived. MAPAM's member Moshe Eram pulled no punches in depicting the situation in the transit camps. To him, they were sites of destitution and poverty; "This estranged daughter (second Israel) is raging; she is filled with bitterness, despair, and disappointment, and justly so."[49] The real problems, Eram contended, could only be solved institutionally—in the Knesset and the Jewish Agency and by the municipal authorities. However, the First Israel chose to use the police against the Second Israel. The Yishuv did not want to see its misery; it did not want to see the transit camps; teachers went there reluctantly, and giving anything to their people was accompanied with a sense of superiority. Entire communities of immigrants were rotting in the transit camps, he concluded.[50]

In addition to assigning blame for the conditions of the newcomers to the institutions, MAPAM figures also argued that the problem was racial, as an official publication stated:

> In the land exists a regime of discrimination in matters concerning labor, housing, and so on. This regime has led, among other things, to desperation, which pushes the newcomers into the bosom of fascism (*Herut*) or cosmopolitanism (MAKI). The Division of the Communities of the East of MAPAM should explain to the public that this discrimination was instigated by the majority party of the land, and with a change of the regime that governs the state and a strong position to MAPAM, we can end this discrimination.[51]

Reflecting the party's position, the Hebrew press of MAPAM (populated mostly by its Ashkenazi writers) was more sympathetic to the needs of the residents. Re'uven Shalgi's story "The Transit Camps in the Circle of Suffering" describes the transit camp in Talpiot as something "the likes of which we do not see in the first world." This place, moreover, was not built by the poor but rather by the state itself.[52] Writing about Sakiyya, Shalgi underscores the fact that it was extremely difficult for the people in the camp to find jobs in factories in Tel Aviv; for these newcomers, "Tel-Aviv is a paradise they yearned for."[53] In Khayriyya, he notes, the denizens (80 percent of whom were Iraqis) are fed only with promises. The families could not afford housing or Hebrew lessons that would enable their integration into society.[54] Shlomo Giv'on's piece on the same topic suggests that if one wants to know the Second Israel, one should go to the central bus station in Tel Aviv. The bus to Ramat Gan comes very often, while the bus to Kfar 'Ana comes less often. "What does the citizen know about Kfar 'Ana?" he wonders. He goes on to describe a space where people frequent the local café because it was one of the few places with electricity in the entire camp.[55] Ora Tamdor, echoing the colloquial Iraqi expression *maku* ("there isn't") which she heard in Talpiot, penned a story, "In the Transit Camp of Talpiot *Maku* Order." This title came from an Iraqi woman who told her: "*Maku* food, *maku* meal, *maku* milk." In fact, the camp was a site of "perpetual *maku*."[56]

Shlomo Shva visited all the camps in the Or Yehuda district and titled his reports "The Road of Poverty." In a story about Khayriyya, he also concludes that the space represents the antithesis of a socialist community.[57] Shva's stories describe the small size of the shacks in which large families were crammed; the lack of proper toilets; the insufficient food rations; the sick individuals without access to proper medical care; the poor education system in the camps and the gaps between the students in camps and the students in the cities; the infrequent buses to the Tel Aviv; and the struggle to get basic services like water and telephones.[58] Perhaps the most striking depiction was of the labor market: Shva describes how some of the Iraqi workers in Khayriyya go to the unemployment bureau, while others stand in front of the Elite Chocolate factory in Petach Tikva. He also provides data on the Iraqis' occupations in Iraq and listed the low wages workers receive for their work, which consisted of running after tractors to collect potatoes that had fallen and not having potable water to relieve their thirst.[59] The stories by Shva and his comrades attempted to dispel the common assumption that Iraqis were lazy and incompetent. Shva emphasizes the preference given to Ashkenazi migrants over Iraqis in housing and labor, yet observes that families with educated individuals (doctors, clerks, engineers) managed to get out of the camps faster, while the poor were left behind.[60] He sums up his experiences as follows:

> Here is a new man—the man of the transit camp, and he is very, very distant from the people of the land of Israel. One hundred thousand individuals live like this, they sit in shacks made of wood, cloth, and tin, on the margins of the roads.... They live in dark centuries of superstition, ignorance, and fear.... The sin of the authorities is that it has become commonsensical and accepted that these people will sit on the side of the roads ... and fight in their places a cruel and difficult battle for existence. The sin of the authorities is that their practices and dress, their superstitions and ignorance have become natural.[61]

Shva attributes the immigrants' ignorance and backwardness to their Arab and Iraqi origins. In this, his discourse echoes that of MAPAI. But he convincingly argues that it is not the Iraqis' fault that they lacked a decent employment, education, and water, but rather the fault of the state. Shva was always quick to dismiss the claims of the directors of the camps that it was easy to move from the camps into permanent housing. The veracity of Shva's reporting was bolstered by the many interviews he did with Iraqi immigrants. Most commonly, MAPAM, unlike the communists, did not connect racism toward Mizrahim to Israel's general approach to Arab culture. But its journals did present a much more balanced picture of the sufferings of the Iraqis and let their voices be heard.

Iraqis, many of whom had identified as socialists and communists in Iraq, joined MAPAM, although in elections the party failed to win votes in the transit camps. 'Ozer Basri, Edward Aharon, 'Ezra Gabbai, David Cohen, and Latif Dori worked for the party in the transit camps. To recruit potential voters, MAPAM surveyed the social conditions in each camp, asking on what date people had arrived in Israel, what the camp's social conditions were like, and about the numbers of Mizrahi Jews and of those who had been sent to a kibbutz.[62] MAPAM's Iraqi activists organized May Day celebrations in Ramla and Sakiyya and made house visits to talk to Iraqis. The party focused its recruitment efforts in the transit camps of Holon, Ramat ha-Sharon (which was a key center), Ijlil, Ness Ziona, and Nahlat Yehuda. Their way was blocked by the all-powerful MAPAI, whose members tried to sabotage MAPAM's efforts. MAPAM members were creative: when MAPAI broke up their meetings, they moved them to a nearby transit camp. MAPAM activists brought a loudspeaker to the Zarnuga camp to overcome the silencing of their speakers there, and they gave speeches elsewhere in Arabic.[63] The party ran a soup kitchen in Talpiot, and its members organized classes in Hebrew and pushed for their men to be appointed as heads of local committees.[64]

In trying to enlist more newcomers to join its ranks, MAPAM used the same tools MAPAI did. One tool of indoctrination of both parties was the ideological seminar. The Histadrut ran some seminars for its members in the transit camps and Iraqis from Sakiyya and Khayriyya were sent there.[65] MAPAM also followed MAPAI in establishing its own department for the Communities of the East ('Adot ha-Mizrah). The party's seminars explained socialism, Arab Jewish peace, and the party's commitment to integration and housing to the Iraqis.[66] Its Iraqi members also were encouraged to participate in a governmental body called "A Council of Mizrahi Jews," which included MAPAI's Bechor

Sheetrit and Shlomo Hillel, MAPAM's Latif Dori, David Cohen, and the Syrian Avraham 'Abbas from the Histadrut, among others. 'Abbas talked about the discrimination in the realms of education and labor toward those with the "dark faces," and members worked together to put an end to this.[67] However, in other settings Mizrahi members of different parties fought each other viciously.

The involvement of Iraqis in MAPAM activities did not prevent them from expressing their disagreement with the party's leadership. Iraqis who wrote for *Al-Mirsad* were unafraid to state bluntly that the state's melting pot politics did not work. Sami Refael and Avraham 'Akri wrote ground-breaking articles on Arab culture and literature for the journal, ignoring those in their own party who proclaimed the superiority of Hebrew culture. Mustafa Kabha has called attention to the writings of MAPAM members Latif Dori and David Cohen on the abuses of both Palestinians and Iraqis. Cohen wrote twenty articles about the transit camps in 1952 alone; both authors addressed their messages to their Arab brethren.[68] Bryan Roby further analyzed the rise of MAPAM's journal *Al-Mirsad* as an indispensable platform for Mizrahi writers like David Cohen, Latif Dori, and others, to discuss issues or racial discrimination in Israel, a platform whose importance increased after 1954.[69] In internal meetings, members such as David Salman, who worked for the party in the transit camps of Or Yehuda, complained about the view within the party that the Mizrahi Jews were not to be trusted.[70] Iraqis pointed out that the emissaries from the kibbutzim did not even try to reach the transit camps, and that they got little help from more established members in the running of Hasbara election campaigns in Arabic and in French. Latif Dori and David Cohen emphasized that the melting-pot paradigm would work only when the gap between the pay of Jews from Asia and Africa and that of immigrants from Europe was eliminated. Aharon 'Abbudi, reporting on MAPAM's failure in the transit camp in Ramat ha-Sharon, observed that the spirit of racial discrimination was alive and well in MAPAM, although its members still suffered from the rule of the MAPAI's ruling clique as well. Yusuf Kubeiba echoed this sentiment and bemoaned the fact that MAPAM ignored the Mizrahi intelligentsia; the Iraqi teachers, doctors, and engineers, who could be valuable members of society, were not recruited into the party. Esther Sarur summed it up: "the party dismisses us."[71]

Other Iraqis stayed more closely to the party line, which held that discrimination in Israel was based on class, not on ethnicity.[72] Shlomo Faraj contended that it was the Mizrahi Jews who were fighting for integration, and that they should not be blamed for having been born in primitive countries. It was the task of MAPAM to educate the Mizrahi immigrants, and yet the party did nothing.[73] Yet the more radical arguments of the Iraqi activists about racial discrimination did have some influence on the leaders of the party. For example, MAPAM's members organized a rally to protest sectarianism in Natanyia,[74] and adopted into its platform a call for abolishing the transit camps.[75]

The most radical member of MAPAM was Latif Dori. Born in 1934 in Baghdad, Dori arrived in Israel in 1951. In just a year, he was coordinating the activities of MAPAM in Khayriyya and Sakiyya. He was involved in the establishment of MAPAM's Arab youth group in 1954, and oversaw the party's activities directed at Israel's Arab citizens. Like the Iraqi MAPAM activists mentioned above, he was very critical of his party's position toward Iraqi Jews. He acknowledged that the party addressed two groups in Israel, the Arabs and the Mizrahim, who were discriminated against, yet argued that the Mizrahi matter was completely neglected. He suggested connecting with the Mizrahi people themselves, promoting the Arabic-speaking intelligentsia into the ranks of the party, adding a Mizrahi reporter to the party's journal *Al ha-Mishmar*, and giving legal aid to Mizrahim who clashed with the state.[76]

While Dori is famous for a series of articles he wrote in 1955 about his visit to Auschwitz, his most noted achievement in the 1950s was bringing to light the first evidence of the massacre of Kafar Qassem. On 29 October 1956, on the eve of the war against Egypt, the Arab population was declared subject to a curfew from 5:00 P.M. till 6:00 A.M. (normally curfew started at 9:00 P.M.). The villagers of Kafar Qassem, who did not know of the change in the hours of curfew and were found outside their homes, were shot by the Israeli Border Brigades at close range. Forty-nine people, including women and children, were killed. Following the decision of an investigation committee which was convened later, the Border Patrol Brigade and its commander were tried and convicted for killing the victims in cold blood. Some received substantial prison sentences that were later reduced (the last of the convicted was released at the beginning of 1960, less than a year and half after the trial).[77]

Ben Gurion ordered that there be no reporting on the event. Three weeks after the massacre, MAKI members Meir Wilner and Tawfiq Tubi went beyond police barriers and interviewed the survivors. They tried to publish their findings in the media but were censored. At the time Dori lived in Kibbutz Horashim, which was close to Kafar Qassem. He managed to enter and meet the *mukhtar* (the village's leader); later, at the Beillinson hospital, he recorded the survivors' testimonies. Dori sent his account to *Al ha-Mishmar* many times, but his story was censored. It was only published on the 20th of December, a month after the massacre, when censorship limitations were finally lifted.[78] Most importantly, the evidence that Dori gathered was used in the trial of the border police. *Haaretz* described Dori's visit to the village in 2006: "Latif Dori arrived this week in Kafar Qassem and barely managed to cross the street. The peace activist, who is seventy-two years old, is considered a local hero. Every time he arrives, passersby, even strangers, recognize him, stop him, shake his hand, and congratulate him. Drivers passing by honk and wave their hands. The local council gave him honorary citizenship."[79] Dori's activities illustrate what an Iraqi Jew could do in MAPAM. On the one hand, he fought for democracy in Khayriyya and Sakiyya, trying to organize cells in the camps themselves. Marginalized within his own party, he reminded party members of the racism not only of MAPAI but also within the kibbutzim of MAPAM. And his knowledge of Arabic, which the party's Ashkenazi members lacked, allowed him to reach out to Palestinians and Mizrahim. Dori believed that the full weight of Israeli military force was directed at the Arab citizens of Israel in order to pressure them to vote for MAPAI. Without the tools of protest and demonstration, the Palestinians were "led like lambs to the ballots."[80] Dori described the meeting he attended after the massacre, which was organized by the government to mark the reconciliation between the villagers of Kafar Qassem and the state. "This was humiliating," he said: poor peasants from Kafar Qassem were coerced into meeting with the minister of police, Bechor Sheetrit, and the mayor of Petach Tikva, and "I stood there and nearly cried myself."[81] In his analysis, both Arabic-speaking Jews and Palestinians were merely pawns in the cynical game that was Israeli democracy. During his lifetime, Dori challenged both his party and his state. In September 1982, Dori and his fellow journalist 'Oded Liftshtiz, found themselves yet again collecting testimonies from Palestinian victims of another, more horrific massacre, that of Sabra and Shatila. The evidence that he assembled was used by the Kahan Commission, which investigated Israel's responsibility for the events.

Ahdut ha-'Avoda, the more nationalist faction that left MAPAM, expressed views very similar to those of MAPAI with respect to the Aliyah. Its short-lived Arabic publications, *Al-Nidal* (The Struggle) and the Arabic supplement its newspaper of *La-Merhav*, promised their readers that the party would guide them in the ways of the Israeli state and provide instruction in socialist Zionism. *Al-Nidal*'s opening editorial from April 1952 boasted that it would be different than the rest of the Arabic newspapers, whose editors adjusted their publications to the needs and desires of the Arab citizens.[82] Akin to both MAPAI and MAPAM, Ahdut ha-'Avoda employed Iraqis, including a key Iraqi activist who worked in the newcomers' camps and in the Histadrut labor bureaus, Shoshanna Arbeli Almozlino. The latter played a seminal role in assisting Iraqis, writing letters on their behalf to various institutions, assisting women in finding employment and placing children in kibbutzim, and making sure teenagers would not be abused in the Israeli labor market. Her connections were useful to her own family and she managed to place only her siblings in a kibbutz; sadly, and perhaps predictably, her own mother was rejected because she was deemed too old for the kibbutz.[83]

Class and Race: The Communists

The Israeli communist party, MAKI, opened its gates to Iraqis. Out of all parties, the ostracized MAKI was willing to explore and expose discrimination against Iraqi Jews. It also led the way in organizing major demonstrations, strikes, and petition campaigns, through which newcomers could voice their concerns. But as open as the party was to hearing what Iraqis had to say, it could offer very little of substance to them. Some middle-class Iraqis had been angry at the communist party back in their homeland, thinking that the involvement of Iraqi-Jewish youth with the illegal Iraqi communist party had bred suspicion of Iraqi Jews as a whole, resulted in arrests, and forced the community to intervene on their behalf at great danger. Most importantly, because of MAPAI's negative position regarding the party, to be a communist was to be a national pariah. Joining MAKI meant that at any time one could be fired from one's position; be discriminated against for jobs, if unemployed; have one's children suffer in school; and have one's name be put last in the lists for housing or transfer to a better location.[84] A MAPAI election poster presented the communists as objecting to donations from the United States, which could actually help the Israeli industry and the newcomers, and as a party which did not support the Jewish Aliyah, while supporting the right of Return for Armenians and Palestinians.[85] Another thing that curtailed the appeal of the party was that although many Iraqi Jews were active as communists, none of them became part of the political hierarchy of MAKI, and its members in the Knesset were either Ashkenazi or Palestinian.[86]

The positions of the party were encapsulated in a piece that appeared in *Kol ha-'Am* (the party's newspaper) about Ben Gurion's trip to the United States. Ben Gurion, it was suggested, claimed that all Jews were brothers, yet the poor Jews, crammed into rundown neighborhoods, became the cannon fodder of the state's wars, while the Arabs were locked up in ghettos. His lofty words about Western democracy concealed the fact that Israel was a democracy in name only; Ben Gurion offered the poor the same freedoms that Truman offered blacks in the United States.[87] MAKI argued that it saw to the needs of all newcomers. For the dwellers in the transit camps, party members demanded fair working conditions and the eventual abandonment of the camps and the establishment of neighborhoods, and in the meantime, improvements in the transit camps in the way of potable water, basic sanitation facilities, and political representation of all residents. The demand for the closure of the transit camps and the moving of residents into decent housing appeared frequently in its election pamphlets and official publications.[88]

The communists found that their status as pariahs actually gave them certain advantages. A non-Zionist party, MAKI was not at all wedded to the idea of Hebrew as the language of the land, and indeed it published pamphlets in Romanian, Yiddish, Hungarian, Polish, Russian, Persian, French, and many other languages. Arabic in particular was a very important language for MAKI. It printed pamphlets, journals, and notices in Arabic for Middle Eastern Jews and Palestinians. Indeed, Palestinian members of the party wrote in Arabic to address the Iraqis.[89] Many of the communist activists, including Eliyahu 'Ezer, Hesqel Qujaman, Musa Huri, Menashe Khalifa, Sami Michael, and Shim'on Ballas had been members of the illegal Iraqi Communist Party. As such, they were used to persecution, to clashing with the state, and to challenging the norms. Some had been arrested and jailed in Iraq; communists like Michael had worked as organizers in factories and schools. They were not easily scared and they brought to MAKI their invaluable expertise, endurance, and ideological commitment. Moreover, all the major Iraqi-Jewish intellectuals, notably Sasson Somekh, Shim'on Ballas, Sami Michael, and David Semah, wrote for the communist press, specifically MAKI's Arabic newspaper *Al-Ittihad*, its cultural journal *Al-Jadid*, as well as for the Hebrew journal of the party, *Kol ha-'Am*.[90] MAKI also focused on the youth, as it was assumed that they would be more willing to take risks than their parents.[91] MAKI was the most successful party in organizing demonstrations, petitions, and rallies. The party considered demonstrations to be a valuable tactic and was active in organizing and supporting the Iraqi demonstrators.[92]

In the Iraqi-Jewish context, MAKI propaganda focused on a few major enemies. MAPAI was discredited as responsible for the misery of the newcomers, with Ben Gurion and Golda Meir being the main targets. According to communist publications, MAPAI was a party that did not care for the newcomers, provided help only in times of elections, and took advantage of their marginal status to use them as laborers. It was characterized by duplicity: it pretended to be socialist yet was enslaved to the interests of the Americans and to their militaristic agenda. The more radical and pro-Russian (until 1956 at least) MAPAM was chastised for its duplicity as well, as an opposition party that chose to collaborate with MAPAI at crucial points instead of fulfilling its function to critique the state. The position toward MAPAI is exemplified in a pamphlet addressed to the workers of Petach Tikva:

> Like wild animals, the parties of the rich and the people of MAPAI are attacking the Eastern Jews [edot ha-mizrah]. Perhaps they [the Mizrahim] were born to save them on Election Day. Where were you when hundreds of children, mostly Mizrahim, were thrown out from schools to the streets? . . . And today, kindergartens are open to the children of the rich and the profiteers. . . . But for the children of the worker and the Mizrahi there is no such privilege.[93]

MAKI acknowledged the reality of the racial discrimination against Mizrahi Jews, as its communist Iraqi members made repeated mention of it in *Al-Ittihad*, *Al-Jadid*, and *Kol ha-'Am*. Doing so provided a boost to MAKI in election campaigns. MAKI Knesset member Esther Wilenska declared that MAKI fought for decent conditions for the inhabitants of the poor neighborhoods and for "the masses, Sephardi, Yemeni, Iraqi and other Mizrahim," who were discriminated against by local municipalities, for health services; and that it was "a loyal defender of the interests of the Mizrahim that are centered in the most remote corners of the cities and the villages, in poor neighborhoods and deserted neighborhoods."[94] In October 1959 Wilenska suggested that a national meeting of Iraqis be held in the city of Ramat Gan in order to strengthen their commitment to MAKI.[95]

MAKI's Iraqi writers knew how to appeal to the pains of the Iraqis. An Arabic publication that MAKI circulated for the 1955 elections, titled *I'rif al-haqiqa* (Know the Truth), presented data on low payments of workers in Israel; attacked police brutality; featured quotes from Israel Rokach, Golda Meir, Ben Gurion, and the leaders of MAPAM which indicated their indifference to the hunger and poverty of Iraqi Jews and their desire to send them to the Negev; and printed a story on an Indian woman (whose family name indicated she was of Baghdadi origins) who committed suicide because of the hunger of her family. The publication also featured a cartoon of two newcomers, dressed in rags and sitting on a bench under a tree, saying that this bench is the only home they can afford under the rule of MAPAI.[96]

The right-wing Herut Party drew fierce attacks from MAKI members. The greatest fear of MAKI was that Herut would attract Iraqi Jews and other Mizrahim, embittered by MAPAI, toward anti-Arab policies. Taufiq Tubi emphasized the need for propaganda against Herut, because of its dark past (its links to fascist forces), its pogroms against the Arab population in Israel, and its hypocrisy embodied in the fact that it pretended to care for ordinary citizens yet supported a capitalist regime that objected to raising taxes on the rich.[97] An editorial in *Kol ha-'Am* counseled Iraqi Jews not to direct their anger toward the Palestinians. The acts of the British agent Nuri al-Sa'id were not the fault of the Palestinian population, and Herut, "the party of fascism," was attempting to turn the attention of the people from the true battle for decent living conditions to chauvinism and violence.[98] MAKI warned the Iraqi newcomers not to listen to the false claims made by Herut that they cared for the little man, as they were nothing more than fascist demagogues who collaborated with the rich at every opportunity. It was the party of war and the enemy of the labor unions.[99] An article the MAKI distributed in the 1959 elections described how Herut members, essentially thugs, tried to break a meeting of MAKI supporters in Ha-Tikva neighborhood, where Iraqi, Yemenite, and other Mizrahim resided. The article's conclusion was clear: "Cutting the fascist fist and standing against the party of Begin's thuggery is a holy duty of all antifascists."[100]

MAKI seized upon the issues faced by the Mizrahim as a key context in which to challenge the State of Israel's self-definition as Jewish and democratic. On the one hand, the party made use of all the opportunities the democratic system in Israel presented for an outcast opposition party. Members worked very hard so that party representatives could be included in the local committees set up to control every transit camp; they ran as candidates in municipal and general elections; and they demonstrated in the camps themselves. MAKI held public meetings in the transit camps, mostly to tackle the lack of social services in the camps, but also to discuss global affairs, from the trial of the Rosenbergs in the United States to the importance of the October Revolution. Moreover, MAKI was unrelenting in voicing the opinion that democratic mechanisms in Israel did not function: it complained about the corruption that marked local elections, that MAPI's agents spied on MAKI party members, that MAPAI and Herut hired thugs to disrupt meetings, and that proper electoral procedures in the transit camps were not followed, so that communists were excluded.[101] The communist press maintained a focus on issues related to the rights of the Palestinians, such as the military regime, the abuse of political prisoners, and undemocratic land confiscations, and the Mizrahi issue complemented these issues by showing the slippage of racism and chauvinism to the Jewish sector. It suggested, in fact, that the state neglected both populations.

At key moments, however, MAKI neglected the battle against racism faced by Iraqi Jews, insisting that class, rather than race, was the main source of discrimination in Israel. MAKI warned against parties representing specific Jewish communities because only a struggle that united Jews and Arabs, Ashkenazi and Mizrahi Jews would yield results. A pamphlet addressed to the newcomers suggested that they should not vote for the Sephardim Party because they bore the responsibility for the economic crisis and the enslavement of Israel to warmongering colonialists, just as much as the other parties.[102] MAKI's leadership was also far less willing to acknowledge the needs of the Iraqis as Iraqis. The party's objection to "sectarian" parties, together with the fact that none of the prominent members of MAKI (Knesset members and general secretaries) were Iraqi underlines the fact that MAKI itself was unwilling to fully recognize the racial realities in Israel. Meir Wilner articulated this position. Young newcomers, he said, faced an intolerable predicament:

> Many promises were made to them before their arrival in the country; they were promised free education, professional education, a life of culture and learning, and yet when they came to this country they found out they had been lied to.... Most of them live in the transit camps [60 percent] in conditions [characterized by] crowdedness, dirt, lack of culture, and are abandoned to degeneration and hunger. The reactionary powers try to promote separatism between the youth of one country and the other, between Ashkenazi and Sephardi youth.[103]

Subscribing to a communist narrative that saw ethnicities, religions, and races as mere smokescreens in the battle of the working classes, he promoted a vision of unity. When MAKI ran for the Histadrut in Jerusalem, it boasted that its slate included Kurdish Jews and a Polish Jew, and declared in its elections pamphlets distributed in the municipality of Jerusalem that "all members of all sects are brethren."[104]

MAKI therefore had to walk a fine line in reconciling its recognition that racism existed in Israel toward the Mizrahim and its decision to stay above such divisions. The Iraqis were not always happy with this situation. In 1954, the party discussed the affairs in the transit camps and the residents' struggle for their rights, where concerns were voiced about the party's neglect of the Iraqi sufferings.[105] In March 1959 the communists initiated discussion of a potential meeting of Iraqi comrades, during which Albert Qujman and Musa Huri suggested that Iraqis had unique problems—"Iraqi problems," as Huri put it. However, their struggle was belittled, with the response being that "this is not a sectarian movement. We are part of our people, but against sectarian discrimination based on class."[106] Shim'on Ballas, a key member of the party and *Kol ha-'Am*'s editor for Arab affairs, depicts how the party Jewish leadership was ignorant with respect to the history of Jews in Arab lands and the history of the Arab peoples more generally.[107] MAKI was indifferent to cultural questions, such as the debate among Iraqi intellectuals of the party about whether to write in Hebrew or Arabic, and refused to open a true space, within its extremely rigid doctrinal beliefs, for the Iraqis to articulate their vision. Palestinian members like Emile Habibi were far more open to discussing such issues than the Ashkenazi leadership of the party was; Michael, Ballas, and Somekh worked more closely with the Palestinians and felt more comfortable with them. Ballas explained this in an interview:

> I remember meeting Meir Wilner, one of the leaders of the Party, in the very first weeks after emigrating and he started asking me all kinds of questions about Syria, about the people, general information. . . . This was a shock for me. . . . Here was a leader of the Party, for the first time in my life I was talking to a Party leader, a member of parliament, and he was asking me, a new immigrant from Iraq, the most trivial questions. It took me a long time to figure out that, essentially, I represented a different world altogether and this somehow always obligated me to explain something. No matter where I was[,] when something happened in the Arab world, people would ask: "What do you say about that, what's your opinion?"[108]

Later, however, when Ballas voiced his critical opinions about Nasserism that contradicted the party line, he ceased to be the local informant and he was censured and edited.[109] Their rigidity cost them key members: Michael left official duties in 1955, Ballas followed a few years later; intellectuals like Somekh (who were not official members) ceased publishing in the party's journals in the mid-1960s.

The inability of the party to deal with issues of race within the Jewish community was manifested plainly after massive riots in the Wadi Salib slum in Haifa. In 1959, the entire slum, populated by North African Jews, rioted for three days. The government was in a state of panic. MAKI made a clumsy attempt to address the rioters, as indicated its *Epistle to the Workers from Asian and North African Lands*. The pamphlet acknowledged that Mizrahim were discriminated against, and provided numbers showing that most Mizrahim lived in appalling poverty. It blamed the government for labeling the Wadi Salib riots as the outcome of incitement, while noting that the government's discrimination was the reason for the "justified bitterness amongst the Mizrahim." But it ended with the following words:

> Look around you: every place where Mizrahim live in poverty, you can find by them Ashkenazi workers who also suffer from cruel exploitation. The blame for the suffering of the workers, the poor, of all communities, lies with the government which cares only for the rich and deserts the poor. If you, and your community, are discriminated against, [know that] the aim of the government is that all the hatred and bitterness you feel will be directed at the whites (Ashkenazim), among whom there are penniless people like you, and not at the real entity to be blamed—the government that does not provide work and cheap housing, and is not concerned with decent living conditions. Pay attention: they are united. In the organization of the industrialists sit together rich Ashkenazim and Sephardim, and together they exploit workers of all communities. In the government as well sit Sephardi ministers responsible for the discrimination policy, and the unemployment. . . . The exploiters want white workers to fight black workers, Jewish workers to fight Arab workers, and the other way around. But our power, the power of the workers, of the poor, is in our unity! The enemy of the Mizrahi is not the Ashkenazi worker but the Sephardi and Ashkenazi employers together![110]

The pamphlet acknowledged that racial discrimination exists in Israel, yet sought to assure the Mizrahim that a shared struggle with the Ashkenazim is the only way to challenge racial discrimination. The communists, in theory, should have been delighted that workers in slums were rebelling against the state, but here the Ashkenazi character of the party's Jewish leadership figured in the dismissal of the radical potential embodied in Wadi Salib.

ILLIBERAL LIBERALS: HERUT AND GENERAL ZIONISTS

The capitalist Israeli parties in theory had more to offer to the Iraqis. Their critique of socialism and specifically of MAPAI's corruption, monopolization of the economy, and control over the migrants' lives resonated with Iraqis who had been members of the middle class of Baghdad and Basra. But both capitalist parties had also problematic agendas as far as the Iraqis were concerned. The General Zionists Party had a very important constituency among their voters, whose profits were increased by paying low wages to Iraqi Jews and who objected to the state providing benefits to the newcomers. Herut, on the other hand, supported granting more benefits to the newcomers. However, that party was marked by a rightist agenda, especially toward the Arabs, which was far more open than any other Zionist party.

Herut members were persecuted by MAPAI on the domestic front: like the communists, they were denied positions and spied on. Consequently, Herut had a common interest with MAPAM and the communists in bringing about an end to MAPAI's rule, although its campaigns viciously attacked both parties. It decried MAPAI's one-party rule of Israel, where state monopolies controlled the economy. Herut called for a constitution that would limit MAPAI's power and ensure a system of checks and balances; an end to nepotism and the bloated bureaucracy; and the termination of censorship of the press and the espionage on private citizens. And they protested the atrocious status of Israel's absorption policies.[111] Herut's leadership tried to show Iraqis that its liberal-economy platform fit their interests. Herut generally accepted more Mizrahim to its ranks, and emphasized the fact that both Irgun and the Stern Gangs had Mizrahi members who heroically fought the British, and were admired by the party's members, Ashkenazi and Mizrahi alike. In this context, the party's newspaper, *Herut*, wrote about the pains of Iraqis as they left Iraq; it protested the fact that the Iraqi police had defiled the Torah scrolls of the migrants on their way to the motherland, and lamented the slow pace of migration from Iraq.[112]

During the second Knesset elections, Menachem Begin toured the transit camps. His circuit included those in the south and the Sharon region. When he visited Rehovot, he used a truck (which other politicians did as well) to move from place to place and as a platform from which to make speeches, the truck being decorated with the photos of Jabotinsky and Israeli flags. In the rally, Begin said he came to the camp with mixed feelings: he was happy because his brothers had returned to the homeland, and sad because millions had not managed to come to Israel and those who had come lived under MAPAI's regime of poverty, nepotism, and abuse of liberties. Begin told his audience that the Irgun had fought the British and paid with the lives of its members, while MAPAI had collaborated with the British (throughout his speech, MAPAI's members were referred to as snitches and collaborators who gave up East

Jerusalem and Hebron). After recounting his somewhat creative version of Zionist history, Begin turned to what mattered to the newcomers. He said that MAPAI's policy was based on fear, which paralyzed those who dreaded the loss of their livelihood. However, if the masses ceased to fear, if they stopped being slaves, they could challenge the ruling party.[113]

In a Herut rally in Tirat ha-Carmel in 1955, Begin repeated this liberal massage to his Mizrahi audience:

> You should know that this country does not belong to MAPAI, the General Zionists, or MAPAM . . . nor to us. This country belongs to the people of Israel, and to every Jew. . . . You are not dependent on MAPAI or the government. On the contrary, they depend on you, as they depend on the rest of the citizens of Israel. As for the right to labor, I tell you simply and honestly that if a government is formed one day under the leadership of the Herut movement, the right to work would be accorded to any member of MAPAI, MAPAM . . . and the communists—to every citizen and denizen in Israel. Because we are disciples of Z. Jabotinsky, who taught us that the rights to a livelihood and the right to existence are not, and cannot be, tied to a party, a view, or an opinion. They are given to every Jew, to every citizen, to every human being.[114]

The message is ostensibly democratic, but we notice here the very dangerous slippage between "citizen" and "Jew." It is not entirely clear whether Arabs were entitled to these democratic rights. And yet for the Iraqis, this vision was very attractive.

The party's Arabic newspaper, *Al-Huriya*, propagated Herut's views to the Iraqis. The Iraqi editor of *Al-Huriya*, Menashe Za'rur, assured readers that the purpose of the newspaper was to discuss their problems. Indeed, the journal published many articles on the sufferings of the newcomers in the transit camps and dedicated much space to the activities of Iraqi Zionists who affiliated themselves with the party.[115] *Al-Huriya*'s hundredth issue boasted the fact that the people of Herut battled against discrimination, called for unity between the people of the homeland, and motivated people for patriotism and sacrifice.[116] Those subscribing to leftist, socialist, and communist goals were presented in its pages as inhibiting the growth of Israel's economy, and as trading the God of Zion for the God of socialism.[117] Underlining the party's own religiosity, *Al-Huriya* depicted how the men of the Histadrut privileged the red flag over the national flag during the Hannukah celebrations, as a sign of their disdain of both Judaism and nationalism.[118]

More generally, in its propaganda efforts Herut attempted to present the counterimage of MAPAI's ideology and politics. If in MAPAI's publications the Histadrut, Kupat Holim, and the Jewish Agency were hailed as doing all in their power to assist the newcomers, in Herut's publication these very same institutions were represented as the embodiment of corruption, exploitation, nepotism, and inefficiency. Herut targeted the Jewish Agency, sometimes referring to it as Vichy's Agency and condemned the politicized treatment of the newcomers (al-a'idun al-judad) by the Jewish Agency's transit camp directors.[119] A 1954 Herut pamphlet from Khayriyya underlined the party's effort to serve the public's interest (maslaha), which it contrasted with the self-serving politics of MAPAI. Four years after the establishment of the camp, the pamphlet read, Khayriyya's residents were still given false promises; their tents were not replaced with appropriate housing, as the Jewish Agency failed them yet again, leaving them to suffer in the winter. In fact, the Jewish Agency used money given to newcomers to build new houses for Histadrut members. The people of Herut, however, would strive to rid the people of this evil.[120] A 1955 Herut poster featured a cartoon which reduced Ben Gurion into an image of four talking heads, each wearing a headdress representing a different Middle Eastern country. The different Ben Gurion heads were quoted as saying: "I am Kurdish," "I and Abraham, our father, came from Iraq," "I and Moses came from Egypt," "I am Yahya and I came from Yemen."[121] The implication was clear: this leader would say anything in order to get elected by Mizrahi voters, but it is merely a charade. Herut posters of the 1959 elections, after a few sectarian riots, including that of Wadi Salib, emphasized the ethnic tensions in Israel even further. They spoke of racial discrimination and terror, and blamed MAPAI for dividing the nation into Ashkenazim and non-Ashkenazim.[122] Another poster mocked the party's new star, military hero Moshe Dayan, suggesting that he remembered the poor voters only before the elections, and yet, when speaking to the rich, he conveyed the view that "unemployment and hunger in the dwelling of the famished do not matter; the important thing is development!"[123]

On a more practical level, Herut, like all other opposition parties, tried to expand its bases in the transit camps, in the hubs of Khayriyya, Sakiyya, and Kfar 'Ana, as well as in the transit camps of Amisav, Kfar Ono, Nahariya, Tira, Holon, Nahlat Yehuda, Zarnuga, Hadera, and Ramat ha-Sharon.[124] Herut's key activist in the transit camps and among Iraqi Jews was an Iraqi Jew, Avraham Salem Levy, who worked with other activists like the intellectual Na'im Zilkha and Latif 'Ezer.[125] Levy was a strong supporter of Aliyah. He described Iraqi Jews before their departure as appearing as if each and every one of them faced execution, and called to bring every Jew to Israel. He also spoke to the party's leadership about the need to stand up against the discrimination against Mizrahi Jews.[126] Menachem Begin further stressed the need to have constant presence in the transit camps, and not only before elections.[127] The party's leadership dedicated a committee to the affairs of the newcomers, which included Levy, the Bulgarian Benjamin Arditi, and the Yemenite, Haim Maguri-Cohen, among other members.[128] To increase their popularity in the transit camps, Yohanan Bader suggested that Herut train between ten to fifteen men to leadership roles in all communities.[129] In a discussion about the need to increase the party's influence in the transit camps of Nahariyya, Tira, and Talpiot, Herut member Avraham Drori depicted how young men from Iraq and Tripoli eagerly attended the party's club in Nahariyya. This indicated to him that people were less fearful and that Herut should send more materials to the transit camps.[130] Herut wished to communicate in Yiddish, Arabic, and Ladino to all newcomers, and Arditi emphasized the need not only to work with the Iraqis in Arabic, but also to form a Ladino newspaper for Turkish residents of the transit camps.[131]

The party collected membership fees in a few transit camps and its activists tried to enter the local committees, especially the unofficial ones, to sell the party's newspapers in the transit camps, and to organize rallies and protests.[132] Beyond its propaganda efforts, Herut members raised concerns that actually mattered to Iraqis. Herut protested the fact that hundreds of newcomers resided in horrible conditions in villages located on the border. These people were merely a "human shield" to stop infiltration of Arabs, yet the state failed to provide them with electricity, telephones, and barbed wire to protect their communities.[133] Herut likewise raised the issue of the rent that Amidar charged in its shacks in the transit camp of Nahlat Yehuda, which, as we have seen, was a concern that troubled many newcomers.[134] A Herut leaflet in Arabic that circulated in the transit camps sharply criticized the police for their violent tactics and arrests without trial, drawing a parallel between the contemporary situation and life under the British mandate.[135]

Herut, however, encountered many difficulties in promoting its agenda to Iraqis. Individuals identified with the movement could be fired or transferred to another transit camp.[136] The party organized conferences dedicated to its ideology, yet individuals were afraid to show up.[137] In the Petach Tikva camp, supporters faced beatings and arrests.[138] Moreover, Herut activists knew painfully well that despite the resentment Iraqi Jews felt toward MAPAI, the Jewish Agency, and the Histadrut, there was not much the party could do on their behalf, because it could not assist newcomers in questions relating to health, housing, and employment, which were provided by institutions close to MAPAI and the Histadrut.[139] Herut pushed for having its labor organization (Histadrut ha-'Ovdim ha-Le'umit) and health organization (Kupat Holim Le'umit) provide services to the residents of the transit camps, but failed.[140] In their correspondence with the Jewish Agency, party activists demanded political representation in transit camps, the opening of party's clubs, or owning a shack that could serve as local headquarters, but were often denied permission.[141] Party leaders complained that in the absence of clubs, members had to hold meetings in cemeteries.[142]

The party suffered from irregularities in election campaigns, which were common with respect to all political parties not affiliated with MAPAI, as in one instance in the transit camp of Hartuv. Herut members contended that MAPAI's representatives had threatened to withhold food and housing from those who attended a Herut rally. David Nathan, a newcomer and a Herut supporter in the camp, pleaded with the state's investigation committee into the matter to be allowed to testify without the transit camp's director being present in the room, but was denied. Nathan then begged the director not to hold his testimony against him and asked for his forgiveness. At this point, other Herut representatives present in the committee's discussion asked that the director be removed, because it was unfair that a witness with control over Nathan's livelihood should be present. The MAPAI representatives refused, and the hearing was closed without a resolution.[143]

Despite these herculean obstacles, Herut managed to increase its power in the third Knesset (almost doubling its number of seats). In 1964, a fraction identified with Herut entered the Histadrut, despite ideological objections from the old guard of the party. At this point, party members who identified with "Second Israel" pushed its leadership to assume positions within an organization that could benefit poor Israelis.[144] Nevertheless, the party's ideology presented a few challenges for its Iraqi voters. Its support of a free market and liberal ideology did not always fit the economic needs of the Iraqis, who had to rely on the state to provide for many of their basic needs. While Menachem Begin supported the rise in minimum wage, arguing that as a human being and a Jew he was profoundly moved to see people suffering, other members of his party objected, suggesting that raising the minimum wage meant that factories would close down, and industry would suffer.[145] Herut also upheld the Zionist ideal of the merger of exiles, to which all Zionist parties subscribed,[146] yet Begin refused to secure a seat in the party's leadership for an Iraqi from Or Yehuda.[147] Potential Iraqi candidates for leadership roles were rejected partly because they were deemed unqualified and partly because the party felt that any person who had not mastered Hebrew could not appear as a public speaker.[148]

Despite Begin's liberalism, he was depicted in the same faltering terms as Herut's political rivals depicted their own leaders. When *Herut* covered Begin's visit to the Rehovot transit camp, the report noticed that the people of the camp, "mostly Iraqis," shouted, "Ya'ish Begin! Ya'ish Begin!" ("Long live Begin! Long live Begin!"), and "running from all sides, the entrances to the tents lifted, thin and brown bodies [*gufot tznumim u-shhumin*] escaped . . . from the tents to the square. Pretty soon the place was filled, and thousands gather . . . and cheered not only the commander of ATZEL [Begin] but also his escorts. Cheers welcomed the Iraqi representatives [of Herut], Saleh Meir and Yosef Zamir."[149] More generally, the party's ideology and praxis presented a very strange mixture of liberalism, pluralism, romanticism, racism, and Jewish chauvinism, and its propaganda efforts reflected these inner conflicts. The rabid anti-Arab and anti-Palestinian publications of *Al-Huriya*, the party's hailing of the militarist spirit (with lengthy explorations of the value of sacrifice for the sake of the nation and the purity of the nation), and its expansionist policies, did not go unnoticed. The Israeli left feared the party's latently hostile stance toward Arab residents and its influence in the transit camps. The leftist parties, though willing to collaborate with Herut at the camps against MAPAI, identified Herut as fascist. Not only MAKI but also MAPAM referred to Herut in its Arabic publication as "Hitler's ally" (*khalifat Hitler*), based on the Stern Gang's negotiations with the Nazis in order to bring more Jews to Israel and the admiration of some members of this group for Benito Mussolini in the 1930s. It its electoral campaign it introduced a poster featuring a red-faced Menachem Begin, holding a gun, under the caption, "Begin in Power? Stupidity and Disaster!" ("Begin la-shilton? Ivelet ve-ason!").[150] The fear of Herut is illustrated by the case of a demonstration orchestrated by Herut in Tiberias in 1951, calling for the execution of two Arabs in Israel for every Jew killed in Iraq. In response, MAKI printed pamphlets and editorials advising Iraqis not to collaborate with the Jewish fascists from Herut, whose practice of persecuting the minorities was no different than those of the Iraqi fascists who persecuted the Iraqi Jews. All fascists, they argued, sought to promote war between nations, race baiting, and murder.[151]

An alternative to Herut was the General Zionists (Ha-Tziyonim ha-Klaliyim). This party had been established in the 1930s in Poland with a platform of Zionism and economic and political liberalism. It won seven mandates in the first Knesset, and became the second largest party in the Knesset and a formidable opponent of MAPAI in the second elections, due to its critique of the austerity regime and the state's control of the economy.[152] Like all parties in Israel, it published an Arabic newspaper edited by Iraqis, *Nashrat al-Markaz* (Central Edition). The Iraqi-Jewish lawyer Yehezkel (Hesqel) Murad argued that Iraqis should join the party, since "the newcomers from Iraq were more used to the life of free enterprise and were free professionals. We need to live in Israel according to the same principles so that we should . . . free ourselves from the shackles that burden us."[153] The party absorbed the tiny Sephardim Party in the second Knesset, based on a shared liberal agenda. Despite MAPAI's vigorous attempts to stop them, party representatives were a persistent presence in the transit camps and newcomer villages for the purpose of recruitment.

Iraqis, however, had reasons not to support this party. The General Zionists were accused by other parties of wanting to limit the scope of Aliyah for economic reasons, accusations they denied. As Orit Rozin notes, the party was divided between the liberal wing and the farmers' wing, whose "culture was not democratic and whose horizon ended with their farms."[154] The farmers, as well as small factories owners who also supported the party, benefited from the cheap labor of people from the transit camps. The mayors and heads of municipalities who belonged to the General Zionists were not at all happy to receive newcomers and resisted the building of transit camps in their territories. The private press, *Haaretz*, *Maariv*, and *Yedi'ot Ahronot*, and especially the party's own journal, *Ha-Boker*, depicted the Iraqis as lazy and out to scam the system.[155] However, its merger with the Sephardim Party convinced Iraqis that the party was still liberal and deserved their votes.

THE SEPHARDIM PARTY

An important venue where the Iraqis could air their grievances was the Sephardim Party. In the first Knesset election it won four mandates, with its leader, Bechor Sheetrit, being appointed minister of police. Sheetrit defected to MAPAI and in 1951 the party won only two mandates, and consequently merged with the General Zionists. In the third Knesset election, they ran independently but did not receive enough votes to qualify.[156] The party's Iraqi representative was Benjamin Saleh Silas Sasson (1903–89), a lawyer trained in the

United Kingdom and a graduate of Oxford, who had immigrated to Mandatory Palestine in 1931. Sasson served as a judge in 1951 in Tel Aviv, and decided to run for the second Knesset as a member of the Sephardim Party. He served on a number of significant Knesset and government committees, and moved on to the General Zionists when the merger occurred. In the Knesset he was a tireless advocate for the Iraqi community. He constantly called on the state to bring the case of the Iraqi Jews, essentially refugees with no property, before the United Nations, and to investigate the extent of the property that Iraqi Jews lost when they left Iraq. Moreover, he blamed the state for ignoring the plight of "the ordinary man": "And in this case, this man sits in a tent and thinks that he is a victim for the creation of the State of Israel . . . and it seems to him that nothing is being done for his sake. Meanwhile he experiences a great deal of difficulty and he does not know whom he should address."[157] Sasson made a point of seeking to resolve the particular issues faced by the immigrants: for example, he asked the minister of interior why newcomers from Iraq needed a special permit to import goods, such as cars.[158]

Another Knesset member (who also moved to the General Zionists) was Salman Shina. A member of the Iraqi parliament and a former editor of the Jewish Iraqi newspaper *Al-Misbah*, Shina, too, wrote about the discrimination against Mizrahi and Iraqi Jews in Israel. He struggled to achieve recognition of the activities of Iraqi Zionists and also attended to immediate needs of the immigrants—from poverty to the inability of Mizrahi Jews to build synagogues in the Jewish state.[159] To discredit Shina's Iraqi voters, in 1955 MAPAI printed a particularly vicious election poster. The poster featured a cartoon of an Arab man broadcasting from radio Damascus, with a caption suggesting that Shina was a man promoting a sectarian regime that divided the people and was supported by the haters of Israel in Syria.[160]

The Sephardim Party, however, was the boldest in depicting ethnic and racial relations in Israel. As it courted Jews of Middle Eastern descent, it set aside all talk of a successful melting pot and instead evoked themes of segregation, discrimination, and racism. It was a Zionist party, and its radical critique was always relevant only to the group it represented, and not to other oppressed groups in Israel, most notably the Palestinians, yet it was probably the party that stressed most consistently the concerns of Iraqi Jews. A poster that the party produced in 1955 was addressed specifically to "our brethren, the sons of the Babylonian community!" It constituted a petition signed by forty Iraqi Jews who called their brethren to vote for the Sephardim Party. They noted their joy that

Iraqi Jews were finally living in a Jewish state after hundreds of years in exile. However, despite the state's pretense of upholding the ideals of equality, upon their arrival in Israel, Iraqi Jews discovered that they were discriminated against in all possible domains, from housing to occupational opportunities, while the political parties neglected their concerns. "The source of discrimination originates from the fact that we do not have representatives in top governmental institutions who will hear our demands and serve as our speakers." The forty Iraqis reminded the Iraqi voters that the party included prominent Iraqis, as well as members who fight against the discrimination of the Sephardim, among them Benjamin Sasson, "a son of a family we knew for generations in Babylon, India, and England, and whose sons served the community, and the nations in which they dwelled, in honor and pride for hundreds of years." The alternative, the Iraqis suggested, was horrific: "Heaven forbid that we become indifferent; that we turn into slaves in our holy land; that we agree to be second-class citizens."[161]

The Iraqi supporters of the party underscored facts that mattered to Iraqi Jews; that Sasson came from a notable family whose history the members of the community knew well; that they were currently denied political representation; and that some members of the community were paralyzed in face of discrimination. They offered their party as the only Jewish-Iraqi solution. This message was repeated during the 1955 elections, the posters of which called for an end to placement in jobs and positions based on political affiliations and for the establishment of a national labor bureau (meaning an organization independent from the Histadrut and its workers' councils). The party was depicted as representing "Sephardim and the communities of the East, craftsmen, merchants, newcomers, veteran citizens [*vatikm*], and independents," to shift away from the language of the leftist parties, which spoke of workers, peasants, and farmers.[162]

The party built on the networks of Sephardi organizations that predated the founding of Israel and provided assistance to Iraqis on an individual basis. This took the form of donations, placements in schools and jobs, the publishing of journals and bulletins, offering Hebrew classes, and providing training and vocational opportunities. For example, sewing machines were sent to transit camps, girls' education was cultivated, and Iraqis were assisted during the harsh winters. The party's members, especially in the Knesset, repeatedly challenged racial discrimination against Sephardi and Mizrahi Jews, supporting their claims with statistics about the percentage of members of these communities among high school graduates and in professions such as judges, lawyers, and clerks. But the party's small size led to its joining bigger parties with different agendas. In addition, especially in the case of Bechor Sheetrit, MAPAI worked to dilute Sephardi power. Ben Gurion appointed Sheetrit, a Sephardi Jew who called for more Sephardim in Israeli institutions, to be the minister of police. Thus, it was Sheetrit who frequently stood up in the Knesset to defend the harsh treatment of the immigrants by the police, labeling the Iraqis and other Mizrahim rioters and provocateurs.[163]

The party had several publications aimed at Iraqi Jews, which served as outlets for reporting on the discrimination the latter faced. The party's journal, *Hed ha-Mizrah* (The Echo of the East), was foremost in this effort. Iraqi intellectual Avraham Ben Ya'aqov, who became one of the most important historians of the Iraqi community in Israel, traveled to the transit camps and detailed their struggles. In a story about Beit Lid, he characterized Iraqis as willing to work, but that, since language was a barrier, they could not understand the camp's Ashkenazi Hebrew teacher. He wondered why the government did not call upon Iraqi Jews who had been living in Israel for some time to help their newly arrived brethren.[164] In another story Ben Ya'aqov recounted that the immigrants, having left almost all of their possessions in Iraq, were enduring the confiscation of what little property they had brought by the clerks of the Jewish Agency.[165] He stressed that Iraqis wanted to become part of the greater Israeli community, to join the army, and to learn Hebrew, but were not granted the chance of doing so.[166]

Hed ha-Mizrah cast Iraqi Jews as Zionist patriots whose integration was prevented by bureaucracy, nepotism, and neglect. Dan Hason was another reporter for *Hed ha-Mizrah* who covered the Iraqi Jews, in particular those who were placed near Jerusalem. Visiting the camp of Talpiot, he was told by a Baghdadi Jew that he had come to Israel because "it is our land." Hason contrasted this positive outlook with the attitudes of other Iraqi Jews crammed in the camp, which once had been populated by soldiers of the Jordanian Legion. One told him that they had come there to die. Another Baghdadi declared that he wanted to work but could not get a license to open a shop, and that his wife had miscarried because there was no phone to contact a doctor or a car to take her to one. Hason concluded this story by saying, "This is no way to absorb Aliyah. This is no way to gather the diaspora [in Israel]. This is how you create human dust."[167] In this story, "human dust," an expression used by Ben Gurion and others to depict the Holocaust survivors, signifies what one became in the State of Israel through the authorities' negligence. Hason's knowledge of Arabic enabled him to converse with the newcomers and gain deeper insight into their state of mind.

Articles in *Hed ha-Mizrah* did not shy from making the claim that racism had infected the uppermost strata of Israeli society. One article, "Race Theories in Israel," took issue with an article by Shalom Ben Horin, in which Ben Horin argued that,

> Herzl said we are one nation. But Herzl was wrong. Herzl did not know the Jews from Morocco and Iraq, the masses of Jews from Yemen and the Jews of the caves [Jewish communities from the Atlas Mountains]. We ourselves did not know the Oriental [*orientalim*] and African Jews who have become the majority among us [Israelis]. . . . One can barely call us one nation now. Was the Zionist cause a worthy one, if the primitive communities of Jews are [now] the striking majority? . . . One Zionist who comes to the land because of a clear Zionist consciousness is better, from a Zionist perspective, than a thousand refugees and the herdlike people [*anshey ha-'eder*]!

Hed ha-Mizrah thus advised individuals to vote for the candidates of the Sephardim parties "lest you become a second-rate citizens like the blacks in America."[168]

The party tried repeatedly to drive home the point that all political parties associated with European Zionism had no desire to include Eastern Jews. Yet *Hed ha-Mizrah* engaged in its own project of self-Orientalizing—referring, for example, to the new migration from Iraq as the Ali Baba migration. The party was too small to operate successfully on its own, and party leaders were careful to highlight their Zionism when needed. In many ways, however, they paved the way for the sectarian parties that emerged in the 1980s, especially SHAS (Hit'ahadut ha-Sfaradim Ha-'Olamit Shomrey Torah; The Global Unity of Sephardim Loyal to the Torah), parties that designated intra-Jewish ethnic relations as the chief component of their political agenda.

WELCOME TO THE ZIONIST CIRCUS! THE KNESSET PLENARY AND THE QUESTION OF ABSORPTION

Contrary to popular and historiographical opinion, Mizrahi-Ashkenazi relations were the subject of discussion all throughout the 1950s in the Israeli parliament, as MAPAM, MAKI, and Herut raised issues that concerned Iraqi and Mizrahi Jews. This opened up a space in which Iraqi Jews could represent their concerns. They related their grievances to newspaper reporters and to local activists who resided in the camps. The opposition Knesset members gathered information from their people in the camps and carefully read the newspapers, looking for stories that would embarrass MAPAI. As the party dominating the Knesset and government committees that managed the camps, MAPAI was a convenient target. Opposition members used an institution called "inquiry during question time" (*she'ilta*) in which Knesset members presented queries in the Knesset Plenary (*meli'a*) to the responsible minister, in order to force the ministers of MAPAI to acknowledge the colossal failures of the Jewish Agency and MAPAI's absorption policy.

The Knesset seemed like an unwelcoming venue at first, since over 90 percent of its members were Ashkenazim. But since the Aliyah was a national matter, all Knesset members were concerned with water, sanitation, health, unemployment, and housing. Significantly, the opposition parties reported on dozens of individual cases in the form of inquiries to ministers or as speeches. Names of individuals and their complaints were thus being heard on the most prominent podium in Israel. For example, MAKI Knesset member Avraham Berman brought to the Knesset's attention the case of the Aslan family in the Zarnuga camp: the head of the family (of ten) was sick and the family's eldest child, a thirteen-year-old girl, was ill as well. Another MAKI Knesset member, Esther Wilenska, related the situation of Naji Zarai of the transit camp of Kfar Ono, who had an ill baby girl. The doctor stated that she was entitled to receive state support, but the support was not enough for the unemployed father.[169] Most cases were heartbreaking: instead of statistics, Knesset members heard real stories of Iraqi individuals rotting in the camps.

Typically, in Knesset debates regarding the plight of the Iraqi immigrants, opposition members would take their side, and a minister would represent the state. Esther Wilenska brought up the case of Gurgi Shabta'i in the transit camp of Rosh Pina, who was a sick father of six, and received thirty liras per month from the Ministry of Welfare. His children were going to school hungry, she explained. The minister of welfare, Moshe Shapira, replied that his ministry was supporting the man, and that Shabta'i and his children were fed by the Feeding Project (Mifaʿal Hazana). The fifth child lived with his mother, who had left Shabta'i because of his drinking and violence. Shabta'i had been given a loan to open a cantina in Khayriyya, but the cantina had failed because of "his treatment of his clients and his personal characteristics." Nevertheless, the welfare office was trying to guide him down the road to independence.[170] In another case, Wilenska informed the Knesset about Yitzhak Shav, who staged a sit-in in the transit camp of Ramat ha-Sharon because he had been unemployed for three months and his seven children were hungry. Golda Meir, the minister of labor, gave a detailed account of the man's labor record: he had been fired from his job in a factory in March 1954, and had worked eight days in October, twenty-four in November, twenty-two in December, and sixteen in January.[171] Having one's case presented was not without risk. As mentioned, Minister Shapira defended the denial of benefits to Shabta'i by publicly smearing his reputation. But at times, the details forced ministers like Meir to acknowledge the poor living conditions endured by individual Iraqis; even those who were categorized as working men, like Yitzhak Shav, did not have enough work to support their families.

In May 1955 the Knesset discussed an altercation between Gurji Semah, a resident of the transit camp of Kfar Ono, and the secretary of the labor bureau there, Shlomo Samocha. MAKI's Avraham Berman claimed that on July 1954 the secretary of the labor bureau had beaten up Gurji and broken his glasses. Gurji had complained to the police in Ramat Gan, but nothing was done. Bechor Sheetrit, the minister of police, presented a different version, suggesting that on July 16th a group of unemployed people had attacked the secretary of the labor bureau, who had run away and hidden. A policeman, Naji Yonah, came on the scene. The minister argued that Gurji was an old man, "chronically unemployed, who [held] a grudge toward the secretary." He incited the crowd, and two policemen had to prevent an attack on the secretary, who scolded Semah, pushed him aside, and while being pushed, his glasses fell off. The police were more than fair; they did not even file a complaint against Semah for illegal assembly and incitement. It was up to him to take his complaint to court.[172] The situation in the Knesset, in some ways, mirrored the situation in this camp. There, three Iraqi Jews were fighting with one another: Gurji on the one hand, and Shlomo Samocha and Naji Yonah, on the other. Then, when these complaints were brought to the Knesset, a communist pariah stood up for Gurji, while MAPAI's Mizrahi minister took the side of the police and the secretary. These discussions, then, rehashed in a wider public setting the processes that occurred in the transit camps and, in a sense, all over Israel.

Similarly, just as some Ashkenazi families quarreled with one another about whether they should take in Mizrahi children during the winter, Knesset members blamed each other's parties and public organizations for not taking in Mizrahi children. General Zionist Party Knesset member Shoshana Persitz was very much involved in efforts to help migrant children and women. When she complained that children were being neglected by the state, the following exchange was recorded:

> *Shlomo Lavie* [MAPAI]: Did you give [these children] a room of your own?
>
> *Eri Jabotinksy* [Herut]: And how many newcomers did your kibbutz take?[173]

Other complaints were less specific and dealt in broad terms with the situation in the transit camps. Knesset member Hannan Rubin (MAPAM) asked Minister Yosef Burg why two thousand people in the transit camp of Yad ha-Ma'avir lived without a telephone. Burg was forced to admit that the only phone was seven hundred meters from the camp. Rubin then asked Golda Meir which jurisdiction Yad ha-Ma'avir was located in, because there was no lighting in the camp, sanitary facilities were lacking, and there was no road to it. He went on to ask about unemployment, the politicized and corrupt administrations of the transit camps, lack of adequate housing, and child labor.[174] When he brought up the harsh conditions of life in the transit camp of Nahlat Yehuda, Rubin found that no one would take responsibility: the minister of health stated that his ministry was not in charge of providing sanitary services to the camp; he himself was worried about the spread of diseases. When Rubin asked whether laws needed to be passed to remedy the situation, the minister asked for a second memo.[175] This particular discussion with the minister of health shed light on the bureaucratic maze with which Iraqis had to grapple, and that government officials, in this case the minister, were well aware of the miserable conditions in the camps.

The debates in the Knesset were very theatrical. Members were apt to lose their tempers and speak more candidly than they might wish. When Bebah Idelson (MAPAI) suggested that not every migrant should immediately be put to work, a very angry Shlomo Lavie (MAPAI) retorted that the Knesset members were attacking the state as flies attacked an open wound. In America, the pioneers had lived modest lives, just like the Zionist pioneers. Now people were simply living on money collected for them from Zionist Jews abroad, a phenomenon which undermined the Zionist pioneering efforts. The people who lived off the state, Lavie added, were just like the Apaches who threatened the American pioneers.[176]

Lavie was not alone in his views, as MAPAI members, as well as other ministers, regularly rejected complaints about racial and ethnic discrimination. When Knesset member Avraham Herzfeld (MAPAI) mentioned that Yemenite Jewish workers were paid less than Ashkenazi, his fellow party members replied that the former needed less money, since they were accustomed to living in tents and shacks from their time in Yemen.[177] His colleague Eliyahu Ben Elisar (Sephardim) inquired why there were no Mizrahi judges; Pinhas Rozen, the minister of justice, responded that "we do not appoint [people] based on sectarian affiliation."[178] When Ben Elisar demanded that more Sephardim be appointed in the welfare bureau, the minister, Moshe Shapira, repeated the argument, saying that the ministry did not hire based on sectarian considerations.[179]

In another session dedicated to the question of whether sectarian discrimination existed in Israel, religious Zionist Knesset member Yitzhak Refael (Ha-Mizrahi) observed that mixed marriages occurred between Mizrahim and Ashkenazim very rarely, and that the communities prayed in separate synagogues. For their part, the newcomers believed that the Ashkenazim see them as inferior and incapable. Yosef Sprinzak, the chairman of the Knesset, called for a cautious approach to the discussion of the "sectarian discrimination." Yisra'el Rokach, the minister of interior (whose own family had lived in Ottoman Palestine since the eighteenth century and who was now a member of the General Zionists), called himself both a Sephardi and a Yemenite. Rokach argued that the Knesset should not even discuss this topic. When he was mayor of Tel Aviv, he continued, he was happy to open synagogues for Yemenites. There were also talented Mizrahi singers, and mixed marriages did occur. Hannan Rubin was more skeptical. This was not a cultural issue, he argued, but rather a social one. The level of the schools in the transit camps was not equal to that of schools in Tel Aviv, and within that city, the type of schools in north Tel Aviv (where mostly Ashkenazim studied) differed from schools attended by Mizrahim in other parts of the city, which were geared toward vocational rather than academic training. These realities created the discrimination, he concluded.[180]

The minister of labor, Golda Meir, was the protagonist of many of the theatrical confrontations in the Knesset. Undaunted, herself dramatic, at times bitter and cynical, at times expressing genuine concern, Golda gave the impression that she was doing everything humanly possible for the Iraqi Jews. The opposition members did not have many opportunities to accomplish things, and so could only criticize the efforts of others. Knesset members ambushed Meir, showering her with inquiries and complaints. In response, Meir corrected Knesset members, questioned their professional training and understanding of the situation, and educated them. Yitzhak Refael was schooled by the minister when he challenged her view of the situation of the transit camps in Jerusalem. He initially addressed her respectfully, saying he was not among the protesters and the instigators, and was "fully appreciative of the government's efforts and the absorption institutions of the Zionist movement." He did, however, wish to bring up two transit camps in southern Jerusalem that were exposed to gunfire from across the Jordanian border. Meir refused to believe that the gunfire was coming from Jerusalem. Refael tried to convince her:

> *Refael*: "Yesterday I was in the transit camp."
> *Meir*: "This is indeed a very important event."
> *Refael*: "I have been in the transit camps more than you have."
> *Meir*: "Shall we break down the statistics?"

Moreover, she added, no great change occurred from the fact that a Knesset member by the name of Refael visited the transit camps yesterday or the day before yesterday.[181] The matter in fact was more serious than Meir cared to admit, because it indicated that West Jerusalem, the capital of Israel, was in fact a border city, and an unsafe one at that, especially for those forced to settle near it. This had immense political implications and was a real concern to the Iraqis in Talpiot and Makor Haim transit camps.

The state, Meir believed, knew what was best for the immigrants. In a heated debate initiated by Moshe Sneh and Haim Yehuda (MAPAM), the latter argued that a citizen could not be a patriot when he was being called "a resident of transit camps" (*toshav ma'abarot*) and forced to work for low wages. Meir dismissed Sneh, saying that his love of Israel was shown by the fact that he and his communist friends did nothing in response to Egypt's bellicosity. Yehuda continued by saying that other states allowed immigrants to become citizens within seven years. Meir replied that there was no use comparing Israel to other states. Israel was special: "Every Jew who comes to the land is blessed, even if he is forced to suffer . . . because of the difficulties of the state. I have no doubt that with the growth of the stream of newcomers—and I want this growth—more will suffer; nonetheless I am sure that we will do, as we have done in the past, all that we can, and even more, to decrease the level of suffering."[182] Meir's words expose, in the most brutal terms, the government's policy: the Aliyah was a necessity, regardless of their suffering. Furthermore, it was the state that realized what the best interest of Iraqi Jews was, even if Iraqi Jews failed to recognize it themselves.

Settlement in the periphery was Meir's answer to most complaints. When Esther Wilenska and Moshe Sneh rebuked some officials for their refusal to meet with twenty unemployed men from Ramla, Meir alleged that the unemployed knew that she would send them to work during the olive harvest, and would not be pressured to make any other decision. Wilenska reminded her that these people wanted decent wages, not temporary, low-paying jobs. Meir then retorted to Wilenska that instead of educating "these masses to the reality in this country and to good deeds . . . [people] come and educate them to demand [literally: cry] 'Factory,' although they know that a factory has not yet been built there. Let the people of Ramat Gan, Ramla, Khayriyya, and Sakiyya go to the settlements." The dialogue continued by Wilenska saying, "There is unemployment in the settlements as well"; and Meir responding, "These people have to move!" Then Meir added sarcastically: "I am not jealous of people whose share in the state's affairs is organizing demonstrations and incitement." Wilenska then wondered whether demanding work constituted incitement. Meir retorted that there was not a single secretary in the employment and labor bureaus who had not been attacked by angry newcomers. When asked by another member of MAPAM how employment could be increased, she answered again: "Settlement!"[183]

On another occasion, Wilenska accused Meir more directly; the state, she contended, feared meeting with those who were suffering, and would rather invest in the police and army, which quench their complaints. Avraham Berman backed her up, saying that "the people of the transit camps are disillusioned— they know that the promises of the government are worthless."[184] Meir threw the accusations back at him: these people stay put, and the opposition party members convince them not to move. The responsibility was on the shoulders of those who did not move to a better place.[185] She considered the refusal to live in faraway settlements a form of disobedience that merited discipline. When Hanan Rubin asked why twelve individuals still lived in Nahlat Yehuda in a single wooden shack that was eighteen square meters in size, and inquired whether more families lived under such conditions, Meir dismissed him by saying that they had been offered housing in either Rehovot or the settlements in the periphery, but that they wanted to stay in the transit camp. She continued, "It seems to me that it is neither in the interest of the state, nor ultimately in the interest of these people, if we . . . agree to such demands."[186]

The real work—the making of operational decisions, the reading of reports, and the discussion of budgets, the nepotism and bureaucratic inertia notwithstanding—was done by the committees of the Knesset and the government, where MAPAI and its collation members did invest much efforts. With small budgets and a growing number of newcomers, ministers did try to draft plans to assist Iraqis and other migrants. The Knesset Plenary was, by contrast, often guilty of rhetorical excess. But this theatricality was extremely helpful to the Iraqis. The narratives of successful absorption advanced by Golda Meir were challenged and ridiculed, and her responses exposed her harsh settlement politics. This platform, then, allowed for the calling into question of MAPAI's policies. It is doubtful whether members of MAPAM, MAKI, or Herut had better solutions, considering their parties' platforms. But all opposition parties pointed out the neglect, racism, and suffering experienced by Mizrahi and Iraqi Israelis. And while the Israeli system itself was not democratic, and the Knesset was almost totally Ashkenazi, in the Plenary, members of political parties who were considered pillars of the community—being Ashkenazi, socialist, Zionist, and signators of the Israeli Declaration of Independence—had the freedom to repeat what the Iraqis said among themselves, as well as what they said in their Arabic press, Arabic leaflets, and protests: the state was failing miserably in their absorption.

CONCLUSION

Many of the features of Israeli political life during the 1950s indicate that the state was far from democratic. Elections were indeed free, but many Iraqis felt pressured to vote for MAPAI. Bribes, threats, and the fear of loss of job or housing were very effective in influencing voters. MAPAI, then, won democratic elections in many undemocratic ways. The other parties in Israel tried to appeal to the Iraqis as well. All parties, despite their immense ideological differences, had common structural features. All were led by Eastern European men, who had a great say in internal party discussions and who did much to shape party newspapers and propaganda efforts, whether it was Ben Gurion (Green), Ya'ari (Weld), Begin, or Wilner. The discourse of all political parties was often vociferous and violent. And into this very complex, Eastern European and Zionist mix, Iraqis were to be integrated.

Elections in Iraq had also been marked by corruption, but nonetheless more than a few Jews there were active politically, as senators, parliament members, and members of both legal and illegal parties.[187] In Israel, they took advantage of a system that used their weakness and dependence on the state. Iraqis, however, knew their votes were needed and used this to their benefit. The Hasbara campaigns of each party helped Iraqi writers and intellectuals, because the parties' Arabic publications provided them with work. Some Iraqis, especially those in MAPAI, tried to generate change from within and managed to create some space within the hegemonic party for their claims to be heard. Iraqis also managed to find a foothold in the political system: their grievances were heard in the Knesset, the opposition press covered the horrific situation in the camps (especially the Arabic publications, in which Iraqis could tell their stories themselves), and the boundaries between transit camps and cities were eroded as a result. With the exception of the communists, all parties offered Iraqis some version of the following bargain: if the latter accepted the Zionist parameters of the state, its ideology, and its ruling bodies, they could benefit from the party's institutions and parliamentary activity.

Nevertheless, there was not a single political party that could offer an ideal solution to Iraqis. Having been urban, free professionals, clerks, and merchants in Iraq, they were less attracted to the socialist and communist parties. Even those Iraqis who leaned in that direction found the Israeli left to be problematic. Within MAPAM and MAKI, Iraqi members consistently complained about discrimination. In addition, MAPAM offered them the same Zionist solutions, especially settlement, that MAPAI did. MAKI was so committed to its rigid ideology that it failed to identify the revolutionary potential of Israel's most important ethnic riots, those of Wadi Salib. The Sephardim Party's agenda was clear and aligned with Iraqi interests, but the party was too small. The General Zionists supported a free market, which would effectively deny the few benefits the Iraqis had actually received.

Most interesting, perhaps, was the tendency represented by Herut, whose members were willing to offer Iraqis roles in their party, as long as participants adhered to the party's right-wing and chauvinistic ideology. Herut's gatherings in the transit camps were described in its publications with much pathos and kitsch. Begin always spoke to "the masses," who always greeted him enthusiastically, and Israeli youth in Betar uniforms accompanied him to the transit camps, where he told the newcomers how he longed for a greater Israel on both sides of the Jordan River. The vision he offered to the Iraqis, however, seemed appealing already during the 1950s: a liberal economy, less intervention by the state in the lives of its Jewish citizens, freedom of assembly, the openness of his party to welcoming Mizrahim, including Iraqis, as members, and the acknowledgment of Israel's racist attitude toward them. In 1977, when Herut, then operating within the larger Likud Party, won the Israeli elections, this vision seemed more attractive than ever.

4 ELEMENTS OF RESISTANCE

IN 1953, a fourteen-year-old girl refused to let a reporter take her photograph for a story he was writing on the transit camp in Talpiot. She told him: "We know you; you take our picture; [you photograph] our poverty and our shacks made of tin; then, you send the pictures to America and get money that should be ours, but we do not see it. It disappears, and we continue living in shacks made of tin and cloth, while you build neighborhoods and houses for yourselves."[1] This incident raises important questions regarding political representation and possible courses of political action on the part of the Iraqi Jews who had become Israeli citizens. First and foremost, how could and did the Iraqi immigrants challenge the all-powerful political apparatus? The girl from Talpiot, it seems, understands politics well; she knows that representing her poverty via the press is not intended to alleviate her suffering and her appalling living conditions, but rather to further the Zionist agenda both domestically and internationally. Thus in order to protest these politics, she takes a small yet astonishing step: she refuses to have her picture taken. She resists.

Focusing on the issue of political action, this chapter uncovers many similar cases as it explores elements of resistance to the state. Despite being poor migrants, Iraqi Jews became active political actors. As Bryan Roby has pointed out, the newcomers were not passive victims but rather active political agents.[2] In fact, in many of the protests in 1950s Israel, Iraqis led the way as organizers and participants. Some protests and demonstrations took place in transit camps, others in the streets of cities and towns. Some were successful in that they managed to secure livelihoods for unemployed individuals, and improve their living conditions (notably, being moved from tents to wooden shacks). Other protests were less successful in achieving the newcomers' goals, but they were effective in another way: they raised public awareness of the status of Iraqi Jews, and they broke the invisible, yet very rigid, boundaries between the marginalized transit camps and the poor neighborhoods, on the one hand, and mainstream Israeli society, on the other.

Not all forms of protest were as dramatic as public demonstrations. Others included attempts of Iraqi Jews to achieve some degree of autonomy over their own bodies and the future of their children. Such acts involved squatting, sit-ins, and writing dozens of petitions to official bodies in Israel, as well as letters to Israeli newspapers. All these forms of protest and resistance, however, indicate that Iraqi Jews, having realized that their citizenship rights in terms of labor and housing had been denied, were pushing to gain them. Moreover, these Iraqis came to the conclusion that their rights were being denied not only due to concrete budgetary considerations but also because of ineffective bureaucracy and ethnic discrimination. Understanding that change was possible, they demanded it.

PROTECTING BODIES AND HOMES: INDIVIDUAL RESISTANCE

From the moment Iraqis arrived in Israel, they used whatever modest means they had at their disposal to resist public policy, and maintain some control over their bodies. For example, Iraqi mothers refused to have their children spayed with DDT.[3] Women also decided to take control over the way they gave birth to their children. Initially, mothers who resided in transit camps were encouraged to give birth at home. Nurses themselves dreaded the long ride, often in a truck rather than in an ambulance. In 1954, the policy was changed and mothers received grants for delivering babies in hospital.[4] However, women preferred to give birth at home, because they remembered the humiliation of giving birth publicly when the ambulance was late arriving at their camp or because they were afraid their children would be kidnapped. They used midwives and local Iraqi doctors at the transit camps, and did not go to public hospitals.[5] Because of their fears that their children might be kidnapped, mothers refused to leave their children's beds when they were hospitalized and did not want to place their toddlers in daycare facilities.[6]

During the harsh winters some parents were afraid of letting their children be taken to more comfortable, safe lodgings because of the risk that they would not return. Esperance Moreh-Cohen describes how she refused to let the women's organization take her two children from her: "The children would die of hunger but I will not give them to any other human being. I am their mother and no one would take better care of them than me." Nevertheless, she was at her wit's end:

> After the polite women left, disappointed at the "primitive Iraqi woman" who was willing to die with her children of hunger, and [would] not put them in the hands of the civilized women who came to rescue them from the dankness of the Middle Ages, I didn't even have a glass to ask for some milk for them. I was not ashamed to look in the garbage and I was happy to find an empty sardine box.[7]

She washed the box and begged the authorities for help. She managed to get hot chocolate and milk for them, as her husband tried to stabilize their tents. She cried throughout the process, but managed to keep them with her.

While some parents pushed their teenage children to work because of difficult economic conditions, other Iraqi parents, especially mothers, realized the significance of education and they refused to yield to the dictates of the state concerning the instruction of their children. Gurjia Salman went on a hunger strike because she wanted her children transferred to proper educational institutions and because they were hungry.[8] In 1954, twenty-four couples arranged a strike in a transit camp because they did not want to send their children to religious schools. Moreover, they contended that their children were not accepted into high school because of sectarian and racial discrimination.[9] Five parents from Beit Dagon protested the raise in tuition in schools in front of the Ministry of Education.[10] Esperance Cohen recounts how she refused to send her children to vocational schools (she was successful; one son became a medical doctor and another an engineer for NASA).[11]

Parents were not enthusiastic about the activities organized by GADNA (an abbreviation of Gdudey No'ar, or "Youth Brigades"). Established in 1940 as part of the Haganna, this organization assumed great importance in June 1949, as the preparatory mechanism for young adults about to be drafted.[12] The communist activist Elihayu 'Ezer, editor of the journal *Sarkhat al-Ma'abarot* (Cry of the Transit Camps), argued that the difficult circumstances under which the youth in the transit camps lived encouraged them to join the GADNA. The government, the journal argued, was wrong to fund this paramilitary group rather than education.[13] Ironically, educational supervisors complained that children from the transit camps of Khayriyya and Sakiyya who attended the GADNA events had fun rather than being ideologically instructed.[14]

Protest was not just the business of the parents; the students also tried to shape their education. Students in transit camps demonstrated against the school's authorities, made the lives of state officials quite unpleasant, and protested when popular school employees, such as janitors and cleaners, were fired. One such protest took place in Khayriyya.[15] In another case, seventeen students in a transit camp staged a three-day sit-in, protesting the decision to close down the eighth grade.[16] One anecdote that illustrates the anarchy in schools and the battles between parents and the state's representatives is the case of a child from Khayriyya who was not allowed to enter the sixth grade. The family believed that their son was wrongly denied entrance; when the boy tried to do so, the principal of the school stopped him and summoned the police. The policemen threatened to lock the child, naked, in the toilet if he disrespected his teachers in the classroom. The minister of education, Ben Zion Dinur, favored the school's position, pointing out that the child had failed Hebrew and math and had misbehaved in school. The parents threatened the principal and tried to beat him up, while the boy's brothers threw stones. The police had to be called.[17] Whether we accept the family's version or that of the state, the case gives us a window onto the situation in the transit camps, one characterized by the frustration of the parents, on the one hand, and the willingness of educational officials to resort to violence and arrests, even to the extent of abusing a young child, on the other.

The transit camps and the poor neighborhood incited a popular protest culture. Protest songs in the Iraqi-Jewish dialect were chanted between shacks and tents. As Ella Shohat notes, such songs underlined a deep regret about leaving Iraq and the longing to return to it. The lines of these songs that Shohat translated capture the misery of Iraqi immigrants, but also the way they used the songs to present a counternarrative to the narratives of the Jewish Agency; "You perturbed the whole universe," Iraqi Jews sang about Ben Gurion; "A bug drove us nuts and we all rushed headlong," they added, representing the act of migration as an act of insanity; and, referring to their Iraqi Muslim neighbors, who warned them not to come to Israel, they sang, "Much as they warned us we just didn't believe it!"[18] In another song, people mocked the representatives of both Israel and Iraq, depicting their Aliyah to Israel as follows: "They bought us; they sold us; they brought us."[19] Making jokes about Ashkenazim, especially bureaucrats and employers, was common; pranks were also utilized as a way of showing displeasure over state politics. The disrespect to officials and the surrounding Ashkenazi community was such that Iraqi Jews used the term *yahudi*, meaning "Jew" in Arabic, to depict only Iraqi Jews; the rest, given their callous behavior, did not seem so Jewish.

In the transit camps, Iraqi Jews sought to have some measure of control over their living situation; people constantly tried to find better shacks and tents than the ones to which they were assigned. Wooden shacks and tin shacks were occupied as soon as they became vacant, without permission from the Jewish Agency, which punished invaders to no avail.[20] Older denizens would tell a new arrival about an available shack that was bigger than the one assigned. When blind people were evacuated from wooden shacks in which they had been housed, other migrants took possession of them.[21] Residents would also try to find an empty tent for newlyweds so that they could spend their wedding night in some privacy.[22] This situation created friction in the camp; there was much envy of those who lived in shacks, and battles over who would get to live in them were fierce. On the other hand, there were many cases of solidarity, in which residents helped each other to locate such shacks. This was part of a larger culture of solidarity; in the absence of fire services, men in the transit camps rushed to save babies when tents and shacks caught on fire, and risked their lives to help children who fell into channels and ditches during times of flooding.[23]

The response to acts of squatting was often violent. The police were called in to remove individuals who had invaded tents, shacks, and deserted property.[24] Yona Shalom, fifty years old, disabled, and the father of five, squatted in a shack that was not allotted to him because his previous shack had burned down and the roof of the replacement leaked. He was jailed for two weeks, and the police destroyed the shack, in which he had installed new windows.[25] At other times, squatters could negotiate their housing solutions within the transit camps' administration. An Iraqi family in the transit camp of Ramat ha-Sharon, for example, spotting a more stable tent than the one assigned to them, settled in it. The better tent, however, was to be settled by a European family, following the decision of the Jewish Agency. The Iraqi family refused to leave. They finally managed to convince the officials in the camp that their seniority and harsh living conditions merited a larger tent.[26] In other cases, Iraqis built shacks in the transit camps so that they could serve as small business in defiance of the Jewish Agency's instructions; some managed to negotiate with the police and the authorities and keep these places.[27]

Iraqi Jews moved illegally between different transit camps and left their camps unlawfully in order to settle in cities. The Jewish Agency distributed propaganda posters warning people of the "sick desire to travel" (that is, of wanting to leave the transit camps); its key official, Giora Yoseftal, bemoaned the mass migration from camps to cities and from villages to cities.[28] Golda Meir acknowledged in a speech to the Knesset that people were moving between camps, stating that fifteen hundred families were squatting in tents after fleeing the north and the south. As a deterrent, she vowed that the squatters in Nahlat Yehuda, Bney Brak, Tel Aviv, and Petach Tikva would receive no benefits.[29]

In cities, Iraqis tried to live in deserted public property, especially Palestinian property.[30] Immigrants came from locations near and far: in one case, nine Iraqi families left the village in the Negev where they had been settled because of the lack of food and water. Upon their arrival in Jerusalem, they went to city hall to protest their living conditions. The communists provided some assistance, taking some of the Iraqis into their homes and printing a leaflet on the matter. The police responded with arrests of the protesters.[31] This was not a unique case; the police response to such acts of invasion was swift and forceful; Iraqi families were evicted by force and occasionally policemen confiscated the belongings of squatters.[32] In Rehovot, the police drove out sixty-five Kurdish Jews who wanted to settle in shacks. Punitive measures were taken as well.[33]

In other cases, Iraqis wanted to stay put. Individuals refused to move to permanent housing once they discovered the poor quality of the houses, apartments, and shacks they received. Families from Ashkelon, for example, refused to occupy apartments that were smaller than what they had been promised.[34] The most insistent resistance to state housing politics occurred in the transit camps of Khayriyya, Sakiyya, and Kfar 'Ana, whose residents resisted their evacuation to other camps or border regions and the appropriation of the territories into nearby cities. The Iraqis petitioned, demonstrated, and withstood the cutting of services for three years to keep their shacks so that they could be close to their places of work in Tel Aviv and nearby cities.[35] They were successful.

The state naturally objected to this high number of squats and illegal constructions, and tried to limit it, arguing that since the Iraqis were individuals with no capital, relying on the state for benefits and funding, it was for the authorities to decide where the Iraqi newcomers would live. As Esther Meir— Glitzenstein explains, the settlement of border zones was a priority, both as a deterrent to Arab invasion and as a way to reduce population density in the center of Israel, and the state saw the migrants as ideal candidates for border settlements. Iraqis were therefore sent to the Negev and the Galilee. Even when Iraqi immigrants possessed enough capital to build houses in the center of the country, they were pressured to settle at the periphery. The Iraqis, for their part, had good reasons for resisting the state's politics. In particular, those Iraqis who were of a middle-class background wanted to stay close to big cities where they could eventually find jobs.[36] Given the poor conditions of the newcomers' villages in the north and the south, there was little reason for the newcomers to have faith in the promises of the government. They therefore squatted, settled, and migrated illegally.[37] In November 1951, Yoseftal noted in his diary that that Iraqis at first did not want to go to the settlement region in the Negev, and that the Ashkenazi settlers were more amenable. He thus supported administrative measures to force them to stay put.[38] When the people of the transit camp of Nahlat Yehuda protested the inadequate sanitation facilities (the lack of showers in particular), Minister of Labor Mordechai Namir justified the fact that services were not provided to the people of the camp because the denizens refused to move to a new settlement.[39]

Some Iraqis turned their backs on mainstream Israeli society altogether. Poverty and living in deserted border regions forced them into a life of crime. A Mizrahi-Palestinian gang assisted in the hiding of six Palestinians from the Triangle who had moved there. This was part of a successful smuggling business of goods and people run by a rabbi and a group of Palestinians, Iraqis, and Yemenites. The police were never able to break up this gang.[40] While I may understand the state's concerns, I cannot help but admire this cooperation of all faiths and ethnicities in defiance of state regulations and borders created in the region after 1948.

SELF-RULE? THE STRUGGLE OVER THE LOCAL COMMITTEES

Iraqis had to fight for the right to govern their own political affairs, especially since municipal councils did not want Iraqi Jews to vote in their districts.[41] As Bryan Roby suggested, an important mechanism for self-rule by the people of the transit camps was the local committee. But as with everything else in the transit camps, bureaucracy and incompetent state policies limited the effectiveness of the committees. The local committees came into existence as a result of the struggle between the Jewish Agency and the Ministry of Interior. Since the Jewish Agency appointed the directors of the transit camps, the Ministry of Interior, the agency's rival, viewed them with suspicion.[42] Dov Rozen of the

Ministry of the Interior saw local committees, elected by the camp's residents, as counterweights to the directors (appointed by his rivals from the Jewish Agency), and sided with them in accusing directors of interfering with their work. The ministry worked through the secretary of the local committee, and the agency, through the director; and these officials often clashed, being obliged to defend the interests of the body that paid them. Complaints about corruption, especially against directors, were numerous. Because directors had a say in hiring, work placement, deciding who among many candidates could open a store, and assigning shacks, they wielded a great deal of power over the daily lives of the newcomers. They were also the main points of contact with outside officials on such matters as housing or sanitary conditions, such the conditions of showers and toilets and their maintenance. Many petitions complained about their corruption and their nepotism.[43]

The official aim of the local committee was to give the new citizens a sense of belonging. The local committees were accorded jurisdiction over certain matters, such as housing, education, and religion, but were to be subordinated to the Ministry of Interior. First they were appointed, and later elections were held to establish their members. Elections were held in Sakiyya, Kfar 'Ana, Bet Lid, and Zarnuga for local committees, but the process took a long time. The ministry was to support and empower them through the creation of infrastructure, notably roads and drainage, sewage, and electricity systems.[44] They were also to supervise the implementation of the mandatory educational law and to appoint a local contact person for the Ministry of Education.[45] The fact that the local committees had a say in education meant that they were in charge of organizing celebrations of holidays, which would ostensibly boost their popularity and power.[46]

The experience of the local committee in Khayriyya can serve as an example. It took a while to elect it, because the Jewish Agency transferred some people from Khayriyya to Kfar 'Ana, and some escaped in the process.[47] The local committee addressed the Jewish Agency, pleading with its officials for clean houses and replacement of tents. "Our lot is bitter and horrendous," they wrote, but the agency took no action. The committee members themselves could not be counted on to attend meetings, for a variety of reasons. The transit-camp director, Mr. Roger Zalman, and the secretary, Sha'ul Havia, were able to provide cultural activities, such as film viewings and the celebration of holidays, but as with all major projects, they relied heavily on the state. For example, they could not even buy the furniture they needed, and asked to be exempted from the heavy taxation on wood products.[48] Zalman's long history as an activist in the Zionist movement in his home country of Romania did not help, as his letters were ignored, and consequently he asked to be transferred.[49]

The elections for the committees were not conducted properly and thus the committees were rejected by the people of the transit camps. Yoseftal contended that in transit camps populated by Ashkenazim, local committees were active; their members might have complained, but they still collaborated and could be treated as partners. Elsewhere, however, there were difficulties.[50] Facts that might have escaped Yoseftal are that the committees, because of their corruption and because of outside intervention in their affairs, were unpopular, and moreover, that many were dominated by Ashkenazim. A letter to the head of the secretaries and committees in the transit camps from the Ministry of Interior lists just three Mizrahi secretaries of local committees out of a total of fourteen. Ashkenazi secretaries were in place in camps that had vast concentrations of Iraqis, such as Zarnuga, Khayriyya, and Hartuv, and in the Yemenite camps of Rosh ha-'Ayn.[51]

Understandably, then, this local leadership was often challenged. In many instances, the transit camps generated their own unofficial leadership, composed of organizers and activists. Such leaders were people connected to political parties opposing MAPAI, from Herut to the communists, or who had been respected teachers and writers in Iraq and wanted to lend a hand to their fellow Iraqis; some rose up from within the camps themselves. Many letters and petitions accusing the directors of corruption and demanding their replacement were written by these individuals. More importantly, in some camps people elected their own local committees, which operated in tandem with the committees appointed by the state. For example, the people of the transit camp in Cessariya set up their own management, whose members petitioned the state for a new local committee.[52] In Sakiyya and Khayriyya the residents refused to accept the local committees recognized by the Jewish Agency and the Ministry of Interior.[53] The alternative committees went so far as to interact directly with the government. For instance, the self-appointed committee for Social Aid of the Committee of Iraqi Jews submitted their own reports to Yoseftal about the horrendous conditions in the camps of Bney Brak and Petach Tivka.[54]

The independent local committee in Sakiyya was a modest success story. Alongside the official committee, an independent committee made up of activists was established through a spontaneous election. Called "the collective committee," it oversaw the affairs of both the Sakiyya and Kfar 'Ana camps.

It operated until 1960 and even managed to meet with state officials, despite having no relationship to the official local council.[55] One of its achievements was the appointment of a new doctor to the camp. The currently serving doctor spoke only Yiddish, and Iraqis felt he treated them like "primitive immigrants." The alternative committee located an Iraqi doctor, Shlomo Atrakchi, and fought with the local health officials in Kupat Holim and Ramat Gan concerning the validity of his credentials, and he was finally appointed.[56]

Despite these successes, the committees elected by the residents of the transit camps were at odds with the administration in the transit camps; officials and bureaucrats simply ignored them. A tragic case was that of the transit camp of Makor Haim, which was so poorly managed that its inhabitants were jealous of the camp of Talpiot because it had a paved road. The camp's independent committee sent a number of letters and petitions all throughout 1951 pleading for help, pointing to the suffering of children during the winter, but the letters were ignored by state officials because the committee was not elected properly.[57]

"DEAR STATE OF ISRAEL": LETTERS AND PETITIONS

Not all the interactions with the state were face-to-face and confrontational. Iraqi Jews also petitioned government officials, seeking to improve their quality of life. Dozens of them are found in various state archives. Some were written in a pleading tone, hoping to evoke sympathy by describing their horrendous or miserable living conditions. Others were letters of protests, which would go as far as to threaten a strike or sabotage if the petitioners' concerns were not addressed. Petitions lamented the death of mothers that happened because there were no doctors on call to deliver the babies, and demanded the dismissal of corrupt bureaucrats who were to blame. The authors wrote to every official body they could, a sign both of their desperation and of their recognition that they were citizens and, as such, had democratic rights.

Most petitions included hundreds of signatures. Four hundred people from Khayriyya, for instance, demanded that a synagogue be established and that an election for a religious affairs committee in the transit camp be held.[58] Typically, petitions were addressed to several authorities, first and foremost the ministries of labor and welfare and the Jewish Agency. The majority had to do with the living conditions in the camp. In another petition from Khayriyya, the petitioners addressed the prime minister, the chairman of the Knesset, the ministers of interior, labor, justice, and police, all the political parties, the Jewish Agency, the city of Tel Aviv, the Histadrut, and the workers' councils in Ramat Gan and Giv'atayim, as well as all the newspapers in Hebrew and Arabic. Their grievances were directed against the Jewish Agency, which wanted to move their tents to another location and refused to build wooden shacks for 150 families. Winter was nearing, they noted, and they expressed amazement that nothing had been done; consequently, the writers threatened to strike.[59]

The Jewish Agency was the target of many complaints, as Iraqis tried to show that it was incapable of running the affairs of the transit camps. Four hundred ninety-two people from Kfar 'Ana wrote that they were living in houses made of cloth or in tents. In addition to the Jewish Agency, however, they pointed to a range of institutions and people responsible for their predicament: those in charge of work placement, who allotted jobs based on nepotism; thugs who scared people in the camp; and dishonest merchants. They demanded clean water, permanent housing, a doctor on call, a clerk for a tax bureau, a regular supply of food, work for the unemployed, bread, and a special house for the babies of the camp.[60]

Sometimes the petition writers made use of the prevailing political discourse, thinking that a socialist or a Zionist framing would help them obtain their demands. A petition from the people of Khayriyya from 1955 contended that their living conditions were unworthy of a civilized man (*adam tarbuti*).[61] While the state proclaimed that it was providing the Iraqis with culture and guidance, the people countered that the state was actually causing them to live in an uncivilized fashion. Another good example of such a petition was sent by the denizens of Kfar Ata, one originally written in Arabic and translated into Hebrew that listed the names of all the Iraqis in the transit camp. It was addressed to the prime minister, though copies were sent to the ministers of agriculture, religion, and the Jewish Agency. The petitioners wrote that they wished to turn the attention of the prime minister to "the grave and miserable conditions under which we are living." They then recounted their suffering and their hunger because of having only bread to eat; they had no soap and lived amid piles of garbage; the synagogue was in miserable shape; the water supply system was dysfunctional; and all of them were unemployed. Reminding the government of its ideals, they represented themselves as grateful: "We thank God that we live under the protection of a workers' government, which defends the rights of the miserable worker." Their grievances, based on this framing, therefore were addressed broadly to the state's elites with their socialist consciences, but also targeted one person in particular, the transit-camp director:

> He does not know how to read and write in Hebrew, and does not have the experience or ability to run the camp. In addition, he creates division and discord. He gave a lecture in Yiddish in which he opposed integration with the Easterners [*mukhalatat al-sharqiyyin*], given that they are of the black race [*min al-jins al-aswad*],[62] and one should not interact with them, in his opinion. Such actions cause feuds and divisions between the residents. Let us not forget that we are all brothers, and we came to Israel to defend freedom and equality, of which we dreamed in exile. We ask that the current director be fired and a more honest and intelligent man be appointed, one with knowledge of and experience in the management of such a camp.[63]

Again, adopting the state line, the petitioners emphasized their Zionism: they longed to come to Israel when they were in exile and accept the Zionist axiom that all Jews are brothers. This lays the groundwork for their protest of the fact that as Iraqis they are classified as Easterners and hence discriminated against. Noticeably, they did not demand an Iraqi director of the camp, but simply a better administrator.

This discourse unfortunately did not help them much. The director responded that all residents in the camps were issued food stamps and the camp had two private stores, and therefore no complaints should be made in response to shortage of food. The complaint, in his opinion, was the doing of a disgruntled man who had been transferred from the Halsa transit camp, and was fired from a position as a cleaner and consequently wanted to incite the residents: "All complaints are motivated by a sectarian point of view. The Oriental Jews and the Iraqis in particular see themselves as discriminated against, in comparison to other newcomers in the transit camp, who are from Poland and Romania."[64] Turning the complaint of the people of the camp on its head (and exposing his own racism), the director argued that it was the gullible Iraqis who were behind the unfounded grievances.

When an issue affected a transit camp as a whole, Iraqi petitioners went outside their ethnic group to collect signatures. The independently elected committee of the transit camp in Rishon le-Zion, for example, petitioned the Jewish Agency (with copies to the minister of interior affairs and the mayor of Rishon le-Zion) concerning local grocery store owner, who did not stock certain food products. As was the case with many petitions, the authors also asked for wooden shacks, the replacement of the director of the transit camp, and the delivery of furniture. Judging by the names, the petitioners were mostly but not exclusively Iraqi: the list includes Ashkenazi names, North African (Swisa, Jerbi), Yemenite (Saʿadia, Yahya), and Sephardi (probably Turkish or Greek migrants: Versano, Eliko). People used Arabic, Hebrew, and Latin characters to write their names. Some educated women (probably Iraqi) signed in both Hebrew and English (like a certain Victoria Rabiʿa), and others in English only (like ʿAziza Salman). Thirty-two people used their fingerprints. In total, 308 men and women signed the petition.[65] From the petitioners' names, we can infer that individuals went from shack to shack, from tent to tent, speaking in various languages, in order to protest the subhuman living conditions.

Some petitioners insisted on meeting the high officials themselves and delivering the petition in person. A small delegation from Sakiyya, led by Shaʾul Hayyek and including Nuria ʾIda, Salim Waya, Eliyahu Shammash, and ʿAliza Salman, brought a petition to the Israeli Knesset. None of the delegation members knew sufficient Hebrew, so a translator was brought. The chairman of the Knesset, to whom their petition was addressed, claimed he was busy and not could receive them; they therefore met with the secretary of the Knesset, M. Rozetti, and with A. Govrin, the chairman of the Knesset Committee. The written petition complained about fraud in food distribution, unfair prices, and particularly the lack of potable water, as residents had to stand in line for hours to fill a bucket of water at the nearby transit camp. They demanded the fair distribution of food, bread, a paved road, a medical doctor specializing in pediatrics, proper lighting, a phone, and a school. The petition was signed by 757 residents.[66]

There was no guarantee, however, that the authorities would meet with petitioners, and for that matter, that the former would attempt to meet the demands of the latter. In a meeting discussing a petition of Khayriyya by an elected delegation, asking for assistance with downpayments for key money that would allow them to live in wooden shacks, the government representative, Yosef David, explained that these people, mostly Iraqis, but also Romanian and Egyptians, had refused to move to agricultural communities distant from Tel Aviv. There was thus no reason to provide the desired assistance.[67] Letters from the people of the transit camps of Kfar Nahman, Sakiyya, and Khayriyya to the minister of interior were passed on to another office or subcommittee as a way of not dealing with complaints.[68]

Iraqis as private individuals wrote to official bodies, to newspapers, and to government offices to complain about corruption of camp directors, demand a job, ask for a transfer to a better location, or report about the mistreatment of relatives.[69] One such letter from a resident of Khayriyya told of a director who fired people without good cause and employed a woman simply because he liked her at a salary of twenty liras.[70] Iraqis in Israel also wrote letters of to family members in Iraq (via Europe). Their message was simple: do not come here.[71] Finally, members of local councils wrote to state bodies about their affairs: the councils of Sakiyya, Kfar 'Ana, and Khayriyya demanded to be included in the same regional council and that the quality of education in their camps be improved.[72] A vital outlet for Iraqi-Jewish parents in particular was the writing of letters to the editors of newspapers and to politicians. The opposition press gladly published them. Intellectuals and ordinary Iraqis thus wrote letters to *Al-Mirsad* and *Al-Ittihad*.

As the state's response to the petitions and letters was partial at best, residents of transit camps also addressed other officials they met and told them about their difficult conditions. When American Jewish Zionists working for the American Jewish Joint Distribution Committee visited the transit camps of Ijlil (near Herzliya) and David (near Haifa), they reported that the people of the transit camps showed mission members with questions and grievances, wondering, "Why are we left here to rot?"[73] These individuals challenged the depictions given to the mission by ministers, officials in the Jewish Agency, and bureaucrats.

As we have seen, petitions of Iraqis printed on pamphlets, in which they called on Iraqis to support various political parties, from MAPAI to Herut to MAKI, circulated in the transit camps. One petition, however, from the transit camp of Kfar 'Ana, signed by Ashkenazi and Mizrahi children, stands out. The children, presumably guided by political activists belonging to leftist parties, wanted to protest the death of Arab children by the Israeli border police in the massacre of Kafar Qassem. The letter was sent to David Ben Gurion, shortly after the events related to the massacre became known to Israeli public. It included the following words:

> To the Prime Minister
> D. Ben-Gurion
> <u>The Government Compound</u>
> We are boys and girls in the transit camp of Kfar 'Ana. Having heard of the shocking murder of men, women, and children carried out by the Border Police in Kafar Qassem, we wish to express our deep shock in this lowly murder. We are astonished and ashamed that young Jews are capable of implementing such barbaric methods against the people living among us. These are methods that we, as Jews, have always suffered from.

We demand that the perpetrators be subject to an open trial, in front of the public, in order that the root of this act be exposed and in order to prevent similar acts from taking place in the future. We demand a harsh punishment for those found guilty.[74]

This petition is unique because of the age of the petitioners and because it does not deal with their daily lives in the transit camp. We can reasonably assume that grownups were involved in drafting this petition. And yet, giving the harsh means exercised against members of radical political parties by MAPAI, it is difficult not to admire the children of Kfar 'Ana, and their parents, who, though living in shacks and tents, still took many risks in order to show their solidarity with other oppressed children, whose lot was even worse than theirs.

It is somewhat ironic that in the modern state of Israel the practice of petitioning, which historians have associated with the medieval and early modern periods, experienced a revival. In those earlier periods, people who were illiterate had other people sign their name for them; similarly, in Israel the Arabic-speaking Iraqis who did not know Hebrew needed a group to speak in their name. Indeed, the manner in which Ben Gurion was addressed—he was referred to as "the merciful ruler of Israel," for example—seemed very premodern. Petitions and letters showed two different trends. On the hand, they were signs of desperation. By writing to various offices, to whomever could listen to them, hundreds of Iraqis protested their impossible living circumstances. On the other hand, they show yet again how Iraqis demanded their civil rights. Transit-camp dwellers organized and collected signatures in the effort to have their voices heard. Officials did not attend to all petitions; some were a mere exercise in a collective expression of grievances. But some Iraqis were able to meet with officials and insist upon what was due them as new citizens.

"THE BRIGADE OF STRIKERS WITH THE TORAH SCROLLS": RALLIES, PROTESTS, AND DEMONSTRATIONS

In 1952, David Teneh (1909–72), a German Jewish economist and a leading activist in the bringing of Jewish refugees to Israel from Germany and the rest of Europe, returned to his post in the Jewish Agency, after working for a short while in the Ministry of Finance dealing with "deserted property" of displaced Palestinians. He was now the director of the powerful absorption division in the Jewish Agency. He saw demonstrations on a daily basis. In a letter to David Ben Gurion, he reported: "The Hebrew month of Sivan is blessed with demonstrations. Delegations come on a daily basis, demanding that tents be replaced with wooden shacks."⁷⁵ Knesset member Michael Hazani similarly complained about the fact that "we witness demonstrations of rage every week," which he saw as the fruits of incitement.⁷⁶

Demonstrating, however, like other acts of opposition at the time, endangered the protesters, who could be fired, denied work placements, and punished in other ways by the authorities in the transit camps.⁷⁷ For example, workers who refused to work as agricultural laborers, or protested low wages and arduousness of the work, were denied welfare payments by the Ministry of Labor.⁷⁸ Yet the hostility the Iraqi Jews encountered did not deter them, as they

FIGURE 4. Getting rid of the *pachons*: a woman trying to cook in the *pachon*. Source: CZA, NKH\404365. Reprinted with permission.

recognized the importance of protest and demonstrations as a means of raising awareness of their plight. As one demonstrator said, "We, the newcomers from Iraq, came to this country to live and work! We were given many promises, but instead of promises we are being abused and neglected."[79]

Some forms of protests occurred in the space of the transit camp. Iraqi Jews would stage a sit-in in labor and welfare bureaus; they claimed they were hungry; that they wanted to support their families; and that the state ought to act on their behalf. The police were often called to deal with such cases of "disorderly conduct." Complaints about the breaking of public order in the lines to work placement or in the welfare bureaus were common at the time.[80] The anger at the state's workers and bureaucrats was so intense that bureaucrats at the camps locked themselves inside their offices; Yoseftal demanded a police presence in the camps as a result.[81]

Individuals often directed their attention to the symbols of the state, the Jewish Agency, and MAPAI, and broke meetings of MAPAI and the Histadrut. When the local branch of the Histadrut was established in the transit camp of Khayriyya, the Histadrut planned a big opening celebration. The secretary of the workers' council in Ramat Gan and Giv'atayim, Mr. Abramovitch, was to give a speech, and Reuven Shabat from MAKI and David Salman from MAPAM wanted to challenge this decision. When Mr. Abramovitch arrived to the ceremony, he was not welcomed. The Histadrut representative noted in his report about the arrival of Mr. Abramovitch: "I barely managed to calm down the many people who were there and avoid bloodshed." This was outrageous, he contended, and concluded by saying, "Please punish."[82] The broad support for the two activists is evidenced by the fact that many residents joined the two when they started protesting. That MAPAI could retaliate by denying residents jobs, food stamps, or firing them from positions, is encapsulated in these two words: "Please punish." In another case, this time in the transit camp of Ijlil (Herzliya), MAPAI held a memorial for the Baghdadi Jews killed in Iraq. MAPAM and MAKI, however, stopped the event, demanding MAPAI address more urgent needs.[83]

Other forms of showing anger at and mistrust of the state were acts of vandalism. Disrespect for public property as well as theft were common in the transit camps; schools, public showers, and offices were convenient targets. Since people were poor and lacked everything from forks to plates to cradles to doors, they stole materials from the camps.[84] State officials interpreted these thefts as acts that were a result of the immoral character of the Iraqis. However, in other cases Iraqi Jews organized to burn or damage public property as a sign of organized resistance; it became a weapon in the political arsenal of the transit-camp residents as Iraqis threatened to burn down tents in order to get housing, and sabotaged the offices of the Histadrut. In 1951, for example, Iraqi residents in the transit camp of Ijlil, who protested the fact that the Jewish Agency built shacks made of cloth instead of wood, destroyed eleven houses made of cloth.[85]

The story "Ha-Kombayn asher hushat" (The Ruined Combine), by David Ben Baruch, celebrated this kind of sabotage, taking as its subject Iraqis who live in a transit camp and work on a farm in the Sharon region. The guard of the farm fears the camp dwellers because they come at night to steal pipes and taps. During the day he values them as cheap laborers; they harvest peanuts for him, for which they are paid based on the weight of the peanuts they collect. In the course of the story, the manager of the farm buys a combine, leaving the people of the camp jobless. In protest, they destroy it. In the story, the act of breaking the piece of machinery by people who were both dependent on the farm and abused by its owners is presented as both surreal and heroic.[86]

Unemployment and humiliating labor conditions were the major driving force behind most demonstrations.[87] Far from being compliant, Iraqis were vocal in expressing their dissatisfaction with the situation. The labor bureaus in each camp were sites of long lines and debates; unemployment generated rage against those in charge; and unemployed workers broke chairs and desks and even attacked employees.[88] Iraqi workers also sent petitions protesting the harsh terms of their employment and demanding permanent jobs. Five hundred men petitioned the prime minister, the chairman of the Knesset, the minister of labor, and the workers council of Petach Tivka concerning their perpetual unemployment and demanding work.[89] Workers in Or Yehuda and Kedma organized a strike to protest the withholding of their wages.[90] Protesters from Khayriyya demanded work and compensation for the unemployed, claiming that the local employment bureau privileged workers from Bney Brak and Tel Aviv over the people from the camp.[91] The unemployed by the moshava of Ramatim came to the offices of the local municipality protesting their conditions and received assurances from the head of the local municipality they would be helped.[92] In the Galilee, workers refused to follow the order from the minister of labor to pick cotton and peanuts, and the Histadrut ordered that they be denied their welfare benefits. Mordechai Namir, the minister of labor, stated that his ministry would not help people who asked for employment but would not take agricultural work; there were means of Hasbara and persuasion, he argued, that could convince them to do the work to which they were assigned.[93]

The distress and frustration pushed Iraqis outside of the transit camps, and led them to demonstrate in the cities nearby their camps. Political parties were very much involved in organizing the protests, especially MAKI and MAPAM. For example, when the people of the transit camp of Ramat ha-Sharon tried to protest the poor water situation in Tel Aviv, MAPAM provided trucks so that the demonstrators could travel to express their dissent in front of the offices of Jewish agency in Tel Aviv; water services were provided, but only after a year.[94]

As in the transit camps, the police broke up protests, often using excessive force. Complaints about police brutality in demonstrations were voiced by the protesters themselves, as well as by Knesset members from opposition parties.[95] The most brutal case was the violent suppression of a protest of four hundred unemployed individuals from the transit camp Kfar Nahman who declared a two-day sit-in in front of the municipal offices of Ra'anana in order to protest their conditions.[96] Similarly, when Iraqi Jews from the transit camps close to Ramat Gan organized a protest in the city to dispute the fact that they were once more denied permanent housing, the police responded harshly. The Iraqis gathered in the local synagogue and brought with them a loud speaker to address the public. The police tried to stop them from proceeding from the synagogue, and yet when the negotiations with the people of the transit camps failed, the police arrested five Iraqis. When riots continued, fourteen- and fifteen-year old teens were beaten by its police forces.[97]

As we have seen, many municipalities refused to include the transit camps in their jurisdiction and provide the migrants with social services. Iraqi Jews marched to many towns and moshavot, such as Herzliya, Holon, Ra'anana, Ness Ziona, Rishon le-Zion, Natanyia, Binyamina, and Kfar Saba, Beit Shaan, Bney Brak, and Ramat ha-Sharon, from their transit camps, blocking roads and demanding that the municipalities recognize that the transit camps were found in their jurisdiction and provide them with services, especially water services.[98] Nearly every town, moshava, or city in whose vicinity a transit camp was built witnessed such demonstrations. At times, the demonstrations followed a tragedy that occurred in a camp. In Holon, a delegation of protestors from the nearby transit camp, stood in silent commemoration of the death of the baby who was burned alive when her shack caught fire.[99] On other occasions, the people of Holon were not as quiet; thousands demonstrated in the transit camp demanding wooden shacks and permanent housing. The location of other protests also relied on the ingenuity of the residents. When the residents of Ramat ha-Sharon transit camp had no water for three days, they found an innovative way to deal with the challenge. They heard that General Moshe Dayan lived in the nearby neighborhood of Tzahala and demonstrated in front of his home. The order to fix the water situation was quick to arrive.[100]

The three big cities of Israel—Jerusalem, Haifa, and Tel Aviv—were important to Iraqi demonstrators who aimed to meet with officials from the Jewish Agency and the state's executive and legislative powers. Demonstrations in Jerusalem were more difficult to arrange, because it was difficult to travel from the center and the north to the capital. In August 1950 representatives from the transit camps (mostly identified with communist and other leftist organizations) demanded work, allocation of more benefits, free medication, and the improvement of sanitation in the camps. They also complained that they got food poisoning from bad food, and that the bread rations were insufficient. Whoever asked for more bread was beaten up. *Kol ha-'Am* reported on the conversation that ensued between the delegation members and the chairman of the Knesset, Yosef Sprinzak said, "Whoever was beaten, let them come to me"; to which a delegation member replied: "Should we bring all of them at once?"[101] The comments of the chairman, expressing disbelief that man could be beaten up because he demanded bread, were met with the member's quick retort that the situation was far more desperate than the chairman could imagine. In 1953, after several delegations of different transit camps had already protested in the Knesset,[102] Iraqi Jews representing the transit camps of Petach Tikva, Sakiyya, Khayriyya, Ramat ha-Sharon, Kfar 'Ana, Kfar Ono, Tel Mond, Talpiot, Makor Haim, Kadima, and Beit Lid demonstrated in the Knesset. This was an important achievement, as they depicted their lives in the camps and met with members of the opposition parties.[103]

The city of Tel Aviv was relatively close to many of the transit camps of central Israel, and thus Iraqis traveled there to protest. The striking of a resident of the camp by a director of the labor bureau triggered a demonstration in this location involving hundreds of Iraqis from the camp of Sakiyya in front of the offices of the Jewish Agency in Tel Aviv. The newcomers put forth demands for employment and a school in the camp, but also carried signs that criticized the bureaucracy for allowing them to suffer them.[104] The people of transit camp of Nahlat Yehuda who protested in front of the building of the Jewish Agency sat in the road in a circle and refused to leave until their demands for better housing were met; the police were brutal in their removal of the protesters.[105] In still another case, people from the transit camp of Be'er Ya'aqov came to the offices of the agency to protest the unexpected and excessively high fee they were being asked to pay for some long-promised wooden shacks that were finally being constructed.

In August 1952, three hundred people from the Rehovot transit camp staged a sit-in in front of the offices of the Jewish Agency in Tel Aviv, demanding that their tents be replaced with wooden shacks. They brought Torah scrolls as a sign of the protesters' religiosity and began a hunger strike, demanding employment. Seventy-three Israeli liras were collected from various transit camps to provide for the families of the strikers, and residents of the transit camps around Tel Aviv brought food to the families of the strikers; in Hadera, Iraqi Jews protested in sympathy with the strikers. Members of the Association of Babylonian Jewry finally intervened to bring about a resolution to the protest, which had galvanized the Iraqi-Jewish population across Israel.[106]

Adding to the challenges faced by the demonstrators was the hostility of the mainstream press toward them. The newspaper *Ha-Boker* reported in a dismissive fashion on the hunger strike and a sit-in:

> The denizens of the transit camp of Rehovot have stopped their sit-in by the building of the [Jewish] agency. The war with the authorities is over. The brigade of strikers with the Torah scrolls at its head has evacuated the *occupied territory* in the street of Nahlat Binyamin and returned home. Some settlement was achieved and the dwellers of the tents were kind enough to go back to their new shacks.... The incident will soon be forgotten, and tomorrow there will be an opportunity for people from another transit camp to demonstrate their willingness to die for some other stupid cause.
>
> We have become accustomed to the sight of newcomers in the streets of cities and towns, and we have become accustomed to such a degree that we pay no attention to the reasons for it. Indeed, we did not expect that newcomers from backward countries would become model citizens in the short period of a year or two.[107]

In the report, the sit-in and the hunger strike are depicted in military language as the occupation of an urban space. Moreover, the reporter assumes that the right to use the democratic tool of public protest is reserved for those who truly understand what democracy is, not for people from "primitive countries" who might embarrass the nation. A reporter for *Davar* continued this line of thinking. He reminded readers that such "noise" was made by the people of the camps during the period of rains. It also noted that when the people of the transit camp were offered the chance to move to another place, they had refused: "What is this about the place that makes people want to sacrifice themselves for its sake?"[108]

K. Shabtai, wrote to a number of newspapers, including MAPAI's *Davar*, was far more understanding:

> I know that I shall not gain any glory by adopting this line: to be the one that speaks out against all those who criminalize others; to speak in favor of these "evil Iraqis" from the transit camp of Rehovot who orchestrated their strike a few days ago at the gates of the Jewish agency in Tel Aviv. There are, among us, those who are willing to defend the Yemenites, for they speak Hebrew and know the Psalms and the Midrash; on normal days we are willing to hear a good word about these Moroccans. But to come and to say that justice is not with us, the Ashkenazim, the Yishuv, the Jewish Agency, but with them, with these Iraqis who protest—horrible![109]

Shabtai explained that Iraqi Jews were accused of being communists or black-market swindlers, but that in fact, they worked on behalf of all the people in the transit camps, including the Romanians (who were even more radical than the Iraqis), the Poles, the Libyan Jews from Tripoli, the Yemenis, and the Iranians. All they wanted, Shabtai said in conclusion, was simply not to be removed to a place remote from where they had lived and worked. Shabtai's story echoed many of the stereotypes current at the time, for example, that the Yemenites were a naïve and agreeable people, whereas the Iraqis were spoiled and rebellious. In this story, however, the use of the democratic tool of the demonstration is represented in a positive light as an act that serves the entire population, Ashkenazi and Mizrahi alike.

Other demonstrations occurred elsewhere in Tel Aviv. Nine hundred women, mostly from the transit camp of Ramat ha-Sharon, demonstrated in front of the Ministry of Health requesting a doctor, a nurse, and a midwife for the camp.[110] A delegation from the same camp also staged a demonstration in Tel Aviv demanding employment.[111]

Some of the protests were very theatrical in nature and included artifacts and careful staging of the marches and the sit-ins; loudspeakers, Torah scrolls, and actual bodies were brought to the scene. The people of the transit camp of Rehovot carried the corpse of a seventy-five-year-old woman whom the religious burial services refused to bury until a payment of thirty liras was received at their office.[112] During the great floods in 1951 Iraqis from Khayriyya stood in front of the Jewish Agency in Tel Aviv, demanding wooden shacks instead of their tents. They brandished a torn tent and a sign that read: "We are in Israel and these are our houses. If we stay in these houses we will be corpses."[113] The poor quality of the drinking water in the transit camps was a major concern. In Sakiyya, Iraqis had to drink brown water, which they nicknamed "Coca-Cola."[114] In response, demonstrators from Sakiyya brought with them bottles of the camp water and carried signs saying, "This is the water we drink!"[115]

Most of the demonstrations were Iraqi in nature; they took place in transit camps populated mostly by Iraqis and were organized by Iraqi activists, many of whom belonged to MAKI. The members of the 1953 delegation to the Knesset were almost exclusively Iraqis, and Iraqi Jews wrote short stories and novels about these rallies and riots, and depicted such protests in their memoirs. During the 1950s, Israel witnessed other demonstrations which were organized by newcomers from specific Middle Eastern countries; Iranian Jews, Libyan Jews, and Indian Jews; all strove for the members of their communities, by protesting and demonstrating.[116] In other demonstrations, however, the Iraqis were joined by Ashkenazim and other Mizrahim. But as the number of protests grew, a sense of Mizrahi combativeness tied Iraqis with brethren from other Middle Eastern countries, as evidenced by their response of the protests of the Yemenite Jews. On 25 October 1952, a few Yemenite Jews from the transit camp of 'Emek Hefer (Valley of Hefer) attacked a guard who had severely beaten a Yemenite woman. On the next day, the 26th, the camps' people drove out about twenty-five policemen who came to arrests the offenders. Then, two hundred policemen came and arrested 105 people from the camp. On the very same day, 150 residents from the mostly Iraqi transit camp of Kfar Saba declared a strike and staged a sit-in for twenty-four hours, demanding housing solutions. They were met with the representatives of the municipal council the following day. The same twenty-four hours witnessed the demonstrations of the people of Khayriyya, who threw stones in the camp and smashed public property, in protest of a plan to settle them in a space that had no running water or connection to the electricity grid. Demonstrations also took place in the transit camps of Rehovot, Sakiyya, Tira, and as well as in two other camps populated mostly by Yemenites and Indians. A whole country rioted for two days, as transit-camp dwellers demanded housing, labor, and water.[117] There was nothing new about the protests in Kfar Saba, Khayriyya, and Sakiyya; the demands of the protesters were made in the past, and the tactics of sit-ins and road blockage were employed before. But the scope of the demonstrations, even if uncoordinated, showed that the pains of the Iraqis were shared by many individuals throughout Israel.

These battles on behalf of labor and civil rights, then, colored the political landscape of Israel during the 1950s. They started as individual protests in public offices where frustrated Iraqis broke the public order or staged individualized sit-ins. Recovering from the initial shock of migration, Iraqis began to organize in the transit camps, challenging their unfair housing and labor conditions and perpetual unemployment. Officials complained that the main reason for the demonstrations, protests, and riots was incitement. Such statements naturally ignored the protesters' own agency and pain. However, political parties were very interested in the protests, an interest that increased when the demonstrators left their transit camps and gathered in the municipal councils of the moshavot close to their camps, and, later, when these battles were waged in the larger cities of the country. MAPAI tried to crush the demonstrations, using police power, while MAKI, HERUT, and MAPAM encouraged them. MAKI and Herut in particular circulated dozens of leaflets, sometimes in extremely colorful language, calling people to protest publicly, and reminding Iraqi Jews and other denizens in the transit camps that supporters of MAPAI, their children, and even their pets, received every possible benefit in the state, while the residents of transit camps and poor neighborhoods rotted in shacks and tents and suffered from hunger and humiliation. The activists of political parties, especially the communist Iraqis, stood by the protesters, demonstrated with them, and suffered from the police reaction. The large number of protests and the fact that they brought many Mizrahim together indicate that the residents of these camps believed that they were part of a system, and that the sufferings of the people of Khayriyya were connected to the sufferings of those who resided in Ramat ha-Sharon, Holon, or 'Emek Hefer. Indeed, demonstrations took place concurrently in several transit camps; individuals protested on behalf of Iraqis who lived in camps very distant from their own; residents in one transit camp collected donations on behalf of demonstrators from another; delegations to the Knesset represented a few camps; and in some cases, a whole camp was engaged in a strike: children did not go to school and workers stayed home.[118] Disillusioned by the promises of the Jewish Agency, MAPAI, and the state, fearful of winters, and yearning to be treated as equal citizens, these courageous Iraqi Jews felt that they had nothing to lose and much to gain.

ETHEL AND JULIUS ROSENBERG IN SAKIYYA

I end this chapter with a case study of one resident's attempt to challenge the transit camps' system of governance. In the summer of 1953, a teacher by the name of Yigal (Naji) Eliyahu was angered by the impeding execution of Jewish communists, Ethel and Julius Rosenberg, accursed of espionage. Today, we know much more about the procedures of the trial, the innocence of Ethel, who was framed by her brother, and the American politics that pushed for the execution. But even then, beyond the screen of McCarthyism and disinformation, it was clear to many Israelis that something terribly wrong had happened in the United States. Pro-Soviet and leftist Israeli circles took an interest in the case; it seemed to them a sign of American anti-Semitism. They were sharply critical of the Israeli government for doing very little on behalf of the Rosenbergs. Sasson Somekh published a moving poem in *Al-Ittihad* dedicated to the couple, the speakers of which were the two sons of the Rosenbergs. Even the religious paper *Ha-Tzofeh* covered the case, providing heartbreaking depictions of the rabbi marching ahead of the Rosenbergs, reading verses from the Psalms, as the couple was about to be executed in the electric chair. The couple's letters to their children were translated into Hebrew and appeared in an Israeli edition shortly after their publication in English.[119]

Eliyahu was moved. A leftist with close ties to both communist and MAPAM circles, he turned to his fellow teachers and convinced them to sign a petition condemning the execution of the Rosenbergs. It was addressed to President Eisenhower, and appeared in MAKI's newspaper *Kol ha-'Am*. News of the matter got the school's director, who summoned Eliyahu to his office. In his defense, Eliyahu said that the petition expressed a universal human concern, not a political point of view. Later, however, he admitted that there was a political element to it. The teachers who had signed the petition were quick to repudiate their involvement. In the investigation of the case, one teacher, Hannah Leibovitch, said she had signed it in a rush. Avraham Salman, Sha'ul Mosheh, and Na'im Dallal defended themselves by saying that they were educating the future soldiers of the nation and the motherland. Some testified that Eliyahu told them he would send their petition only to President Eisenhower, not to the Israeli communist press. They also revealed that Yigal Eliyahu followed the teachings of Moshe Sneh; that Eliyahu had directed his students to attend activities of MAPAM's youth movement, Ha-Shomer ha-Tza'ir; and that his brother, Haim, led informal classes on leftist ideology outside of school.[120]

In the investigation by the teachers union (affiliated with the Histadrut), Eliyahu admitted that he had convinced his fellow teachers to sign the letters, but not during instructional time. Eliyahu contended that the letters sent by the teachers as testimony against him were written under the pressure of the school's director, though the latter denied this. Eliyahu admitted that he followed the thinking of Moshe Sneh, but added that his politics were not related to any political party. Eliyahu was so angry he sent a notice to his fellow teachers in the transit camps, accusing them of libel. In an article he published in the journal *Smol* (Left), "What Is Right and What Is Wrong in the Transit Camp of Sakiyya," he pointed out that the political organizations of the left could not hold public meetings in the camp, while MAPAI meetings could not be disturbed. Furthermore, a teacher in the camp could not work for the sake of a political ideal. Yet other teachers were permitted to gather students in the Histadrut club and push them to an anticommunist and antileftist agenda. That said, in his statement to the investigation board of the Ministry of Education, he repeated his earlier statement that humane motivations were behind his actions. Albert Einstein and other European and American scientists and intellectuals, he explained, had supported the Rosenbergs, as did every educated person with a conscience. His letter, he reminded the board, was addressed to Eisenhower, and was meant to promote peace and justice. He was a victim here, he alleged, as his reputation had been tarnished and he was the one who should be suing the school. The political nature of the investigation became apparent when Eliyahu repeated his argument that the pope and Albert Einstein and other leading intellectuals had pleaded for clemency for the couple, to which Y. Geffen of the Histadrut's teachers' union responded, "Let them then publish their petitions in the press of the [Israeli] left."[121]

Eliyahu did use his position for political ends, although at the time, many in his surroundings wrote in support of the Rosenbergs. On the other hand, his actions did not merit the very politicized and hysterical reaction of the school's director, the Ministry of Education, and the Histadrut teachers' union after realizing that a communist and MAPAM supporter existed in their midst. Many of the letters by Eliyahu's fellow teachers who regretted signing the petition are written in the same handwriting and contain identical content. I assume someone composed the original, and then made the teachers sign individual copies. The teachers, probably worried for their own livelihood, were now made to sign a letter not about communists in the United States but about a fellow teacher in Israel. Moreover, an analysis of the investigation shows that Eliyahu's crime was not only that he had used the petition to promote his political ideas in the school, but also that he published his ideas in the wrong newspaper and was a supporter of the wrong parties. In a way, the system itself was far more politicized than the socialist teacher, and its control of the school—from the teachers to the director to the supervisors—is made evident by the case.

The fact that such a minor affair could become such a scandal illustrates how important it was for the system to have the denizens of the camp in line with MAPAI's political vision, and how easy it was to put pressure on fellow Iraqis, who feared unemployment, as a punishment for "unacceptable" political activity. On the other hand, it shows that space for political activities existed, even under such repressive conditions. The press was one such venue. Eliyahu made use of newspapers twice: first, when he published the petition, and second, when he protested his own employment conditions and the politicization of public life in the camp. The state might attempt to silence a dissident voice, but he could still complain and publish in the communist and socialist press. Holding a public position, in this case that of teacher, enabled Eliyahu and activists like him to reach a wider audience: they talked to the students about politics after class (like Eliyahu's brother, who organized activities after school); they composed petitions to be sent to government officials; and they wrote letters within the camp (such as those that Eliyahu sent to his fellow teachers). In addition, activists like Eliyahu relied on personal networks for support, especially family, when siblings and married partners shared their views. Finally, it was vital to Eliyahu to insist, even as he was about to be fired, that the system in which he taught was characterized by malevolent politicization, and that he, as a citizen, had the right to speak his mind.

CONCLUSION

The demonstrations, petitions, and local organizations of Iraqi Jews were simultaneously Iraqi, Israeli, and Mizrahi. They were Iraqi protests because many of the participants in them were Iraqis and identified as such (as well being identified by the press and by state officials). More importantly, some demonstrators utilized skills they had developed in Iraq for taking political action, which included organizing a local committee, writing petitions (often in Arabic), and mobilizing people for demonstrations. It was not a coincidence that Iraqi Jews were well versed in these tactics, as just prior to their arrival in Israel they had witnessed and participated in the Wathba. The Wathba refers to the mass wave of protests that engulfed Baghdad in the winter of 1948, demanding an end to the state's pro-British policies and a domestic agenda based on social justice. Many Jews participated in these events. One could say that Iraqi Jews brought the spirit of the Wathba with them to Israel.[122]

The demonstrations were also Israeli. The Israeli political scene of the 1950s was marked by waves of demonstrations. Those against the reparations agreement with Germany in 1952 were the most dramatic; others were organized by veterans, disabled people, Haredi men (especially in Jerusalem), and housewives protesting the austerity measures. During the 1940s, most protests were directed against the British mandate; after 1948, the State of Israel became the target. Iraqi Jews, no strangers to this form of political expression, were quick to make their voices heard as Israelis. While Iraqi Jews might have missed Iraq

FIGURE 5. Leaving the transit camp; a woman packing. Source: CZA, NKH\404364. Reprinted with permission.

terribly, cursing the moment they left it, they utilized the discourse of the state, representing themselves as citizens and patriots who deserved the same rights as those granted to the rest of the population. At times, they were desperate and their desperation led them to protest violently; they had nothing to lose. But the petitions and the public demonstrations show that Iraqi Israelis were fully aware that their civil rights were being violated, and they demanded a change.

The communist press eagerly reported on these events, by way of challenging MAPAI, but these mass movements did not only depend on the communists. There was also something Jewish about these protests. The people of the Rehovot transit camps brought Torah scrolls to protests; other Iraqi Jews petitioned to build synagogues in the transit camps where they resided; and some Iraqi Jews even wondered how bureaucrats and the policemen, their fellow Jews, could be so cruel. The fact that they were Jewish enabled the Iraqis to protest more vigorously than the Palestinians. The latter were not even allowed to hold public demonstrations, and supervision of their political affairs was in the hands of the army and the police.

Finally, these elements of resistance were Mizrahi. Many of the petitions and the letters mention that the protesters were treated badly by the police and denied housing and benefits, not only because they were poor migrants, but also because their community of origin was Middle Eastern and Arab. Joined in their protests by Jewish immigrants from elsewhere in the Middle East, Mizrahi activism was dismissed in the press as nothing more than antisocial behavior typical of the "backward countries" from which they came. Yet by constantly reminding the Israeli state of its commitment to its citizens and by insisting that they were not just human material to be utilized to populate deserted border towns and to fight Israel's demographic battles, these Iraqi protesters helped move Israeli democracy forward.

5 ISRAELI BABYLONIANS

IN 1954 a very angry Ephraim Matzliah wrote a letter to the director of the national radio station, the Voice of Israel (Kol Yisraèl). On the evening of the holiday of Simhat Torah, thirty Iraqi men had gathered to hear an hour-long radio show that was supposed to broadcast prayers of all the communities of Israel. However, Matzliah complained, the Ashkenazi prayers lasted 41.5 minutes, and a mere 1.2 minutes were allotted to prayers chanted in the Baghdadi style: "Do you take us for fools? Why did you publicize . . . that a Baghdadi band was playing only to broadcast one percent of a song? . . . By what right do you Ashkenazim, whose entire chant consists of a single word: la, la, la, la, get to have 41 minutes allotted to you?" It amounted to "vicious discrimination."[1]

This story reflects Matzliah's keen sense of discrimination based on ethnic considerations. The prayer he desires is an Iraqi one. He identifies a prominent state institution, the national radio station, as Ashkenazi, on the basis of the audience it has clearly targeted. And, importantly, he feels that as an Israeli citizen he has a right that the radio serve the needs of his community.

This story points up three salient identities of the Iraqi-Jewish community that emerged during the 1950s and 1960s in Israel. The first is Iraqi. Sitting in isolated camps, speaking an Iraqi dialect of Arabic, and feeling neglected by the state, Iraq became the Promised Land for many Iraqi Jews; they lamented the loss of cultural inclusion they had experienced there. The second was Arab Jewish. Iraqi-Jewish intellectuals continued writing about Arab affairs, as they had done in Iraq, and communicated in Arabic with other Arabic-speaking members of the Israeli community. Their mastery of Arabic and knowledge of Arabic literature made them very valuable to the Israeli state, particularly as teachers and translators. The third was Mizrahi, an identity shaped within Israel, through the struggle against Ashkenazi hegemony. It was a particular kind of Israeli identity that connected Iraqi Jews to other non-European Jewish groups in Israeli society, those categorized as members of the communities of the East, like the Egyptians, Moroccans, Tunisians, Iranians, Turks, and Syrians.

While these identities were being formed, the Palestinian population of Israel was living under a military regime. Given the hatred that Iraqi Jews felt toward the Israeli establishment, it was conceivable that the two populations could cooperate with one another, and this did occur to a limited extent. From small-scale trade in smuggled goods in the markets from Israel's borders to collaborative activity in the communist party, this collaboration united speakers of Arabic. But living in Israel also set Jews from Iraq against the Palestinians. Iraqi Jews harbored a deep hatred for the Arab radical nationalists who had helped to drive them out of Iraq, a hatred that had led to the emergence of a Zionist underground in Iraq. The Israeli state for its part widened the divide between Iraqi Jews and the Palestinians, by using the former as key elements of the management of the latter. The state needed Arabic speakers, who could staff Israeli mechanisms of security, education, and propaganda in the Arab sector. Working for these state institutions was, for Iraqis, a way out of poverty, a way to gain respectability in Israeli society, and, indeed, a way to gain a sense that they were serving their new nation.

The intertwining of the Iraqi, Mizrahi, and Arab identities, and the complex relationships with the Arabs and the Palestinians, generated processes that created the Israeli Iraqis (Israelis of Iraqi descent), who were very critical of the Israeli Ashkenazi establishment and yet considered themselves Israeli citizens.

A LOST PARADISE: IRAQI IDENTITY

The Iraqi identity of the newcomers survived in the transit camps and cities and was especially pronounced in the early 1950s. Iraqi Jews dressed in Iraqi clothes, spoke in the Iraqi dialect, and listened to Iraqi music. Because the Iraqis were settled in large groups in remote places, such as transit camps, they were isolated during this time from mainstream Israeli society and culture. Yet this Iraqi identity also endured in cities like Ramat Gan and Or Yehuda, and in neighborhoods where Iraqi newcomers resided, like Ha-Tikva in Tel Aviv. In a parallel phenomenon, the Kurdish identity of Jews from Northern Iraq persisted in the transit camps and distant moshavim to which the Kurds were sent.

David Kazzaz, an Iraqi Jew who was trained as a medical doctor at the American University in Beirut and lived in Tel Aviv in the early 1950s, describes how the decision makers, mostly of European origins, were "too obtuse to feel the humanity of the Iraqis."[2] He further explains:

> In the State of Israel I have seen, for the first time in my life, a universe where Jews hate Jews. German Jews, Polish Jews, Romanian Jews, Russian Jews, Iraqi Jews, Yemenite Jews, Sephardi Jews, Ashkenazi Jews, were all deprived of their identity, discriminated against, and hated in some way. . . . It was obvious to everybody that discrimination was a barrier one had to overcome if one needed something from someone, individually or officially. And everybody knew that those with power favored their own kind.[3]

According to Kazzaz, those with power were Eastern and Central European Jews. These ethnic ties mattered when it came to finding a job, being promoted—and even when buying something special in a grocery store.[4]

The Iraqi identity, however, was not only the result of the European / Middle Eastern divide. The Iraqi culture of the Iraqi-Jewish middle and upper classes was profoundly Western, as the Iraqi-Jewish youth were educated in bilingual schools and many graduates of the Iraqi education system read works of Western literature. Communists like Sami Michael and Shim'on Ballas took pride in their rich knowledge of global and leftist literature. The Israeli Iraqi identity, therefore, also emerged when it conflicted with other Middle Eastern identities in Israel. In the transit camp in Tiberias, for example, Jews from Mosul and 'Aqra clashed on occasion. The Arabized Mosuli Jews, according to press reports, felt superior to the latter, who spoke Aramaic, and feelings ran so high that physical confrontations ensued.[5] From the deserted Palestinian village of Lifta, which the state tried to resettle with Kurdish and Yemenite Jews, the latter sent a letter to Ben Gurion in 1952, complaining that the former, whom they described as thieves and murders, were terrorizing them.[6] In the transit camps of Amisav, Iraqi Jews clashed with Iranian Jews, who claimed the Iraqis were favored by the municipal administration of Petach Tikva.[7]

Some of the differences between Jewish migrants from Arab countries were linguistic. Arabic is a language typified by diglossia, in which a formal form is written in all parts of the Arab world and understood by its educated and literate populations, and at the same time a variety of dialects exists in many states and regions. Iraqi Jews knew the Egyptian dialect from films and radio shows. Egyptians, Syrians, and Palestinians resided in Iraq, and taught in Jewish and public schools. These dialects were thus recognizable and understood in the transit camps. On the other hand, Iraqis found it difficult to understand North African Jews, and resorted to French in order to communicate with them and with Romanian Jews. Ge'ula Sehayek al-'Ani describes in her autobiographical novel how she learned to speak the Tunisian dialect in the transit camp of Hartuv from the Tunisian women who were her neighbors.[8] Occasionally, the Iraqi dialect represented a barrier to communication between Iraqis and Palestinians. Tikva Agasi, who worked for the Histadrut, hired a Palestine from Jaffa to translate her speeches into the dialect spoken in Palestinian villages so that she would be understood by local women.[9]

In other cases, the differences between different communities of Middle Eastern Jews were not linguistic, but rather were based on class and place of origin. For example, the Iraqi migrant Shoshana Levy married a Yemenite Jew despite the objections of both families. The Iraqis felt the Yemenites were too religious, less urbane, and less educated.[10] Sami Michael recalled: "There is not too much in common between Iraqis and Yemenites. The Iraqis share much more in common culturally with Yekkes (German Jews) than with Yemenites. . . . So are Moroccans and Persians, Egyptians, and Georgians. They have nothing in common but the fact that they are not Ashkenazim. If I make a Yemenite meet an Iraqi, there will be no Mizrahi language that would connect them, as Yiddish connects the European Jews."[11] Iraqi Jews, Michael continues, who had their own transnational networks that extended to China and India, were snobs with respect to other Middle Eastern communities.

Another community with which the Iraqi Jews had a problematic relationship was the Palestinian Sephardi Jews, or what was called in Israel the "pure Sephardim." These included well-established Jewish families who had inhabited Palestine for centuries as well as poor Sephardim. They tried to reach out to Iraqi Jews, especially through the Sephardim Party, but their efforts were met with a certain degree of suspicion. Some Palestinian Sephardim were among the social elite in the new country, and furthermore had been active in the Zionist movement. Nevertheless, since they were discriminated against by the Ashkenazi elites, and differed in their vision of the state from the Ashkenazi Zionists, the Sephardim were willing to acknowledge that Israeli society was characterized by discrimination based on ethnicity.[12] Not all Iraqis, however, trusted the Palestinian Sephardim. There was a feeling among the Iraqis that the Palestinian Sephardim were too cozy with the establishment, while the Palestinian Sephardim for their part sought to distance themselves from the more Arabized migrants.

An article in *Al-Mirsad* exemplifies these tensions. Its author, Ibrahim al-Nashi' ("Ibrahim the writer"), wonders how the rich Sephardim, who were connected to MAPAI, could represent the interests of poor Easterners (*sharqiyun*). In this article, titled "Thoughts on the Conference of the Sephardim," Ibrahim describes how at the end of the conference, the Sephardi leadership called on Jews to migrate to and settle in Israel. However, very few Mizrahi attended the conference; the majority were wealthy Sephardi politicians. Their parties, especially those associated with the Israeli right, wept "crocodile tears" for the Eastern Jews. But there was little in common between the laboring, suffering Eastern Jews, who had recently migrated to the county, and the Sephardim who spoke on their behalf.[13] The article is not so much about Iraqi identity as it is about the splits within the Mizrahi public. The point of view of those who came in the 1950s, and were relegated to lives in transit camps and slums, the article suggests, was very different from that of the Sephardim who had lived in Israel prior to 1948 and sought to represent the newcomers. The Iraqis' life in the transit camps, unemployment, and the experience of being uprooted from an Arab homeland inevitably undercut their solidarity with the Palestinian Sephardim based on a common Mizrahi identity.

Iraqi Jews had good reasons to be suspicious of Sephardi Jews who worked for the establishment, especially MAPAI. On the one hand, the Mizrahim within the establishment helped to place dozens of Iraqi Jews in jobs, fully aware of the discrimination in Israel. On the other hand, officially they repeated the mantras of MAPAI about the success of the Aliyah. Avraham 'Abbas was a Syrian Jew who facilitated the work of many Iraqi and other Mizrahi men and women in the Histadrut, using his influence in the Histradut's Arab division. But when he spoke about the affairs of the Histadrut to his fellow Sephardim abroad, his rosy depictions were no different than those of his Ashkenazi superiors. Consider his words at the Congress of the Global Federation of Sephardi Jews in Paris: "Emissaries and members of the Histadrut guided them [Jewish migrants] before they came to the country. Our newcomers love labor and hard work, although they were not used to it in exile. The merchant, the grocer, and the landlord in exile, in Israel were made into workers. Our comrades work in the field, in the factory, in the village, and in the city. We have succeeded in all our projects!"[14]

The disdain of the Ashkenazi establishment that Iraqi Jews felt, the gulf between them and the other Mizrahi communities, and their bitter lives in the transit camps during the early 1950s spurred some to illegal attempts to return to Iraq. Many wanted to return but could not do so. Iraqi Jews had no passports when they came to Israel, only travel documents issued specifically for their migration to Israel (so they could not travel to other countries). Getting a passport in Israel was not an easy task, and the authorities often refused to issue passports to newcomers. A state of war had existed between Iraq and Israel and going back was impossible.[15] Consequently, Iraq, for the migrants in Israel, was the object of intense nostalgia: they remembered their homes, their businesses, their social prestige, with love and longing. Happiness in Iraq was contrasted with the situation in Israel. A story in *Al-Mirsad* that focused on the lack of good-quality drinking water in the transit camps reported that water was being sold in the transit camps of Kfar 'Ana: "The old men were reminded of the days in which this practice [of selling water] was common in Iraq, decades ago, and now they see it again in Israel, which became, under the rule of MAPAI, the land of wonders and miracles."[16] This story contradicts the Israeli national narrative, which contrasted Iraqi primitivism with Israeli progress. In this story, Iraq is the country in which people had functioning water systems in houses, and Israel, a land where people live in tents and cannot get decent drinking water, is an undeveloped space only old men can make sense of. As Hesqel Hesqel from the transit camp in Kfar Ono wrote, back in Iraq men had employment, now they came home hungry.[17] A woman identified only as Dalia from Khayriyya (many at the time did not write their full name, probably of our fear of government's response) described in Al-Mirsad the hovels in which suffering Iraqis lived in Israel. To depict these huts, she used the word *akwakh* (shacks), a term that describes the dwellings of poor Shi'ites in Baghdad.[18] By using this term, Dalia suggested implicitly that in Israel Iraqi Jews *become* what the poor Shi'ites in Iraq had been. It reflected more broadly the yearning of many Iraqi men, impoverished in Israel, to return to Iraq, where they had enjoyed a much higher standard of living.

These memories stayed with Iraqi Jews after they left the transit camps and improved their living conditions. The memoirs of Tikva Agasi reflect this Iraqi patriotism coexisting alongside an Israeli patriotism:

> I do not know why Abraham, our father, had to leave Aram Naharayim (Mesopotamia), with her abundance of waters and fertile lands, which quite a few people believe to be a paradise, and come to Palestine, a forsaken desert land....
> It does not mean I do not like Jerusalem, whom God sanctified for the Jews. She is sacred to me, and [is] the pearl of all cities of the East, after we had built it. But I would have liked God to leave Abraham in Aram Naharayim, which was in my

opinion, much more convenient for the worship of God, and for the building of a Temple, than [in] a deserted land like Palestine.[19]

In Tikva's story Iraq is a prosperous paradise, while Palestine is a desert. It is God's will that Jews inhabit the latter land, which she accepts, but His decision seems somewhat inexplicable. To Tikva, Iraq was the measure by which to evaluate all things in Israel. When she and other migrants from her transit camp were taken on a trip to the Jordan River, Tikva explained to the tour guide that "the smallest crick coming out of the Tigris or the Euphrates is wider than this river."[20] In her trips around Israel, she made fun of the attempts to find oil in Israel, compared to its abundance in Iraq.[21] On a tour of the palms tree around the Sea of Galilee, she informed the guide that Iraq had over eighteen million palm trees of various kinds.[22] As these anecdotes illustrate, to a middle-class Iraqi like Tikva, Israel's resources seemed all the more meager in light of Iraq's natural riches.

The literary genius whose work is deeply suffused with this sense of Iraqi nostalgia is Samir Naqqash. Born in Iraq in 1938, Naqqash migrated to Israel at the age of thirteen; he and his family were settled in the transit camp of Amisav. His parents applied to the Ministry of Interior for passports so that they could return to Iraq, but their request was denied. His father died two years after their arrival to Israel; after eight years in the Amisav transit camp, the family moved a newly created neighborhood in Petach Tikva. Naqqash's literary writings were solely in Arabic, and incorporated dialogue in colloquial Iraqi. This was a revolutionary decision: he kept alive a dialect used by Baghdadi Jews in the first half of the twentieth century, while writing in the 1970s, 1980s, and the 1990s. By the 1980s Naqqash was famous in the Arab world, with writers like the Egyptian Nobel laureate Nagib Mahfuz praising his writings. And yet he died in 2004, bitter and disappointed.[23]

In his short story "Fi Manzil al-khiraq wa'l 'aja'ib" (In the House of Rags and Wonders), two grieving sisters bemoan the passing of their relative Menashe. Both sisters never married, and they wonder what would have happened had they stayed in Baghdad; one is a former teacher, the other a graduate of Alliance high school. Baghdad was their "fortress," their heaven; and they speak in French to one another to evoke their Iraqi-Francophile past. We learn about Menashe, and hear his voice, and theirs, through their memories. The story's setting, a retirement community, accentuates an ongoing sense of death; its Iraqi inhabitants are depicted as the living dead, who dwell in a land that kills its own people. The narration moves between past and present and is punctuated by the movement of the clock; time is the real enemy of the elderly. Time, in fact, conceptualized in relation to the longing for the Baghdadi past and the slow decay in Israel, is the protagonist of the story. The story is global and extremely local at the same time. It takes place in Israel, but very few Israelis, Jews or Palestinians, can fully understand its historical references to events in Iraq during the first half of the twentieth century, and its interpolations of the Jewish Iraqi dialect, peppered in Ottoman Turkish words. The sisters in the story are very Iraqi, but also very Chekhovian (unmarried women recalling their potential pasts, presents, and futures appear in many of his plays); the time is Israeli and Iraqi, but also Shakespearean (see especially Sonnet 12). Yet, significantly, Naqqash's language and allusions could be understood only by Iraqi Jews of his generation, who shared this history.[24]

Naqqash's short story "Laylat 'araba" (The Night of the Willow) also deals with memories from Iraq. It takes place during Sukkot, as the protagonists remember how the Muslims used to visit them during the holiday and describe in detail the Iraqi-Jewish way of celebrating it. Iraq is their promised land, as they bemoan its loss and the disappearance of its Arab-Jewish culture. They likewise remember their friends from Iraq who now lived in the transit camps, like Salim, a famous 'ud player in Iraq, who became a poor garbage collector and lived in poverty in the Ha-Tikva neighborhood in Tel Aviv. He broke his 'ud, in fact, out of anguish and anger and married an insane woman. His Iraqi friends wonder if he is still alive. Death is very much alive in the minds of the protagonists of this story, manifested in the lighting of candles in memory of the dead during the holiday. As in the previous story, Israel symbolizes a space of decline for people who are about to die. Baghdad, and Iraq more generally, is the land of the living, the land of music—the land to which its Jewish sons yearn to return, but cannot.[25]

Not all Iraqi Jews were as radical as Naqqash. More commonly, the Iraqi background served as a basis on which to organize and offer mutual help. Iraqi Jews formed a number of groups and clubs in Israel, the most active of which was the Association of Aram Naharayim. Its membership included more established Iraqi Jews who had migrated to Palestine during the mandate era. "Aram Naharayim" was the Hebrew name for Mesopotamia in biblical times, the land from which Abraham came to Canaan. The group's members also referred to their old homeland as "Babylon," an expression that has remained extremely popular in Israel to this very day. These biblical names accentuated the ancient nature of this Jewish community, whose first members had come to Mesopotamia after the destruction of the First Temple in Jerusalem, and the fact that this community was responsible for assembling one of the most formidable works of Jewish law, the Babylonian Talmud. At the same time, the name Babylon distanced Jews from the negative connotations of "Iraq," an enemy Arab state.

The Association of Aram Naharayim was well aware that they were discriminated against like other Middle Eastern Jews, but chose to focus on the needs of Iraqis in particular. The group's aims were to represent the community in a positive light to the Israeli public and to have Iraqis elected to municipal posts, the Knesset, and the Histadrut.[26] In September 1950 the association, which counted Yehezekel Sofer (editor of the *Journal of The Youth of Aram Naharayim*), historian Avraham Ben Ya'aqov, and Benjamin Silas Sasson among its members, called on Iraqi Jews who had come to Israel before that year to help the newcomers find work and housing and teach them Hebrew. In fact, they wondered why the state had not asked more-established Iraqi Jews to help with the settlement of their new brothers.[27] Iraqi migrants wrote to the group's paper and expressed their frustration as Iraqis, complaining that the bureaucrats in Israel "did not understand the soul of the Iraqi Jew."[28]

Iraqi Jews also operated as a bloc within and across political parties. Both MAKI and MAPAI had special sections consisting of Iraqi Jews. In 1959, sixty Iraqi members of all political parties met in Ramat Gan to call for unity, map out a plan for battling discrimination against the Mizrahim, improve the image of the community, and strategize about how to attain fair representation in both political and nonpartisan institutions. The members of MAPAI, 'Ezra Gabbai and Nissim 'Ezra, admitted in this meeting that their own party discriminated against their community.[29]

The most important venue for writing about Iraq, its history, its present, and its significance to Iraqi Jews in Israel, was the leftist press. The communists in particular wanted to stress that Israel, a land that lauded itself as an island of democracy and progress in a sea of Middle Eastern oppression, did no better in the treatment of minority groups than Iraq did. Whereas the state consciously underscored the differences between Iraq and Israel, the former being a space of exile and the latter a homeland, the pamphlets and publications of MAPAM and especially MAKI suggested no such distinction could be made. Moreover, the prominence of Iraqi Jews in Iraqi leftist movements was seen as a model for the Israeli left.

The Iraqis of MAKI identified any attempt to create a state based on ethnicity with the right-wing elements that had engaged in anti-Semitic campaigns in their old homeland. Consequently, they took a critical position toward another form of ethnic nationalism, Zionism, in Israel. A pamphlet signed by Iraqi-Jewish communists Eliyahu ʿEzer, Yaʿaqub and Albert Qujman, Hesqel (Yehezkel) Sadiq (the brother of the Jewish communist Yehudah Sadiq, who had been executed in Iraq in 1949), poet David Semah, and journalist Shimʿon Ballas (under the pen name "al-Adib al-qass") urged their fellow countrymen to vote MAKI for these reasons.³⁰ They pointed out that the Iraqi Community Party (ICP; Al-Hizb al-Shuyuʿi al-ʿIraqi) struggled against fascism and did not pay any heed to anti-Jewish sentiment. Those who had called themselves patriots in Iraq had accused the communists of being traitors. This happened in Israel as well: MAKI was condemned for collaborating with the Arabs because it struggled against ethnic nationalism.³¹ Not only Iraqis, but also Palestinians, used the memory of the Iraqi past to convince Iraqis to support MAKI. Emile Habibi wrote favorably about the ICP and the heroism of its members.³²

In a MAKI pamphlet addressed to the workers in Holon, the author noted that "we did not struggle against the enemies of the people in Iraq to bow our heads in Israel."³³ Iraqi-Jewish communists and members of MAPAM went even further, drawing comparisons between Iraq and Israel in various political domains. Elihayu ʿEzer, the editor of the journal *Sarkhat al-Maʿabarot*, compared the paramilitary Israeli organization, the GADNA, to *Al-Futtuwa*, a paramilitary youth movement in Iraq, established by profascist elites in the 1930s. He depicted the GADNA as fostering a "military spirit," a term taken from the arsenal of metaphors used by profascist elites in Iraq during the 1930s. By linking such policies to the IDF the journal insinuated that there was no difference between right-wing parties in Iraq and the governing body in Israel.³⁴

The parallels between Israel and Iraq were also drawn in the context of the anti-Herut campaigns run by MAPAM and MAKI. Herut was likened to the right-wing, antidemocratic Al-Istiqlal (Independence) party in Iraq, and to nationalist Iraqis who had persecuted Iraqi Jews. The journal *Sawt al-Maʿabarot* (The Voice of the Transit Camps), edited by Yaʿaqub Qujman, compared Hertu's leader Menachem Begin to the leader of Al-Istiqlal, Muhammad Mahdi Kubba. In a story titled "Muhammad Mahdi Kubba Cares for the Denizens of the Transit Camps" the author wrote that "it is no coincidence that the leaders of the fascists in Israel, Muhammad Mahdi Kubba, sorry, Menachem Begin, tours the transit camps in the service of American dollars."³⁵

Iraqi-Jewish communists drew on their experiences in Iraq in making the case for their potential as members of MAKI. Letters written in Arabic by Iraqis who wished to join the party, such as Eliyahu Cohen and Avraham Cohen, noted that they had been persecuted by the Iraqi regime for their ICP activities as a way of establishing their communist credentials.[36] Iraqi-Jewish communists continued to follow the Iraqi press so that they could inform readers, Ashkenazi and Iraqi alike, about the situation in Iraq. A story published in *Kol ha-'Am* in 1950 about the abuse of rights of political prisoners included references to stories published in Iraqi newspapers, such as the paper of the social democrats, *Sada al-Ahali*, and the ICP paper *Al-Qa'ida*. A story on the notorious prison of Nuqrat al-Salman noted that "our reporter in Baghdad" was the source of details about the event, indicating that by November 1950, there were connections between communists in the two countries.[37] During the 1950s, *Kol ha-'Am* reported on Nuri al-Sa'id's campaigns against the communists in the broader context of the persecution of the left in Arab states, the history of the ICP from its establishment to the execution of its leaders, and the 1952 mass demonstrations against the regime (known as the intifada).[38]

For many Iraqi leftists, the Wathba, the series of demonstrations in the winter of 1948 against the Iraqi regime's pro-British policies and social conservatism, was the example par excellence of a successful battle of both Jews and Arabs against the state. MAPAM's Arabic journal *Ila al-Amam* commemorated this event. MAPAM activist David Cohen wrote that when he was a prisoner in Iraq, he saw the day of the Wathba as a great day for Iraqi independence. We, the Jews, he added, were a minority in Iraq, but we stood with the Iraqi people, and even today we send the Iraqis our greetings. His hope was that in the next commemoration of the Wathba, peace would prevail between Jews and Arabs.[39] MAPAM's *Al-Mirsad* featured articles that praised the left in Iraq, wrote about Iraqi communist prisoners, and emphasized the Iraqis' desire for peace.[40] Similarly, the Israeli communist cultural magazine *Al-Jadid* ran a story about a poetry reading that the communists held in Haifa to commemorate the Wathba and published David Semah's poem "Al-Wathba al-ula" (The First Wathba), in which the speaker yearns for a second Wathba, and more broadly, for a revolution in the Middle East.[41] In the poem, the speaker pledges his love for Baghdad, swearing that he could and should not forget his childhood, the landscape of his country, his old house, and his dear friends. He sends his greetings to his city and its revolutionary people, yearning that its slaves be liberated. Semah had already attempted to publish poems in Baghdad in honor of the martyrs of the Wathba, but was dissuaded from doing so by the leadership of the Jewish community. In Israel, however, thanks to the communist Arabic press, he was able, not only to get a poem published that called for a revolution in Iraq (and implicitly in Israel), but also to express what was an absolute taboo in the mainstream Israeli press, his longing for his old homeland, Iraq.[42]

To provide evidence of the desire of the Iraqi people for peace, a young intellectual, Sasson Somekh, translated a poem by the Iraqi leftist poet Muhammad Salih Bahr al-'Ulum, which appeared as a MAKI pamphlet in 1955. The poet resided in Iraq and dedicated his words to communists in Israel. The poem spoke of the friendship between the two nations whose peoples are being tortured by tyrants who despise freedom and whose regimes are founded on war. Yet both people should struggle for a common future, lest darkness prevail:[43]

> People of Israel, we are brothers,
> Two ancient nations,
> Whose hearts are intertwined,
> In the fields of love we blossomed,
> Like roses in the spring,
> And our breathing turned one,
> Like those of lovers,
> We were, and still are,
> Stronger from this war,
> And from the ploys of the merchants of death.
>
> As our nations rise to strike
> The heads of all the robbers,
> As our desires turn
> Into fists of an eternal truth,
> We shall save both our nations,
> From the jaws of foreigners!

Both nations, continued Bahr al-'Ulum, were twins brutally separated from one another by ruthless foreigners. The poem called on "the people of Mikunis" (communist Jewish leader Shmu'el Mikunis) to rise against these evil foreigners:

> This shall be your revenge against your rulers,
> Like my revenge against mine,
> Our fists combined together,
> We will bring death upon the tyrants.[44]

Bahr al-'Ulum might have known Iraqi-Jewish communists who convinced him to write the poem. But the significance of the poem lies in the parallels it draws between the two nations, and the reception it received, thanks to Somekh's efforts. MAKI's most noted intellectual, Hebrew poet Alexander Penn, read the poem and replied in a poem of his own. I do not know what the poet's face looks like, wrote Penn, and yet he has touched him because the power of his poem, "As if I wrote it in Hebrew // Only under a different name and in a different country."[45]

The breadth of these efforts by Iraqi Jews to maintain their connections to an Iraq past and present bespeaks their eagerness to retain their Iraqi identity. It was a country whose Arabic dialects Iraqis spoke, whose culture they celebrated, and memories of which they cherished *in Israel*, for them an inhospitable land of destitution and discrimination. Politically, left-leaning organizations used their experience in Iraq as a model. MAKI's Iraqi-Jewish members kept their Iraqi memories alive to provide templates for action in Israel and constantly evoked comparisons between Iraq and Israel. And although there were immense differences between Iraqis like Tikva Agasi, who missed the Tigris and the Euphrates, Samir Naqqash, who refused to write in Hebrew, and communist writers like David Semah, to all Iraqis, the Israeli state's pretense of being a haven for the oppressed sons of the Iraqi exile seemed somewhat ridiculous.

ISRAEL'S VOICE IN ARABIC: ARAB-JEWISH IDENTITY IN ISRAEL

During the time period under study, Hebrew and Arabic were the official languages in the Jewish state. The 160,000 Palestinians who resided in Israel legally, plus around 46,000 deported Palestinians who had made their way illegally to Israel, spoke Arabic as their mother tongue. They were joined by 123,300 Iraqi Jews, 48,300 Yemenite Jews, 45,400 North African Jews, 31,000 Libyan Jews, and 8,800 Egyptian Jews. In total around 462,000 people living in Israel spoke Arabic, in a dialect variant, as their first language. The country had also taken in 321,500 Jews from European countries, who spoke a variety of languages, as well as 56,400 Jews who spoke Persian and Turkish. In the 1950s and 1960s, then, the mother tongue of most of the people in Israel was not Hebrew; it was a multilingual society, where most citizens were bilingual to some degree.[46]

The state made a tremendous effort to normalize this multilingual context, especially through the teaching of Hebrew in the transit camps. Men with academic degrees were entitled to Hebrew classes, although those were not offered regularly in most camps. The state developed excellent instructional institutions in Hebrew and the competition to be admitted to them was strong among newcomers. Applications for positions that were not manual labor required knowledge of Hebrew; many documents regulating food and labor and most official notices in the transit camps were printed in Hebrew. Special divisions in the Ministry of Education were formed for the aim of spreading Hebrew culture through teaching, but also through theatrical performances, with help from the IDF. Hebrew was key to social mobility and the Iraqi newcomers realized that the faster they became fluent in Hebrew, the sooner they would have a wider set of opportunities.[47]

The Arabic of the newcomers was suppressed. Children and grownups were asked to change their names either in Shaʿar ha-ʿAliyah or by teachers and guides in the transit camps. Fahima Irbili became Shoshanna Arbeli, Amal Salih became Tikva Agasi, Fuʾad Amir became Elie Amir, and Salih Kemal Menashe became Sami Michael, and so on. In the kibbutzim doing so was often mandatory. The campaign against Arabic was part of a campaign against foreign languages in general. Yiddish, the mother tongue of most Ashkenazim, was considered particularly perilous and public performances in this language were banned. German was also a pariah language and was banned from radio broadcasts, cinematic screenings, and theatrical performances. The censoring of the German language went hand-in-hand with official and unofficial boycotts of German goods and cultural products (it was not until 1965 that diplomatic relations were established). However, as recent studies have shown, these languages survived in Israel as spoken and written languages, despite state policies.[48]

The Arabic language and culture of Iraqi Jews thus had to contend with a hostile environment. Nuzhat Qassab Darwish describes her meeting with her five-year-old nephew, who was born in Israel, after she arrived from Iraq:

> I approached to kiss him, but he rejected me, with some hate. Of course we had no shared language. The little boy spoke only Hebrew. My brother-in-law apologized and said: "The kid thinks you are Arabs, and the Arabs killed Jews here during the war, among them friends and neighbors of ours." The father—in Hebrew, and us—in our language, which the child did not understand, tried to explain to him that we were Jews, his relatives, that we loved him and . . . yearned to see him. Thus, slowly . . . he made peace with us, but seemed to remain estranged from us for a while.[49]

For an Israeli child, then, Jews speaking Arabic and looking Arab was an oddity he could not comprehend. Furthermore, speaking in Arabic in certain places in the public Israeli-Jewish domain was not tolerated. Iraqi educator Victor

Mu'allim recalls a bus ride he took from the Sakiyya transit camps with two teachers. One of them, Avraham Yehezkel, had a transistor radio, a rare and expensive commodity in those days, and the three listened to the news in Arabic. Some passengers were displeased, and said to them, "Arabs, you are Arabs . . . stop speaking in Arabic and making others listen to Arabic." He asked them politely:

> "So why are you speaking Yiddish and not Hebrew?" . . . We were more than patient and told them: "You know Arabic is our mother tongue and you cannot free us from it at once." But they didn't let us go, and continued shouting loudly: "You are Arabs, turn off the radio, you are not Jewish." Avraham Yehezkel told them forcefully: "This is our mother tongue and we will not stop listening to it." Immediately one of the lads stood up, snatched the transistor radio from Avraham Yehezkel, and threw it from the bus window. . . . We begged the driver to stop the bus and let us pick up the radio, but to our surprise instead of stopping, the driver burst into laughter and started cursing us, justifying the tossing out of the Arabic-speaking transistor radio.[50]

The three then went to the police station in Tel Aviv to complain. Those who had thrown the radio out of the bus said it had been too loud and that it had fallen out of their hands accidentally, and the matter was dropped. Speaking or listening to Arabic in public, then, marked these Iraqi Jews as Arabs. That every Israeli they met, from the bus driver to the criminals to the policemen, was hostile to Arabic-speaking Jews, caused these Jews to feel like strangers in their new country. And we note that Arabic here is being pitted against the other forbidden tongue, Yiddish, as the speakers of these respective languages try to render each other even more foreign.

Arabic, however, was used as a language of daily communication with Palestinians. Interactions relating to trade, commerce, and even hiding illegal infiltrators, were conducted illegally between people in the transit camps of Kfar Saba, Petach Tikva, and Ramat ha-Sharon. One Iraqi man recalls that when he worked near Kiryat Shmonah, which was close to the border with Lebanon, he had excellent an relationship with the Arabs across the border.[51] More radical Jews adopted Arabic as a way of challenging racial realties in Israel and connecting with the Palestinians. This was the case with Sami Michael:

> I was a journalist. I was a leader in the communist underground. All of a sudden everything that I knew was not only worthless because it is not in Hebrew, but

also was associated with the Arab enemy. I came with the culture of the enemy, with the language and traditions of the enemy.... When I spoke Arabic, they (the Israelis) thought I was an Arab. It is difficult to count how many times I was taken off a bus for security checks. They thought I left my village without a permit from the military governor.... I was called by my Iraqi name, Saleh (Salih), and obviously this did not help.... I was ashamed to tell them I was Jewish. In Iraq... I [had] battled against any aspect of hostility toward the Jews, and here I was treated with hostility as an Arab. I remembered my Arab friends in Iraq, who identified with me, and fought for me.... I was very sorry that those who behaved like that toward me were Jewish. And at the end they always shouted at me: "Why didn't you tell us that your father's name is Menashe?"[52]

For Michael, resisting classification and being identified with the Arabs was a way of preserving the feeling of the shared Arab-Jewish solidarity in Iraq and of protesting the separation between Jews and Arabs in Israel.

Nonetheless, despite the state's efforts and the public hostility toward Arabic, Arabic persisted as the language of Iraqi Jews in Israel in many domains, including in the public sphere. Broadly speaking, three kinds of Arabic bilingualism existed in the Iraqi community in Israel: the first was that of older Iraqi Jews, whose first language was and remained Arabic and who knew another language like English, French, or Turkish. The second, of Arabic and Hebrew, was that of Iraqis between the ages of sixteen and fifty-five, who had been educated in Arabic but who were able to learn Hebrew as a second language, as a result of working in Israel (if older) and furthering their education (if younger). A speaking knowledge of Hebrew came first; reading and writing came later. Young adults in particular acquired native proficiency in both languages. Finally, there was the Arabic of younger children either born in Iraq or born to Iraqi parents in Israel. They heard Arabic at home, and could often speak or understand it, but could not read and write it. Hebrew thus became the language with which they communicated and in which they read and wrote.

Arabic culture survived in Israel for many years. Arabic music broadcast on Syrian and Egyptian radio stations was played in cafés in the transit camps and the new neighborhoods of newcomers, much to the dismay of state officials.[53] Arabic music was played in wedding parties, and other family celebrations to which Iraqi artists were invited.[54] In Iraq, Jews were leading musicians in their country, as Shoshana Gabai showed in an important article.[55] Salih and Da'ud al-Kuwaiti, two of Iraq's most prominent musicians—the Iraqi king himself had begged them not to leave—were relegated in Israel to a life of poverty.

They and other Iraqi-Jewish musicians found work playing for parties in marginal spaces, notably Café Noah in Tel Aviv. But nevertheless they continued to perform for Iraqi audiences in their new country. In the 1960s, Iraqi artists like Filfel al-Gurgi released records in Arabic for Iraqi Israelis. While their records were never played on official radio stations, and most Israelis did not hear about them, they did become popular at weddings and parties of Iraqi Jews, especially in the 1960s and 1970s, when more people could afford such celebrations.[56]

Arabic was also a language of much importance to the state. Because Arabic-speaking Jews could vote, political parties sought to reduce the barriers to communication and addressed them in Arabic. Each major party had a newspaper in Arabic, staged rallies in Arabic, and distributed leaflets in the transit camps in Arabic. Moreover, the state saw value in having citizens with knowledge of Arabic because it was the language of the enemy. The Israeli state needed to monitor and supervise the Palestinians who had become Israeli citizens, and it was in a state of war with its Arab neighbors, while the Israeli leadership constantly feared an Arab invasion. Consequently, hundreds of Arabic-speaking Jews were employed in domains relating to the management of the Palestinian population and the gathering of intelligence about Arab countries. Mostly, the commanders or directors at the top were Ashkenazim, but Iraqi Jews played a leading role in the collection and analysis of meaningful information and in staffing the state's propaganda and teaching mechanisms geared toward the Palestinians.

The central information-gathering unit of the Israeli intelligence, Intelligence Service 2, specifically drafted Iraqi Jews. The unit was an outgrowth of the intelligence arm of the Haganna and the 1948 War. In 1949, the unit employed 250 men and women, a number that would increase over the following two decades (during which time the unit was given a new name). Two Iraqi Jews, 'Ezra Mani (1915–2005) and Avraham Sharoni (b. 1918), who had immigrated to Mandatory Palestine during the interwar period, established the foundations for the unit's research methods, which involved the collection of materials from Arab lands, the translation of newspapers, transmissions, and letters from the Arab world, the training of new generations of soldiers to decipher such materials, and the composition of dictionaries of the various Arabic dialects to this end. This network of communication intelligence was staffed in part by immigrants from Arab lands, including many Iraqis. In 1948 most of those who deciphered the radio transmissions and wires were either Syrian or Iraqi Jews. The Iraqi

Jews in the unit assisted in the creation of Hebrew dictionaries of Iraqi terms, as they were familiar with the Muslim-Iraqi dialects. The Iraqi Jews had not learned Arabic as a "dead language" in Israeli high schools and in universities; their Iraqi schools (both private and public) had provided excellent instruction in Arabic language and literature, and they possessed cultural sensitivities that others in the unit did not have.[57]

Iraqi Israelis also worked for both the Shin Bet (General Security Service) and the Mossad (the institution of intelligence and other special missions), especially in the 1960s and onward. Both, the former in charge of security within Israel, the latter of gathering information outside Israel, came into existence in the early 1950s and were under the direct authority of the Israeli prime minister. Israel needed more spies in Arab states after 1948, but the Arab citizens of Egypt, Syria, and Lebanon were reluctant to collaborate with the Israelis; after the Lavon Affair, the number of agents declined further. Iraqis were drafted and trained to pass as Muslim Arabs, which entailed learning everything from Arabic proverbs to Muslim forms of prayer. Ironically, they became more Arabized as a result of their training in Israel than they were in Iraq. One Iraqi-Jewish agent, for example, recalls that his speech about the Arab predicament, as an undercover student agent, was so convincing that Egyptian students even gave him a signed photo of Gamal 'Abd al-Nasser.[58]

Iraq was a particular concern of the Israeli government in the 1960s. The performance of Israeli intelligence in Iraq, during the years 1949–51, was far from perfect; two Zionists were caught and executed and the coordination between the different branches operating in Iraq was poor.[59] When Israeli diplomats and intelligence agents later worked with Iraqis and in Iraq, they were more organized and much more successful. An Iraqi Jew was able to convince an Iraqi pilot to defect to Israel, with his Mig aircraft, in July 1966; messages in code to the pilot were also transmitted via Israel's Arabic broadcasting service.[60] During the postcolonial era, Israel reached out to non-Arab and anti–Pan Arab players in the Middle East, such as Iran, Turkey, and the royalists in Yemen. The Iraqi Kurds were an important ally, especially after 1963 when a pro-Egyptian government came to power in Iraq.[61] In the years 1966–70 there were close ties between Israel and the Kurdish powers in northern Iraq. Sami Michael recalls that the state wanted him to serve as a liaison to the Kurds:

> I was amazed that even though, at the time, I was ostracized for being communist, they constantly made me enticing offers. They even pressured me. All of them. Intelligence, Military Intelligence, Shin Bet.... The dumbest idea was that

I would return to Iraq, and they would make sure I was imprisoned, and there I would link up with the Kurdish leadership in prison.⁶²

Other Iraqi Jews were more amenable to collaborating with the intelligence forces. They were included in the groups of doctors, agricultural experts, and military advisers who moved between Iran, Iraqi Kurdistan, and Israel, as Israelis trained Kurdish troops in northern Iraq and Kurds visited Israel. The Kurdish leader Mustafa Barazani visited Israel and met with a Jewish family who had helped his father in Ottoman Iraq.⁶³ Operations in Iraq assumed much greater importance after the rise of the Ba'ath to power in 1968. The new regime persecuted the Jewish community, jailed and tortured dozens of Jews, and carried out public executions of Jews in 1969; in the years 1969–71, members of the Jewish community were smuggled outside of Iraq with Israeli help.⁶⁴

Domestically, Iraqi Jews were integral to the government's management of the Palestinian population in Israel. The Palestinians in Israel did hold Israeli citizenship, but intelligence was gathered about every aspect of their lives, from the content of songs sung at weddings to the education system.⁶⁵ A tiny unit in the 1950s, Ulysses, comprised of Iraqi and other Middle Eastern Jews, trained Jews to pass as Arabs and settled them in Arab villages in Israel. The Iraqi Jews who joined learned the Qur'an, Islamic history, and the Palestinian dialect, in order to pass as Palestinians. The operation, which involved a few dozen men, was a failure, however—the agents did not provide meaningful information, and the operation was terminated.⁶⁶

A more successful and stable venue for Iraqi Jews to contribute to Israeli society based on their background was education. Palestinian teachers were under the supervision of the Israeli authorities. After the national education law was passed, Arab children were sent to Israeli schools as was mandated by the new law. Despite the fact that the state carefully screened the teachers, Arab students and teachers alike continued to commemorate the Nakba and considered the Egyptian president 'Abd al-Nasser, and not Ben Gurion, their true leader.⁶⁷ In light of this situation, the state needed Jews with good command of Arabic. Although they did not speak the same dialect as the Palestinians, a number of Iraqi Jews did have teaching experience, having worked in the prestigious Jewish educational system in Iraq and in Iraqi public schools. In 1950–51, there were a hundred schools for Arab children staffed by 628 teachers, of which 80 were Jewish. Initially, education officials had reservations about the Iraqis' participation. The authorities feared that the Iraqi-Jewish teachers would not be comfortable in a "pure Arab environment," and thus the Iraqi teachers were only placed in mixed cities (Haifa, Jaffa, Acre, and two schools in Jerusalem). Furthermore, Israeli officials felt that Iraqi Jews could not teach Israeli values to Arab students, since they did not know much about the country themselves.[68] Other Iraqis found positions teaching Arabic in Jewish schools (elementary and high school) to Hebrew-speaking students, once their level of Hebrew was adequate.

The historian Shira Robinson was the first to bring to light the immense impact of Iraqis on the Arab education system in Israel from around 1950 through the 1960s. Robinson showed that the initial hesitation about Iraqi Jews had dissipated by mid-1950, and Iraqis were teachers, inspectors, curriculum writers, and seminary instructors, as well as authors of textbooks that expressed the ideals of the state. During the 1950s and 1960s, these teachers worked not only in the mixed cities but also in villages. As Robinson illustrates, the state favored Iraqi Jews over Arab teachers, so that a system was created in which the Arab education division was run by Ashkenazi directors who supervised Iraqi teachers, who in turn prepared texts for, taught, and evaluated Arab teachers and students.[69]

Another major institution that employed Iraqi Jews was the Histadrut's Arab division. By collaborating with the Histadrut, Palestinians could attain a higher standard of living, get professional training, and ensure education and budgets to municipalities and villages. The Histadrut operated branches and coordinated activities in Arab villages and in the cities to bring about the Israelification of—and MAPAI control over—the Palestinians. The Iraqis played the role of mediator in these processes. Some notable figures were Eliyahu Agasi, Esperance Cohen, Tikva Agasi, and especially Nuzhat Qassab, who founded and ran the Arab women's division of the Histadrut.[70] This division had as its mission the development of cultural and professional activities in Arab villages and cities, such as the establishment of Histadrut clubs for women in Nazareth, offering classes in home economics, Hebrew, and literacy skills, and organizing an Arab cultural festival in Haifa, at which Nuzhat Qassab spoke in Arabic about a Hebrew poetess. Qassab arranged for politicians to speak in Arab villages (Golda Meir visited the village of Julis, for example), cultivated connections with Palestinian writers like Salim Jubran, and coordinated the state's propaganda efforts in Arab villages and cities.[71] In many cases the participants in the activities were Christian or Druze. The events were reported about in MAPAI's Arabic publications, such as the daily *Al-Yawm* and *Haqiqat al-Amr*. The Iraqi women who participated in these efforts saw themselves as feminists and as promoting feminism within the "Arab sector" of Israeli society. They were not always welcomed, depending on the activity, and sometimes faced outright hostility, as when organizing celebrations of Israeli Independence Day in Arab cities like Nazareth. Qassab, in fact, feared "hostile elements,"[72] and reports that an Arab boy told the Arab women involved in these efforts that "you are celebrating Independence Day; but this is not our country: may it burn."[73] The women who worked with her, however, attacked the boy, saying that if the state burns, he will be burned with it. After 1967 the activity programs were extended to East Jerusalem.

Another governmental initiative that employed Iraqi Jews in particular was the state's Arabic-language propaganda machine. The state radio had a broadcasting service, the Sawt Isra'il bi'l 'Arabiya (Voice of Israel in Arabic), which operated in the 1950s, and hired Iraqi Jews. Initially, the station's purpose was to counter Arab propaganda outlets, especially the popular Egyptian *Sawt al-'Arab*, established in 1956. Its signal was strong enough that its programming could be heard across the entire Middle East. The Mossad and the Shin Bet were involved in its operation and used it for their purposes. The state had a great deal of influence on programming, and in fact one of its satirical show put together by Egyptian Jews was a direct result of Golda Meir's displeasure at the sketches about her broadcast the Egyptian radio station; she wanted her own show as a countermeasure and she got it. The director of the Voice of Israel in Arabic was Sha'ul Bar Haim, an Iraqi Jew, as were many of the producers, scriptwriters, and program directors, while the broadcast hosts were Palestinians. The local Hebrew press lionized the service for telling the truth, which the Arabs of the entire region wanted to hear, even in Egypt, where Nasser was lying to his people. Iraqi Jews put together a variety of programs on music, women's affairs, and educational, health, and legal matters, during which listeners' questions were answered and Qur'an quizzes were held. Some of its programs, especially those on health, were popular all over the Middle East. While initially a propaganda tool, during the 1950s and 1960s Iraqis such as Salim Fattal, Murad Mikha'il, Nuzhat Qassab, Ishaq Bar Moseh, Nir Shohat, Eliyahu Nawi (a Basran Jew and the mayor of Beersheba, whose popular show featured Arabic proverbs and fables), Menashe Somekh, Arieh Elias, Edmond Sahayyek, and many others used the Voice of Israel in Arabic as a means to express their love of Arabic culture, music, and literature.[74]

The Voice of Israel in Arabic had its own orchestra, which hired many Iraqi-Jewish musicians during the 1950s. The orchestra not only played background music and short musical interludes between shows, but had its own music shows and, later, concerts that featured original material alongside more familiar songs from the Middle Eastern repertoire. It absorbed gifted Iraqi musicians who worked for the Iraqi radio and played with the greatest singers in Iraq; they now played alongside Egyptian-Jewish musicians. While many of the performers never attained in Israel the fame they had enjoyed in Iraq, and were paid a pittance to play in the radio, they did find an appreciative audience among the Iraqis, Mizrahim, and Palestinians.[75]

A few Iraqi actors found work in government-sponsored theater productions directed at the Arab population. Ze'ev Yosifun (Yoskovich) ran a company called TELEM (Te'atron la-Ma'abarot) for the people of the transit camps. His shows were an element of the campaign by the Ministry of Education to spread Hebrew among the newcomers, and the company put on plays in the transit camps, such as Kazablan. However, since Yosifun founded the company also to divert Jews from drinking arak, Iraqis searched for other alternatives.[76] Arieh Elias, an actor trained in Baghdad, tried to get into auditions by more-established theaters in Israel. However, when he read the part of Shylock in an Arabic accent in his auditions, the managers of theaters and theatrical troupes burst out laughing. While it was perfectly acceptable and in fact was the norm for the Ashkenazi actors to play characters from Shakespeare and Tennessee Williams in heavy Russian accents, Arabic accents were met with derision. Elias, along with Egyptian-Jewish actors, took to performing for Arabic-speaking audiences—notably the Palestinians—shows such as Ahmad Shawqi's *Majnun Laila*. In the 1960s, he directed and starred in films, one of which was featured in the Venice Film Festival, and yet continued to perform in Arab villages like Kafar Yasif and Kafar Qassem leading amateur theatrical groups; he felt this public truly appreciated his craft.[77]

The state also published Arabic newspapers, which were intended for both the Arabic-speaking Jewish and the Palestinian readerships. These were a source of employment for young Iraqi intellectuals like Shmu'el Moreh and his sister, Esperance Cohen; Murad Mihka'il; and Nissim Rejwan. These sang the praises of Israel and published kitschy poems about peace and coexistence. At the same time, the Iraqi authors wrote about the marginalization of Mizrahim in Israeli society and the platform gave Iraqi writers the opportunity to discuss Arabic culture, poetry, and prose.[78]

These state institutions offered Iraqi Jews a path toward mainstream Israeli society. More than just stable, professional work, this form of employment gave Iraqis the sense that they were contributing to the Israeli national project, especially through their work among the Palestinians living in Israel and in the state's operations overseas. Their knowledge of Arabic culture and language was not only acceptable, it was desirable. At the same time, Iraqis seized the opportunity to go beyond mere propagandizing, and in the theatrical, intellectual, and educational domains particularly they sought to enrich the Arab culture of Israel.

A story that exemplifies the Zionization of Arab-Iraqi identity in Israel is "'Al Gehalim" (On the Burning Coal), by Rahamim Rejwan. Set in the Israel of the 1970s, the story presents Sha'ul, who has worked for twenty-seven years as an accountant for the Ministry of Interior (he is sixty-seven years old as the story takes place). Sha'ul frequents a small restaurant in Holon, owned by a Palestinian, Abu Sami. The restaurant caters to Iraqi Jews, who had come to Israel during the 1950s and who continue speaking in the Iraqi dialect. Despite the fact that Abu Sami's menu is overpriced, the Iraqi Jews love the restaurant because it serves delicious meat and fish cooked over burning coals in the Iraqi style (the restaurant's oven had been made in Gaza) to the sounds of the music of singers Farid al-Atrash and Umm Kalthum, as well as Iraqi singers. Avi, a beautiful young man, is the cook; he makes the best Iraqi-style fish in the restaurant. In conversations between the regulars and Abu Sami, Avi's identity is revealed; his real name is Ibrahim and he is actually a Palestinian from Khan Yunis. This news is alarming to the Iraqi-Jewish clients, as Avi/Ibrahim dates Jewish women. One Iraqi Jew, 'Ezra, threatens to kill his daughter for dating Avi/Ibrahim. Gradually, all of Avi/Ibrahim's girlfriends leave him when they find out that he is Palestinian. Avi/Ibrahim is upset and wants to know who told the clients he is an Arab. Sha'ul replies:

> "Don't you think it's our right, Ibrahim?"
> "What right? You are foreigners here."
> "What do you mean?"
> "Leave politics out of it. I don't like to argue about this subject."[79]

Avi/Ibrahim gets drunk, but Abu Sami does not want to fire him since his fine cooking still attracts the Iraqi Jews. But Avi/Ibrahim cannot handle the tensions. At the end of the story he prepares a meal for an Iraqi family, with all the Iraqi ingredients they love. He also puts poison in their food. The father of the family dies as a result.

The story takes place after 1967. At this point, Palestinians from the West Bank hold the low-paying jobs, which were the domain of the Mizrahim before 1967. On the one hand, the story emphasizes what ties the Jews and the Arabs together: the love of Arab music and food and the Arabic language. Abu Sami, a Palestinian, runs an Iraqi café in Holon, where a transit camp populated by Iraqi Jews once existed. Avi/Ibrahim moves from Khan Yunis, a city close to Gaza, to a richer place; like many Mizrahi Jews during the 1950s, he is forced to erase his Arab identity, most notably by changing his name to Avi, short for Avraham. Avraham/Ibrahim is the father of both Arabs and Jews in the Abrahamic faiths. Here, the Palestinian character needs to identify clearly with one religion in order to survive in the Jewish city. The Iraqi Jews are upset about his real identity; this would have happened in Iraq as well, as intermarriage between Jews and Muslims was something Jews rarely accepted. And yet what marks the difference between Iraqi Jews and Palestinians, despite their shared culture, is that the Palestinian protagonist sees Sha'ul as one of the foreigners who took over his land. Moreover, his bitterness at being driven out from the café leads him to acts of violence. Most significantly, the Iraqi-Jewish writer of the short story cannot imagine a possibility where Avi's Jewish lovers might still maintain their relationships with him after he reveals himself as Ibrahim. Nor can he imagine any other possibility for Avi/Ibrahim to live with the people who share his Arab culture other than conflict and death. Cultural links between Arab and Jews are meaningless politically and socially after 1967; to Rejwan, fluidity is dangerous.

Arabic, however, was also the language of radical and leftist Iraqi Jews. In radical circles, being a Jew who was comfortable in Arab culture signified being a Jew who was sympathetic to the concerns of Arabs throughout the region and in particular to the suffering of the Palestinian citizens of the state. MAPAM and the communists both addressed Arab affairs in their print outlets. Latif Dori from MAPAM wrote poetry expressing solidarity with the people of Algeria in their struggle for independence. In *Al-Mirsad*, there were calls for equal rights for the Arab minority (*aqaliyya*),[80] protests about land confiscation, reports on the demonstrations by Jewish and Arab crowds to better the conditions in "their shared country" (*bi-biladina al-mushtariq*),[81] and critiques of the poor Arab education system.[82] However, as noted, MAPAM's own kibbutzim benefited from land confiscation after 1948 and the party's Zionist outlook and commitment to the agricultural settlement policy as a solution for the problem of unemployed migrants deterred both Arabs and Mizrahim from voting for its candidates.

MAKI emphasized much more strongly the shared nature of the struggle of Palestinians and Mizrahim against the state because both groups had the same Arab culture and similar experiences of persecution. The communists emphasized regional solidarity: they reported about events in the Arab world and declared that they shared the sorrows of fellow revolutionary Arabs across the Middle East. The slogans on posters carried by May First demonstrators reflected the assumption that Jews and Arabs needed to work together toward common goals: "May the battle of the Algerian People for Freedom and Independence Win!"; "We carry brotherly greetings to the Iraqi masses that freed themselves from their enslavers!"; "Long Live Peace between Israel and Arab countries"; and "Let Israel join the winning march for freedom of the peoples of Asia and Africa!"[83] Nesia Safran, who was a member of the Petach Tikva branch of the communist youth movement (and an Ashkenazi), recalls in her memoirs that she wrote poems in honor of Jamila, the Algerian freedom fighter, and considered the Jordanian communist Raja, a sixteen-year-old killed in a demonstration, a heroine.[84]

Communist Jewish writers proposed that there was indeed a connection between Iraqi Jews and the Palestinians—a connection of suffering. MAKI's Palestinian authors wrote about the treatment of Iraqi Jews, both because they cared for Iraqi Jews and because they sensed that this treatment presaged what would happen to the Palestinians. Sami Michael's sketch from Kol Ha-'Am protested police brutality through the telling of the story of one of its most prized dogs, Zuzu, which patrols the border zones and takes part in campaigns dedicated to searching Palestinians who smuggle the border back to Israel, destroying Arab homes, and exiling people.[85] Michael was troubled by the fact that the families of the Palestinian refugees who returned illegally were given the option of turning them in or being jailed for harboring an illegal infiltrator. "Do you know the meaning of blaming a father and a mother for not turning in their son who has come back home? I escaped Iraq before the Jews became the objects of harsh persecutions. I came here and discovered that the situation of the Arabs . . . under the military regime was equally bad."[86] Michael was also devastated to see the Palestinians of Jaffa living in a ghetto. And again, Iraqi-Jewishness served as the measure against which he esteemed the situation of the Palestinians: "Every once in a while some Jewish thugs would break into the Arab ghetto [in Jaffa], kicking and rioting, just like the gangs of thugs who invaded, under Nazi influence, the Jewish quarters [in Iraq]. . . . I identified with the defenseless Arabs."[87] The Arabs of Jaffa were thus experiencing what his Jewish Baghdadi brethren had suffered in 1941: brutality at the hands of ultranationalists that was permitted by the ruling party.[88] A writer for *Kol ha-'Am* drew a similar parallel when describing the difficulties of the denizens of Migdal Gat. The reporter noted that after the city was cleansed of its Arab inhabitants, now political pressure and abuse were directed toward the denizens of the transit camp. The comparison between the two groups and the relationship of the state toward them was hard to miss.[89]

In the field of Arab culture, Iraqi Jews active in communist publications made a noticeable contribution to the Arabic literature in Israel. Iraqi-Jewish intellectuals, such as Sasson Somekh, Shim'on Ballas, Sami Michael, and David Semah, wrote for the communist press, namely *Al-Ittihad*, its cultural journal, *Al-Jadid*, and the Hebrew journal of the party, *Kol ha-'Am*. These authors and poets had been personally acquainted with Iraqi writers, and had been exposed to a range of literary and poetic innovations in Baghdad. They continued to champion this work after immigrating to Israel, being strong proponents of social realism in prose and modernism in poetry.[90] MAKI attracted the most brilliant Palestinian writers, like the novelist and satirist Emile Habibi and the poets Samih al-Qasim and Mahmud Darwish. Palestinian writers at the time were endeavoring to both preserve and develop the Arab culture of their homeland at a time when they were cut off from the greater Arab world. They were interested in Iraqi poetry and literature not only because of their innovative qualities but also because of its themes. The noted Iraqi progressive poet 'Abd al-Wahhab al-Bayati wrote extensively on the sufferings of the Palestinian refugees, for example. After the 1958 revolution, which thrust the communists to center stage in Iraq, more poems by al-Bayati appeared in *Al-Jadid*: the paper printed "Aslak sha'ika" (Barbed Wire), one of Bayyati's most celebrated poems about the Palestinian refugees.[91] The communist Arabic literary scene was thus a crucial site of creativity and protest in the face of censorship, the military regime, and the difficult political conditions.

One organization that did a great deal to encourage Iraqi-Jewish literary activity in Arabic was the Club of the Friends of Arabic Literature in Israel (later the Hebrew-Arabic Literary Club), whose members hoped to facilitate interaction between Arab and Jewish writers. The club was established largely due to the efforts of Somekh, Semah, and Ballas. In March 1954, Somekh and Semah wrote a letter to *Al-Jadid* asking for help in raising the profile of Arab culture in Israel.[92] *Al-Jadid*'s editorial board responded to this call: Jabra Nicola, the editor, and Sami Michael, who already worked in MAKI's publishing ventures, came from Haifa to meet with the young Iraqi writers. Ballas, Somekh, and Semah began to publish in *Al-Jadid* and invited more Iraqis to do so.[93] Ballas recalls that he "stressed that Arabic is a fundamental component in our identity as human beings, and in that we [were] no different than other people in the region, and therefore we should preserve this identity in our writings."[94]

The openness of the Palestinian writers toward Iraqi Jews stood in contrast to the hesitant responses of the Ashkenazi communists who did not understand the cultural dilemmas of Iraqi-Jewish writers.[95] Shim'on Ballas in particular was critical of the cultural conservatism of his Ashkenazi peers. Although he wrote extensively about Arab affairs in *Kol ha-'Am*, his involvement in Arabic literary circles was frowned upon:

> It was reality that pushed me into fulfilling some sort of a function here, of serving as a connection to this world that was not only seen as being in a state of war and perpetual hostility but was totally and absolutely alien. And this includes everyone, not just the Zionist parties or the right but the Communist Party as well. I wrote a lot on Arabic literature and culture. I also did the anthology of Palestinian stories that came out in 1969. You begin to think that if you don't do these things then no one else will, so it becomes a role that you have to fulfill, a duty that you have to take upon yourself.[96]

Generally speaking, Iraqi-Jewish authors believed in the theory of *iltizam*, which called on writers to be committed to the society in which they lived, engage in politics, and use their literary gifts for the sake of society. Both Ballas and Michael wrote short stories in Arabic about the sufferings of the dwellers of the transit camps. Significantly, many Arabs in Israel read these stories, because they were published in Palestinian journals and newspapers and not by MAPAI's Arabic press. Iraqi-Jewish poets also addressed Palestinian issues in their writings. Sasson Somekh's poem "Tilka al-qulub" (These Hearts) expressed the view that there was no point in celebrating the virtues of poetry as long as heroes were locked up in jails and exiled, as long as the blacks were being executed (in America), and as long as Palestinians were being banished from their villages.[97]

The Palestinian-Iraqi-Jewish alliance crystallized during the massacre in Kafar Qassem, in which the Israeli Border Brigades shot forty-nine Palestinians at close range. Many of those killed were teenagers and children (twenty-two of the dead were under the age of eighteen). I have mentioned Latif Dori's response to the massacre in a previous chapter. The intellectual David Semah was blunter. Shortly after the slaughter took place, Semah published his poem, "Sawfa ya'udu" (He Shall Return), which was dedicated to the people of Kafar Qassem. The poem is constructed as a dialogue between a mother and her daughter, who asks the mother repeatedly where her father is. The mother imagines a few returns: she initially answers that the girl's father will return, bringing roses for his daughter. Then she says the father is about to return; he is in a faraway place. Next, she feels that he might return, his hands handcuffed with iron bars, after toiling in the field for no pay. Finally, the daughter confronts her mother, urging her to tell the truth, as she has heard from the people of the village that "they have killed him. . . . My father shall never return!" The mother then admits that the father will not return, and yet she prophesizes that in the future crowds will pour into the streets and ignite a revolution against the oppressors; this will bring an end to their miseries; then her father will return.[98] While other Palestinian poets commemorated the women and children massacred, Semah chose to write about those who survived. The very Palestinian perception that the return should not be conceptualized as the return of individuals but rather should occur as a result of a political struggle circulated in the Arabic literary culture of time and is also conveyed in Semah's powerful words.

The prolific studies of Reuven Snir and Shmu'el Moreh have uncovered a whole archive of Iraqi-Jewish literary activity in Arabic in Israel, by poets like Salim Sha'shu'a, Ibrahim 'Obadiah, Murad Mihka'il, and fiction writers like Ibrahim 'Akrai, who were not communists. Their works, 'Obadiah's poetry in particular, represent a significant contribution to the Arabic literary scene in Israel. These intellectuals refused to abandon their language of creation and expression, and expressed their nostalgia for Iraq and longing for peace in Israel in Arabic.[99] The Iraqi-Jewish communist writers, not surprisingly, adopted a much more critical stance. They refused to join the mainstream press in its praising of the new state. They were radicals, and for them, the sufferings of Iraqi Jews in the transit camps and the sufferings of Palestinians in Israel were outcomes of the same system. They were not Arab nationalists; they had a deep score to settle with the Iraqi right, which had emphasized ethnic nationalism at the expense of other groups in the state. But out of a profound sense of justice and shared victimhood, they collaborated with and wrote in support of Palestinians. The bonds between them remained strong after the Iraqi Jews left MAKI.

To a large extent, the Arab culture of Iraqi Jews survived in Israel, though this truth has not been widely acknowledged until recent years. Israel of the 1950s and 1960s was a bilingual space in which many Jews spoke Arabic. They did so despite the general contempt for a language identified with the Arab and Muslim enemy and the marginalized Arab citizens of the state. Iraqi Jews had immigrated to a state that strongly believed in its Hebrew ideology and sought to suppress all other languages, Ashkenazi and Mizrahi alike. However, Arabic survived and even flourished in the isolated transit camps, in the cafés of Iraqi Jews, and in the print media outlets of both the government and its opposing bodies. Arabic was also a useful language. Fluency in Arabic offered a way out of destitution in the transit camps and the slums of the cities, if one was willing to use his or her knowledge of the language in the service of the state. The forms of governmental employment Iraqis chose varied; there is a world of difference between being a spy in an Arab community (either in Israel or abroad) and a musician who is revered by fellow Arabs for his artistic prowess. But all these people who made use of Arabic, from the most radical communist to the intelligence officer working on a military dictionary for the IDF, show how profoundly connected Iraqi Jews were to their mother tongue and how numerous political bodies in Israel took advantage of this love.

THE RISE OF THE DARK-BROWN: MIZRAHI IDENTITY

Perhaps the most important mentality that came to be constructed in the new state of Israel following the mass migration from Arab states was Mizrahi identity. Jewish writers in Iraq had defined themselves as *sharqiyyun*, members of the East. The discussion of the differences between East and West had preoccupied the Arab public sphere since the nineteenth century; within this context Iraqi Jews conceptualized their identity as members of the Jewish communities of the East.[100] The idea that Sephardi and Ashkenazi Jews varied in their practices of Judaism was accepted in Ottoman and Mandatory Palestine; in fact each community had its own chief rabbi under British rule. In Israel, being Eastern, or in Hebrew, "Mizrahi" (and at times *ben 'edot ha-mizrah*, "son of the communities of the East"), meant something different. It meant being an Israeli whose family had come from Muslim lands and who was discriminated against because of these origins. In Israel, then, much more so than in Iraq, Iraqi Jews came to realize that the lot of Jews who came from Middle Eastern countries was similar to theirs. The Ashkenazi elites who were tasked with the absorption of the Iraqi Jews often did not know the differences between Egyptian, Iraqi, Turkish, and Persian cultures. All looked alike and were similarly suspicious in their eyes. While transregional connections, such as trade, a shared print market, and religious ties connected Jews from Iraq to Jews in Iran, Egypt, and the Levant before their arrival in Israel, Mizrahi solidarity in Israel was forged in the transit camps, schools, kibbutzim, and the Israeli labor market, and grew stronger through the protesting of the state's policies.

The rise of Mizrahi identity had to do with the Israelization of Iraqi Jews and their acceptance of the notion that they were Israeli citizens and that as Jews they deserved rights and privileges in the Jewish state. The Israeli-Jewish identity of Iraqis was cemented during these years and connected them to the state. During the 1960s, those who managed to leave the transit camps spoke Hebrew in their workplaces. In schools, children learned about Israeli holidays, national and Jewish religious; these holidays were celebrated in the transit camps, with special food rations and days off from work (for those who did) on holidays.[101] Latif Dori reported enthusiastically in *Al-Mirsad* how the Iraqi migrants celebrated Israeli Independence Day and stood for a moment of silence in remembrance of the souls of the Jewish martyrs who had died in

FIGURE 6. Children together in a transit camp. Source: CZA, NKH\404401. Reprinted with permission.

this great war (*arwah shuhada' al-harb al-kabira*).[102] Flag-raising ceremonies in schools and in the transit camps bolstered the nascent identity of Iraqi Jews as Israeli citizens. Membership in youth movements, political organizations, and women's organizations all strengthened the relationship of Iraqi Jews to the Israeli state.[103]

The Ashkenazim, against the foil of which Mizrahi identity was formed, were not a monolithic group. Iraqis greatly resented the Ashkenazim who had come to Mandatory Palestine before World War II because the latter were well represented in MAPAI's bureaucracy and government bodies. Other Ashkenazim were Holocaust survivors, who like the Iraqis and other Middle Eastern Jews had arrived penniless, were processed in Sha'ar ha-'Aliyah, sprayed with DDT, and settled in transit camps. There were clashes in the transit camps between Ashkenazim and Iraqis, because the Ashkenazim managed to leave the transit camps earlier and because in some camps Ashkenazi directors favored the new Ashkenazi migrants.[104] However, there were instances of Ashkenazi and Iraqi migrants signing the same petitions and helping one another in times of difficulty. Iraqi Jews got to know Holocaust survivors in newcomers' camps (*mahanot 'olim*) and in the cities, especially in neighborhoods built for newcomers. Nuzhat Qassab recalls that in Jerusalem, her family came to know one such family. They related their life story to their Iraqi neighbors and both families cried together; the families grew close and helped each other overcome the difficulties of life in their new land.[105] Latif Dori wrote moving articles about his visits to the death camps in Poland, and, as an Iraqi Jew, informed the Israeli public in its entirety about the horrors of the Holocaust. Sami Michael heard stories about the Holocaust from survivors he met in the camps for newcomers. He perceived that they, too, were discriminated against—Israelis saw them as miserable people who went as lambs to the slaughter. The establishment, he felt, adopted a patronizing attitude toward these Jews, who had suffered far more than he had, as an Iraqi. Since they spoke Yiddish or Polish or Hungarian, Michael conversed with them in English about authors they liked, such as Pushkin, Beckett, and Shakespeare.[106] Iraqi teenagers also met teenagers who were Holocaust survivors in kibbutzim. In the transit camps themselves, children befriended children from all communities; they shared with them certain experiences like having to change their names to Hebrew names. [107] These Iraqi-Israeli children grew up in transit camps, hearing Yiddish, Polish, and especially Romanian.[108]

The connections to other groups of Jews, including Ashkenazim, facilitated the acceptance of the fact that Israel was now the home of Iraqi Jews. Despite the desire of many Iraqi Jews to return to Iraq, younger Iraqis called to increase the number of Jews coming to Israel. Moreover, in their demonstrations against the persecution of Jews in Iraq, they waved both Israeli flags and black flags, which they termed "the symbols of the Holocaust."[109] Accepting the fact that Israel was now their home, however, also meant that Iraqi Jews came to the realization that the Israeli political sphere should be the arena for their battles for equality and justice. The Mizrahi identity therefore was formed first and foremost in the context of the struggle with the state's Ashkenazi elites, especially the bureaucrats, an essentially domestic struggle to end discrimination by Jews against other Jews.

Autobiographies, press items, and petitions sent from Iraqis to different government bodies unpack the meanings of Mizrahi in various Israeli contexts. First, the word, as uttered by Ashkenazim, signified Arabness and at times blackness. In the press, the skin color of Iraqis and Mizrahim in general was "dark-brown" (Hebrew: *shahum*; plural: *shhumin*), a blend between the word "black" (*shahor*) and "brown" (*hum*). While Jews from Middle Eastern countries were also called a variety of derogatory terms meaning "black," the coining of a term to describe a black-brown color indicated something new: something in between the color of the dark Arabs and the Ashkenazi Jews. Ashkenazi Jews, who had often been perceived as dark and black in Europe, now reenvisioned themselves as white and European vis-à-vis the Arabs and the Jews of the Middle East.[110] Iraqis recall the unbelievable ignorance regarding their culture: Ashkenazim assumed they came from desert lands where camels roam the streets and where Western culture was virtually unknown.[111] They report that Ashkenazim were placed in better jobs, that teachers and professors made derogatory remarks to Iraqi students and humiliated them in class, and that promotions in the workplace were denied based on origin. They also noted that they stayed longer in the transit camps, while Ashkenazi families were evacuated to other neighborhoods. In some cases, this long stay formed bonds of friendship between Iraqi, Egyptian, Tunisian, and Iranian Jews who stayed with them in the transit camps, especially among children.[112] These experiences, be it that of a young Iraqi woman begging an Ashkenazi professor to let her continue with her studies in the university, or a woman being told that her children would amount to nothing more exalted than carpenters and welders, made them realize that their problem was not only an Iraqi problem, it was a Mizrahi problem.[113]

Iraqi Jews addressing the state's officials and institutions during the 1950s protested discrimination and identified themselves as Mizrahim. As early as 1950,

Eliyahu Nissan, writing to the journal of the Association of Aram Naharayim, called for "awakening, unity, and the formation of an ideological, political, and militant force for changing the political, *one-sect-based* [*had-'adati*] order,[114] which reigns in the state, which hurts us and all the other non-Ashkenazi communities. Your slogan in your journal should be: equal rights, in law and in practice." If not, cautioned Nissan, we will become "the dirt of the land."[115]

Iraqis buttressed their arguments about the discrimination they faced with facts. A fellow Iraqi, Ephraim Nahum, similarly complained that the name Iraqi had become a slur. They are being called Schwarze Juden (Black Jews). As an example he cited the Ministry of Religious Affairs, "which is more Ashkenazi than Israeli in its conduct and manners."[116] Young Iraqis began to collect data not only on the number of Iraqis with positions in state institutions but also on the number of Mizrahim, whom they believed were beginning to constitute the majority of the country's population. The historian Avraham Ben Ya'aqov noted that the Mizrahi communities in Israel made up about 42 percent of the population, but were not represented proportionally. He acknowledged that the prime minister was trying to rectify the situation, but that low-level bureaucrats were thwarting the rise of the new generation.[117] Shlomo Ben Menachem 'Eini represented the discrimination in the Israeli Internal Revenue Service in numerical terms: it employed only three Sephardi clerks out of a hundred (in addition to twelve supervisors). When he recommended an Iraqi trainee he was told there was no job for her.[118]

Iraqi-Jewish educator Victor Mu'allim explained in 1957 how race divided Jewish Israel into a first and second Israel. Israel was composed of two branches: European and Eastern. Mu'allim also pointed to the demographic paradox of Mizrahi life in Israel. On the one hand, Mizrahi families were told to have many children in the interest of national security (so that a sizeable Jewish majority will come into being). On the other hand, the state did nothing to support these children. He proposed that gap between second Israel and Ashkenazi Israel was deepening; the second Israel consisted of thousands of souls, living in densely populated apartments and in slums, who did not graduate from high school or attend universities.[119] In a letter to the newspaper *'Al ha-Mishmar* following the riots in Wadi Salib, he denounced the violence of the rebels, yet added:

> For years we warned the heads of the majority party to stop classifying people based on their country of origin.... In Wadi Salib, Migdal ha-'Emek, and Beersheba, there were days of tensions as a result of the existence of poverty, destitu-

tion, unemployment, bitterness, ignorance, and sickness. The problem of the discrimination of the people of the East is a problem of a social nature.[120]

The riots about which Mu'allim is speaking here involved North African Jews for the most part. While he did not condone the violence, he was sympathetic to the participants' concerns as Mizrahim: they were discriminated against and deserved the support of fellow Iraqis. Being Mizrahi signifies here being victimized by the state despite being Israeli citizens.

In the Arabic publications of Iraqi Jews, the word *Ta'ifiyya*, which in Iraqi national discourse signified confessionalism and sectarianism, was used to describe ethnic divisions between Jews of different ethnicities. As Arab national discourse (which Iraqi Jews knew from Iraq) called for an end to sectarianism for the sake of national unity, Iraqi Jews called for an end to sectarianism in Israel to ensure the unity of Jews within that country. By writing about the marginalization of their culture, some Iraqi Jews were suggesting that the melting-pot ideology simply did not work and that a multiplicity of cultures should and could exist in the land; neither was better than the other. Others called for a unity of communities in Israel, but argued that the melting-pot ideology, or the merger of exiles in Israel—a very worthy Zionist cause—could not be realized in Israel because of ethnic divisions and sectarianism.

The attention to race was strong in the leftist press, despite the fact that both MAPAM and MAKI believed that class, and not race, was at the core of the problems of Mizrahi Jews, and despite MAPAM's official line of favoring the melting-pot ideology. The leadership of MAPAM was willing to recognize, because of its hatred of MAPAI, that sectarian divisions existed in Israel. *Al-Mirsad* reported that on his visit to Kfar 'Ana, Knesset member Hannan Rubin raised the issue of sectarian separation (*tafriq ta'ifi*), decrying the fact that one race lived in fine houses and the other did not.[121] MAPAM's journal, *'Al ha-Mishmar*, which printed a few supplements in Arabic, stressed that it sought to address the *unique* needs of Eastern Jewry, whose situation was very vulnerable.[122] Many articles in *Al-Mirsad* from the first issue on, especially those by David Cohen and Latif Dori, characterized the racial (*'unsuri*) divisions in Israel as resembling apartheid. They proposed that the government actively prevented the merger of exiles and that Israel was based on separation, which created two racially different groups, one employed and the other not, and starving as a result. David Cohen wrote in MAPAM's *Ila al-Amam* that this division into two communities (*tawa'if*) of Ashkenazim and Mizrahim (*abna' al-tawa'if al-sharqiyya*) hindered the rise of the next generation of Israelis.[123] *Ila al-Amam*, which circulated mostly in the transit camps of Or Yehuda, called for an end to the racist divisions between communities in Israel.[124]

Ibrahim Shamash, from Khayriyya, continued this line of thinking in his article "The Cry of Hunger," in *Al-Mirsad*. The new division created by the government, Shamash contended, separated the people into slave mongers (*musta'abid*) and slaves. The idea was to keep people hungry so that they would vote for MAPAI: "We migrated from our country to be one nation," he wrote, and yet faced this ethnic division. He found some hope, however, in the fact that history showed that the hungry would eventually rise up to break their shackles.[125] The article reflects the desire of the Mizrahim to be integrated into Israeli society, and yet it points out that the regime in Israel was seeking to enslave people of a particular race and color. The solution was to rise against the oppressors (*tugha*)—in Israel.

Demography was frequently a topic in *Al-Mirsad*, as a number of articles noted that the Eastern community was becoming a majority. One author, Syrian-Jewish Avraham 'Abbas, acknowledged this fact while resisting the implication that it should embolden Mizrahim to put forward their concerns at the expense of other groups.[126] 'Abbas was more cautious because he believed in the merging of communities and exiles, but other readers were less optimistic and wrote about an ethnic regime that was taking shape before their eyes. One reader observed, for example, that while a great deal of attention was given to Soviet Jewry in other countries, the unemployed Jewry from Eastern lands in Israel were ignored.[127]

The parallel and antagonistic trajectories of Israelization and the battle against discrimination comes up in letters written by Iraqi youth who lived on kibbutzim (associated with all branches of labor Zionism). The teenagers called for the unity of all the communities in Israel.[128] Avraham Yehezkel, from Gan Shmu'el, connected what was happening on his kibbutz to the reality throughout Israel:

> "Discrimination" . . . is a word that comes from the mouths of every Mizrahi newcomer. And this discrimination that everybody complains about is about all sorts of things; in the government, and among the Ashkenazi residents in the country. For example, in the transit camps you see that the newcomers who come to [this] country from Europe can get housing from the [Jewish] Agency in a short time, and where they want. And the Mizrahim are given housing in places they do not want and after a longer time. The discrimination between ourselves and the people of the country exists, as if we are strangers and not one Jewish nation, in the sense that most of the people of the land are Ashkenazim,

and we, the Mizrahim, are a minority. For this reason the Ashkenazim think they have more rights than the people of the East. They think that the Jews of the East are less educated than they are. The opposite in fact is the truth. I do not wish to argue against the people of the West, but I would like to say that this problem causes great hatred among the Jewish people.[129]

These young men were fully supportive of the idea of labor Zionism—that Israel is a Jewish and socialist state. But they suggest that the mistreatment of the Mizrahim on the kibbutz and throughout the country goes against Zionist ideology, which emphasizes Jewish unity within Israel, and against socialist ideology.

The communist press was less committed to the idea of the merger of exiles and spoke more about the merger of classes. Like MAPAM, communist writers wrote about the rise of a particular Mizrahi identity in Israel, and, importantly, connected it to the discrimination against Palestinians. In their reports, uniquely, Israel was not a land of its Jews, but of all of its ethnic and religious groups. A. Peck wrote as early as 1949 in *Kol ha-'Am* that the Mizrahim (*'edot ha-mizrah*) suffer from "social oppression and sectarian [*'adatit*] discrimination." This discrimination, in the fields of employment, education, social services, and military service, positioned the Mizrahi Jews in the lower ranks of society. Another danger, however, was looming large since "many of the Mizrahim have yet to understand the connection between the racial [*giz'it*] discrimination against the Arabs and the sectarian [*'adatit*] discrimination with respect to them."[130] A pamphlet in Arabic from December 1957, addressed to the people of the transit camp in Rehovot, presented more explanation of the racial tensions in Israel: "The policy of MAPAI and its reactionary allies [toward the Mizrahim] is the same policy addressed against the Arab minority in this country, which now clearly concerns all publics in Israel. By [the creation of] racial blocks [*kutal 'unsuriyya*] now planned for the Jewish citizens, as was done before with the Arab citizens, they want to bring their supporters to power."[131] The pamphlet, then, suggested that just as the Arab-Palestinian population was divided into Christians and Muslims, the Jewish population will become racially divided between Ashkenazim and Mizrahim, all for the benefit of the present hegemonic party.

Writers like Sami Michael and Shim'on Ballas addressed the discrimination against Mizrahim in Israel. They recognized that the Arab culture of the Mizrahim was the focal point of the prejudice and that a new Mizrahi identity was being born out of the experience of discrimination. Sami Michael expressed this Mizrahi solidarity in his Arabic short stories, whose protagonists were not only Iraqis and Palestinians, but also Egyptians, Yemenites, and Moroccans. "Hadha abbi" (This Is My Father) focuses on a Mizrahi teenager whose father is killed when the transit camp's guard mistakes him for an Arab; "Tabaraka al-rabb" (Praise Be to God) deals with the discrimination against the Yemenites; and "Al-Aswad" (The Black) centers on a Moroccan teenager about to commit suicide. In all these stories, the marginalization and persecution of the Mizrahim in Israeli society, and the tragic outcomes of these processes, are important themes.[132]

Michael based a Hebrew short story on an event that occurred in August 1950 in the camp of Pardes Hannah, where Avraham Harosh, a forty-eight-year-old man and father of five, was beaten to death by policemen after he demanded work and housing. In response, dozens of newcomers rioted. In the course of the riots, four people were arrested and one man, 'Abdallah Sha'ul, fifty-five, was severely beaten, while two of his sons were among those arrested. The official response by the police was that Harosh died from a sudden stroke and that the rioters caused a great deal of damage and stoned the Hadera police force.[133]

In response, Michael penned a short story, which follows two newcomers, the Iraqi Avraham and the Egyptian Moshe, who live in a transit camp. Avraham had worked for Iraq's rail authority but was fired because of his participation in a strike. Moshe is a Zionist; he hopes for a better future and trusts the state, although he misses Egypt very much: "His old house stood, almost as it was there, in front of his eyes. He imagined himself sitting pleasantly, reading satirical newspapers, with his wife busy with their children, in an atmosphere filled with happiness and bliss." Moshe cannot stand Avraham's constant critique of the Israeli state. In the course of one of their arguments, Moshe asks his Iraqi friend:

> "Well, why did you come here after all and leave your Arab friends?" He pronounced the word "Arabs" with contempt and with rage.
>
> Avraham ... replied calmly ... : "Thousands are asking themselves why they came. You ask this very same question in moments of pessimism. You thought that your coming here would put an end to persecution. I came here hoping to find a livelihood; apparently I had illusions as well. But as you can see in this transit camp, no solution is to be found.... As for returning to my Arab friends, the time has passed, and there is no need for that. Had I stayed there, I would have fought ... for better conditions there. I can do the same here.

However, it is Moshe, the Zionist, who finally succumbs, while Avraham survives. Told by officials in the employment office in the camp that there is no work for him, Moshe begins to shout, frustrated by his repeated, unsuccessful efforts to secure even a modest livelihood for his family. Two policemen arrive to calm him down; while he begs for mercy, the policemen beat Moshe to death. He "dropped down unconsciously, not realizing how a Jew could be beaten by a fellow Jew."[134]

In the story, Michael turns the victim of police violence into a Zionist Egyptian Jew. Furthermore, for both Iraqi and Egyptian Jews, the travel from Arab lands to the Jewish homeland is not represented as the passage from an oppressive exile to a blissful paradise, but rather as the continuation of oppression and exploitation—in fact, the deterioration of one's living conditions—and eventual death. The text, importantly, demands of its readers that they ask why the Iraqis and the Egyptians came to Israel and what happened to them there. Being Mizrahi in this text means that memories of the Arab past shape the characters' views of the Israeli present and that solidarity is fostered between Jews of different Middle Eastern states against discrimination and violence in and of the state of Israel.

To conclude, the concept of Mizrahi-ness was an Israeli creation and was born out of the fact that Middle Eastern Jews accepted Israel as their homeland, albeit with much difficulty and resentment. A Mizrahi Jew could be a Zionist who believed in the merger of exiles or a radical communist who shared his sorrows with the Palestinians. He or she may have spoken Arabic, Turkish, Persian, or Georgian, or have been sons and daughters of native speakers of these languages. But this Mizrahi identity—for all—was forged out of the recognition that racial and ethnic discrimination existed in Israel. During the 1950s and 1960s Iraqi Jews, especially in their writings in Arabic, but also in their letters, petitions, and protests, articulated a sense of Mizrahi-ness. They identified the ethnic divide in their new country; they pointed to the correlation between ethnicity and socioeconomic privilege; and they used harsh words—division, sectarianism, separation, and partition—to describe the realities of disunion created after the mass migration. The realization that they shared a great deal with other Middle Eastern Jews led to harsh critiques of the Ashkenazi leadership of the country, its hegemony, and its callous bureaucracy, as well as a call for Mizrahi solidarity and the demand that all Israeli citizens be able to enjoy their civil rights.

CONCLUSION

This chapter underscores a few processes relating to various kinds of Iraqi-Jewish identity formation in Israel before 1967. These identities were not monolithic but were intertwined with one another; often Iraqis felt themselves to be Mizrahi and Iraqi at the same time. The oscillation between Mizrahi, Iraqi, and Arab-Jewish identities allowed Iraqi Jews to maintain strong ties with the Arab world and yet simultaneously separate themselves from this world. In the early 1950s, Iraqi and Arab identities were dominant. Iraqi Jews spoke Arabic in the transit camps and intellectuals wrote in that language. Iraqi Jews missed Iraq and longed to return to it. With the realization that theirs was a destiny shared with other Jews, with Iraqi-Jewish children being raised as Israeli citizens, and with increased opportunities for employment, their outlook began to change. More and more Iraqi Jews saw themselves as Mizrahi. Furthermore, their knowledge of Arab culture ceased to be a radical tool by means of which to form bonds with the Palestinians, as communist intellectuals had hoped, but was turned to the service of the state, and helped it to protect its regional and geostrategic interests.

Iraqi Jews, nonetheless, were far from satisfied with the State of Israel. As Mizrahim they fought discrimination and wrote about their marginalization in a state that aimed to be secular, socialist, and Jewish; they demanded their rights as Jewish citizens in a Jewish state. These rights were not always accorded to them, but the construction of the Mizrahi identity helped Iraqi Jews to clearly articulate their demands. This process produced individuals who loved Arab and Iraqi food, loved Iraqi culture and music, but operated exclusively within Israeli-Jewish parameters. While communist radicals spoke of a joint battle with the Palestinians, the majority chose another route, as they tried to survive discrimination and unemployment. The state's policies of dividing different populations were highly successful in this regard. Despite their love of Umm Kalthum, Iraqi Jews realized they lived in the land of Golda Meir. And they acted accordingly.

CONCLUSION

The Death of Arab Jewishness

IN THE FALL OF 2015, Palestinians and Israelis lived through yet another "wave of violence." In one noteworthy incident, an Israeli man stabbed another Jew in Kiryat Ata. The attacker was searching for an Arab to kill to avenge the death of fellow Jews. His victim, the twenty-three-year-old Uriel Razkan, recaptured his experiences in an interview with IDF radio: "I heard a shout: 'You deserve it, you deserve it, Arab bastards!' When I turn around I see a Haredi man. I shouted to him, 'I'm a Jew,' but he tried to continue. I just ran away; otherwise I would have been killed."[1] Tragically, some sixty years after the mass migration of Iraqi and other Middle Eastern Jews to Israel, it is still dangerous for a Jew to look like an Arab in the Jewish state. And given the Arab-Israeli conflict, it will continue being dangerous for years to come.

The fear of not being able to distinguish between Arabs and Jews, and the state's consequent desire to create a clear separation between the two groups, deeply affected Iraqi Jews, a community of Arabic-speaking Jews, whose members experienced the pains of migration and displacement when they arrived in Israel in the early 1950s. The Iraqi-Jewish migrants were utterly dependent on the state that had taken them in as the provider of their food, clothing, housing, and employment. The state's leadership sought to Westernize, Zionize, and discipline the Iraqi migrants, yet lacked the most basic resources to do so. Nonetheless, every failure of the state's integration and absorption policies was presented as the migrants' fault, being attributed to their "primitivism" and "lack of knowledge of Western norms." These newcomers were also seen as a voting bloc bound to MAPAI's, Israel's ruling party, whose members used their party's control over the transit camps in which the newcomers lived to ensure their party's reelection. The extent of the sufferings of the Iraqi and Mizrahi Jews, the deaths of migrants in transit camps, and the phenomenon of child and teenage labor, have not yet been fully documented, and I hope that this book will shed some light on this case of historical injustice, which has not been treated in depth in Israeli historiography and is virtually unknown in the United States.

Iraqi Jews resisted state policies. They exercised political agency by squatting, demonstrating, writing petitions, working within the Israeli political parties to generate change, organizing within radical leftist and communist organizations, and most especially by struggling to maintain their human dignity and normalcy under destitute conditions. Mothers fought for their children to get a decent education, fathers took possession of wooden shacks and empty apartments so that their families would have a roof over their heads, parents stole boxes and pieces of wood to improvise furniture in shacks and tents, and writers insisted on preserving their Iraqi and Arab cultural heritage in a state that celebrated its Hebrew culture. In a sense, these Iraqis were some of the first to battle for social justice and equality in the new state.

Iraqi Jews slowly became Israelis. Education in the new state, acquisition of Hebrew speaking and reading skills, the rise of a new generation of Israelis of Iraqi origins, and the realization that being Jewish in the Jewish state was connected to privileges, enabled Iraqi Jews to integrate into the new state during the 1960s and 1970s. Many Iraqis, moreover, worked within the state bureaucracy, using their skills, especially their mastery of Arabic language and culture, to serve Israel's Hasbara, security, and educational efforts. Iraqi Jews, moreover, framed their demands to obtain citizenship rights not only as citizens but also as Jews. This inevitably created some fissures between them and the Palestinians. Moreover, the state fostered such divisions by pitting Palestinians against Mizrahim or at least keeping them in separate communities. Transit camps were located on the lands of depopulated Palestinian villages, and former Palestinian neighborhoods and villages, especially in southern Tel Aviv, became slums populated by Iraqis and other Mizrahim. While Eastern and Central European Jews who had come to Ottoman and Mandatory Palestine before 1948 gained the most from the deportation of the Palestinians and the confiscation of their lands, Iraqi Jews fathomed well the message that the state broadcast to them in every possible venue: in the Jewish state, it is better to be a Jew. On the other hand, Iraqi Jews had a different vision of Judaism than that of the state's elites; they did not identify with the state's attempts to turn Judaism from a faith into a secular and national ideology, as attested, for example, in the difficulties of many Iraqi youth to adjust to the secular culture of the kibbutzim.

The conditions faced by the Iraqi-Jewish community changed after the 1967. Palestinians from the occupied West Bank entered the Israeli labor market and took jobs in services and construction once held by Mizrahim. The Iraqi-Israeli community was divided between more-established members who managed to find a foothold in Israeli society, relying on social capital acquired either in Iraqi or on Israeli educational institutions, and those who could not find a way out of the cycle of poverty, and who lived in poor neighborhoods, such as Ha-Tikva and Salameh in Tel Aviv, and in towns in the periphery of Israel.

In the 1970s, the political landscape of Israel changed. The 1973 war against Egypt and Syria, during which over two thousand Israeli soldiers were killed, left many Israelis with the sense that MAPAI had not done enough to protect the state's security. Corruption charges against MAPAI's members fueled more anger toward that party. Beginning in 1971, the Mizrahi Black Panthers movement was active nationally, with a particularly strong presence in Jerusalem. The Panthers organized demonstrations, protesting socio-ethnic discrimination in Israel. Although North African Jews mostly headed the movement, Iraqis did play a role, especially the charismatic Kokhavi Shemesh, an Iraqi Jerusalemite who attended a historic meeting between the leaders of the Israeli and the American Black Panthers; Angela Davis represented the American side. The Panthers brought to the public sphere a new-old radical Mizrahi agenda—and they were crushed by the state in the mid-1970s as a result. And yet, their protests should be seen against the background laid out in this book, one of ongoing social protests and demonstrations dating back to the 1950s. Those gave rise to the protests of the second generation, who shared the pains of their parents.[2]

The Israeli elections of 1977 marked another change. A second generation of Mizrahim, no longer fearful of MAPAI, and resentful of the discrimination against their parents, voted for Likud, a right-wing party that emerged out of Herut. The party, still under the leadership of Menachem Begin, supported the Mizrahi agenda. As we have seen, however, Begin had articulated such views during the 1950s, when he toured the transit camps in his election campaigns. As the Israeli premier, Begin embarked on projects meant to renovate slums and improved the educational system in poor neighborhoods and development towns. Paradoxically, the long-time Iraqi MAPAI members of the Knesset, like Shlomo Hillel and Shoshanna Arbeli Almozlino, now found themselves in opposition to Mizrahi Knesset members, especially young North African Likud members, who represented a new Mizrahi leadership. The Israeli right offered much, but this came with a certain price; and the price was almost always at the expense of the Palestinians. Housing opportunities, for example, were now ample and cheaper, partly because the affordable housing projects were located in settlements in the West Bank and Gaza, a result of the right's embracing of the Messianic (and Ashkenazi) Jewish settlement movement in the West Bank.[3]

Mizrahi Jews, according to many polls, continue to vote for right-wing parties, claiming they are more patriotic than members of parties associated with labor Zionism.[4] This, despite the fact that the neoliberal policies of right-wing parties in the last two decades further marginalized poor Mizrahim. Given the narrative of this book, especially MAPAI's attitude toward the Mizrahim, it is not surprising that many Mizrahim resent the Israeli labor movement. While some Iraqis remain loyal members of parties associated with labor Zionism and liberal Zionism, and in fact are leading figures in them, voting patterns in such places as Or Yehuda or southern Tel Aviv evidence consistent support for parties that are to the right of the Israeli center. Seemingly, this reality can be seen as the failure of MAPAI: instead of breeding a generation of faithful voters, the party created the communities that led to its demise. On the other hand, if MAPAI's aim was to Zionize Iraqi Jews and separate them from their Arab heritage, the success is well beyond what the MAPAI leadership of the 1950s could have hoped for.

The 1980s and 1990s saw the rise (and fall) of sectarian Mizrahi parties that designated the Mizrahi agenda, and only the Mizrahi agenda, as their main concern. The most important of these is the highly successful Shas Party, which emerged out of ultraorthodox circles, where the discrimination against Mizrahim was extremely blatant. Led by Rabbi 'Ovadia Yosef, an Iraqi rabbi who is famous for innovative ruling granting, Shas (albeit Haredi) seemed like a new alternative. It appealed mostly to North African Jews, and to Mizrahim on the periphery of Israel, who relied on its educational and social services. Its members early on collaborated with the centrist government of Yitzhak Rabin, with 'Ovadia Yosef declaring that it was permissible to give land to the Arabs to achieve a permanent peace (Yosef had also positioned himself as a moderate voice after the 1967 war, cautioning believers not to violate the sanctity of Temple Mount / Al-Haram al-Sharif in Jerusalem). Shas, however, as an orthodox religious party, angered liberal Zionist parties, because of its adherence to Halachic law, including Sabbath and dairy strictures. Shas was also unable to form a true opposition to the state. Relying on state support for its educational and rabbinical institutions, Shas mostly desired to collaborate with Israeli governments.[5] One of its leaders, Elie Yishay, who rose to prominence in the 2000s, was noted for his racism, especially toward non-Jewish labor migrants and African asylum seekers.

Over the years, the Iraqi community preserved its identity surrounding the circles of belonging I described in this book. The Babylonian-Iraqi identity was, and remains, very strong; Iraqi Israelis raised funds and built a distinguished museum, the Center for the Heritage of Babylonian Jewry, in Or Yehuda. The site commemorates the community's history prior to the arrival in Israel. Iraqi-Jewish intellectuals formed the Society for Exiled Iraqi-Jewish Academics, which publishes and documents various aspects of Iraq's Jewish culture and history in the books it prints in both Arabic and Hebrew. The city of Or Yehuda still retains its Iraqiness; its host of restaurants and cafés, in what is called "Little Baghdad," offer Iraqi food cooked by and for Iraqi Jews (as well as others). The second generation of Iraqi Israelis celebrates this Iraqi sense of identity. Grandchildren of Iraqi musicians are revisiting the music of the Iraqi past and returning to the Mizrahi cafés of the 1950s, and produce cover versions of old Iraqi songs: Dudu Tasa (Da'ud al-Kuwaiti's grandson) has recorded his grandfather and great uncle's music. Other Iraqi musicians, like Ya'ir Dallal, play Iraqi music both in Israel and abroad and collaborate with the former members of the Orchestra of the Voice of Israel in Arabic. Young writers like Almog Behar, Elie Eliyahu, and Mati Shemoelof narrate the silenced history of their grandparents in their poetry, short stories, and novels. A recent Israeli film, based on a best-selling novel by Elie Amir, "The Dove Flier," told the story of the migration of a Jewish family from Baghdad. The Israeli cast, mostly comprised of second-generation Iraqi Jews, spoke in the Iraqi-Jewish dialect. The film was a smashing box-office success.[6]

The digital age has connected between Iraqi Jews in Israel and fellow Iraqis in Iraq and in the diaspora via websites, chat groups, and other modes of social media, and has enabled Iraqis of different faiths, after years of separation, to converse about the past and the present. Iraqi Muslims and Christians, in fact, have shown a great interest in Jewish-Iraqi history and cultural activities. Baghdadi publishers and writers produce works about Iraqi Jews: the biographies of Shmu'el Moreh and Sasson Somekh, as well as literary texts written in Hebrew by Iraqi Jews, have appeared in Arabic translations in the global Arab press and in Iraq. In Israel, Facebook groups, formed to preserve Iraqi heritage have become popular. While some Iraqis connect their Iraqi-Jewish identity to broader Mizrahi and Palestinian circles, others, like the members of the Facebook group Preserving the Iraqi Language (Meshamrim et ha-safa ha-'iraqit), focus chiefly on their Iraqi identity.[7] The members of this Facebook group see themselves as Israeli patriots who care deeply about their Iraqi heritage. The group offers Arabic classes in the Iraqi-Jewish dialect for the younger members of the Israeli-Iraqi community, circulates photos and pictures from Iraq before the migration and photos from the 1950s, maintains connections with the Iraqi diaspora, and posts YouTube videos in the Iraqi dialect.

The Mizrahi identity is strong among the newer generation of Iraqi Jews, and is reflected upon in the works of some of the young poets like Almog Behar.[8] Third-generation Israeli Iraqis are finding ways to identify with the suffering of other Mizrahim as part of a broader struggle for social justice. The debates on color and race in Israeli society changed in the last generation. The migration of Ethiopian Jews in 1988, currently one of Israel's most underprivileged groups, meant that there were now Jewish groups more "blackened" than the Mizrahim, who were once conceptualized as black vis-à-vis the Ashkenazi European white. In a recent wave of demonstrations during the spring of 2015, Ethiopian Jews protesting their discrimination identified with African Americans in Baltimore and Ferguson.[9] Mizrahim and Ethiopians sometimes work together, but at other times, the groups are pitted against one another. In Or Yehuda, for example, racial tensions arose between the older residents of the city and the poorer Ethiopians.[10] The Russian migration to Israel following the fall of the Soviet Union had an interesting and unexpected outcome. It represented a major wave of Ashkenazi migrants, who were sent initially to development towns and absorption centers. While the educational and social capital of the Russian Jews enabled their relatively easy integration to the labor market, these newcomers, unlike many others, insisted on a politics of cultural pluralism and strove, successfully, to maintain their culture in Israel. Its multicultural vision has proven inspirational to Mizrahi Jews as well.

The accentuation of the Mizrahi identity was a defining characteristic of a newer organization, Ha-Keshet ha-Demokratit ha-Mizrahit (the Democratic Mizrahi Rainbow), which was active in the 1990s. Established by Mizrahi Jews, this organization put forth an agenda based on Mizrahi-Ashkenazi equality, social justice, unprejudiced distribution of resources in Israel, peace with the Palestinians, and a just solution to the Arab-Israeli conflict. In this Pan-Mizrahi organization Iraqi voices were heard clearly: Yehouda Shenhav, Yossi Yona, and Shoshanna Gabai were among the leaders and intellectuals of this movement. In the academic field, Ella Shohat's appearances on Israeli TV, and the translations of her works into Hebrew, shaped the nature of Mizrahi studies in Israel. The sociologist Yehouda Shenhav's discussions of the concept of "the Arab Jews," his interviews on *Haaretz*, and his studies of Israel's relations with the Iraqi-Jewish community have created a new language and a new research agenda. Shenhav's importance also emanated from his position within Israeli academia. His editorship of the prestigious journal *Te'oriya u-Bikoret* (Theory and Criticism) and the seminars he has been arranging on the topic at the Van Leer Institute in Jerusalem have inspired a whole generation of Israeli researchers, who have studied how Jewish communities from Muslim lands were imagined and othered in Israel. *Te'oriya u-Bikoret* was also instrumental in reconfiguring the Israeli literary canon by focusing attention on Mizrahi writers like Sami Michael and Shim'on Ballas.[11]

Indeed, Ballas and Michael, long after they left MAKI, became important writers in Israel. They wrote in Hebrew about Iraqi, Arab, Palestinian, and Israeli experiences. The first Hebrew novels by Ballas and Michael depicted the transit camps. Ballas, in fact, was the first to use the term *Arab-Jew* when writing for an Israeli audience. Michael's 1992 best-selling novel, *Victoria*, focuses on Jewish women in interwar Baghdad, while his novel *Trumpet in the Vadi*, which has been included in the Israeli school curriculum, deals with a Palestinian family in Haifa during the 1980s. Ballas, Michael, and Sasson Somekh continued working in translation. Michael translated Mahfuz's Cairian trilogy into Hebrew, Ballas edited anthologies of translated Palestinian literature, and Somekh translated Arabic short stories and dozens of poems by Mahmud Darwish, Samih al-Qasim, and many others. Now, celebrating his ninetieth birthday, Michael is still involved in politics as the president of the Israeli Civil Rights Association. In the summer of 2012, he delivered a keynote speech at the Israel studies conference. Shocked by the pogroms against African labor migrants in Tel Aviv, Michael showed that he had not changed much from his radical days in the Israel of the 1950s. Michael spoke about his own pains as a migrant, about racial discrimination in Israel, and about his sympathy for the victims. *Haaretz* reported that some of the attendees were utterly dismayed, complaining that this was the most anti-Israeli speech they had heard in their lives.[12] Ballas, Somekh, Semah, and Moreh became professors of Arabic literature and established the study of modern Arabic literature within Israeli academia.

Today, Iraqis and Mizrahim live in an Israeli context typified by contradictions. On the one hand, a Mizrahi revival is currently taking place. Silenced histories like the kidnapping of Yemenite babies are discussed publicly, and the Ministry of Education revised teaching programs to integrate Mizrahi history and literature into the curricula of all schools in Israel. Every day there appears yet another article, essay, or work of art exploring ethnic divisions among Israeli Jews.[13] The majority of Mizrahim, however, do not speak Arabic. Mizrahi poets, historians, social scientists, novelists, and writers, among them many Iraqis, are doing much to reflect on Jewish life in Muslim lands and unpack the systems of discrimination that exist in Israeli society to this day. A clear indication of this spirit, which rose high in the beginning of the Arab spring, was a letter written by Mizrahi Jews to fellow Arab rebels:

> We, as the descendants of the Jewish communities of the Arab and Muslim world, the Middle East and the Maghreb, and as the second and third generation of Mizrahi Jews in Israel, are watching with great excitement and curiosity the major role that the men and women of our generation are playing so courageously in the demonstrations for freedom and change across the Arab world. We identify with you and are extremely hopeful for the future of the revolutions....
>
> We are Israelis, the children and grandchildren of Jews who lived in the Middle East and North Africa for hundreds and thousands of years. Our forefathers and mothers contributed to the development of this region's culture, and were part and parcel of it. Thus the culture of the Islamic world and the multigenerational connection and identification with this region is an inseparable part of our own identity....
>
> We, too, live in a regime that in reality—despite its pretensions to being "enlightened" and "democratic"—does not represent large sections of its actual population in the Occupied Territories and inside of the Green Line border(s). This regime tramples the economic and social rights of most of its citizens, is in an ongoing process of minimizing democratic liberties, and constructs racist barriers against Arab-Jews, the Arab people, and Arabic culture. Unlike the citizens of Tunisia and Egypt, we are still a long way from the capacity to build the kind of solidarity between various groups that we see in these countries, a solidarity movement that would allow us to unite and march together—all who reside here—into the public squares, to demand a civil regime that is culturally, socially, and economically just and inclusive.[14]

Recently, however, many radical Mizrahim have taken a more sectarian position, focusing exclusively on the Mizrahi struggle. These Mizrahi activists argue that the liberal Zionist left, or what they called "the white left," has done nothing for the sake of the Mizrahim, not even recognizing the horrors of the 1950s or battling to close socioeconomic gaps within Israel society today. Some Mizrahi activists still see the solution to this predicament in a joint alliance with Palestinian activists against state politics. Many others, however, contend that any position that seems to echo a liberal Zionist concern, not to mention a radical pro-Palestinian one, is detrimental to attempts to create Mizrahi solidarity, which must include left- and right-leaning Mizrahim. They likewise argue that the divisions between left and right become meaningless in Israeli politics. In the 2015 elections, the slogan "Mizrahim vote for Mizrahim" assumed much popularity in some circles. Radical Mizrahim, moreover, are presently facing a harsh dilemma. There are Likud members who promote the Mizrahi cause and are willing to invest money in development towns and poor neighborhoods. When it comes to Mizrahim, these right-wingers produce very subtle observations about hegemony, oppressed Mizrahi cultures and histories, and the problems of secular liberalism. Unfortunately, when it comes to the rights of the Palestinians, all such sensitivities quickly disappear; chauvinism, oppression, and bigotry replace passionate support of multiculturalism and critical approaches to Israel's past; revisionism, to them, is a privilege preserved only to the Jewish victims of the state.

The roots of these debates should be located in the 1950s, when some Iraqi Jews chose to focus on exclusively the Mizrahi and Iraqi struggle, while others, like Ballas, Semah, Somekh, and Michael, sided with the Palestinians. Looking ahead, it seems very plausible that Israel will become a more segregated and sectarian society. Most Palestinians will be relegated to miserable lives within a subordinate Palestinian authority and in disaster-stricken Gaza, and Palestinian-Israeli citizens will be discriminated against as third-rate citizens. And the group of marginalized Jews, who once lived in Arab countries such as Iraq and still partake in Mizrahi Arab culture as produced in Israel, will ignore (or even cheer) this segregation, while battling against the discrimination they still face in the state. They will not argue, as Golda Meir has done, that a tent in Israel is better than a house in Baghdad. They will simply battle to attain a better house in Israel. Hopefully, thought, shared notions of victimhood and a joint battle for justice and historical recognition will unite various groups in Israeli society and create a better future for Israel-Palestine. For all its people. Right now, though, this future seems painfully far off.

APPENDIX
Main Transit Camps

NORTHERN DISTRICT
- 'Afula
- Halsa
- Mansi
- Rosh Pina

HAIFA DISTRICT
- Binyamina
- Kfar Ata
- Tira
- Zichron Ya'aqov

CENTRAL DISTRICT
- Agrobank
- Amisav / Petach Tikva
- Beit Lid
- 'Emek Hefer
- Kfar Nahman

JERUSALEM DISTRICT
- Hartuv (Har Tov)
- Makor Haim
- Talpiot

TEL AVIV DISTRICT
- Ijlil/Jalil
- Kfar 'Ana
- Khayriyya
- Kiryat Ono
- Ramat ha-Sharon
- Sakiyya

SOUTHERN DISTRICT
- Be'er Ya'aqov
- Kastina
- Kubeiba
- Zarnuga

ABBREVIATIONS

ASA   Department for Self-Rule (Agaf le-Shilton 'Atzmi)
CWJ   Councils of the Workers of Jerusalem (Mo'ezet Po'alim)
CZA   Central Zionist Archive (Ha-Archiyon ha-Tzioni ha-Merkazi), Jerusalem
DRP   Dov Rozen Papers, collected in: Dov Rozen, ed., *Ma'abarot ve yeshuvey 'olim be-aspaklariya shel misrad ha-pnim* (Tel Aviv: Misrad Ha-Pnim, 1985)
ISA   Israel State Archives (Ginzach ha-Medina), Jerusalem
JDS   American Jewish Joint Distribution Committee (online and in New York City)
LA   Lavon Archive (Ha Machon le-Heker Tn'uat ha-'Avoda 'al shem Pinhas Lavon), Tel Aviv
MYO   Mahlaka le-Yishuv 'Olim (Department for the Settlement of 'Olim)
MZ   Metzudat Ze'ev, Beit Jabotinsky, Tel Aviv
NLI   National Library of Israel, Posters Collection, Jerusalem
OWM   Organization of Working Mothers (Irgun Imahot 'Ovdot)
RK   Records of the Knesset (Divrey Yemey ha-Knesset), Jerusalem
YT   Yad Tabenkim Archives, Ramat Efal, Israel
YY   Yad Ya'ari, Kibbutz Giv'at Haviva, Israel

NOTES

INTRODUCTION

1. Records of the Knesset, State of Israel [henceforth: RK], vol. 23: 784; 3rd Knesset, session 403, 3–5/February/1958.

2. For the number of newcomers to Israel, see Chapter 1, p. 22.

3. Theodor Herzl, *Der Judenstaat: Versuch einer modernen Lösung der Judenfrage* (Leipzig: Breitenstein, 1896); for an important analysis of concepts of exile in Jewish history more broadly, see: Amnon Raz-Krakotzkin, "History, Exile and Counter-History: Jewish Perspectives," in *A Companion to global Historical Thought*, ed. Prasenjit Duara, Viren Murthy, and Andrew Sartori (Chichester: Wiley Blackwell, 2014), 126–35.

4. Aziza Khazzoom, "The Great Chain of Orientalism: Jewish Identity, Stigma Management, and Ethnic Exclusion in Israel," *American Sociological Review* 68:4 (2003): 481–510.

5. Michelle Campos, *Ottoman Brothers, Muslims, Christians, and Jews in Early Twentieth-Century Palestine* (Stanford, Calif.: Stanford University Press, 2011); Abigail Jacobson, *From Empire to Empire: Jerusalem between Ottoman and British Rule* (Syracuse, N.Y.: Syracuse University Press, 2011).

6. Hanna Yablonka, *Survivors of the Holocaust: Israel After the War*, trans. Ora Cummings (New York: Palgrave Macmillan, 1999); Tom Segev, *The Seventh Million: The Israelis and the Holocaust*, trans. Haim Watzman (New York: Hill and Wang, 1991, 1993).

7. Adam McKeown, "Global Migration, 1846–1940," *Journal of World History* 15:2 (2004): 155–89.

8. Keith David Watenpaugh, *Bread from Stones: The Middle East and the Making of Modern Humanitarianism* (Berkeley: University of California Press, 2015); Benjamin Thomas White, *The Emergence of Minorities in the Middle East: The Politics of Community in French Mandate Syria* (Edinburgh: Edinburgh University Press: 2012); Seda Altug, "Sectarianism in the Syrian Jazira: Community, Land, and Violence in the Memories of World War I and the French Mandate (1915–1939)," Ph.D. diss., Utrecht University, 2011.

9. On Jewish migration to Israel after 1948, see: S. N. Eisenstadt, *The Absorption of Immigrants* (London: Routledge and Kegan Paul, 1954); Dvora ha-Kohen, *'Olim bi-s'ara, ha-'Aliyah ha-gdolah u-klitatah be-Yisra'el, 1948–1953* (Jerusalem: Ben Tzvi, 1994); Moshe Lissak, *Ha-'Aliyah ha-gdola bi-shnot ha-hamishim, kishlono shel kur ha-hituch* (Jerusalem: Mosad Bialik, 1999); Mordechai Na'or, ed., *'Olim u Ma'abarot, 1948–1952* (Jerusa-

Yad Ben Tzvi, 1986); Dalia Ofer, ed., *Ben 'Olim le-Vatikim, Yisra'el ba-'aliya ha-gdola, 1948–1953* (Jerusalem, Yad Ben Tzvi, 1996); Orit Rozin, *Hovat ha-Ahava ha-qasha: Yahid ve-kolektiv be-Yisra'el bi-shnot ha-hamishim* (Tel Aviv: 'Am 'Oved, 2008).

10. For a useful comparison on how Depression-era reformers looked at the Jews and the Italians of the Lower East Side, see: Suzanne Wasserman, "'Our Alien Neighbors': Coping with the Depression on the Lower East Side," *American Jewish History* 88:2 (2000): 209–32.

11. For a brilliant analysis of state politics toward Mizrahim, see: Ella Shohat, "Sephardim in Israel: Zionism from the Standpoint of Its Jewish Victims," *Social Text* 19:20 (1988): 1–35.

12. For an excellent analysis of how migration to new urban spaces affects race relations and the African-American working class, see: Joseph Heathcott, "Black Archipelago: Politics and Civic Life in the Jim Crow City," *Journal of Social History* 38:3 (2005): 705–36.

13. On the productive ways of thinking of W. E. B. Du Bois's notion of outcasts and strangers in their homeland in the context of race relations in the United States, see: Thomas C. Holt, "The Political Uses of Alienation: W. E. B. Du Bois on Politics, Race, and Culture, 1903–1940," *American Quarterly* 42:2 (June 1990): 301–23.

14. Shira Robinson, *Citizen Strangers: Palestinians and the Birth of Israel's Liberal Settler State* (Stanford, Calif.: Stanford University Press, 2013).

15. Esther Meir-Glitzenstein, *Ben Bagdad le-Ramat Gan: Yotz'ey 'Iraq be-Yisra'el* (Jerusalem: Yad Ben-Tzvi, 2008), 111–12.

16. The fifth Annual Study Mission of the United Jewish Appeal to Israel, Europe and Muslim Lands, *The Other Side of the Coin: A Report to American Jewry*, October 29–November 9, 1958, American Jewish Joint Distribution Committee online archives [henceforth: JDC], http://search.archives.jdc.org/multimedia/Documents/NY_AR55-64/NY55-64_ORG_066/NY55-64_ORG_066_0962.pdf (accessed 7/March/2017).

17. For an excellent parallel on how Jews retain their eastern European culture in the United States, see: Rebecca Kobrin, "The Shtetl by the Highway: The East European City in New York's Landsmanshaft Press, 1921–39," *Prooftexts* 26:1–2 (2006): 107–37.

18. Attestations of this nostalgic approach around found in Tzila Dagon, *Sippura shel ma'abara be-Ramat ha-Sharon* (Ramat ha-Sharon: Ha-Merkazim ha-khilatiyyim Ramat ha-Sharon, 2007). The book includes fifty-nine testimonies of mostly Iraqi Jewish residents of the camp, and some former employees, that depict their daily experiences there. See also: Ines Elias, "Yaldey ha-Ma'abarot kotvim et ha-historia ha-mushteket," *Haaretz*, August 18, 2016, www.haaretz.co.il/gallery/.premium-1.3041521 (story on the children of the transit camp of Ness Ziona) (accessed 29/October/2016).

19. Thomas C. Holt, "Marking: Race, Race-Making, and the Writing of History," *American Historical Review*, 100:1 (1995): 1–20; see also: Mary Corbin Sies, "The Everyday Politics and Spatial Logics of Metropolitan Life," *Urban History Review/Revue d'Histoire Urbaine* 32:1 (2003): 28–42.

20. The foundational texts, influenced by modernization theory, are: S. N. Eisenstadt, *The Absorption of Immigrants* (London: Routledge and Kegan Paul, 1954), and *Es-*

says on Sociological Aspects of Political and Economic Development (The Hague: Mouton Press, 1961). For the changes in this ideology see: Daniel Gutwien, "From Melting Pot to Multiculturalism; or, The Privatization of Israeli Identity," in *Israeli Identity in Transition*, ed. Anita Shapira (Westport, Conn.: Praeger, 2004), 215–33.

21. Shlomo Swirski, *Israel's Oriental Majority* (London: Zed Books, 1989); Lissak, *Ha-'Aliyah*; Hannan Hever, Yehouda Shenhav, and Pnina Motzafi-Haller, eds., *Mizrahiyim be-Yisra'el, 'iyun bikorti mehudash* (Jerusalem: Van Leer, 2002); Gai Abutbul, Lev Grinberg, Peninah Motsafi-Haler, eds., *Kolot Mizrahiyim: Likrat siah mizrahi hadash 'al ha-hevra ve-ha-tarbut ha-Yisraelit* (Tel Aviv: Masada, 2005); Sammy Smooha, *Israel: Pluralism and Conflict* (London: Routledge and Paul Kegan, 1978); Aziza Khazzoom, *Shifting Ethnic Boundaries and Inequality in Israel; or, How the Polish Peddler Became a German Intellectual* (Stanford, Calif.: Stanford University Press, 2008); As'ad Ghanem, *Ethnic Politics in Israel: The Margins and the Ashkenazi Center* (London: Routledge, 2010); Oren Yiftachel, *Ethnocracy: Land and Identity Politics in Israel/Palestine* (Philadelphia: University of Pennsylvania Press, 2006); Khazzoom's excellent study in particular focuses on the formation of Mizrahi identity through allocation of resrouces, while paying heed to the Iraqi case .

22. Rozin, *Hovat*; Deborah S. Bernstein, "Ha-Ma'barot bi-shnot ha-hamishim," *Mahbarot le-mehkar u-le-bikoret* 5 (1980): 5–47; Meir-Glitzenstein, *Ben Bagdad*.

23. Scholars of Mizrahi history and politics, Sami Shalom Chetrit in particular, have argued that major Mizrahi resistance to the state began in 1959 with the riots of North African Jews in the Haifan region of Wadi Salib, and developed into a full-fledged resistance movement with the Mizrahi Black Panthers in the 1970s, and the more organized political movements of the 1980s and 1990s, like the SHAS party and the Democratic Mizrahi Rainbow. Sami Shalom Chetrit, *Intra Jewish Conflict in Israel: White Jews, Black Jews* (London: Routledge, 2010).

24. Bryan K. Roby, *The Mizrahi Era of Rebellion: Israel's Forgotten Civil Rights Struggle, 1948–1966* (Syracuse, N.Y.: Syracuse University Press, 2015).

25. For resistance in Palestinian-Israeli context: Joel Beinin, *Was the Red Flag Flying There? Marxist Politics and the Arab-Israeli Conflict in Egypt and Israel, 1948–1965* (Berkeley: University of California Press, 1990); Ilana Kaufman, *Arab National Communism in the Jewish State* (Gainesville: University Press of Florida, 1997); Maha Tawfik Nassar, "Affirmation and Resistance: Press, Poetry, and the Formation of National Identity Among Palestinian Citizens of Israel, 1948–1967" (Ph.D. diss., University of Chicago, 2006); On Palestinian communists, culture and literature, see: Ibrahim Taha, *The Palestinian Novel: A Communication Study* (London: Routledge/Curzon, 2002).

26. In Judaism, a division exists between Ashkenazi (literally, "German") and Sephardic (literally, "Spanish") communities. Ashkenazi denotes the Jews who lived in European lands and originated in Germany, whereas Sephardic means the Jews who were exiled from Spain in 1492 and found refuge in territories belonging to the Ottoman Empire, as well as in some European countries like the Netherlands. This division, which has been commonly understood in the Jewish world for centuries, excludes major Middle Eastern Jewish communities, whose roots date back to antiquity. Such com-

munities, however, were also called Sephardic because their prayers were based in part on formulas written in medieval Spain and they followed the rulings of Jewish scholars from Spain. See Ella Shohat, "The Invention of the Mizrahim," *Journal of Palestine Studies* 29:1 (1999): 5–20. On Mizrahim in Israel, see: Yehouda Shenhav, *The Arab Jews: A Postcolonial Reading of Nationalism, Religion, and Ethnicity* (Stanford, Calif.: Stanford University Press, 2006); Ella Shohat, *Taboo Memories, Diasporic Voices* (Durham, N.C.: Duke University Press, 2006).

27. Ussama Makdisi, "Pensée 4: Moving Beyond Orientalist Fantasy, Sectarian Polemic, and Nationalist Denial," *International Journal of Middle East Studies* [henceforth: *IJMES*] 40:4 (2008): 559.

28. Max Weiss, "Practicing Sectarianism in Mandate Lebanon: Shi'i Cemeteries, Religious Patrimony and the Everyday Politics of Difference," *Journal of Social History* 43:3 (2010): 708–9.

29. On Iraqi Jewish history, and its involvement in the Iraqi middle classes and the state's cultural and social elites, see: Orit Bashkin, *New Babylonians: A History of Jews in Modern Iraq* (Stanford, Calif.: Stanford University Press, 2012); Reuven Snir, ʻArviyut, Yahadut, Tziyonut: Ma'avak zehuyot bi-yetziratam shel yehudei ʻIraq (Jerusalem: Yad Ben Tzvi, 2005); Nissim Kazzaz, He-Yehudim be-ʻIraq ba-me'a he-ʻesrim (Jerusalem: Yad Ben Tzvi, 1991); Nissim Rejwan, *The Jews of Iraq: 3000 Years of History and Culture* (London: Weidenfeld and Nicolson, 1985).

30. On Yemen, see: Esther Meir-Glitzenstein, "Operation Magic Carpet: Constructing the Myth of the Magical Immigration of Yemenite Jews to Israel," *Israel Studies* 16:3 (2011): 149–73; on North Africa, see: Avi Picard, ʻOlim bi-msura: Mediniyut Yisra'el klapey ʻaliyatam shel yehudey tzfon Africa, 1951–1956 (Jerusalem: Mosad Bialik, 2013); Anat Mooreville, "Eyeing Africa: The Politics of Israeli Ocular Expertise and International Aid, 1959–1973," *Jewish Social Studies* 21:3 (2016): 31–71; on the changes in the historiography of Jewish community in the Middle East, see: Orit Bashkin, "The Middle Eastern Shift and Provincializing Zionism," *IJMES* 46:3 (2014): 577–80; see also: Meir-Glitzenstein, *Ben Bagdad*, 10–11.

31. Meir-Glitzenstein, *Ben Bagdad*.

32. Bashkin, *New Babylonians*, 58–99.

33. On Hebrew ideology see: Michael Levin et al., "Diyun: Ha-Tzmiha ve-ha-hitgabsuht shel tarbut ʻivrit mekomit u-yelidit be-eretz Yisra'el, 1882–1948," *Katedra* 16 (July 1980): 161–233.

34. Lital Levy, *Poetic Trespass: Writing between Hebrew and Arabic in Israel/Palestine* (Princeton, N.J.: Princeton University Press, 2014).

35. Liora Halperin, *Babel in Zion: Jews, Nationalism, and Language Diversity in Palestine, 1920–1948* (New Haven, Conn.: Yale University Press, 2014.

36. Naʻama Rokem and Amir Eshel edited a volume of *Prooftext* (33:1) dedicated to the interactions between German, Jewish, and Hebrew cultures. See also their introduction to the volume: "German and Hebrew: Histories of a Conversation," 1–8.

37. Ella Shohat, "The Question of Judeo-Arabic," *Arab Studies Journal* 23:1 (2015): 14–74.

38. Snir, *'Arviyut*; Reuven Snir, "'Till Spring Comes': Arabic and Hebrew Literary Debates Among Iraqi-Jews in Israel (1950–2000)," *Shofar: An Interdisciplinary Journal of Jewish Studies* 24:2 (2006): 92–123.

39. Beinin, *Was the Red Flag*, in particular: 67–73; 76–79; Avi Bareli, *Authority and Participation in a New Democracy: Political Struggles in Mapai, Israel's Ruling Party, 1948–1953* (Brighton, Mass.: Academic Studies Press, 2014); Robinson, *Citizen Strangers*; for a list of MAPAI's governments, ministers, and Knesset members, see the website of the Israeli Knesset, www.knesset.gov.il/faction/heb/FactionPage.asp?PG=77 (accessed 30/October/2016).

40. Beinin, *Was the Red Flag*, 15–17, 31–40, 79–84; on relations with MAKI see in particular, ibid., 117–25; Aviva Halamish, *Meir Ya'ari* (Tel Aviv: 'Am 'Oved, 2013); Aviva Halamish, "Loyalties in Conflict: Mapam's Vacillating Stance on the Military Government, 1955–1966; Historical and Political Analysis," *Israel Studies Forum* 25:2 (2010): 26–53.

41. For pre-state communism, see: Beinin, *Was the Red Flag*, 26–31; on MAKI as a party, see: ibid., in particular, 50–55, 125–37 (on Seneh's movement from MAPAM to MAKI), 137–41, 235–39 (on the split in the party); Kaufman, *Arab National Communism*; Nassar, *Affirmation and Resistance*.

42. Nassar, *Affirmation and Resistance*.

43. Snir, *'Arviyut*; Snir, "'Till Spring Comes.'"

44. Avraham Diskin, ed., *Me-Altalena 'ad hena, gilguleha shel tn'ua: Me-Herut le-Likud* (Jerusalem: Carmel, 2011); Yahiam Weitz, *Ha-Tza'ad ha-rishon le-kes ha-shilton, tnu'at ha-Herut, 1949–1955* (Jerusalem: Yad Ben Tzvi, 2007).

45. Palestinian Sephardim refers to Sephardim who were born in Ottoman or mandatory Palestine. Campos, *Ottoman Brothers*.

46. *Al-Yawm* sold fifteen hundred issues in 1950, two thousand issues in 1953, three thousand to four thousand issues in 1960, and four thousand issues in 1966. The party continued the publication of a pre-state newspaper, *Haqiqat al-Amr* (Matter of Fact), which sold two thousand issues in 1950, twenty-five hundred issues in 1953. Mustafa Kabha, "Yehudim mizrahim ba-'itonut ha-'aravit be-Yisra'el, 1948–1967," *'Iyunim bi-tkumat Israel* 16 (2006): 453.

47. *Al-Mirsad* sold two thousand issues in 1952–54, two thousand to three thousand issues in 1955–58, three thousand issues in 1959–62, and four thousand issues in 1963–67. *Sawt al-Ma'abir* sold fifteen hundred issues to two thousand issues in 1955–58. Kabha, "Yehudim mizrahim," 456. The party also published an Arabic supplement to its journal *'Al ha-Mishmar*; see Ya'aqov Yehoshu'a, "Skira 'al toldot ha-'itonut ha-'aravit-yehudit ba-aretz be-hamishim ha-shanim ha-ahronot" (1956), reprinted in Ya'aqov Yehoshu'a, *Reshimotav shel effendi ntul sachar sofrim* (Tel Aviv: Ha-Kibbutz ha-Me'uhad, 2016), 76–78.

48. *Al-Ittihad* sold three thousand issues in 1948–50, four thousand to five thousand issues in 1952–55, six thousand in 1956–62, three thousand issues in 1959–62, and six thousand to seven thousand issues in 1963–67. *Al-Jadid* sold three thousand to four thousand issues in 1952–55, four thousand in 1956–62, and four thousand in 1963–67. See: Kabha, "Yehudim mizrahim," 459.

CHAPTER 1: HUMAN MATERIAL

1. Israel State Archives [henceforth: ISA] G 5558/20, 30/November/1951, from Dr. Shaʻul Zalodokovsky to David Ben Gurion: "the situation in the Maʻabarot."

2. Ibid.

3. For data on the migrants to the state, see Moseh Sikron, "Ha-ʻAliyah ha-hamonit, memadeha, meʼafyeneya va-hashpaʻoteha," in Naʼor, ed., ʻOlim, 31.

4. Ibid., 34.

5. Bashkin, *New Babylonians*, 183-228.

6. Esther Meir-Glitzenstein, *Zionism in an Arab Country: Jews in Iraq in the 1940s* (London: Routledge, 2004); Meir-Glitzenstein, *Ben Bagdad*, 52-56; Abbas Shiblak, *The Lure of Zion: The Case of Iraqi Jews* (London: Al-Saqi Books, 1986), 64-128.

7. The more critical view of Israel and the Zionist underground is expressed in: Bashkin, *New Babylonians*, 183-228; Shiblak, *Lure of Zion*, 67-71; 103-27. For more traditional accounts, see: Moshe Gat, *The Jewish Exodus from Iraq, 1948-1951* (London: Frank Cass, 1997); Haim Cohen, *Ha-Peʻilut ha-tzionit be-ʻIraq* (Jerusalem: Ha-Sifriya ha-Tzionit, 1969).

8. Bashkin, *New Babylonians*, 183-228; Shlomo Hillel, "Ha-Mahalachim sheholidu et ha-ʻaliya ha-hamonit me-ʻIraq," in *Mi-Bavel li-Yerushalim: Kovetz mehakrim u-teʻudut ʻal ha-tsiyonut ve-ha-ʻaliya me-ʻIrak*, ed. Tzvi Yehuda (Tel Aviv: Merkaz Moreshet Yahadut Bavel / Mabat, 1980).

9. Tzvi Tzameret, "Ben Gurion ve Lavon: Shtey ʻemdot klapey ha-klita ha-reʼuya shel ha-ʻolim ba-ʻaliya ha-gdola," in Ofer, ed., *Ben ʻOlim*, 73-98; Yitzhak Refael, "Ha-Maʼavak ʻal ha-ʻaliya ha-hamonit," in Naʼor, ed., ʻOlim, 9-19.

10. Yehouda Shenhav, "The Jews of Iraq, Zionist Ideology, and the Property of the Palestinian Refugees of 1948: An Anomaly of National Accounting," *IJMES* 31:4 (1999): 605-30.

11. Ibid.

12. On debates within the Jewish American community and decline in American Jewish donations, see: ha-Kohen, *ʻOlim bi-sʻara*, 88-90; on the economic situation, see: ibid., 90-91.

13. On fears of the nature of the newcomers, and demands to limit Aliyah, see: ha-Kohen, *ʻOlim bi-sʻara*, 105-9.

14. Sahlav Stoler-Lis and Shifra Schwartz "'Nilhamot ba-baʻarut u-be-hergelim ne-hshalim: Tfisot u praktikot shel ahayot ve-rofʼim klapey ʻolim ba-ʻaliya ha-gdola shel shnot ha-hamishim," *Israel* 6 (2004): 41-43.

15. Tzameret, "Ben Gurion ve Lavon."

16. Refael, "Ha-maʼavak"; ha-Kohen, *ʻOlim bi-sʻara*, 301-37.

17. Shlomo Hillel, "Tomar la-yehudim she-yavoʼu aval she lo yemaharu," Naʼor, ed., *ʻOlim*, 141-42.

18. Ibid., 142.

19. ISA HZ 2397/14, 1/December/1950, Ministry of Foreign Affairs, conversation with Haim Sarid [Aliyah Office], Shamay Kahana [Middle East Department], Shmuʼel Ben Dor [U.S. department]; Meir-Glitzenstein, *Ben Baghdad, 105-107*

20. Association of the Youth of Aram Naharayim, *Journal of The Association of the Newcomers from Babylon in Israel* 17 (1/April/1951).

21. Nancy Jo Nelson, "The Zionist Organizational Structure," *Journal of Palestine Studies* 10:1 (1980): 80–93.

22. Victor Muʻallim Dror, *Bi-Ntivey Hayim: Zichronot ve-eruʻim she-einam nischahim* (Or Yehuda: n.p., 2000), 34–36.

23. Abu Sifin was a poor Jewish neighborhood in Baghdad.

24. Rahamim Rejwan, "Ba-derech la-maʻabara," in *ʻAl Gehalim: Kovetz sippurim* (Tel Aviv: ZHL/IDF, Mifkedet Hinuch Rashi, Misrad ha-Bitahon-Hotzaʼa la-Or, 1985), 11–12.

25. Rejwan, "Ba-derech," 16.

26. Dagon, *Sippura shel maʻabara*, 31, 125.

27. Ibid., 22; Meir-Glitzenstein, *Ben Bagdad*, 107–8; ha-Kohen, *ʻOlim bi-sʻara*, 83–84.

28. A conversation with Elie Amir, Yaʻaqov Besser, and Dan Tzalka, conducted by Dr. Mordechai Naʼor, Shulamit Meshulam, David Amit, and Tzvi Tzameret, "'Oley Shnot ha-hamishim ke-sofrim," in Naʼor, ed., *ʻOlim*, 197; Hezzi Luffben, *Ish yotze' el ehav* (Tel Aviv: ʻAm ʻOved, 1967), 161–62.

29. Luffben, *Ish*, 161–63; Meir-Glitzenstein, *Ben Bagdad*, 107–10; ʻEzra Haddad, *Avney Derech: Le-toldot ha-yehudim be-ʻIraq me hurban ha-bayt ha-rishon ve-ʻad la-thiya ha-leʼumit* (Tel Aviv: Irgun Yotzʼey Iraq be-Yisraʼel, 1969), 161–62.

30. Luffben, *Ish*, 163–65; RK vol. 5: 1475; on the density in Shaʻar ha-ʻAliyah, see: ha-Kohen, *ʻOlim bi-sʻara*, 84–85; on the difficulites of a young child to deal with the sanitary conditions and the food, see: Ran Cohen, *Saʻid*, Tel-Aviv: Ha-Kibbutz ha-Meʼuhad, 2016, 49–51.

31. Meir-Glitzenstein, *Ben Baghdad*, 107–8; Luffben, *Ish*, 163; Dagon, *Sippura shel maʻabara*, 46–47; 65, 130–31.

32. Muʻallim Dror, *Bi-Ntivey*, 38–40.

33. Rejwan, "Ba-derech," 23.

34. Meir-Glitzenstein, *Ben Bagdad*, 107–8; ha-Kohen, *ʻOlim bi-sʻara*, 3–84.

35. Association of the Youth of Aram Naharayim, *Association of the Newcomers from Babylon in Israel* 14 (1/January/1951); Giora Yoseftal, *Giora Yoseftal: Hayav u-Poʻalo, Mivhar ktavim, dvarim she-baʻl peh, yomanim, mikhtavim*, ed. Shalom Warm (Tel Aviv: Mifleget Poʻeley Eretz Yisraʼel, 1963), 18.

36. Luffben, *Ish*, 188–89; Miriam Kachenski, "Ha-Maʻabarot," Naʼor, ed., *ʻOlim*, 69–87; Daneil Plesentstein and Daneil Shahar, "Ha-geografia shel ha-Maʻabarot," in ibid., 87–97.

37. Within this order, Um Khaled was annexed to Natania, Sarafand annexed to Ness Ziona, Hirbat ʻAzun to Raʻanana, Sindi ʻAli and al-Haram to Herzliya, Tel ʻArish, to Holon, and Feja to Petach Tikva. Dov Rozen, ed., *Maʻabarot ve yeshuvey ʻolim be-aspaklariya shel misrad ha-penim* (Tel Aviv: Misrad ha-Penim, 1985) [henceforth: DRP, Dov Rosen's Papers], Document 6, 16/April/1950 to: Division of Self-Rule from: director of the Division for the Settlement of ʻOlim.

38. ISA, G 956/8 Dov Rozen, Ministry of Interior, to Jewish Agency.

39. DRP, Document 9, Jerusalem, 15/May/1950, from: the Department for Self-Rule [Agaf le-Shilton ʻAzmi; henceforth: ASA], to the director of the Division for Self-Rule.

40. ISA, G 1900/28, 18/September/1952, a petition by the people of the transit camp in Khayriyya, tent 10A; Dagon, *Sippura shel ma'abara*, 47; 149–50; Geula ben Shim'on (Geula Rahamim), "Yaldut bi-shechunat Shaviv be-Herzliya," http://ravdori.co.il/previewpage.aspx?str=1379 (accessed 30/October/2016).

41. Dagon, *Sippura shel ma'abara*, 54.

42. DRP, data collected, 1/January/1953.

43. ISA, G 149/22, 30/May/1954, petition from the Iraqi Jews of the transit camp of Kfar Ata to the prime minister and the ministers of Aliyah, agriculture, religion, the Jewish Agency in Jerusalem; Mu'allim Dror, *Bi-Ntivey*, 68–74.

44. DRP, Document 5/d Diary of Iyar ASA, Mahlaka le-Yishuv 'Olim [Department for the Settlement of 'Olim: MYO], April 1950–May 1950; DRP, Document 5 Diary of Tevet ASA, MYO, December 1949–January 1950.

45. ISA, K 91/29, February 1955, a petition of the people of Khayriyya to the Knesset; 16/February/1955, discussion of the subcommittee for the labor committee, the housing in the transit camp of Khayriyya.

46. RK vol. 18: 2090, 2nd Knesset, session 619, 27/June/1955; RK vol. 18: 2091, 2nd Knesset, session 619, 27/June/1955.

47. RK vol. 22: 2294, 3rd Knesset, session 319, 3/July/1957.

48. Dagon, *Sippura shel ma'abara*, 32.

49. 'Ezra Murad, *Ohalim-Shirim* (Tel Aviv: Alef, 1980), 18–19.

50. On the electricity situation in Yad Ha-Ma'avir, see: RK vol. 18: 1645, 2nd Knesset, session 595, 17/May/1955.

51. RK vol. 21: 766, 3rd Knesset, session 224, 16/January/1957; Yoseftal was not eager to have Iraqis move from various kinds of temporary housing, and regretting the shift from various temporary forms of housing. See: Giora Yoseftal, "Siha 'im tz'irey ha-kvutzot," Bet Berl, 1959, in Yoseftal, *Hayav*, 132; on wooden shacks prices, see: ha-Kohen, *'Olim bi-s'ara*, 209–10.

52. Murad, *Ohalim*, 20: "Who could we forget"; the word *Tnuva* refers to a Histadrut cooperative specializing in milk and dairy products.

53. In 1952, 336 people in the transit camp of Kordoni B used one shower; 53 used one toilet in Karkur; in the transit camp in Zichron 23 families used one faucet and in the Talpiypot camp 25 families. The transit camps in Petach Tikva and 'Afula had in 1952 very few functioning toilets, and Ra'anana had only two. The camp in Kfar Ono had no trash cans, and the camp in Herzliya was not connected to water in its first year. ISA, G 149/20, 26/March/1953, letter from A. Amrami, the Sanitation Division, to Mr. Ziggel, Jewish Agency, Absorption Division. ISA, G 5557/20, 8/May/1952, from Dr. Pfiffer, the Bureau of Public Hygiene, the Ministry of Health, to Mr. Zibel, absorption division; ha-Kohen, *'Olim bi-s'ara*, 264–65.

54. DRP, Document 5/c ASA, MYO, March 1950–April 1950; on the problems relating to water in Zarnuga camp, see: DRP, Document 5/d Diary of Iyar, MYO, April 1950–May 1950. See also the discussion of the committee in the Or Yehuda camps, and the account on the Holon in DRP, Document 5/f Diary of Tamuz ASA, MYO, June 1950–July 1950; on the help given to Kfar 'Ana to pay for its water service, see: DRP, Document

5/g Diary of Av, ASA, MYO, July 1950–August 1950; on the water conditions in Holon, see: DRP, Document 5a Diary of Shevat, ASA, MYO, January 1950–February 1950; on the water in Sarafand, Holon, see: Document 5b Diary of Adar, ASA, MYO February 1950–March 1950.

55. RK vol. 16: 2571; 2nd Knesset, session 483, 31/August/1954.

56. Moshe Huri, "Ha-Ma'abara," in Na'or, ed., *'Olim*, 178–79.

57. Ge'ula Sehayek al-'Ani, *Ganevet ha-tarnegol: Yomana shel yaldat ma'abara* (Kiryat Ono: Safra, 2011), 10; testimony of Kochava Safi [née Yosef], in "Ha-Morah Rina ve talmideha be-ma'abarat Talpiyot," in Na'or, ed., *'Olim*, 158.

58. ISA, G 149/22, 30/November/1952, health report; on lice, bugs, and mosquitoes, in the transit camp of Petach Tikva, see also the account by Sami Michael, *Al-Ittihad*, 29/May/1953.

59. ISA, G 149/22, 6/November/1952, letter from H. Shoval, vice director in the Health Ministry to Health Ministry—Petach Tikva, and Sanitary Division; ISA, 14/160-G, 28/August/1951, Mina Meir, Zehava Gefen, the Central Histadrut for Zionist women to Yosfetal.

60. DRP, Document 142 to the committees in the transit camps; from: MYO, the Interior Ministry [M. Weiss, assistant director], 17/November/1952.

61. ISA, G 149/22, 5/May/1954, from the chief medical officer, Dr. A. Frenkel, to Ministry of Interior Affairs, the Department for Settling Newcomers, health departments in districts of Petach Tikva; ISA, G 160/14, 7/February/1952, from Dr. Matan, director of the Branch for Public Hygiene, to Dr. Noah, the District Health Bureau.

62. Dvora ha-Kohen, "Ha-Yishuv ha-vatik mul 'olim: rashuyot mekomiyot mul ma'abarot," in Offer, ed., *Ben 'Olim*, 98–117; ha-Kohen, *'Olim bi-s'ara*, 234–39; 241–46.

63. DRP, Document 7, Jerusalem, 8/May/1950, a report by Ministry of Interior—MYO.

64. Ha-Kohen, "Ha-Yishuv ha-vatik"; ha-Kohen, *'Olim bi-s'ara*, 234–39; 241–46.

65. DRP, Document 62: ASA, MYO to Jewish Agency Absorption Division, 25/December/1950.

66. *Kol ha-'Am* 10/November/1952, no. 1740, 4; *Kol ha-'Am* 11/November/1952, no. 1741, 4; *Kol ha-'Am* 13/November/1952, no. 1743, 4.

67. ISA, G 14/160, 28/August/1951, Mina Meir, Zehava Gefen, the Central Histadrut for Zionist women to Yosfetal; *Kol ha-'Am* 20/October/1952, no. 1722, 4.

68. On disconnecting services around the city of Netanya, see: *Davar* 18/November/1955, *Haaretz* 18/November/1955; on the difficulty of the city of Rishon le-Zion to provide water supply to the transit camp see: ISA, G 1901/8, 15/May/1952, A. Scheftel, Rishon Le-Zion, to the Ministry of Internal Affairs, ASA, MYO.

69. DRP, Document 62: ASA, MYO, to Jewish Agency Absorption Division, 25/December/1950.

70. ISA, G 149/22, 28/May/1951, from Dr. Yequtiel by Dr. A. Matan, Health Ministry. See also the demand of the agency that the state pays for beds rather than the agency doing so: ISA, K 82/18 1st Knesset, 15/January/1951 meeting in the Health Ministry.

71. *Kol ha-'Am* 4/December/1953, no. 2086, 4.

72. RK vol. 18: 1296–97; 2nd Knesset, session 580, 1/January/1955; RK vol. 15: 569–70 2nd Knesset, session 349, 5/January/1954.

73. On the situation in Holon, see: Lavon Archive [henceforth: LA] IV-250-26-50 to the transportation division in the city of Holon, from Yosef Gold, the organizer of the transit camp by the Histadrut, 14/August/1951; on the situation in Ra'anana, see: RK vol. 18: 1657, 2nd Knesset, session 596, 18/May/1955; on truck service in Ra'anana and its poor conditions, see: RK vol. 18: 2105, 2nd Knesset, session 620, 28/June/1955.

74. Rozin, *Hovat*, 215–19; see also: ha-Kohen, *'Olim bi-s'ara*, 191–92, 195–97, 200.

75. In Petach Tikva transit camp no doctor, nurse, or night services were available; in the transit camp of Bney Brak a walk of fifteen minutes was needed to get to the local clinic. In the early 1950s, seventy-nine transit camps reported to the government that they had no medical service of any kind. Sixty-three transit camps did have clinics, mostly run by Kupat Holim (sixty out of sixty-three), which were open six days a week. In Kfar Nahman and the Sakiyya camps no doctors were on call: RK vol. 18: 2090, 2nd Knesset, session 619, 27/May/1955.

76. The welfare bureaus were connected to the Welfare Ministry. The word in Hebrew used at the time is *Misrad ha-Sa'ad*, meaning "Assistance Ministry," and *Liskhat ha-Sa'ad*, "Assistance Bureau."

77. ISA, G 4243/6, 5/February/1954, report of the Committee of Ministers for Health Matters in Border Places and Villages (Yishuvey Sfar ve Kfar); Dr. T. Yeshurun to Dr. N. Batish, director general of the Ministry of Health, Jerusalem, 19/September/1954; Ministry of Health, "the problem of village doctors," 23/June/1954; ha-Kohen, *'Olim bi-s'ara*, 191–92.

78. ISA, G 14/160, 23/October/1951, General Union of Nurses to the Histadrut.

79. ISA, G 5557/20, 30/November/1951, from Dr. Sha'ul Zalodokovsky to David Ben Gurion: "the situation in the Ma'abarot"; government officials expressed concern that the lack of medical care, with little assistance from the Jewish Agency, with very few nurses would result in the spread of eye and skin diseases; see: ISA, K 82/18, 1st Knesset, 15/January/1951, meeting in the Health Ministry; ha-Kohen, *'Olim bi-s'ara*, 191–92, 195–97, 200.

80. ISA, G 160/14, 10/April/1952, a letter by Yusuf [Yosef] Za'rur.

81. Dani Dvir, *Tzuf ha-Dvora* (Tel Aviv: Dani Dvir, 2014), 55.

82. On Beit Lid camp, see: RK vol. 15: 1055 2nd Knesset, session 386, 3/March/1954; RK vol. 18: 1296–97; 2nd Knesset, session 580, 1/January/1955; on Holon see: RK vol. 16: 2344: 2nd Knesset, session 467, 1–11/August/1954; on Be'er Ya'aqov see: RK vol. 16: 2571; 2nd Knesset, session 473, 17/August/1954; RK vol. 16: 2571; 2nd Knesset, session 473, 17/August/1954.

83. RK vol. 22: 2612, 3rd Knesset, session 340, 3/July/1957.

84. LA IV-250-64-1-204, A. Rotem, the Division of Camps and Transit Camps, to the general director of the postal services, Ministry of Transportation, 14/September/1952; LA IV-250-64-1-204, A. Abramovitch to the Ministry of Transportation, 20/July/1952.

85. Rozin, *Hovat*, 219–22.

86. ISA, G 4243/6, 5/August/1954, Dr. Z. Avigdori to M. Lachover, Ministry of Labor.

87. Huri, "Ha-Ma'abara," in Na'or, ed., *'Olim*, 179.

88. ISA, G 257/22, 9/August/1951, Ministry of Finance, review of the supply in the transit camps; ISA, G 257/22, 9/August/1951, Ministry of Labor—Ma'abarot, a report of the labor bureau (*lishkat 'avoda*).

89. Dagon, *Sippura shel ma'abara*, 66.

90. RK vol. 7: 994–95: session 223, 6/February/1951; ISA K 82/18 1st Knesset, 5/February/1951, from Central Mashbir to T. Govrin; on suppliers arriving late to Talpiot: ISA, G 20/5557, 24/October/1951, Government of Israel, Ministry of Labor, a report on distribution based on the request of the Ministry of Labor; ISA 4/October/15, a protocol of the meeting held in the food division of the Jerusalem district with the representatives of the Jewish Agency and Ha-Mashbir.

91. ISA, G 257/22, 9/August/1951, Ministry of Labor—Ma'abarot, a report of the labor bureau (*lishkat 'avoda*).

92. Meir-Glitzenstein, *Ben Bagdad*, 158–91; see in particular her comparison to the state of Iraqi Jews in 1983, 884–89.

93. Swirski, *Israel's Oriental Majority*; Lissak, *Ha-'Aliyah*.

94. A survey that looked at the occupations of male Iraqi and Iranian immigrants to Israel from 1948 to 1952 (before arrival to Israel) showed that 28.4 percent worked in craftsmanship and industry, 28.8 percent commerce and selling, 15.5 percent worked in bureaucracy and administration, 5.0 percent worked in free and technical professions, and only 9.2 percent worked in agriculture. A general survey of the occupations of male immigrants to Israel from Asia and Africa from 1948 to 1954, years in which most newcomers were from Iraq, showed that only 3.4 percent worked in free and technical professions, only 6.3 percent in bureaucracy and administration, and 7.1 percent in commerce and selling. The numbers of those employed in agriculture were much higher: 16.8 percent were defined as working in agriculture, and 10.6 percent were agricultural laborers. Also, 23.3 percent were unskilled workers, 24.5 percent dealt in craftsmanship, industry, and construction, and 12.6 percent worked in the public sectors. Based on Sikron, "Ha-'Aliyah," 42.

95. Tikva Darvish, *Yehudey 'Iraq ba-kalkala* (Ramat Gan: Bar Ilan University, 1987).

96. Ya'aqov Nahon, *Megamot ba-ta'asuka, ha-meymad ha-'adati* (Jerusalem: Machon Yerushalayim le-Heker Israel, 1984). See also: Ya'aqov Nahon, *Dfusey Hitrahvut ha-haskala u-mivneh hizdamnuyot ha-ta'asukra* (Jerusalem: Machon Yerushalayim le-Heker Israel, 1987); Meir-Glizenstein, *Ben Bagdad*, 180–89; on the professional promotion options of Mizrahim see also Khazzoom's insightful study, Shifting, in particular 89-161.

97. LA IV-250-64-1-204 Histadrut, Va'ad Poel, Aliyah Division, Branch for Professional Training, 10/January/1952.

98. RK vol. 9: 1787–1802, session 253, 16/May/1951, 1st Knesset; RK vol. 15: 2228 2nd Knesset, session 4561, 28/July/1954; RK vol. 13: 550–54, 2nd Knesset, session 175, 26/January/1952.

99. Meir-Glitzenstein, *Ben Bagdad*, 175–79.

100. Meeting of the government, 9/November/1952, present David Ben Gurion, Levy Eshkol, Y. Burg, B. Dinburg, H. Cohen, P. Lavon, G. Meirson, G. Norok, P. Naphtali, M. Shapira; Meir-Glitzenstein, *Ben Bagdad*, 175–76.

101. RK vol. 24: 2385; 3rd Knesset, session 500, 23/July/1958; vol. 24: 2248; 3rd Knesset, session 504, 30/July/1958.

102. LA IV-250-26-79 Y. Tesler, public work division, the union of construction workers, Holon; RK vol. 27: 644; 3rd Knesset, session 393, 15/January/1958.

103. Dagon, *Sippura shel ma'abara*, 23.

104. Ibid., 49.

105. The major laws passed regulated insurance rights regarding termination and health and pension benefits (*hok ha-bituah ha-le'umi*, 1953), labor organization (*hok irgun ha-pikuah 'al ha-'avoda*, 1959), women's labor rights (*hok ta'sukat nashim*, 1954), and wages (*hok haganat ha-sachar*, 1959). See also: LA IV-104-1233-3-744, the law of organized supervision on labor (*hok irgun ha-pikuah 'al ha-'avoda*, 1954).

106. Dagon, *Sippura shel ma'abara*, 47.

107. Ha-Kohen, *'Olim bi-s'ara*, 213–14.

108. Mu'allim Dror, *Bi-Ntivey*, 71–72; Meir-Glitzenstein, *Ben Bagdad*, 176; on labor bureaus, see: ha-Kohen, *'Olim bi-s'ara*, 214.

109. Testimony of Kochava Sagi [née Yosef], in "Ha-Morah Rina," Na'or, ed., *'Olim*, 163.

110. On complaints from Safad, see: RK vol. 16: 2389; 2nd Knesset, session 472, 16–18/August/1954; on the workers in Kiryat Shmonah, who waited for three months for their wages because the Ministry of Labor and the local municipality did not coordinate the pay and on workers in Or Yehuda who were not paid because the workers' council did not coordinate its work with those of Ramat Gan and Sakiyya: see RK vol. 18: 1295; 2nd Knesset, session 580, 1/January/1955; on the transit camp of Kfar 'Ana workers where did not pay during the winter of 1954 because of lack of coordination with the Ministry of Finance; RK vol. 16: 2249–50: 2nd Knesset, session 462, 2–4/August/1954; on workers in Ramat ha-Sharon where wages were withheld between Nov 1954 to January 1955, see: RK vol. 18: 1297; 2nd Knesset, session 580, 1/January/1955; On Sakiyya, were workers waited for four months to be paid because the director of the transit camp employed workers without a permission of the state: see: LA IV-250-64-1-204, A. Abramovitch to A. Zigel, Jewish Agency, absorption division, 14/July/1952.

111. RK vol. 16: 2390; 2nd Knesset, session 472, 16–18/August/1954; RK vol. 25: 431; 3rd Knesset, session 661, 22–24/December/1958.

112. See, for example, the case of Mordechai Gabbai, who was fired from the Sakiyya school because he had another job. LA IV-250-64-1-204 Mordechai Gabbai to the Council of Workers in Ramat Gan and Giva'tayim, Khayriyya B.

113. LA IV-250-64-1-204 Mordechai Gabbai to the Council of Workers in Ramat Gan and Giva'tayim, Khayriyya B.

114. LA IV-208-1 G. Rojinksi, Municipality of Rehovot, to minister of the interior, 25/August/1952, regarding Sakiyya, Zarnuga, Giv'on.

115. In Rosh Pina camp, workers had to march for three kilometers to reach the labor bureau; when the camp was dissolved and the people moved the town of Hazor, no labor bureau was to be found there. See: RK vol. 23: 1031; 3rd Knesset, session 418, 24–26/February/1958; workers had to travel from Kfar Nahman to Ra'anana where the

local labor bureau only registered people at noon. See: RK vol. 24: 2558; 3rd Knesset, session 508, 5/August/1958; RK vol. 24: 2385; 3rd Knesset, session 500, 23/July/1958.

116. RK vol. 13: 550–54, 2nd Knesset, session 175, 26/January/1952.

117. Sami Michael, *Gvulot ha-ruah, Sihot 'im Ruvik Rosenthal* (Tel Aviv: Ha-Kibbutz ha-Me'uhad, 2008), 44–45.

118. The welfare bureau in the local transit camp in Kiryat Benjamin stopped support of needy people because it had no funding; Kiryat Shmonah did not pay support for needy people for three months. The city of Holon closed down its welfare bureau because of lack of appropriate budgets. Months took for budget to arrive from minister of finance to minister to the welfare offices. See: RK vol. 21: 661–62, 3rd Knesset, session 127 7–9/January/1957.

119. RK vol. 18: 2104, 2nd Knesset, session 620, 28/June/1955.

120. Report—Survey in the Maabara Amishav, June 1959–June-1961, JDC, http://search.archives.jdc.org/multimedia/Documents/NY_AR55-64/NY55-64_CR_016/NY55-64_CR_016_0613.pdf (accessed 31/October/2016).

121. Sha'ul Haddad, "Mishma'at Barzel be-bet sefer Shahmon," *Neharde'a, Bit'on Merkaz Moreshet Yahadut Bavel* 31 (Fall 2010): 36.

122. Journal of the Association of the Youth of Aram Naharayim, (1/January/1951).

123. On the thugs, see the story of Sami Michael on how the state used drug addicts and criminals in the service of MAPAI (*Al-Ittihad* 7/November/1952); Michael connected the thugs to the phenomena of police brutality in the transit camps. He also noted that the people of the transit camps who resist this violence are called terrorists while the thugs are ignored (see his story on Ramla, *Al-Ittihad* 26/June/1953).

124. Mu'allim Dror, *Bi-Ntivey*, 95–97.

125. LA IV-250-64-1-204 from the councils of the workers of Ramat Gan, to the Loan Division of the workers in Ramat Gan (Kupat Milve).

126. RK vol. 7:1475: session 200, 13/December/1950 1st Knesset.

127. DRP, Document 145 to the committees in the transit camps; from: the Interior Ministry, MYO [M. Weiss, assistant director], 29/January/1953.

128. For example, in 1951 five grocery stores in the camp of Bney Brak served two hundred Iraqi families with no butchers. In the camp in Petach Tikva no milkman was to be found and two butchers served seven thousand people, 80 percent of whom were Iraqi Jews. ISA, G 6/16/32 Association of Iraqi Jews to Yoseftal, 30/December/1951.

129. LA IV-250-64-1-204 H. Davidovich to the director of the transit camp of Khayriyya, 14/May/1952.

130. Dagon, *Sippura shel ma'abara*, 34–35, 78.

131. ISA, G 28/1900, 8/September/1952, the religious committee of Khayriyya B to the minister of religion, and the chief rabbis in Tel Aviv, the minister of the interior.

132. *Al ha-Mishmar* 28/August/1955, in CZA, S71/109 [Ma'abarot]; *Al-Mirsad* 14/May/1951, 4.

133. Dagon, *Sippura shel ma'abara*, 49.

134. Ibid., 23–24, 65, 88, 126.

135. LA IV-208-1, 3/January/1952, union of social workers to the city of Haifa.

136. Nahon, *Megamot*; Darvish, *Yehudey.*

137. LA IV 250-361-1-2455, the Histadrut, the Councils of the Workers of Jerusalem [CWJ], the Organization of Working Mothers [OMW], a brochure for the activities of the organization and Hasbara, March 1958; the Histadrut, CWJ, OWM, a brochure for the activities of the organization and Hasbara, July 1958; the Histadrut, CWJ, OWM, activities of culture and Hasbara (under the organization of Shulamit Palgi), 4/December/1955; the Histadrut, CWJ, OWM, activities of culture and Hasbara (under the organization of Shulamit Palgi), 26/December/1955; the Histadrut, CWJ, OWM, activities of culture and Hasbara (under the organization of Shulamit Palgi), 5/November/1955; CWJ, OWM, activities of culture and Hasbara (under the organization of Shulamit Palgi), 9/August/1955; the Histadrut, CWJ, OWM, activities of culture and Hasbara (under the organization of Shulamit Palgi), 17/August/1955, the Histadrut, CWJ, OWM, brochures 3/October/1954; 24/October/1954.

138. RK vol. 16: 2249–50: 2nd Knesset, session 462, 2–4/August/1954.

139. Dagon, *Sippura shel ma'abara*, 39, 66, 76, 166–67.

140. Ibid., 150–59.

141. LA IV-250-64-1-204 to the committee of the transit camp of Sakiyya by the IDF, from Magen David Adom directorship, 20/January/1952; Captain 'Ovadia Abraham, commander of the Sakiyya camp for the IDF, complaint on Magen David Adom, 30/December/1951.

142. DRP, Document 5/h Diary of Elul ASA, MYO, August 1950–September 1950.

143. RK vol. 7: 944–55: session 211, 3/January/1951.

144. Mu'allim Dror, *Be-Ntivey*, 47.

145. An official investigation committee that looked into what is called in the Israeli media "The Yemenite Babies Affair," looked at 745 cases of missing babies and found 711 to be dead. Of these cases, 30 were European and American, 19 from Asia; 94 from Arab countries, 5 from Israel, 83 from North Africa, and 450 from Yemen. Yossi Zolfan and Ogen Goldman, *Va'adat ha-hakira ha-mamlachtit le-'inyan hey'alman shel yeladim mi ben 'oley Teyman,* submitted to the Knesset environment and internal affairs committee, 20/June/2001, www.knesset.gov.il/mmm/data/pdf/m00334.pdf (accessed 31/October/2016). The events were reported also in the 1950s: Maariv, 26/February/1954; *Davar* 25/September/1950; *Davar* 29/September/1950; Boaz Sanjero, "Be-Ein hashad ein hakira amitit, duah va'adat ha-hakira be-'inayan parashat he'almutam shel yeladim mi-ben 'oley Teyman," *Teoriya u-bikoret* 21 (2002): 47–76; ha-Kohen, *'Olim bi-s'ara*, 194.

146. Zolfan and Goldman, *Va'adat*, www.knesset.gov.il/mmm/data/pdf/m00334.pdf (accessed 31/October/2016).

147. For a full list of disappearing children by country, look the website of AMRAM, www.edut-amram.org/databases/countries/ (accessed 4/February/2017).

148. See the testimony of Abraham Yitzhak, www.edut-amram.org/testimonies/nissim-avraham/ (accessed 31/October/2016).

149. Esperance Moreh-Cohen, *Mi-Gdot ha-Hidekel le-gdot ha-Yarkon: Sippurim ve zichoronot* (Jerusalem: Agudat ha-Akadema'im Yotz'ey Iraq, 2006), 41; on her biography,

see: Mahmud 'Abbasi and Shmu'el Moreh, *Tarajum wa-athar fi'l adab al-'arabi fi Isra'il, 1948–1987* (Shifa' 'Amr, Israel: Dar al-Mashriq Li'l Tarjama Wa'l Tiba'a, 1987), 199.

150. Dagon, *Sippura shel ma'abara*, 34–35, 78.

151. Rozin, *Hovat*, 21–81, 219–22, 227.

152. Testimony of Kochava Sagi [née Yosef], in "Ha-Morah Rina," in Na'or, ed., *'Olim*, 158; on the fear that children would fall to the holes in the ground used as toilets, see also: Dagon, *Sippura shel ma'abara*, 88.

153. Testimony of Amalia Juna [née Shemesh], in "Ha-Morah Rina," in Na'or, ed., *'Olim*, 159.

154. Stoler-Lis and Schwartz, "'Nilhamot,'" 31–62; Rozin, *Hovat*, 199–223.

155. Stoler-Lis and Schwartz, "'Nilhamot,'" 46.

156. Ibid. Stoler and Schwarz, however, note that the attitude was not uninterrupted; toward 1954, especially after a visit of the anthropologist Margaret Mead to Israel, and the rise of local Israeli anthropologists, the elitist attitude of nurses changed.

157. RK vol. 25: 431; 3rd Knesset, session 661 22–24/December/1958.

158. Dagon, *Sippura shel ma'abara*, 24.

159. Ibid., 37–38.

160. Ibid., 52.

161. LA IV-208-1, 6/July/1949, a report by the appeal committee of the labor bureau in Ramat Gan.

162. Born into a family from Irbil, and raised in Mosul, Shoshanna Arbeli became a member of the Zionist underground in Baghdad; as a result she was jailed and escaped to Mandatory Palatine in 1947 and lived in Kibbutz Sdeh Nahum. She started out working for MAPAM and Ahdut ha-'Avoda, and eventually found her way to MAPAI. She was first elected to the Knesset in 1962, and served for over three decades. As the chairwoman of the Labor Committee, the Committee of Internal Affairs and the Environmental Committee, and as the minister of health, she attended to labor and health rights.

163. Nadav Peress, "Shoshanna Arbeli Almozlino: Zot she-hetzila otanu," *Haokets* 14/July/2015, www.haokets.org/2015/07/14/%D7%A9%D7%95%D7%A9%D7%A0%D7%94-%D7%90%D7%A8%D7%91%D7%9C%D7%99-%D7%90%D7%9C%D7%9E%D7%95 D7%96%D7%9C%D7%99%D7%A0%D7%95-%D7%96%D7%95-%D7%A9%D7%94 D7%A6%D7%99%D7%9C%D7%94-%D7%90%D7%95%D7%AA%D7%A0%D7%95/ (accessed 31/October/2016).

164. For experiences of women in the Israeli labor market, see the following memoirs: Moreh-Cohen, *Mi-Gdot*; Shoshanna Arbeli Almozlino, *Me-ha-Mahteret be-Bavel le-Memshelt Israel* (Tel Aviv: Ha-Kibbutz ha-Me'uhad, 1998); Tikva Agasi, *Mi-Baghdad le-Yisrael* (Ramat Gan: Kolgraph, 2004); Shoshana Levy, *'Al Em ha-derekh* (Tel Aviv: Shoshana Levy, 2001); Nuzhat Qassab [Katzav] Darwish, *Snuniyot ha-Shalom, 'Im ha-nashim ha-'araviyot va-ha-druziyot be-Yisra'el* (Or Yehuda: Ma'ariv, 1998).

165. *Kol ha-'Am* 26/November/1952, no. 1757, 3.

166. Phyllis Shalgi and Miriam Goldwasser, "Hafra'at ishiyut tipusit li-kvutzat nashim 'iraqiyot le'or ha-reka' ha-tarbuti shel 'adatan," *Megamot* 6:3 (1955): 236–42.

167. Rozin, *Hovat*, 236. On an Iraqi mother who took a ride from her transit camp in the Galilee to visit her son who was hospitalized in Haifa and had to escape when the driver who tried to rape her, see: Levy, 'Al Em,' 88; on a young girl who went to the clinic and was touched inappropriately by a male nurse, see: al-'Ani, *Ganevet*, 57; 4; See also the series of articles published in *Al ha-Mishmar* on June 12–17 by Shlomo Sheva in CZA, S71/109.

168. Dagon, *Sippura shel ma'abara*, 52.

169. RK vol. 18: 1675, 2nd Knesset, session 5957; Rozin, *Hovat*, 236; on brothels in Kfar 'Ana, Meir-Glitzenstein, *Ben Bagdad*, 152.

170. RK vol. 24: 2525, 3rd Knesset, session 508, 5/August/1958.

171. Miriam Kachenski, "Ha-Ma'abarot," MATAKH's [Merkaz le-Techonologia Hinuchit] electronic library, http://lib.cet.ac.il/pages/item.asp?item=12939 (accessed 31/October/2016).

172. Another company, called Halamish, was also involved in construction. On 'Amidar's relationship with the state, see: Yoseftal, diary entry, 13/November/1952, in Yoseftal, *Hayav*, 172–73; ha-Kohen, *'Olim bi-s'ara*, 179; 180–82, 31, 191–92; data is available on 'Amidar's website: www.amidar.co.il/wps/portal/!ut/p/c1/04_SB8K8xLLM9MSSzPy8x Bz9CP00s_gQAzdTQ09LYwMDP0s3AyM_z5BAX3MvA3dTU_1wkA6cKgyMjCDyBj iA04G-n0d-bqp-QXZ2mqOjoiIA37Eq_w!!/dl2/d1/L2dJQSEvUUt3QS9ZQnB3LzZfVD BGNTFJOTMwME45RjAyTklUUU03SjBHMTA!/ (accessed 31/October/2016).

173. RK vol. 10: 500–501, session 253, 28/November/1951, 2nd Knesset; RK vol. 18: 1298; 2nd Knesset, session 580, 1/January/1955; RK vol. 18: 1299; 2nd Knesset, session 580, 1/January/1955; RK vol. 20: 1585, 3rd Knesset, session 110, 22/March/1956.

174. RK vol. 22: 2294, 3rd Knesset, session 319, 3/July/1957.

175. Yoseftal, diary entry 2/July/1953, in Yoseftal, *Hayav*, 177; Meir-Glizenstein, *Ben Bagdad*, 113–138, 171–180.

176. DRP, February 1951, Document 18A—budgets to settlements of 'olim outside of a municipal council.

177. LA IV-208-1302-8, 29/August/1958; statement to the editorial of *Be-Terem* from Zelig Lavon, Shikun 'Ovdim, LTD; LA IV-208-1302-8, 5/October/1954, lecture by Zelig Lavon, to the Board of Directors, Shikun 'Ovdim, LTD.

178. LA IV-208-1302-8, 24/June/1951; statement by Zelig Lavon, Shikon 'Ovdim, LTD.

179. LA IV-208-1302-8, 6/October/1955; lecture by Zelig Lavon, to the Board of Directors, Shikun 'Ovdim, LTD.

180. RK vol. 24: 2258, 3rd Knesset, session 510, 5/August/1958; RK vol. 23: 1031, 3rd Knesset, session 418, 24–26/February/1958; RK vol. 23: 2504, 3rd Knesset, session 516, 4/August/1958; RK vol. 25: 431, 3rd Knesset, session 667–69, 22–24/December/1958.

181. RK vol. 16: 2389, 2nd Knesset, session 472, 16–18/August/1954.

182. LA IV-208-1302-8, 27/January/1959; to the secretary of the Histadrut, Pinhas Lavon to Zelig Lavon, Shikun 'Ovdim, LTD; statement by Zelig Lavon, 15/August/1958.

183. LA IV-208-1302-8, 5/January/1957; meeting of the board of Shikun 'Ovdim; to the secretary of the Histadrut, Pinhas Lavon from Zelig Lavon, Shikun 'Ovdim, LTD, 9/June/1957.

184. LA IV-208-1302-8, 6/October/1955; lecture by Zelig Lavon, to the Board of Directors, Shikun 'Ovdim, LTD.
185. Meir-Glitzenstein, *Ben Bagdad*, 112–13.
186. RK vol. 18: 1645, 2nd Knesset, session 595, 17/May/1955.
187. Mu'allim Dror, *Bi-Ntivey*, 93; ha-Kohen, *'Olim bi-s'ara*, 298–301.
188. Ofer Aderet, "Ha-Layla bo hu'alu toshavey ma'abert Kfar Saba le-masa'iyot," *Ha-Aretz (Haaretz)* 8/July/2016, www.haaretz.co.il/news/education/.premium-1.3000651 (accessed 31/October/2016); David Sela', Mered ha-Ma'abarot, Atar Nostalgia online (transcript of a an interview in the program Shishi Ishi with Moshik Timor, broadcasted on Kol Israel, Reshet Bet radio station on 11/February/2011), www.nostal.co.il/Site.asp?table=Terms&option=single&serial=13444&subject=%EE%F2%E1%F8%E5%FA# (accessed 31/October/2016); Kfar Saba City Museum, *Ha-ma'abara "ne'elma" be-ishon layla*, www.kfar-saba-museum.org/%D7%90%D7%A8%D7%9B%D7%99%D7%95%D7%9F-%D7%94%D7%A2%D7%99%D7%A8/%D7%9E%D7%95%D7%9C%D7%98%D7%99%D7%9E%D7%93%D7%99%D7%94-%D7%9C%D7%A6%D7%A4%D7%99%D7%99%D7%94-%D7%95%D7%94%D7%95%D7%A8%D7%93%D7%94/%D7%9E%D7%99%D7%93%D7%A2-%D7%94%D7%99%D7%A1%D7%98%D7%95%D7%A8%D7%99/32-%D7%90%D7%A8%D7%9B%D7%99%D7%95%D7%9F-%D7%94%D7%A2%D7%99%D7%A8/%D7%9E%D7%95%D7%9C%D7%98%D7%99%D7%9E%D7%93%D7%99%D7%94-%D7%9C%D7%A6%D7%A4%D7%99%D7%99%D7%94-%D7%95%D7%94%D7%95%D7%A8%D7%93%D7%94/%D7%9E%D7%99%D7%93%D7%A2-%D7%94%D7%99%D7%A1%D7%98%D7%95%D7%A8%D7%99/334-%D7%94%D7%9E%D7%A2%D7%91%D7%A8%D7%94-%D7%A0%D7%A2%D7%9C%D7%9E%D7%94-%D7%91%D7%90%D7%99%D7%A9%D7%95%D7%9F-%D7%9C%D7%99%D7%9C%D7%94 (accessed 31/October/2016).
189. Report—Survey in the Maabra Amishav, June 1959–June-1961, http://search.archives.jdc.org/multimedia/Documents/NY_AR55-64/NY55-64_CR_016/NY55-64_CR_016_0613.pdf (accessed 31/October/2016).
190. *Davar* 8/July/1955; *Al ha-Mishmar* 19/June/1956; *Ma'ariv* 5/July/1955; *Davar* 27/12/1955; *Davar* 8/August/1960; *Ma'ariv* 7/8/1960 (in this story, the newcomers from Iran orchestrated a demonstration asking to be returned to Iran); *Davar* 12/April/1961; 23/May/1962 (on MAPAI's control), *Herut* 9/July/1959.
191. Mu'allim Dror, *Bi-Ntivey*, 81–86; Meir-Glitzenstein, *Ben Bagdad*, 151–59.
192. Meir-Glitzenstein, *Ben Bagdad*, 151–59; Meyer Schwartz, *Or-Yehuda: A New Immigrant Development "Satellite Town" in the Conurbation of Tel-Aviv-Yafo* (Jerusalem: n.p., 1968); Eric Cohen, *Kehila Ktana be-merhav metropolin: Mehkar khilati 'al Or Yehuda be-ezor Tel-Aviv* (Jerusalem: Eliezer Kaplan School of Economics and Social Sciences, Hebrew University, 1966).
193. Tzvi 'Akirav, "Hug Bavli be-shnat 1953," *Neharde'a, Bit'on Merkaz Moreshet Yahadut Bavel* 31 (Fall 2010): 48–49; Memi Pe'er, ed., *Ramat Gan: City of Gardens*, (Ramat Gan: Municipality, Publicity Department, 1998); Meir-Glitzenstein, *Ben Bagdad*, 145–57.
194. On the group, see Chapter 5, 206–207.

195. Adriana Kemp, "Medabrim Gvulot: Havnayat teritoriya politit be-Yisra'el, 1949–1957" (Ph.D. diss., Tel Aviv University, 1997); Ra'anan Weitz and Avshalom Rokach, "Ha-'aliya ha-hamonit u mif'aley ha-hityashvut ha-hakla'it," in Na'or, ed., 'Olim, 64.

196. Weitz and Rokach, "Ha-'aliya," 53–68; ha-Kohen, 'Olim bi-s'ara, 139–40; 143–45.

197. Yoseftal believed that one could not settle Yemenites and other Jews in the same village. See: Yoseftal, diary entry 14/January/1951, in Yoseftal, Hayav, 149, ha-Kohen, 'Olim bi-s'ara, 141–42, 143–45; Kemp, Weitz, and Rokach, "Ha-'aliya," 53–68; Petition to Prime Minister David Ban Gurion, 2/November/1952, from May Naftuh committee, CZA, www.scribd.com/doc/78885810/%D7%90%D7%A8%D7%9B%D7%99%D7%95%D7%9F-%D7%A6%D7%99%D7%95%D7%A0%D7%99 (accessed 31/October/2016); data on Kurdish villages is also found in the blog of Kurdish Jews in Israel, www.tapuz.co.il/blog/net/viewentry.aspx?entryId=1311187 (accessed 31/October/2016). Baghdadi Jews also felt that the Kurdish Jews were better fitted to agriculture. As Ezra Haddad noted, "The problem of the absorption of Kurdish Jews was not that difficult, [since] from their nature they were used to physical labor and as famers they found their place in a few agricultural villages." Haddad, Avney Derech, 83.

198. Meir-Glitzenstein, Ben Bagdad, 134–35.

CHAPTER 2: CHILDREN OF IRAQ, CHILDREN OF ISRAEL

1. Al-'Ani, Ganevet, 48.

2. Ibid., 49.

3. ISA, G 149/22, 30/November/1952, health report; on lice, bugs, and mosquitoes, in the transit camp of Petach Tikva, see also the account by Sami Michael, Al-Ittihad 29/May/1953; ISA, G 149/22, 6/November/1952, letter from H. Shoval, vice director in the Health Ministry to colleagues at Health Ministry–Petach Tikva and to Sanitary division; ISA, G 14/160 28/August/1951

4. In 1947 the infant mortality rate among the Jewish community was 29 per thousand. In 1949 the number rose to 51.71 per thousand. The breakdown is important, however: on the kibbutzim the ratio was 16.5 per thousand, whereas among the newcomers, it was 157 per thousand. By 1951, the number had dropped to 81 per thousand; the following year it was 52.5 per thousand, and in 1953 it was 47.5 per thousand. In some months, of 100 deaths of children in hospitals, 10 were of children from cities and 90 were of children in transit camps. Rozin, Hovat, 228–31.

5. ISA, K 12/6 29/October/1957 the committee of public services, the 3rd Knesset, third seat.

6. The meeting of the third government, 11/October/1952.

7. Rozin, Hovat, 220–21.

8. The Ministry of Education and Ministry of Interior agreed that a warm glass of milk would be provided to all students in transit camps that were not under the jurisdiction of an official municipality. Parents were to pay for the milk, but they were advanced a year's worth of credit. DRP, Document 141/A to: the committees in the transit camps; from: the Ministry of Education, 8/9/1952.

9. ISA, G 14/160 28/August/1951 Mina Meir, Zehava Gefen, the Central Histadrut for Zionist women to Yosfetal; Rozin, *Hovat*, 231.

10. Rozin, *Hovat*, 231.

11. Luffben, *Ish*, 193–95; 204.

12. Herzl Hakak and Balfour Hakak, "Te'omim bi-Yerushalayim," in *Safrut yeladim ve-na'ar* 100 (1998), ed. Gershon Bergson, reprinted in the brothers' blog, Herzl and Balfour Hakak, Zehut Kfula, www.hakak-twins.com/articles/bikur3.asp (accessed 28/November/2016).

13. RK vol. 4: 1070: meeting 122 of the 1st Knesset, 20/March/1950.

14. YT 35 (MAKI) Series: Districts, Box 13: file 6, a pamphlet (in Hebrew and in Arabic) to the people of the transit camp of Holon, 28/January/1954.

15. ISA K 82/18 1st Knesset, 16/January/1951, the activities of the Knesset in the transit camps.

16. *Kol ha-'Am* 26/October/1952, 1727; *Al ha-Mishmar* 9/November/1952, in CZA S71/109 [Ma'abarot] 4.

17. *Kol ha-'Am* 26/October/1952, 1727, no. 4.

18. ISA, G 6/70/44, 12/May/1953; 3/August/1952, to Golda Meir, Ministry of Labor from Z. Elmaliach, transit camp of Semah.

19. YT 35 (MAKI) Series: Districts, Box 14: file 2, a pamphlet to the people in the transit camp David [Mahane David]; *Kol ha-'Am* 24/October/1952, no. 1752, 4; *Haaretz*, 23/November/1952, CZA S71/108 [Ma'abarot].

20. Al-'Ani, *Ganevet*, 13.

21. *Al-Mirsad* 14/May/1951, 4.

22. RK vol. 23: 383, 3rd Knesset, session 383 24/December/1957.

23. RK vol. 23: 698; 3rd Knesset, session 396 21/January/1958.

24. *Al-Ittihad* 31/July/1953; quoted in Kabha, "Yehudim mizrahim," 458.

25. Rejwan, *'Al Gehalim*, 184–92.

26. Al-'Ani, *Ganevet*, 53–85.

27. DRP; Document 143 to: the committees in the transit camps; from: NYO, the Ministry of the Interior [M. Weiss, assistant director], 14/January/1953.

28. ISA, P 4800/10 16/March/1953, a letter to the financial adviser, Ministry of Education.

29. On the battles to have religious schools in the transit camps, especially with respect to Yemenite children, see: Tzvi Tzameret, *Yemey Kur ha-hituch, Va'adat hakira 'al hinuch yaledy ha-olim* (1950; repr., Be'ersheba: Ben Gurion University Press, 1993).

30. LA IV-215-1200 from Y. Niv to Y. Gefen 19/March/1953; ISA GL 1153/29 letter by Y. A. Rimon, the department of the implementation of the public education law to Prof. Rigger, 19/February/1952; the secretary of the local committee in Zarnuga to the Ministry of Education, division for the implementation of the public education law, Jerusalem, 7/November/1951; the secretary of the local committee in Zarnuga to the Ministry of Education, division for the implementation of the public education law, Jerusalem, 5/November/1951.

31. ISA GL 1153/29 letter by Y. A. Rimon, the department of the implementation of the public education law to Prof. Rigger, 19/February/1952; the secretary of the local committee in Zarnuga to the Ministry of Education, division for the implementation of the public education law, Jerusalem, 7/November/1951; the secretary of the local committee in Zarnuga to the Ministry of Education, division for the implementation of the public education law, Jerusalem, 5/November/1951.

32. LA IV-215-1132 General report 26/June/1952; a letter to Miriam Shapira, education bureau—the director of the school for working youth, from Mister Haya; ISA GL 1124/28 A. Etz-Hadar to director of supplies division, the absorption division of the Jewish Agency 7/July/1953.

33. ISA GL 1124/28 9/February/1953 Bathsheba Me'iri, report on my visits for arts and crafts lessons.

34. LA IV-250-64-1-204 Mordechai Gabi to the Council of Workers in Ramat Gan and Giv'atayim, Khayriyya B 2/November/1952.

35. LA IV-215-324 Beith Hinuch/Sakiyya B to Ya'aqov Sarid, 17/June/1953; LA IV-215-324 Ze'ev Halperin, to Miriam Shapria [Sakiyya B] 1/January/1953; letter to Y. Sarid, from center of education, Sakiyya B, 25/October/1951.

36. LA IV-215-324 Ari Mor, director of Beit Hinuch, Sakiyya B, to Ya'aqov Sarid, 11/January/1953.

37. LA IV-215-324 from Ya'aqov Sabagh, transit camp, Khayriyya, to Y. Gefen, 11/January/1953.

38. LA IV-215-1200 Y. Gefen to Miss H. Bert, directory of department of special education, 5/January/1953.

39. LA IV-215-324 from Ya'aqov Sabagh, transit camp, Khayriyya, to Y. Gefen, 11/January/1953.

40. Dagon, *Sippura shel ma'abara*, 52, 137–38.

41. ISA GL 1124/28 9/February/1953, Bathsheba Me'iri, report on my visits for arts and crafts lessons.

42. RK vol. 16: 2154 2nd Knesset, session 456 14/July/1954.

43. LA IV-215-1200 from Y. Gefen to S. Abir, direct of school in transit camp Be'er Ya'aqov, 12/January/1953; Gefen to Levey, Beit Hinuch in the transit camp of Be'er Ya'aqov.

44. LA IV-215-324 to Y. Gefen from G. Farber [Manshiya School] 10/July/1953; to Miss Sh. Farber, from Y. Gefen, 25/June/1953; to Ben Zion Dinur, minister of education, from Sara Barka'it, 27/April/1953.

45. LA IV-215-1200 from Y. Niv to Y. Gefen, 19/March/1953.

46. LA IV-215-1200 from Zvi Kremer (Beit Eliezer) to Y. Gefen (supervisor of schools of the workers) 19/March/1953; see also the accounts from the camp of Khayriyya: LA IV-215-324 to Ben Zion Dinour, minister of education, from Y. Geffen, 23/November/1952.

47. LA IV-250-64-1-204, the Histadrut, division of Aliyah—the division for professional training, 26/September/1952.

48. LA IV-215-1200 letter to A. Arnon, general director in the Ministry of Education from Y. Gefen 6/February/1953; letter from Y. Gefen to Dr. Avidor, 6/February/1953.

49. LA IV-250-64-1-204, A. Abramovitch to KKL, 16/July/1952.

50. LA IV-215-1200 from Y. Gefen to S. Abir, direct of school in transit camp Be'er Ya'aqov, 12/January/1953; Gefen to Levey, Beit Hinuch in the transit camp of Be'er Ya'aqov.

51. Dagon, *Sippura shel ma'abara*, 96.

52. Ibid., 170–71.

53. ISA, G 20/5558 1/February/1952, letter from Kalman Kahana to David Ben Gurion, report dated 24/January/1952.

54. ISA GL 1477/28 from Miriam Bloomberg [teacher] to supervisor Hannah Rothberg 21/January/1954.

55. Le'ah Na'or, ed., "Ha-ma'abarot ve-anahnu: Zichronot me-Herzliya shel-pa'am," www.Naorlea.co.il/biography.asp?id=7 (accessed 4/February/2017).

56. Rozin, *Hovat*, 206.

57. ISA GL 9/1250 State of Israel, Ministry of Education, note on our activities in the month of July. 13/November/1956; LA IV-250-64-1-204, protocol of the meeting of the local committee Yad ha-Ma'avir, 11/November/1952; protocol of the meeting of the local committee Yad ha-Ma'avir, 23/October/1952; protocol of the meeting of the local committee Yad ha-Ma'avir, 21/October/1952.

58. LA IV-250-64-1-204, protocol of the meeting of the local committee Yad ha-Ma'avir, 11/November/1952; 23/October/1952; 21/October/1952.

59. DRP, Document 113 to: the secretaries and committees in the transit camp, from: MYO, the Interior Ministry, Jerusalem [Dov Rosen] 24/January/1952; topic: preparation for Tu be-Shvat.

60. DRP, Document 114 to: the committees in the transit camps; from: MYO, the Interior Ministry, Jerusalem [M. Weiss] 14/January/1952; LA, IV-208-1; from: the municipality of Tiberias to the center of culture and Hasbara: 13/February/1952; LA IV-215-1200 Sakiyya school 29/January/1953.

61. DRP, Document 114 to: the committees in the transit camps; from: MYO, the Ministry of the Interior, Jerusalem [M Weiss] 14/January/1952; LA, IV-208-1; from: the municipality of Tiberias to the center of culture and Hasbara: 13/February/1952; LA IV-215-1200 Sakiyya school 29/January/1953.

62. ISA G 22/390 3/February/1953 minutes of a meeting attended by Yosef Kariv, A. Aven Shoshan (Ministry of Education), GADNA representative; D. Rozen, Ministry of Interior; Y. Kevesh, youth division by the agency.

63. DRP, Document 108 to: all municipalities and local committees from: MYO, the Ministry of the Interior, Jerusalem [Dov Rosen], April 1952.

64. DRP, Document 109 to: all local committees outside the municipal zone from: MYO, the Ministry of the Interior, Jerusalem [Dov Rosen] March 1952.

65. Robinson, *Citizen Strangers*, 113–53, in particular 116–33, 140–48, 196.

66. LA IV-215-1200 Y. Gefen; protocol of teachers meeting, 18/November/1952.

67. LA IV-215-1132 general report, 26/June/1952; a letter to Miriam Shapira, education bureau—the director of the school for working youth, from Mister Haya.

68. ISA GL 1151/4, 20/July/1953; a report on the visit to the transit camp of Rehovot.

69. LA IV-215-1200 Y. Gefen; protocol of teachers meeting, 18/November/1952.
70. Mu'allim Dror, *Bi-Ntivey*, 74–75.
71. Ibid., 62, 69–70, 98–99.
72. Agasi, *Mi-Baghdad*, 109–10.
73. Ibid., 110.
74. On Shalom al-Kativ / Shalom Kattav, see: 'Abbasi and Moreh, *Tarajum*, 192–93.
75. Shalom Kattav, *Likuey me'orot, me-shirey eretz Yisra'el ha-ahat* (Ramat Gan: Zoharim, 1978), 38.
76. Shlomo Swirski, *Ha-hinuch be-Yisra'el, Mahoz ha-maslulim ha-nifradim* (Tel Aviv: Brerot, 1990).
77. Dagon, *Sippura shel ma'abara*, 126, 137–38.
78. RK vol. 23: 784; 3rd Knesset, session 403 3–5/February/1958; RK vol. 24: 2264; an appendix to session 490 9/July/1958.
79. Beit Jabotinsky, Mezudat Ze'ev [henceforth: MZ] H1/2/4, 3/June/1954; discussions of the Committee on Newcomers Affairs; Dagon, *Sippura shel ma'abara*, 175.
80. *'Al ha-Mishmar* 12/June/1955; *'Al ha-Mishmar* 14/June/1955; *'Al ha-Mishmar* 19/June/1955; *'Al ha-Mishmar* 21/June/1955; CZA in S71/109.
81. Some recordings are available in Dudi Patimar's YouTube channel: www.youtube.com/channel/UCvJYx7y7UObywoBu-bZNIIA/videos?shelf_id=1&view=0&sort=dd (accessed 28/November/2016).
82. Al-'Ani, *Ganevet*, 71–103.
83. RK vol. 23: 969; 3rd Knesset, session 415, 18/February/1958.
84. Dagon, *Sippura shel ma'abara*, 147.
85. Kfar Saba City Museum, *Ha-ma'bara "ne'elma."*
86. Dagon, *Sippura shel ma'abara*, 34, 39, 66.
87. Ibid., 126–27.
88. Ibid., 145–46.
89. *Kol ha-'Am* 19/October/1952, no. 1721, 4.
90. RK vol. 24: 1747; 3rd Knesset, session 452 3/August/1958.
91. RK vol. 19: 576 3rd Knesset, session 43 20/December/1955.
92. LA IV-215-1132 General report 26/June/1952; a letter to Miriam Shapira, education bureau—the director of the school for working youth, from Mister Haya.
93. *Davar* 23/November/1953 in S71/110 [Ma'abarot].
94. *Al-Mirsad*, 28/May/1953, p. 4.
95. Victor Mu'allim Dror, *'Avar lo rahok: Sippurim ve-eru'im she-lo nash leham* (Tel Aviv: n.p., 1985), 108.
96. Ibid., 109–10.
97. Kattav, *Likuey me'orot*, 27.
98. Ibid., 26.
99. Al-'Ani, *Ganevet*, 43.
100. RK vol. 5: 1475: meeting 139, 15/May/1950.
101. RK vol. 7: 994–95: session 223 6/February/1951; appendix—the notice of the committee for transit camps affairs, 7: 1025; on the operation, see: Rozin, *Hovat*, 233–34.

102. RK vol. 7: 994–95: session 223 6/February/1951; appendix—the notice of the committee for transit camps affairs, 7: 1025.
103. *Kol ha-'Am* 29/December/1950, no. 1180, 1; *Kol ha-'Am* 7/January/1951, no. 1187, 4.
104. Dagon, *Sippura shel ma'abara*, 133.
105. Giora Yoseftal, diary entry, 14/January/1951, in Yoseftal, *Hayav*, 144.
106. Ibid.
107. Letter from the chairperson of the Committee of Babylonian Jews in Jerusalem to the Jewish Agency [Jerusalem], 14/February/1950 in CZA S59/197.
108. DRP, Document 100, 22/November/1950 to: all regions, from: settlement division.
109. Rozin, *Hovat*, 232–34.
110. Na'or, "Ha-ma'abarot," www.Na'orlea.co.il/biography.asp?id=7.
111. Ibid.
112. RK vol. 7: 994–95: session 223 6/February/1951; appendix—the notice of the committee for transit camps affairs, 7:1025.
113. Rozin, *Hovat*, 233.
114. Giora Yoseftal, diary entry 14 January 1951, in Yoseftal, *Hayav*, 147.
115. *Kol ha-'Am* 29/December/1950, no. 1180, 1.
116. *Kol ha-'Am* 7/January/1951, no. 1187, 4; DRP, Document 101, from Jewish Agency, D. Zimand, to Ministry of the Interior, MYO, 13/December/1950; Document 102 summary of a meeting with the chief of staff with the Ministry of the Interior, MYO, 14/December/1950.
117. On the GADNA, a paramilitary organization established in 1940, abbreviation of Gdudey No'ar, "youth brigades," see p. 190.
118. ISA K 82/18 1st Knesset, 16/January/1951, the activities of the Knesset in the transit camps; ha-Kohen, *'Olim bi-s'ara*, 280–88.
119. RK vol. 10: 783–84, 2nd Knesset, session 35 20/December/1951.
120. Yoseftal, *Hayav*, 139–44.
121. *Kol ha-'Am* 24/December/1951, 1476, 4.
122. DRP; Document 103: telegram to the minister of interior, Mr. Shapira, from Dov Rozen, 20/December/1951, Document 106, from minister of interior, ASA, MYO; Memo to the secretaries of transit camps and camps, Mahane Israel, Beit Lid, Rosh ha-'Ayn, Sakiyya, 'Ana, Mordechai, Zarnuga, Yanveh, 'Akir, Bayt va–Gan [by Yavni'el], southern Tira, Ramat ha-Sharon [from Tov Rosen], 17/December/1951; *Kol ha-'Am* 23/December/1951, 1475, 4.
123. Yoseftal, *Hayav*, 161.
124. ISA, G 14/160 28/August/1951, Mina Meir, Zehava Gefen, the Central Histadrut for Zionist women, to Yosefetal.
125. Giora Yoseftal, diary entries dated 17/December/1951, in Yoseftal, *Hayav*, 151.
126. Giora Yoseftal, diary entries dated 24/December/1951, in Yoseftal, *Hayav*, 154–57.
127. *Kol ha-'Am*, 23/December/1951, 1475, 4.
128. Ibid.
129. DRP, Document 106, minister of interior, ASA, MYO; Memo to the secretaries of transit camps and camps, Mahane Israel, Beit Lid, Rosh ha-'Ayn, Sakiyya, 'Ana,

Mordechai, Zarnuga, Yanveh, 'Akir, Bayt va–Gan, southern Tira, Ramat ha-Sharon [from Dov Rosen], 17/December/1951.

130. Giora Yoseftal, diary entry dated 31/December/1951, in Yoseftal, *Hayav*, 163.

131. Giora Yoseftal, diary entries dated 17/December/1951; 24/December/1951, in: Yoseftal, *Hayav*, 151–54.

132. Giora Yoseftal, diary entry dated 14/December/1951, in Yoseftal, *Hayav*, 139–41.

133. Giora Yoseftal, diary entry dated 17/December/1951, in Yoseftal, *Hayav*, 151.

134. Giora Yoseftal, diary entries dated 24/December/1951, in Yoseftal, *Hayav*, 157.

135. Giora Yoseftal, diary entries dated 31/December/1951, in Yoseftal, *Hayav*, 162.

136. Giora Yoseftal, diary entries dated 24/December/1951, in Yoseftal, *Hayav*, 157.

137. ISA, G 14/160 26/October/1951, NAHAL command, GADNA command, Yitzhak Rabin, commander, operation division, to the minister of security, prime minister, Jewish Agency.

138. Sami Michael went on to depict the winter in the transit camps as a battle scene (*ma'araka*), see his story on the transit camps battle with the winter: *Al-Ittihad*, 27/September/1952.

139. ISA, K 92/1 the subcommittee for the affairs of children in the transit camps, 7/December/1953.

140. RK vol. 19: 170–71: 3rd Knesset, session 15 26/October/1955; on the cycle of disastrous winters, see also Sami Michael's story "another winter" (*shita' akhar*) in *Al-Ittihad* 24/September/1954; see also his story about how the rains politicized the newcomers: the storm (*'asifa*) of the newcomers would be stronger than those of the winter *Al-Ittihad* 2/October/1953.

141. While the kibbutzim to which the children were sent belonged to different political parties within labor Zionism, I did not find any meaningful differences between kibbutzim identified with MAPAM, MAPAI, and Le-Ahdut ha-'Avodah with respect to both the behavior of the members of the kibbutzim members and the children's attitudes; thus I treat them all as one unit in this chapter.

142. David Ben Baruch, *Bi-svach kurey ha-klita: 'Al ha-murkavut be-klitat havarot 'iraqiyot ba-tnu'a ha-kibbutzit ha-hilonit ba-shanim, 1950–1952* (n.p., 2006); Meir-Glitzenstein, *Ben Bagdad*, 302–10.

143. Levy, *'Al Em*, 83–95 (on Kibbutz Mishmar ha-'Emek); on parents taking their children out of kibbutzim, see the letter of Noga Alafi from Glil Yam, in *Bederch ha-Hagshama: Alon ha-'Aliyah ha-Bavlit ba-Kibbutz ha-Me'uhad*, 24/December/1946–21/January/1947, reprinted and annotated in: Mordechai Bibi, *Ha-Mahteret ha-tziyonit ha-haluzit be-'Iraq*, 4 vols. (Jerusalem: Yad Ben Tzvi, 1988), 3: 556; Cohen, *Sa'id*, 73–74.

144. Menashe Yarden, "Eich hitragalnu la-'avoda," *Tnu'at ha-halutz bi-Yirushalayim* 12/June/1945–10/July/1945, reprinted in Bibi, *Ha-Mahteret*, 2: 663.

145. Levy, *'Al Em*, 83; Bashkin, "on jails"; on adjustment to kibbutz life, see the letter of Batia Mizrahi from Kibbutz Dafna: *Bederch ha-Hagshama* 24/December/1946–21/January/1947, reprinted and annotated in: Bibi, *Ha-Mahteret*, 3: 554–55; on positive depictions of celebrating holidays in kibbutzim, see: a letter from Tikva Sofer Shotat in Kibbutz Gesher, *Derech ha-Halutz bi-Yirushalim* 12/June/1945–10/

July/1945, in Bibi, *Ha-Mahteret*, 2: 658–59; Meir-Glitzenshtain, *Ben Bagdad*, 303–21; Cohen, Saʻid, 74-82.

146. Almozlino, *Me-ha-Mahteret*, 51–53; see also the account of Yaʻaqov Kaduri, published in *Igeret ha-Tnuʻa-be-Sdeh ha-Hagshama* July 1947, reprinted in Bibi, *Ha-Mahteret*, 4: 727.

147. Ben Baruch, *Bi-svach*.

148. David Ben Baruch, *Ha-Sippurim me-ha-megira ha-emtzaʻit* (n.p.: n.p., 2010), 13.

149. Ben Baruch, *Bi-svach*, 28; see also Elie Amir's autobiographical account on his stay in the kibbutz where he depicts the dress code there and the problems for girls wearing shorts, in Elie Amir, *Tarnegol kapparot*, 40th ed. (Tel Aviv: ʻAm ʻOved, 2015), 50, 53, 68.

150. Ben Baruch, *Bi-svach*, 13–14; on tensions between native Israelis, different newcomers, and Iraqis in Kibbutz Bet Oren and Kibbutz Givat Brener and relationship with counselors, see the account of ʻEzar Shemesh from Bet Oren, *Igeret ha-Tnuʻa-be-Sdeh ha-hagshama* July 1947, reprinted in Bibi, *Ha-Mahteret*, 4: 731; Cohen, Saʻid, 80-81.

151. Meir-Glitzenstein, *Ben Bagdad*, 302–21.

152. Levy, *ʻAl Em*, 94; on getting to know the Israeli scenery, see the account of Uri Shefer Babay, from Naʻan, in *Derech ha-Halutz bi-Yirushalim* 12/June/1945–10/July/1945, in Bibi, *Ha-Mahteret*, 2: 660–61, and the essay of Margalit Akirav-Cohen, from Naʻan, in ibid., 661–62; on identifying with the desire to bring European refugees to Mandatory Palestine and how the Iraqi youth shared their pains, see the account of Shimshon Ballas in *Igeret ha-Tnuʻa-be-Sdeh ha-hagshama* July 1947, reprinted in Bibi, *Ha-Mahteret*, 4: 712–13.

153. Dagon, *Sippura shel maʻabara*, 54.

154. Association of the Youth of Aram Naharayim, *Journal of the Association of the Youth from Aram Naharim* (17/September/1950); CZA S20/613.

155. Yitzhak Minz, protocol of a kibbutz meeting, Yagur, 18 July 1951, quoted in Ben Baruch, *Bi-svach*, 76–82.

156. Almozlino, *Me-ha-Mahteret*, 52.

157. Ben Baruch, *Bi-svach*, 90–94.

158. Ibid., 95.

159. Amir, *Tarnegol kapparot*.

160. Ibid., 174.

161. Cherka Moria, "Maʼavakam shel nifgaʻey ha-tippul be-gazezet: Ha-omnam maʼavak she-nichshal?" *Maʻasey Mishpat* 6 (2014): 135–36; information on "ringworm children" is given in the Israeli Health Ministry: see: *Hok le-pitzuy nifgaʻi ha-gazezet* (1994); www.health.gov.il/LegislationLibrary/Gazezet_01.pdf (accessed 29/November/2016); the Israeli Health Ministry, *Merkaz he-leʼumi le-nifgaʻey gazezet*, www.health.gov.il/Services/Citizen_Services/tinea_capitis_compensation/Pages/gazezet_center.aspx (accessed 29/November/2016).

CHAPTER 3: THE ONLY DEMOCRACY IN THE MIDDLE EAST

1. RK vol. 10: 798–99, 2nd Knesset, session 35, 2/December/1951.

2. Nir Keydar, *Mamlakhtiyut, ha-tfisa ha-ezrahit shel David Ben Gurion* (Jerusalem: Yad Ben Tzvi and Ben Gurion University Press, 2009); Tzameret, "Ben Gurion ve Lavon."

3. In this context, it should be noted that in the 1st Knesset, 23 seats were occupied

by kibbutz members (out of 120), a number three times more than their proportion in the overall population of Israel.

4. LA IV-208-1302-8 27/January/1959; to the secretary of the Histadrut, Pinhas Lavon to Zelig Lavon, Shikun 'Ovdim, LTD; statement by Zelig Lavon, 15/August/1958.

5. Yitzhak Greenberg, "Hevrat ha-'Ovdim u-klitat ha-'aliya ha-gdola bi-shenot ha-hamishim," *'Iyunim bitkumat Israel* 2 (1992): 94–115; Nahum Gross, *Bank ha-Po'alim: Hamishim ha-shanim ha-rishonot* (Tel Aviv: 'Am 'Oved, 1994).

6. RK vol. 25: 431; 3rd Knesset, session 558 22–24/December/1958.

7. Mu'allim Dror, *Bi-Ntivey*, 72–73; Yitzhak Greenberg, "Ha-Kalkala ha-marhiva shel meshek ha-'ovdim, 1948–1988," in *Hevra ve-kalkala be-Yisrael-mabat histori ve-achshavi*, ed. Avi Bareli, Daniel Gutwein, and Tuvia Friling (Jerusalem: Yad Ben Tzvi/ Machon Ben Gurion le-Heker Yisra'el ve-ha-Tzionut, Ben Gurion University, 2005), http://in.bgu.ac.il/bgi/iyunim/2005/13.PDF (accessed 29/November/2016).

8. ISA, G 333/4 D. Teneh (Jewish Agency) to Gershon Zack (Jewish Agency).

9. RK vol. 10: 633–36, 2nd Knesset, session 31 12/December/1951; on Ben Gurion's approach to the Iraqis, see also: Meir- Glitzenstein, *Ben Bagdad*, 91-6.

10. As public relations officer Mr. Ginton explained, the Ministry of Health ran a propaganda (*hasbara*) campaign "in the field of health and hygiene among the dwellers of the camp." ISA, G 149/22 30/May/1954 statement by B. Ginton, public relations, the Ministry of Health.

11. ISA, G 2388/10 3/January/1951 memo of *Voice of Israel*.

12. LA IV-250-64-1-204 from the Haim Davidovich, absorption division, to the councils of the workers of Ramat Gan.

13. Rozin, *Hovat*, 130–67.

14. Ibid., 105–67.

15. RK vol. 22: 2479, 3rd Knesset, session 332 23/July/1957.

16. LA IV-250-64-1-204 a letter to the local council Or Yehuda from Sakiyya B., 21/April/1954.

17. RK vol. 18: 1297–98; 2nd Knesset, session 580, 1/January/1955.

18. LA IV-250-64-1-204, letter from A. Abramovitch to Arieh Zilberman, 18/September/1952.

19. MZ, H1-9/77, 7/December/1953, discussions of a club in Kfar 'Ana.

20. RK vol. 13: 556, 2nd Knesset, session 175, 26/January/1952.

21. ISA, the protocol of the third government meeting, 16/October/1952–23/November/1953, vol. 17, meeting dated 16/October/1952, present David Ben Gurion, Yosef Burg, Dov Yosef, Pinches Lavon, P. Naftali, Bechor Shitrit, M. Shapira.

22. The meeting of the third government, 11/October/1952.

23. RK vol. 24: 2361; 3rd Knesset, session 495, 16/July/1958.

24. LA IV-208-1302-8, 29/August/1958; statement to the editorial of *Be-Terem* from Zelig Lavon, Shikun 'Ovdim, LTD.

25. RK vol. 10: 799, 2nd Knesset, session 35, 2/December/1951; on the representation of Iraqis as lazy and men of the Levant, see Meir-Glitzenstein, *Ben Bagdad*, 96–101.

26. RK vol. 7: 467–70, 1st Knesset, session 200, 15/May/19501st Knesset.

27. On how the press and the newspapers of other Zionist political parties painted the newcomers as insane, violent, and easily incited, see also the story of Sami Michael, which criticized *Ha-Dor* and the *Jerusalem Post* in *Al-Ittihad* (7/November/1952); see also his critique of the liberal Haaretz, in *Al-Ittihad* 12/November/1954.

28. *Ha-Dor* 8/July/1953, in CZA S71/111 [Ma'abarot].

29. *Ha-Dor* 18/October/1953, in CZA S71/111 [Ma'abarot].

30. *Davar* 26/March/1952, in CZA S71/110 [Ma'abarot].

31. *Davar* 17/August/1955, in CZA S71/109 [Ma'abarot].

32. *Davar* 9/November/1953, in CZA S71/109 [Ma'abarot].

33. *Davar* 15/May/1953, in CZA S71/109 [Ma'abarot].

34. David Ben Gurion, *Khitatuna li'l sanawat al-arab' al-qadima* (MAPAI: Ha-Mahlaka le-Yotz'ey 'Adot ha-Mizrah, 1951); The National Library of Israel [henceforth: NLI], collections of electoral campaign posters (Osef Ta'amulat Bihrot la-Kneset; ser. 2, 1951 elections), V1856/3/56.

35. Yehoshu'a, "Skira," 74–75.

36. Ibid., 75.

37. Ibid., 75–76.

38. On these riots, see Chapter 4, pp. 165–174.

39. Meir-Glitzenstein, *Ben Bagdad*, 239–44; on the Iraqis in MAPAI and their role, see ibid, 230-273.

40. For his autobiography, see: Shlomo Hillel, *Ruh qadim* (Jerusalem: 'Idanim, 1985), on his role in the Knesset, see: www.knesset.gov.il/mk/heb/mk.asp?mk_individual_id_t=380 (accessed 29/November/2016); and Meir-Glitzenstein, *Ben Bagdad*, 257–63.

41. *Davar* 22/May/1959.

42. RK vol. 22: 2293–95, 3rd Knesset, session 319 3/July/1957.

43. Kabha, "Yehudim mizrahim," 450–51.

44. Beinin, *Was the Red Flag*.

45. Yad Ya'ari [henceforth: YY], 129: 2, a paper to the organizational division in the department of the Eastern communities, no. 942, 11/August/1957; Zion Mathityahu, Ramat Gan, 17/December/1956, report.

46. MAPAM, *Ma Tzarich kol po'el lada'at: Keytzad yehuslu ha-ma'abarot?* NLI; collections of electoral campaign posters (Osef Ta'amulat Bihrot la-Keenest); series 2 (1951 elections), V1856.

47. YY 129:2, a paper to the organizational division in the department of the Eastern communities, no. 942, 11/August/1957; see also: Aryeh Magal, "*Al-Mirsad*: Mapam's Voice in Arabic, Arab Voice in Mapam," *Israel Studies* 15:1 (2010): 115–46; on the literary activities of Abraham Musa (Ibrahim al-Akari) in *Al-Mirsad*, see: 'Abbasi and Moreh, *Tarajum*, 7–8; see also Bryan K. Roby, "The Beginning of Oriental Jewish Protests in Israel and the Use of Israeli Police in the Suppression of a 'Mizrahi' Struggle, 1948–1966" (Ph.D. diss., University of Manchester, 2012), 122–23.

48. MAPAM election poster, NLI; collections of electoral campaign posters (Osef Ta'amulat Bihrot la-Kneset, series 3 (1955 elections), V2978.

49. RK vol. 15: 256–57, 2nd Knesset, session 326 25/November/1953.
50. RK vol. 15: 256–58, 2nd Knesset, session 326 25/November/1953.
51. YY 129: 2, a paper to the organizational division in the department of the Eastern communities, no. 942, 11/August/1957.
52. 'Al ha-Mishmar 19/June/1953, in CZA S71/111 [Ma'abarot].
53. 'Al ha-Mishmar 5/July/1953, in CZA S71/110 [Ma'abarot].
54. 'Al ha-Mishmar 3/July/1953, in CZA S71/110 [Ma'abarot].
55. 'Al ha-Mishmar 28/August/1955, in CZA S71/109 [Ma'abarot].
56. 'Al ha-Mishmar 15/November/1953, in CZA S71/111 [Ma'abarot].
57. 'Al ha-Mishmar 19/June/1955, in CZA S71/109.
58. 'Al ha-Mishmar 16/June/1955; Al ha-Mishmar 17/June/1955; Al ha-Mishmar 12/June/1955, in CZA S71/109.
59. 'Al ha-Mishmar 14/June/1955, in CZA S71/109.
60. 'Al ha-Mishmar 16/June/1955, in CZA S71/109.
61. 'Al ha-Mishmar 21/June/1955, in CZA S71/109.
62. YY 123: 12, David Cohen, statement, 15/October/1958.
63. YY 124: 2, the divisions of 'Adot ha-Mizrah, decision of the division, 6/April/1955; 1/April/1955; Haim Yehuda to the propaganda division, 14/March/1955; Haim Yehuda to propaganda division, 14/March/1955; letter from H. Kafri to Y. Nzer, 16/January/1955; letter to Haim Yehuda from S. Cohen, 27/October/1954.
64. YY 124: 1, division for 'adot ha-mizrah, summary protocol, 31/August/1955; meeting concerning East Nahariya, 6/September/1955; meeting on the transit camp in Ness Ziona, 24/September/1955; meeting of the division of the eastern communities (edot ha-mizrahi) in Jerusalem, 17/October/1955, concerning the failure in the elections.
65. LA IV-250-64-1-204 Va'ad Po'el, Y. Geler, to the workers' councils, Ramat Gan, 12/June/1952; Y. Geler to the council of Ramat Gan, 8/June/1952.
66. YY 129:2, letter to the department of the Eastern communities, 7/September/1957.
67. YY 129: 2, protocol of the supreme council for 'Adot ha-Mizrah to the executive committee (va'ad pe'ol) of the Histadrut, 2/April/1958.
68. Kabha, "Yehudim mizrahim," 455–56.
69. Roby, *Mizrahi Era of Rebellion*, 66–85.
70. YY 129: 2, correspondence between David Cohen and David Salman, 3/April/1959 (Cohen to Salman); 29/March/1959 (Salman to Cohen); see also Abraham Cohen to the general secretariat of MAPAM, 6/March/1957.
71. YY 133: 5, A. 'Abbudi, the transit camp of Ramat ha-Sharon, to MAPAM's center.
72. YY 124: 1, protocol of the secretariat of the 'Adot ha-Mizrah 7/July/1960, 21/May/1960.
73. YY 131: 21, the meeting of the 'Adot ha-Mizrah in the south, 26/April/1959.
74. YY 133: 21, report, 2/January/1959; 4/January/1959.
75. YY 123: 12, 10/February/1955, meeting protocol.
76. YY 133: 5, A. 'Abbudi, the transit camp of Ramat ha-Sharon, to MAPAM's center; on Dori's role in MAPAM, see Roby, "The Beginning," 127–32.

77. Ha-Miflaga ha-Komunistit ha-Yisra'elit, *Kfar Kasem: 1956–2006* (Tel Aviv: Ha-Miflagah ha-Komunistit ha-Yisra'elit, 2006), 1–3; Shira Robinson, "Local Struggle, National Struggle: Palestinian Responses to the Kafr Qasim Massacre and Its Aftermath, 1956–66," *International Journal of Middle East Studies* 35:3 (2003): 393–416.

78. Tom Segve, "If the Eye Is Not Blind nor the Heart Closed" (a story about Latif Dori). Haaretz website, www.haaretz.com/if-the-eye-is-not-blind-nor-the-heart-closed-1.203445 (accessed 30/November/2016).

79. Ibid.

80. Latif Dori, "Hamishim ve-hamesh shana la-teveah bi-kfar Qasim," Defeatest Diary website, 24/October/2011, www.defeatist-diary.com/index.asp?p=articles_new 10737&period=4/10/2011–28/11/2011 (accessed 30/November/2016). Moshe Ivgi, interview with Latif Dori, www.youtube.com/watch?v=IU5xnIbgwRQ (accessed 30/November/2016).

81. Ivgi, interview with Dori.

82. Yehoshu'a, "Skira," 77–79.

83. Almozlino, *Me-ha-Mahteret*, 65; on her bio, see: Meir-Glitzenstein, *Ben Bagdad*, 264–66.

84. YT 35 (MAKI) Series: Districts, Box 35: file 1, a pamphlet to the workers of Holon regarding the dismissal of a MAKI's worker from his factory (21/September/1959); a pamphlet about the dismissal of Doris Ezra for political reasons 19/August/1954; YT 35 (MAKI) Series: Districts, Box 13: file 6; S15/4/35 a letter to Ra'anan Weitz from H. Bar-Ilan concerning the expulsion of five communists in Tel Aviv, 22/November/1950; 10/May/1950, a letter to Levy Eshkol, G. Yoseftal, H. Helman from R. Teneh [Jewish Agency] (the letter specified that the transit camp in Acre refuses to accept eleven families because they are communist and the transit camp leadership is afraid of demosrations).

85. NLI; collections of electoral campaign posters (Osef Ta'amulat Bhirot la-Kneset), series 3 (1955 elections).

86. Nesia Safran, *Shalom Lekha Communism* (Tel Aviv: Ha-Kibbutz ha-Me'uhad, 1983), 28.

87. *Kol ha-'Am* 15/June/1951, no. 1320, 4.

88. See for example YT 35 (MAKI) Series: Districts, Box 7: file 1, pamphlet to the workers of Jerusalem 9/September/1955; pamphlet 1954.

89. YT 35 (MAKI) Series: Secretariat, Box 1: file 3, a letter from Taufik Tubi to Emile Habibi, 4/January/1954.

90. Nassar, Affirmation and Resistance.

91. YT 35 (MAKI) Series: Conferences, Box 17: file 5, the seventh conference of the communist youth, December 1957. A sketch by Sasson Somekh was shown in the conference which featured a mother telling her communist son: "red is a rotten color"] [Hebrew].

92. For pamphlets calling for demonstrations, see: YT 35 (MAKI), Series: Publications, Box 7, file 3, pamphlet from the transit camp of Holon (Arabic) (21/May/1951); YT 35 (MAKI), Series: Publications, Box 7, file 3, pamphlet concerning the elections to the

Histadrut, the local municipalities and the Knesset (December 1954); YT 35 (MAKI), Series: Publications, Box 7, file 3, pamphlet in the name of the Rehovot Transit Camp, Kfar Saba Transit Camp and Kfar Ono transit camp (Arabic) (16/February/1951); on protests of Iraqi Jewish activists in the transit camps around Jerusalem, see: YT 35 (MAKI) Series: Districts, Box 7: file 1, a notice from MAKI branch in Talpiot, 1953; on the communist attempts to arrange communist demonstrations in camps, see also: Meir-Glitzenstein, *Ben Bagdad*, 210–17; on MAPAI's violence in breaking down these demonstrations, see ibid., 221–25; on the communists and Iraqi Jews, see also: Meir-Glizenstein, *Ben Bagdad*, 211–25; on the role of the communists in organizing demonsrations, see: Orit Bashkin, "Unholy Pilgrims in a New Diaspora: Iraqi Jewish Protest in Israel, 1950-1959," The Middle East Journal 70:4 (2016), 612-14

93. YT 35 (MAKI) Series: Publications, Box 7: file 1, pamphlet [1955?].

94. YT 35 (MAKI) Series: Publications, Box 6: file 7, Esther Wilenska, "for democratic municipalities, for the people," a publication of the central committee, September 1950.

95. YT 35 (MAKI) Series: Instructions of the central committee to the provinces and the comrades, Box 5: file 3, letter from Esther Wilenska to the local secretariats.

96. MAKI, *I'rif al-haqiqa*, Haifa (4/May/1955), NLI; collections of electoral campaign posters (Osef Ta'amulat Bhirot la-Kneset; series 3 (1955 elections), V2978.

97. YT 35 (MAKI) Series: Particulars, Box 5: file 6, letter from Taufiq Tubi to Comrade Herzberg.

98. *Kol ha-'Am* 20/November/1951, no. 1447, 1; see also Sami Michael accounts from *Al-Ittihad*, which compare Herut's propaganda to the sounds of dogs (12/September/1954).

99. YT 35 (MAKI) Series: Secretariat, Box 1: file 7, pamphlet 1955.

100. NLI; collections of electoral campaign posters (Osef Ta'amulat Bhirot la-Kneset; series 4 (1959 elections); the poster included an article from *Kol ha-'Am* 31/August/1959.

101. YT 35 (MAKI) Series: Districts, Box 8: file 8, municipal election pamphlets and posters; YT 35 (MAKI) Series: Districts, Box 11: file 2 (MAKI activities in Holon and Tel Aviv); YT 35 (MAKI) Series: Districts, Box 14: file 2 (activities in the north), YT 35 (MAKI) Series: Districts, Box 16: file 7 (MAKI activities in the south-central regions); YT 35 (MAKI) Series: Districts, Box 7: file 1 (activities in Jerusalem); YT 35 (MAKI) Series: Districts, Box 11: file 6 (electoral campaigns).

102. YT 35 (MAKI) Series: Districts, Box 7: file 1, pamphlet to the people of Jerusalem 10/March/1958, pamphlet, preparation for first of May, 28/April/1957.

103. YT 35 (MAKI) Series: Conferences, Box 1: file 5, the sixth conference of the communist youth, 19/March/1953.

104. YT 35 (MAKI) Series: Districts, Box 8: file 8, memo to the Histadrut members in Jerusalem, 1969; YT 35 (MAKI) Series: Districts, Box 11: file 6, pamphlet to the voters in Jerusalem.

105. YT 35 (MAKI) Series: Particulars, Box 5: file 1, a letter from Taufik Tubi to the committees in sub-branches, 17/March/1954.

106. YT 35 (MAKI) Series: Instructions of the central committee to the provinces and the comrades, Box 5: file 3, report from 29/March/1959; a letter from the central committee to the members of the district concerning the meetings of Iraqi members, 25/March/1959.

107. Shimon Ballas, *Be-Guf rishon* (Tel Aviv: Ha-Kibbutz ha-Me'uhad, 2009).

108. Ammiel Alcalay, "At Home in Exile: An Interview with Shimon Ballas," in *Keys to the Garden: New Israeli Writing*, ed. Ammiel Alcalay (San Francisco: City Lights Books, 1996), available at www.wordswithoutborders.org/article/at-home-in-exile-an-interview-with-shimon-ballas (accessed 4/February/2017).

109. Ballas, *Be-Guf*, 54; based on his readings of communist newspapers in Arabic, Ballas was much more critical of Nasserism than the party's initial perception of the movement. On MAKI's relationship to Nasserism, see: Beinin, *Was the Red Flag*, 160–203; 212–23.

110. YT 35 (MAKI) Series: Publications, Box 6: file 5, July 1959, epistle to the Workers from Asian and North African Lands from the central committee of MAKI, Tel Aviv.

111. For the party's views and their positions in the 1951 first elections, Menachem Begin, *Basic Outlines of Our World View and Our National Uutlook*, trans. Yonatan Silverman and Ilana Brown, ed. Israel Medad (Jerusalem: Menachem Begin Center, 2007); originally published in 1952.

112. *Herut* 11/July/1952, 1; *Herut* continued asking that newcomers would arrive in Israel all throughout the 1950s and objected to the selection of newcomers from North Africa, see also: *Herut* 24/June/1956, 1.

113. *Herut* 17/July/1951, 1.

114. *Herut* 20/June/1955, 2.

115. *Al-Huriya* 21/December/1954, 1; Kabha, "Yehudim mizrahim," 460; Yehoshu'a, "Skira," 80–82.

116. *Al-Huriya* 22/December/1955, 1, discussed at Yehoshu'a, "Skira," 80.

117. Yehoshu'a, "Skira," 81–82.

118. Ibid.

119. YY *Hizb al-Huriya*, pamphlet no. 38, 11/January/1954.

120. MZ H 1/9/77, pamphlet dated 22/June/1954, *Khayriyya Between Past and Present*; see also the pamphlet addressed to the people of Khayriyya (*ya sukkan Khayriyya!*) in MZ H 1/9/77 pamphlet dated 5/December/1953.

121. NLI; collections of electoral campaign posters, series 3 (1955 elections).

122. Posters collection, 1959 campaign: National Library of Israel website, http://web.nli.org.il/sites/NLI/Hebrew/collections/treasures/elections/elections_materials/Pages/elect_ephemera_1959.aspx (accessed 30/November/2016).

123. Ibid.

124. MZ H 1/9/77, 13/December/1953, to: Herut secretariat (Tel Aviv) from Na'im Zilkha (Khayriyya), concerning contract with the secretaries of Kfar 'Ana and Sakiyya; on activities in Amisav, see: MZ, H1 19/78, letter dated 14/February/1954; from Adam Naji, from the transit camp of Petach Tikva to A. S. Levy; letter dated 27/September/1955 from Zion Baddash to chairman of Herut; MZ H1 6/20, letter from Dr. Shimshon

Yonichman (Jewish Agency) to Herut central committee (Tel Aviv); letter from A. Drori to Jewish Agency dated 22/June/1954.

125. MZ H1 9/78 letters dated 14/March/1953, from Naʿim Zilkha to general secretariat; letters concerning the disagreements between A. S. Levy and Zilkha (the former felt Zilkha was inactive in the party and neglected the transit camps; Zilkha eventually quitted his position).

126. MZ H1/2/4, protocols from the central committee, 16/December/1954; protocols from the central committee, 27/February/1955.

127. MZ H1/2/4, protocols from the central committee, 9/September/1954.

128. MZ H1/2/4, protocols from the central committee, 3/June/1954.

129. MZ H1/2/6, protocols from the central committee, 26/August/1956.

130. MZ H1/2/4, protocols from the central committee, 3/June/1954.

131. MZ H1/2/4, protocols from the central committee, 3/June/1954.

132. MZ H1/2/6, protocols from the central committee, 15/October/1956; MZ H1/2/4, protocols from the central committee, 27/April/1954.

133. MZ H1 6/20, Herut to Jewish Agency, dated 21/March/1955.

134. MZ H1 6/20, letter dated 25/November/1955, from Y. Konigsberg, division of newcomers camps and transit camps, to Herut movement.

135. YY *Hizb al-Huriya*, pamphlet no. 38, 11/January/1954.

136. MZ H1/2/4, protocols from the central committee, 15/October/1956.

137. MZ H1 9/78, letter dated 27/September/1955 from Zon Badash to chairman of Herut; the letter deals with a Herut man who was sent from the transit camp of Amisav to Rehovot.

138. MZ H1/2/6, protocols from the central committee, 15/October/1956.

139. MZ H1/2/4, protocols from the central committee, 27/April/1954.

140. MZ H1 6/20, 21/June/1954, letter from Dr. Shimshon Yonichman (Jewish Agency) to Herut central committee (Tel Aviv).

141. MZ H1 6/20, letter from Dr. Shimshon Yonichman (Jewish Agency) to Herut central committee (Tel Aviv); letters from A. Drori to Jewish Agency dated 22/June/1954; letter dated 29/October/1956 from Dov Donner to Mr. Konigsberg (Jewish Agency).

142. MZ H1/2/4, protocols from the central committee, 3/June/1954.

143. *Herut* 17/July/1951, 1.

144. Yaʿaqov Rot, "Tahalichey hakamat siʿat techelet lavan bi-tnuʿat ha-Herut," in *Me-Hevrat ʿavoda le-irgun ʿovdim: Leket maʾamarim ʿal Histadrut ha-ʿovdim bi-yemey ha-yishuv ve-ha-medina*, ed. Avi Barʾeli, Yosef Gorni, and Yitzhak Greenberg (Kiryat Sdeh Boker: Merkaz le-Moreshet Ben Gurion, 2000), 570–91.

145. MZ H1/2/6, protocols from the central committee, 20/January/1951.

146. MZ H1/2/6, protocols from the central committee, 15/November/1956.

147. MZ H1/2/6, protocols from the central committee, 26/August/1956.

148. MZ H1/2/4, protocols from the central committee, 27/February/1955; protocols from the central committee, 29/May/1955; protocols from the central committee, 5/June/1955.

149. *Herut* 17/July/1951, 1.

150. NLI; collections of electoral campaign posters (Osef Ta'amulat Bhirot la-Kneset; series 4 (1959 elections).

151. Orit Bashkin, "The Barbarism from Within: Discourses About Fascism Amongst Iraqi and Iraqi-Jewish Communists, 1942–1955," *Die Welt des Islams* 52 (2012): 424–26.

152. Amir Goldstein, "Shki'at ha-tzionim ha-klalim ve-kishlona shel ha-alternativa ha-liberalit," *'Iyunim bitkumat Yisra'el* 16 (2006): 343–93; data on the party from the Knesset website: www.knesset.gov.il/faction/heb/FactionPage.asp?PG=81 (accessed 30/November/2016).

153. *Nashrat al-Markaz* 21/December/1954, 1.

154. Rozin, *Hovat*, 143.

155. See for example the article which depicted the newcomers as prone to complaining, in *Ha-Boker* 3/January/1952, in CZA S71/111 [Ma'abarot].

156. On the party in the Knesset, see: www.knesset.gov.il/faction/heb/FactionPage.asp?PG=89 (accessed 30/November/2016); Meir-Glitzenstein, *Ben Bagdad*, 246–57.

157. RK vol. 10: 798–99, 2nd Knesset, session 35 2/December/1951.

158. RK vol. 12: 2379, 2nd Knesset, session 93 25/June/1952.

159. Orit Bashkin, "Salmān Shīna," *Encyclopedia of Jews in the Islamic World*, ed. Norman A. Stillman, Brill Online Reference Works, http://referenceworks.brillonline.com/entries/encyclopedia-of-jews-in-the-islamic-world/shina-salman-SIM_0020160 see also: Salman Shina, *Mi-Bavel le-Tzion: Zichronot ve-hashkafot* (Tel Aviv: Ha-Merkaz, 1955); *Ha-Tzosfeh* 25/July/1955; *Ha-Tzosfeh* 11/February/1957; *Herut* 30/September/1955.

160. MAPAI election poster, NLI; collections of electoral campaign posters (Osef Ta'amulat Bhirot la-Kneset; series 3 (1955 elections), V2978.

161. NLI; collections of electoral campaign posters (Osef Ta'amulat Bhirot la-Kneset); series 2 (1951 elections), V1856/9/1.

162. NLI; collections of electoral campaign posters (Osef Ta'amulat Bhirot la-Kneset); series 3 (1955 elections), V2978.

163. Meir-Glitzenstein, *Ben Bagdad*, 246–57.

164. *Hed ha-Mizrah* 28/April/1950, 9.

165. *Hed ha-Mizrah* 21/April/1950, 6.

166. *Hed ha-Mizrah* 5/May/1950, 13.

167. *Hed ha-Mizrah* 31/May/1951, 6.

168. *Hed ha-Mizrah* 25/August/1950, 7.

169. RK vol. 18: 2088, 2nd Knesset, session 619, 27/June/1955.

170. RK vol. 16: 2249–50, 2nd Knesset, session 462, 2–4/August/1954.

171. RK vol. 18: 1297, 2nd Knesset, session 580, 1/January/1955.

172. RK vol. 18: 1533, 2nd Knesset, session 588, 9–11/May/1955.

173. RK vol. 7: 262, meeting 192, 20/November/1950.

174. RK vol. 16: 1595, 2nd Knesset, session 414, 10–12/May/1954; RK vol. 16: 1680, 2nd Knesset, session 421, 18/May/1954.

175. RK vol. 16: 2142, 2nd Knesset, session 455, 12–14/July/1954.

176. RK vol. 13: 550, 2nd Knesset, session 175, 26/January/1952.

177. RK vol. 7: 467–70, meeting 200, 15/May/1950.

178. RK vol. 15: 1055, 2nd Knesset, session 386, 3/March/1954.
179. RK vol. 16: 2249–50: 2nd Knesset, session 462, 2–4/August/1953.
180. RK vol. 15: 703–5, 2nd Knesset, session 358, 20/January/1954.
181. RK vol. 15: 2234, 2nd Knesset, session 456, 28/July/1954.
182. RK vol. 19: 170–71, 3rd Knesset, session 15, 26/October/1955.
183. RK vol. 15: 109–14, 2nd Knesset, session 316, 11/November/1953.
184. RK vol. 15: 258–60, 2nd Knesset, session 326, 25/November/1953.
185. RK vol. 15: 258–60, 2nd Knesset, session 326, 25/November/1953.
186. RK vol. 15: 2227–28, 2nd Knesset, session 4561, 28/July/1954.
187. Orit Bashkin, *The Other Iraq: Pluralism and Culture in Hashemite Iraq, 1921–1958* (Stanford, Calif.: Stanford University Press, 2009), 17–124.

CHAPTER 4: ELEMENTS OF RESISTANCE

1. *Ha-Dor* 18/October/1953, in CZA: S71/111 [file: Ma'abarot].
2. Roby, *Mizrahi Era of Rebellion*.
3. Dagon, *Sippura shel ma'abara*, 88.
4. Ha-Kohen, *'Olim bi-s'ara*, 200.
5. Al-'Ani, *Ganevet*, 44.
6. Dagon, *Sippura shel ma'abara*, 32.
7. Moreh-Cohen, *Mi gdot*, 30.
8. RK vol. 18: 2104, 2nd Knesset, session 620, 28/June/1955.
9. RK vol. 21: 2081, 3rd Knesset, session 171, 16/October/1956.
10. *Kol ha-'Am* 18/September/1952, no. 1697, 4.
11. Moreh-Cohen, *Mi-gdot*, 41–42.
12. On the role of GADNA in the transit camps: ha-Kohen, *'Olim bi-s'ara*, 166–69.
13. YT 35 (MAKI), Series: Publications, Box 7, file 3, *Sarkhat al-Ma'abarot*, s.d., ed. Eliyahu 'Ezer. Sami Michael also criticized a professor at the Hebrew University who told his Iraqi students not to study but to enlist to military service so that they would absorb the "national spirit" (*Al-Itthiad*, 1/May/1953).
14. LA IV-215-1132, general report, 26/June/1952; a letter to Miriam Shapira, education bureau, the director of the school for working youth, from Mister Haya.
15. LA IV-215-324 to Mr. Nathan Elhanany, the head of Kfar Mesubin [Khariyya], from Sara Barkai'it, director of school for youth, 25/January/1953; to Dr. M. Gat, director of the Ministry of Education chief of staff, 11/January/1953.
16. *Kol ha-'Am* 26/November/1953, no. 2049, 1.
17. RK vol. 15: 850, 2nd Knesset, session 369, 10/February/1954.
18. Shohat, "The Question," 41–42.
19. The words were: *ba'una, ishtaruna, jabuna*. Jada' Gil'adi, *Isra'il nahw al-infijar al-dakhili: al-taqattub bayna al-mustawtinin al-urubiyyin wa-abna' dar al-Islam* (Cairo: Dar al-Bayadir li'l nashr wa'l tawzi', 1988).
20. See, for example, the story of 'Ezra Irbili who left his wooden shack without permission, and invaded another shack by breaking the door; the Ministry of Welfare immediately stopped state support. RK vol. 18: 2104, 2nd Knesset, session 620, 28/June/1955.

21. ISA K 83/16, protocol of the meeting of the Knesset subcommittee for the housing of the Gedera transit camp.
22. Dagon, *Sippura shel ma'abara*, 49.
23. Ibid., 60, 137–38.
24. Luffben, *Ish*, 244.
25. RK vol. 24: 2111; 3rd Knesset, session 477, 18/June/1958.
26. Dagon, *Sippura shel ma'abara*, 62.
27. Ibid.
28. Luffben, *Ish*, 244; Yoseftal, diary entry 14/January/1951, in Yoseftal, *Hayav*, 149.
29. RK vol. 12: 2509, 2nd Knesset, session 102, 2/July/1952; on the invasions to the tents in the center, see also: ISA G 45/5591 D. Teneh (Jewish Agency) to the prime minister, Jewish Agency, Ramat Gan, 10/July/1952.
30. For Iraqi squatting in Jerusalem, see: *Kol ha-'Am* 21/October/1950, no. 1147, 4; on squatting in the cities, see also, Bashkin, Unholy Pilgrims, 617-621.
31. *Kol ha-'Am* 22/September/1950, no. 1098, 6.
32. *Kol ha-'Am* 19/December/1950, no. 1171, 4; *Kol ha-'Am* 1/September/1950, no. 1083, 6; on the fifteen hundred families identified as squatters within the transit camps, see Meir-Glitzenstein, *Ben Bagdad*, 219–20; on squatting in the cities, see ibid., 123–28.
33. On a dramatic case of evacuating newcomers from their homes, see: *Kol ha-'Am* 7/October/1952, no. 1711, 4.
34. RK vol. 23: 644; 3rd Knesset, session 292, 1/January/1958; on the intentional plan to build small apartments, thinking that they serve Eastern European families with small children, see: Yoseftal, "Siha," in Yoseftal, *Hayav*, 133.
35. Mu'allim Dror, *Bi-Ntivey*, 81–86; ISA, G 1900/28 8/September/1952, the religious committee of Khayriyya B to the minister of religion, and the chief rabbis in Tel Aviv, the minister of interior; LA IV-250-64-1-204, letter from Na'im to the Ramat Gan workers' council, 17/April/1952.
36. Meir-Glitzenstein, *Ben Bagdad*, 113–28.
37. Kemp, "Medabrim."
38. Giora Yoseftal, diary entry, 18/November/1951, in Yoseftal, *Hayav*, 149; on the extant of newcomers refusing to live in places allotted to them, see: ha-Kohen, *'Olim bi-s'ara*, 291–93; on benefits denied to them, the ideas that the police would guard them so they do not escape, see: ibid., 294–95.
39. RK vol. 24: 2111; 3rd Knesset, session 477, 18/June/1958.
40. Giora Yoseftal, diary entry, 14/January/1951, in Yoseftal, *Hayav*, 148.
41. For excellent coverage of all unofficial committees, starting in Pardes Hannah, see Roby, "The Beginning," 99–113; see also Roby, *Mizrahi Era of Rebellion*, 86–110.
42. Roby, *Mizrahi Era of Rebellion*, 66.
43. RK vol. 18: 2087, 2nd Knesset, session 619, 27/June/1955; ha-Kohen, "Ha-Yishuv"; ha-Kohen, *'Olim bi-s'ara*, 275–78.
44. DRP, Document 15, municipal care of settlement of *'olim*—a report delivered at a press conference in Jerusalem, 15/May/1951, by Mr. Dov Rozen, the minister of interior; Document 140 to: the committees in the transit camps; from: the Division for

the Settlement of 'Olim, the Ministry of the Interior [M. Weiss, assistant director], 3/September/1952; Document 138 to: the committees in the transit camps; from: MYO the Ministry of the Interior [M. Weiss, assistant director], April 1952.

45. DRP, Document 139 to: the committees in the transit camps; from: MYO, the Ministry of the Interior [M. Weiss, assistant director], 10/June/1952.

46. DRP, Document 112 to: representative from the transit camp, from: MYO, the Ministry of the Interior, Jerusalem [Dov Rosen] 5/November/1952.

47. LA IV-250-64-1-204 to the minister of interior affairs, from A. Abramovitch, the municipal division of the executive committee [va'd ha-po'el], 21/November/1951.

48. LA IV-250-64-1-204, protocol of the meeting of the local committee Yad ha-Ma'avir, 11/November/1952; protocol of the meeting of the local committee Yad ha-Ma'avir, 23/October/1952; protocol of the meeting of the local committee Yad ha-Ma'avir, 21/October/1952; LA IV-250-64-1-204, A. Abramovitch to Ministry of Education, supply division.

49. LA IV-250-64-1-204, letter to Ya'aqov Atias, the director of Yad ha-Ma'avir, from D. Agasi, 14/September/1952.

50. Giora Yoseftal, diary entries dated 18/November/1951, in Yoseftal, *Hayav*, 148.

51. DRP, Document 113 to: the secretaries and committees in the transit camp, from: MYO, the Ministry of the Interior, Jerusalem [Dov Rosen] 24/January/1952.

52. RK vol. 11: 1303, 2nd Knesset, session 55, 13/February/1952.

53. RK vol. 14: 2170, 2nd Knesset, session 200, 10–13/August/1953.

54. ISA, G 6/16/32, Association of Iraqi Jews to Yoseftal, 30/December/1951.

55. Mu'allim Dror, *Bi-Ntivey*, 68–69.

56. Ibid., 74–75.

57. Luffben, *Ish*, 193–204.

58. ISA, G 1900/28, 8/September/1952, the religious committee of Khayriyya B, to the minister of religion, and the chief rabbis in Tel Aviv, the minister of interior.

59. ISA, G 1900/28, 23/October/1952.

60. ISA, G 1900/30, 29/January/1951, a petition from the citizens of Kfar 'Ana to the presidency of the Knesset, the prime minister, the chair of the Histadrut, the Ministry of Health, and the Jewish Agency.

61. ISA G 6/86/13, 1/June/1955, petition of the people of Khayriyya and delegation of the people of the camp to the chairman of the labor committee.

62. The Hebrew translation was even more racial and in it the director of the camp was depicted as calling the Mizrahi residents "dirty Negroes."

63. ISA, G 149/22, 30/May/1954, petition from the Iraqi Jews of the transit Camp of Kfar Ata to the prime minister and the ministers of Aliyah, agriculture, religion, the Jewish Agency in Jerusalem.

64. ISA, G 149/22, 30/May/1954, Division to the Department of Newcomers settlement, from Yehushua Baruchi.

65. ISA, G 1901/8, January 1952, petition of the transit camp of Shikun Mizrah, January 1952, to the Jewish Agency; Absorption Division, copy: minister of interior, City of Rishon le Zion.

66. ISA, K 9/22, a protocol of the meeting of with the denizens of Sakiyya B, 4/November/1951, with M. Rozetti and A. Govrin.

67. ISA K 82/18, 2nd Knesset, subcommittee of the Ministry of Labor in the case of the [transit camp] of Khayriyya.

68. ISA K 71/3, protocols of the meeting of the interior affairs committee, 10/August/1954; discussion of the letter of the people of the transit camp in Amishav; the meeting of the minister of internal affairs, 29/June/1954, discussing the letter of the people of the transit camp in Kfar Nahman; the protocol of the meeting of the internal affairs committee, 1/June/1954; G 6/86/13, 1/February/1955; labor committee, 1/February/1955.

69. ISA G 901/9, 8/May/1955, letter from David ʻAbd, to the interior minister.

70. LA IV-250-64-1-204, Mordechai Gabbai to the council of workers in Ramat Gan and Givaʻtim, Khiriyya B.

71. Sami Zubaida, "Being an Iraqi and a Jew," in *A Time to Speak Out: Independent Jewish Voices on Israel, Zionism, and Jewish Identity*, ed. Anne Karpf, Brian Klug, Jacqueline Rose, and Barbara Rosenbaum (London: Verso, 2008), 267–77.

72. LA IV-250-64-1-204, letter from Naʻim to the Ramat Gan workers' council, 17/April/1952.

73. The fifth Annual Study Mission of the United Jewish Appeal to Israel, Europe, and Muslim Lands, *The Other Side of the Coin, A Report to American Jewry*, 29/October–9/November/1958. JDC, http://search.archives.jdc.org/multimedia/Documents/NY_AR55-64/NY55-64_ORG_066/NY55-64_ORG_066_0962.pdf (accessed on 4/February/2017).

74. A copy of this petition is found in *Mathaf al-Shuhada'*, Kafar Qassem, Israel.

75. ISA G 45/5591 D. Teneh, letter to the prime minister, Jewish Agency, Ramat Gan, 10/July/1952.

76. RK vol. 12: 2509, 2nd Knesset, session 102, 2/July/1952.

77. On the role of demonstrations in Iraq public life, see also: Meir-Glitzenstein, *Ben Bagdad*, 136–47.

78. RK vol. 24: 1746, 3rd Knesset, session 452, 3/August/1958.

79. *Kol ha-ʻAm* 6/October/1952, no. 1710, 4.

80. RK vol. 25: 431, 3rd Knesset, session 558, 22–24/December/1958; RK vol. 18: 1297, 2nd Knesset, session 580, 1/January/1955; RK vol. 23: 383, 3rd Knesset, session 383, 24/December/1957.

81. Luffben, *Ish*, 243.

82. LA IV-250-64-1-204, A. Sharkerman, Histadrut Center in the transit camp of Sakiyya B to the general Histadrut, the workers' councils of Ramat Gan and Givʻatayim, 20/July/1952.

83. *Davar* 10/February/1952.

84. ISA GL 1124/28, A. Etz-Hadar (director of supplies division), to Ben Zion Luria, director of school repairing division, 5/May/1953; RK vol. 18: 2087, 2nd Knesset, session 619, 27/June/1955.

85. *Davar* 28/October/1951; *Davar* 25/October/1951.

86. David Ben Baruch, *Sippurim*, 60–64.

87. On Mizrahi demonstrations in cities, see: Roby, *Mizrahi Era of Rebellion*, 110–37;

on protests against unemployment, see: Bashkin, Unholy Pilgrims, 615, Meir-Glitzenstein, *Ben Bagdad*, 176–177.

88. Journal of the Association of the Youth of Aram Naharayim, (1/January/1951); Meir-Glitzenstein, *Ben Bagdad*, 176.

89. LA IV-215-1670: petition of the denizens of the Patach Tikva transit camp, 5/June/1953.

90. LA IV-250-64-1-204, A. Abramovitch to Ministry of the Interior, 2/July/1952; RK vol. 24: 2385; 3rd Knesset, session 500, 23/July/1958; vol. 24: 2248; 3rd Knesset, session 504, 30/July/1958.

91. *Kol ha-'Am* 23/September/1952, no. 1700, 4.

92. *Kol ha-'Am* 26/September/1952, no. 1701, 4.

93. RK vol. 21: 766, 3rd Knesset, session 224, 16/January/1957; for a case of ninety workers in Amisav who refused to go to their job assignment see: RK vol. 23: 120, 3rd Knesset, session 354, 11–13/November/1957.

94. Dagon, *Sippura shel ma'abara*, 76.

95. RK vol. 4: 708–9: meeting 112 of the 1st Knesset, 1/February/1950; meeting 116 of 1st Knesset, 14/February/1950, vol. 4: 785.

96. *Kol ha-'Am* 5/November/1953, no. 2031, 4.

97. RK vol. 22: 2293–95, 3rd Knesset, session 319, 3/July/1957.

98. On the demonstrations of Kfar Nahman, *Ha-Dor* 22/January/1954; *Davar* 9/February/1954; *'Al ha-Mishmar* 4/February/1954, in CZA: S71/109 [file: Ma'abarot]; on Holon see: see: *Kol ha-'Am* 10/November/1952, no. 1740, 4; *Kol ha-'Am* 11/November/1952, no. 1741, 4; *Kol ha-'Am* 13/November/1952, no. 1743, 4; see also: Bashkin, Unholy Pilgrims, 617.

99. *Kol ha-'Am* 26/October/1952, 1727; *'Al ha-Mishmar* 9/November/1952, in CZA S71/109 [Ma'abarot] 4.

100. Dagon, *Sippura shel ma'abara*, 29.

101. *Kol ha-'Am* 3/August/1950, no. 1058, 1.

102. On the elections in the camps, and MAPAI's involvement in its affairs, see: Gil'adi, *Isra'il*, 130.

103. *Kol ha-'Am* 26/November/1953, no. 2049, 1; on demonsrations in Jerusalem, see also: Bashkin, Unholy Pilgrims, 616.

104. *Kol ha-'Am* 6/October/1952, no. 1710, 4; on the callous approaches of bureaucrats in the camps, and attempts of the camps dwellers to take over the offices within the camps, see: Gila'di, *Isra'il*, 128–29; on demonsrations in Tel Aviv, see: Bashkin, Unholy Pilgrims, 615-617.

105. ISA G 45/5591, a letter by the association of Iraqi Jews on the events on 22 June 1952, 3/July/1952.

106. *Kol ha-'Am* 25/August/1952, no. 1676, 4; *Kol ha-'Am* 26/August/1952, no. 1677, 4; *Kol ha-'Am* 27/August/1952, no. 1678, 4; *Kol ha-'Am* 28/August/1952, no. 1679, 4; *Kol ha-'Am* 29/August/1952, no. 1680, 3; Meir-Glitzenstein, *Ben Bagdad*, 140–42.

107. *Ha-Boker* 5/September/1952, CZA: S71/111 [file: Ma'abarot].

108. *Davar* 28/August/1952, in S71/111 [Ma'abarot].

109. *Ha-Boker* 2/September/1952, in CZA S71/111 [Ma'abarot]; on Shabtai's articles, see: Meir-Glezenstein, Ben Bagdad, 139–42

110. *Kol ha-'Am* 19/August/1952, no. 1672, 4.

111. *Kol ha-'Am* 20/October/1952, no. 1722, 4.

112. *Davar* 27/February/1952; *Ha-Boker*, 27/February/1952, in CZA: S7/108 [file: Ma'abarot].

113. *Kol ha-'Am* 26/December/1951, 1478, 4.

114. Luffben, *Ish*, 237–38.

115. *Kol ha-'Am* 21/December/1951, 1457, 2.

116. Roby documented the relations between ethnicity and protest. On demonstrations of Yemenites, see: Roby, *Mizrahi Era of Rebellion*, 87–91; on Indian protest see: ibid., 116–21; on Iranian demonstrations see: *Maariv* 7/August/1960; *Maariv* 8/August/1960.

117. Shay Fogelman, "The Forgotten Ones," *Haaretz* 21/January/2010; on the rebellion in 'Emek Hefer and other activities in the transit camp, see: Roby, *Mizrahi Era of Rebellion*, 101–3. Read more: www.haaretz.com/israel-news/the-forgotten-ones-1.261857 (accessed 3/December/2016).

118. On demonstrations that paralyzed entire camps, see: *Kol ha-'Am* 27/October/1952, 1728, no. 1; *Kol ha-'Am* 28/October/1952, 1729, no. 1; on the spread of protests to city, see: Roby, *Mizrahi Era of Rebellion*, 86–137.

119. Ethel Rosenberg and Julius Rosenberg, *Michtavim mi-bet ha-mavet* (Tel Aviv: Ha-Kibbutz ha-Me'uhad, 1953); 'Akiva Zimerman, "Me-ha-zug Rosenberg ve-'ad Pollard," *Ha-Tzofeh* 19/May/2003.

120. LA IV-215-1670, letter from Mor Ari to Y. Geffen, educational center, Tel Aviv, 10/June/1953; letter to inspector Geffen from Yosef Yehoshua [teacher, Sakiyya B], 11/June/1953; letter from Avraham Salman, Sha'ul Mosheh, Na'im Dallal to Y. Geffen, 11/June/1953; letter from Y. Geffen to Y. Niv, 11/June/1953, "What is allowed and what is forbidden in the transit camp of Sakiyya," *Smol* 12/June/1953; the statement of comrade Yigal Eliyahu 17/June/1953; the investigation of comrade Y. Eliyahu [Y. Geffen], 17/June/1953; Meir-Glitzenstein, *Ben Bagdad*, 221–222.

121. LA IV-215-1670, letter from Mor Ari to Y. Geffen, educational center, Tel Aviv, 10/June/1953; letter to inspector Geffen from Yosef Yehushua [teacher, Sakiyya B], 11/June/1953; letter from Avraham Salman, Sha'ul Mosheh, Na'im Dallal to Y. Geffen, 11/June/1953; letter from Y. Geffen to Y. Niv, 11/June/1953, "What is allowed and what is forbidden in the transit camp of Sakiyya," *Smol* 12/June/1953; the statement of comrade Yigal Eliyahu 17/June/1953; the investigation of comrade Y. Eliyahu [Y. Geffen], 17/June/1953.

122. Orit Bashkin, "A Patriotic Uprising: Baghdadi Jews and the Wathba," in *Violence and the City in the Modern Middle East*, ed. Nelida Fuccaro (Stanford, Calif.: Stanford University Press, 2016), 151–68.

CHAPTER 5: ISRAELI BABYLONIANS

1. ISA, N 27/4, letter from Ephraim Matzlih to the director of the Voice of Israel, 20/October/1954.

2. David Kazzaz, *Min ha-Hidekel ve-hal'a: Zichronot me-heyehem ve-korotehem shel yehudey 'Iraq* (Tel Aviv: Ma'ariv, 2006), 330.

3. Ibid., 335–36.

4. Ibid.

5. *Davar* 17/August/1955, in S 71/109 [Ma'abarot].

6. A petition from the people of Mey Naftuh to David Ben Gurion, 2/November/1952, www.scribd.com/document/78885810/ארכיון-ציוני (accessed 4/February/2017).

7. *Davar* 8/August/1960; *Herut* 9/August/1961; *Maariv* 7/August/1960; *Maariv* 8/August/1960.

8. Al-'Ani, *Ganevet*, 102.

9. Agasi, *Mi-Baghdad*, 167.

10. Levy, *'Al Em*, 102–7.

11. Michael, *Gvulot ha-ruah*, 21.

12. On the Sephardim, see: Campos, *Ottoman Brothers*; Jacobson, *From Empire*.

13. *Al-Mirsad* 27 May 1954, 1.

14. LA, protocol of the meeting of the Congress of the Global Federation of Sephardi Jews, Saint Lazar, Paris, 12/August/1951.

15. Orit Rozin, "Negotiating the Right to Exit the Country in 1950s Israel: Voice, Loyalty, and Citizenship," *Journal of Israeli History: Politics, Society, Culture* 30:1 (2011): 1–22; excellent data and analysis on immigration from the state of Israel in the 1950s is found in Ori Yeudai, "Forth from Zion: Jewish Emigration from Palestine and Israel, 1945–1960" (Ph.D. diss., University of Chicago, 2013).

16. *Al-Mirsad* 9/July/1953, 4.

17. *Al-Mirsad* 12/March/1953, 1.

18. *Al-Mirsad* 14/May/1953, 4.

19. Agasi, *Mi-Baghdad*, 144.

20. Ibid.

21. Ibid., 145.

22. Ibid., 145–46.

23. 'Abbasi and Moreh, *Tarajum*, 236–337; Neri Livne, "Samir Who?" *Haaretz* 3/August/2004, www.haaretz.co.il/misc/1.988723 (accessed 3/December/2016).

24. Samir Naqqash, *Yawm habalat wa-ajhadat al-duniya* (Jerusalem: Al-Matba'a al-Sharqiyya, 1980), 105–57.

25. Ibid., 159–226.

26. Association of the Youth of Aram Naharayim, *Journal of the Association of the Newcomers from Babylon in Israel* 8 (16/August/1950).

27. Association of the Youth of Aram Naharayim, *Journal of the Association of the Newcomers from Babylon in Israel* 11 (8/October/1950).

28. *Kol Yotz'ey 'Iraq be-Yisra'el* [The Voice of Iraqi Jews in Israel], no. 26, 1/July/1952.

29. YY 133: 21, Avner Me'iri to party secretariat, 7/July/1959.

30. YT 35 (MAKI), Series: Publications, Box 7, file 3, pamphlet addressed to new comers from Iraq, Arabic, ca. 1951 or 1955.

31. Ibid.

32. *Kol ha-'Am* 11/March/1949, 633, 2.

33. YT 35 (MAKI), Series: Publications, Box 7, file 3, pamphlet from the transit camp of Holon (Arabic), 21 May 1951.
34. YT 35 (MAKI), Series: Publications, Box 7, file 3, *Sarkhat al-Ma'abarot*, s.d., ed. Eliyahu 'Ezer.
35. YT 35 (MAKI), Series: Publications, Box 7, file 3, *Sawt al-Ma'abarot*, 30 December 1954, Petach Tikva transit camp.
36. YT 35 (MAKI) Series: Particulars, Box 5: file 6.
37. *Kol ha-'Am* 24/November/1950, no. 1150, 3; see also a similar report on the Wathba by "Ibn Khaldun," *Kol ha-'Am* 9/February/1951, no. 1216, 4.
38. *Kol ha-'Am* 13/November/1949, no. 831, 1; *Kol ha-'Am* 11/March/1949, no. 633, 2; see also the story about the intifada in *Kol ha-'Am* 26/November/1952, no. 1757, 3; *Kol ha-'Am* 7/December/1952, no. 1762, 2–3.
39. *Ila al-Amam* January 1956.
40. *Al-Mirsad* 23 July 1953, 1; see also Latif Dori on the Wathba on 12/March/1953, 4; see also: *Al-Mirsad* 12/December/1953, 4, speech on the Wathba in Khayriyya transit camp.
41. *Al-Jadid* May 1957, vol. 4, no. 5, 42–46.
42. David Semah, *Hatta yaji' al-rabi'* (Tel Aviv: Al-Matba'a al-Haditha, 1959), 61–66.
43. YT 35 (MAKI) Series: Publications, Box 6: file 5, pamphlet dated 1955 [Hebrew].
44. Ibid.
45. Ibid.
46. On Arabic speakers see Hillel Cohen, *'Aravim tovim, ha-modi'in ha-Yisra'eli ve-'aravim be-yisra'el: Sokhnim u-maf'ilim, mashtampim u-mordim, matarot ve-shitot* (Jerusalem: 'Ivrit, 2006), 10.
47. Ben Zion Fischler, "Hanhalat ha-lashon bi-ymey ha-'aliya ha-hamonit," in *'Olim*, ed. Na'or, 145–57; on Hebrew instruction, legislation, and the initiatives of Ben Zion Dinur (the minister of education), see: ha-Kohen, *'Olim bi-s'ara*, 157–60.
48. Nathan Wolfuwitz, "Hershali me-Astropoli be-beyt ha-mishpat," originally published in July 1951, reprinted in *Haaretz* 30/March/2004, www.haaretz.co.il/misc/1.955774 (accessed 3/December/2016); *Haaretz* 10/June/1954, reprinted in www.haaretz.co.il/opinions/today-before/1.1727574 (accessed 3/December/2016); Moshe Zimmerman, *'Avar Germani: Zikaron Yisra'eli* (Tel Aviv: 'Am 'Oved, 2002); Na'ima Barzel, "Ha-Kavod, ha-sin'a, ve-ha-zikaron ba-diyunim be-she'elat ha-pitzuyim ve-ha-shilumim me-Germania bi-shnot ha-hamishim," *Yad va-Shem, Kovetz Mehkarim* 25 (1994), 203–25.
49. Qassab Darwish, *Snuniyot*, 28.
50. Mu'allim, *Be-Ntivey*, 172.
51. Dagon, *Sippura shel ma'abara*, 60.
52. Michael, *Gvolut ha-ruah*, 54.
53. On the voice of Fayruz in the Tiberias transit camp, see: *Davar* 17/August/1955, in S 71/109 [Ma'abarot]; on the approaches to Arabic music, see: Yochai Oppenheimer, "'Od Hozer ha-niggun be-'orkechem: Muzika ve-zehut Yehudit-'aravit," *Pe'amin* 125–27 (2010): 337–408.

54. Dagon, *Sippura shel ma'abara*, 66.

55. Shoshana Gabai, "Ke-she-zahav ha-dorot 'od hitgalgel ba-shechunot," *Haokets* 23/June/2013, www.haokets.org/2013/06/23/%D7%9B%D7%A9%D7%96%D7%94%D7%91 -%D7%94%D7%93%D7%95%D7%A8%D7%95%D7%AA-%D7%A2%D7%95%D7%93 -%D7%94%D7%AA%D7%92%D7%9C%D7%92%D7%9C-%D7%91%D7%A9%D7%9B %D7%95%D7%A0%D7%95%D7%AA/ (accessed 3/December/2016).

56. Ibid.; Shmu'el Moreh, "Salih wa-Da'ud al-Kuwaiti, 'ashiqan min al-Kuwait," *Ilaf* 23/February/2010, http://elaph.com/Web/opinion/2010/2/535813.html (accessed 3/December/2016).

57. Naham Ilan, "Tivuch Tarbuti: Avraham Sharoni, min ha-modi'in ha-tzva'i el ha-milon ha-'aravi-'ivri," *Pe'amim* (2010): 193–211; Avner Ya'qov-Yaron, *Shalom lakh Baghdad* (Jerusalem: Ha-Machon le-Heker ha-Mahteret ha-Tzionit, 2004), 310: Agasi, *Mi-Baghdad*, 169–72; Uri Dromi, "Truma adira le-havant ha-na'ase bi-tzva'ot 'arav, *Haaretz* 25/May/2005, www.haaretz.co.il/1.1013503 (accessed 3/December/2016); see also the website of the unit today: www.yehida.co.il/index.php?option=com_content&view= article&id=56&Itemid=142 (accessed 3/December/2016).

58. Ya'qov-Yaron, *Shalom lakh*, 92.

59. Rafi Siton, Yizhak Shushan, and Eli Tavor, *Anshey ha-sod va-ha-seter: Me-'Alilot ha-modi'in ha-Yisra'eli me-ever la-gvulot* (Tel Aviv: 'Idanim, 1990), 180–81; Yossi Melman and Dan Raviv, *Meraglim lo mushlamim: Sippuro shel ha-modi'in ha-Yisra'eli* (Tel Aviv: Ma'ariv, 1990), 32–38.

60. Michael Bar Zohar and Nissim Mish'al, *Ha-Mosad: Ha-Mivza'im ha-gdolim* (Tel Aviv: Hemed, 2010), 148.

61. Melman and Raviv, *Meraglim*, 78–79.

62. Maya Sela, "Author Sami Michael: Mossad Tried to Recruit Me in 1950s," 1/July/2011, www.haaretz.com/author-sami-michael-mossad-tried-to-recruit-me-in-1950s -1.370530 (accessed 3/December/2016).

63. Shlomo Nakdimon, *Tikva she-karsa, ha-kesher ha-Yisra'eli-Kurdi, 1963–1975* (Tel Aviv: Yedi'ot, 1996), 66, 117, 178, 220–21; Yaron, *Shalom lakh*, 42; Nahik Navot, *Sippuro shel ish Mossad* (Or Yehuda: Kineret, 2015).

64. Nakdimon, *Tikva she-karsa*, 152–53; 312–22.

65. Cohen, *'Aravim tovim*, 157–68.

66. Or Heller, *Mista'aravey ha-Shabak*, Doco10, Channel 10, 6/September/2015, http://docu.nana10.co.il/Article/?ArticleID=1146889 (accessed 3/December/2016).

67. Cohen, *'Aravim tovim*, 171.

68. Y. L. Ben Or, "Ha-hinuch ha-'aravi be-Yisra'el," *Ha-Mizrah ha-Hadash* (1950): 1–8; on a career of an Iraqi intellectual turned into Arabic inspector in Israeli school, see: 'Abbasi and Moreh, *Tarajum*, 228.

69. I am thankful to historian Shira Robinson, who allowed me to use the materials she uncovered in her unpublished seminar paper: "Iraqi Teachers in Israel's Palestinian Arab Schools, 1948–1966," originally submitted in the History Department, Stanford University, November 2003.

70. Sara Osazki Lazar, "Me-Histadrut 'ivrit le-Histardrut Yisra'elit: Hishtalvutam

shel 'aravim ba-irgun, 1946–1966," 'Iyunim bi-tekumat Israel 10 (2000): 381–419; Meir-Glitzenstein, *Ben Bagdad*, 246–75.

71. Qassab Darwish, *Snuniyot*, 108–26; 'Abbasi and Moreh, *Tarajum*, 199.

72. Qassab Darwish, *Snuniyot*, 172.

73. Ibid., 173.

74. Ibid., 38–45 (Nuzhat also refers to how the director trained her to speak in the Palestinian dialect) on the roles of Ishaq Bar Moshe, David Sagiv, Nir Shohat, see: 'Abbasi and Moreh, *Tarajum*, 26–27, 103, 127; Rafi Man, "Mi Shome'a et kol Yisra'el?" *Et-Mol* 237, www.ybz.org.il/_Uploads/dbsArticles/etmol_237-man.pdf (accessed 3/December/2016). S. Segiv wrote a lengthy piece on the radio's role in anti-Nasserite propaganda (*Maariv* 4/August/1959); which was continued by another enthusiastic report the next year by Ram Evron (*Maariv* 8/July/1960); see Ehud Ya'ari's piece on the station's role in the Hasbara to the Arab world (*Davar* 14/May/1967).

75. 'Inbal Perlson and Eyal Dotan, *Simha gdola ha-layla: Muzika yehudit-'aravit ve-zehut mizrahit* (Tel Aviv: Resling, 2006); David Sagiv was also a musical editor, see: 'Abbasi and Moreh, *Tarajum*, 103.

76. ISA GL 9/1250, State of Israel, Ministry of Education, note on our activities in the month of July, 13/November/1956; *Davar* 18/November/1955; *Davar* 20/November/1955; *Davar* 21/February/1960; *Maariv* 26/February/1960; on Te'atron la-'Am, the theater company that toured the transit camps, see: ha-Kohen, *'Olim bi-s'ara*, 153–57.

77. Mati Shmuelof, "Ariye be-Baghdad" (an interview with Arieh Elias), *Anashim* 474 (March 2006): 22–29; see the obituaries posted after Elias's death in Ynet (a website belonging the newspaper *Yedi'ot Ahronot*), www.ynet.co.il/articles/0,7340,L-4654727,00.html (accessed 3/December/2016); Walla website, http://e.walla.co.il/item/2790854 (accessed 3/December/2016); Haaretz website, www.haaretz.co.il/gallery/cinema/1.2631491 (accessed 3/December/2016).

78. Kabha, "Yehudim mizrahim"; on the work of Me'ir Haddad, Shalom Darwish, and Esperance Cohen, in *Al-Yawm* and *Al-Anba'*, see 'Abbasi and Moreh, *Tarajum*, 55, 103, 199. Cohen also edited *Kalimat al-Mar'a*, which was intended for women and was published by the Histadrut as well.

79. Rejwan, *'Al Gehalim*, 169.

80. *Ila al-Amam* January 1946.

81. *Al-Mirsad* 28/August/1954, 1.

82. *Al-Mirsad* 23/December/1954.

83. YT 35 (MAKI), Series: Districts, Box 14, file 7, Pamphlet ICP in the Eastern Galilee, 25/November/1951.

84. Safran, *Shalom*, 93.

85. *Kol ha-'Am* 10/November/1953, no. 2035, 2.

86. Michael, *Gvulot ha-ruah*, 93–94.

87. Ibid., 91–92.

88. Ibid., 99; Michael also depicted the attempts of MAPAI to incite Iraqi Jewish workers to banish Arab workers and take their place, although both are dark and speak Arabic (*Al-Ittihad* 24/April/1953).

89. *Kol ha-'Am* 17/December/1950, no. 1169, 4.

90. Snir, "'Till Spring Comes,'" 101-104; Sasson Somekh, *Life After Baghdad: memoirs of an Arab-Jew in Israel, 1950–2000*, trans. Tamar L. Cohen (Brighton, England: Sussex Academic Press, 2012), 31.

91. *Al-Jadid* 8:9 (1961): 23–27; Sasson Somekh, "Reconciling Two Great Loves: The First Jewish-Arab Literary Encounter in Israel," *Israel Studies* 4:1 (1999) 1–21; on the effects of the revolution in Iraq, see: Beinin, *Was the Red Flag*, 205–7.

92. Somekh, *Life After Baghdad*, 32; Somekh, "Reconciling."

93. Somekh, *Life After Baghdad*, 33–36; Ballas, *Be-Guf*, 41, 44–45.

94. Ballas, *Be-Guf*, 45.

95. Ibid., 48.

96. Alcalay, "Interview with Shimon Ballas," *Keys to the Garden*, 66.

97. The reference to the blacks in American appeared in another poem by Somekh, which compared the situation of the blacks in the United States to that of Iraqi Jews in Israel. The poem was dedicated to Paul Robeson. Snir, *'Arviyut*, 304; Snir, "'Till Spring Comes,'" 105; *Al-Jadid* November 1955, 48–49; *Al-Jadid*, March 1954, 18–19.

98. Semah, "Sawfa," ya'ud, hatta yaji, 41–45.

99. Snir, *'Arviyut*.

100. Bashkin, *New Babylonians*, 15–57.

101. See Chapter 2, p. 77; Fischler, "Hanchalat ha-lashon."

102. *Al-Mirsad* 1/May/1953, 4.

103. See Chapter 2, pp. 77–78.

104. Roby, *Mizrahi Era of Rebellion*, 96–98.

105. Qassab Darwish, *Snuniyot*, 32–33.

106. Michael, *Gvulot ha-ruah*, 18.

107. Dagon, *Sippura shel ma'abara*, 117.

108. Ibid., 132.

109. Association of the Youth of Aram Naharayim, *Journal of the Association of the Newcomers from Babylon in Israel* 15 (1/February/1951).

110. On white and black in Israeli society, see: Eitan Bar-Yosef, *Villa ba-jungel, Africa ba-tarbut ha-Yisra'elit* (Jerusalem: Machon Van-Leer and ha-Kibbutz ha-Me'uhad, 2013).

111. Almozlino, *Me-ha-Mahteret*, 52; CZA S20/613, the journal of the Association of the Youth from Aram Naharayim, brochure dated 17/September/1950.

112. Dagon, *Sippura shel ma'abara*, 82.

113. Levy, *'Al Em*, 98; al-'Ani, *Ganevet*, 66; Qassab Darwish, *Snuniyot*, 54–56.

114. Emphasis in the original.

115. Association of the Youth of Aram Naharayim, *Journal of the Association of the Newcomers from Babylon in Israel* 12 (1/November/1950).

116. *Kol Yotz'ey 'Iraq be-Yisra'el* [The Voice of Iraqi Jews in Israel], no. 25, 1/June/1952.

117. Ibid., no. 28, 1/September/1952.

118. Ibid., no. 23, 23/June/1952.

119. Mu'allim Dror, *Be-Ntivey*, 116–20: letter from Victor Mu'allim, Or Yehuda, June 1958.

120. Muʻallim Dror, *Be-Ntivey*, 121–22; the reference is to an article in *ʿAl ha-Mishmar* 14/August/1958.

121. *Al-Mirsad* 29/April/1954, 3.

122. *Al ha-Mishmar* 1/January/1951, no. 9, 1.

123. *Ila al-Amam*, no. 8, 24/June/1958, 1.

124. Ibid.

125. *Al-Mirsad* 4/February/1954, 3.

126. *Al-Mirsad* 13/May/1954, 1.

127. *Al-Mirsad* 1/January/1953, 4.

128. Moshe Hugi, Yoman Kibbutz Yagur, 30/June/1951, quoted in Ben Baruch, *Bi-svach*, 74.

129. Avraham Yehezkel of the Iraqi youth group Gan Shmuʻel, 7/January/1952. Quoted in ibid., 110–11.

130. *Kol ha-ʿAm* 10/January/1950, no. 581, 4.

131. YT 35 (MAKI), Series: Publications, Box 7, file 3, pamphlet by the name of the committee of Sakiyya, Khayriyya, and Kfar Ono (Arabic), Al-Ittihad Press, 1954.

132. See in particular his short stories "Tabaraka al-rabb," *Al-Ittihad* 20/September/1952; "Hadha abbi," *Al-Jadid* 1:8 (June 1954): 38–44; "Al-aswad," *Al-Jadid* 2 (October 1955): 23–39.

133. *Kol ha-ʿAm* 23/August/1950, no. 1075, 1.

134. *Kol ha-ʿAm* 20/September/1950, no. 1097, 4.

CONCLUSION

1. "Jewish Victim of Anti-Arab Stabbing Laments Racism," *Times of Israel* 14/October/2015, www.timesofisrael.com/jewish-victim-of-anti-arab-stabbing-laments-racism/ (accessed 3/December/2016).

2. Chetrit, *Intra Jewish Conflict in Israel*, 43–224.

3. Akiva Eldar and ʿIrit Zartal, *Adoney ha-aretz: Ha-Mitnahalim u-medinat Yisraʾel* (Or Yehuda: Dvir/Zemorah-Bitan, 2004).

4. Avraham Diskin, ed., *Bhirot u boharim be-Yisraʾel* (Tel Aviv: ʿAm ʿOved, 1988); Michal Shamir, ed., *The Elections in Israel* (New Brunswick, N.J.: Transaction Publishers, 2015).

5. Yoʾav Peled, ed., *Shas: Etgar ha-Yisraʾeliyut* (Tel Aviv: Yediʿot Ahronot/Sifrey Hemed, 2001).

6. On the new generation of Iraqi Israeli writers, see: Levy, *Poetic Trespass*, 189–294; Data on the Dov Flyer [*Mafriah ha-yonim*] is found in the Israeli movie database: www.edb.co.il/title/t0027611/ (accessed 3/December/2016).

7. See Facebook page, www.facebook.com/groups/zahavb (accessed 3/December/2016).

8. For a collection of Almog Bahar's poems in English translation, as well as his short stories, see his website: https://almogbehar.wordpress.com/english/ (accessed 3/December/2016).

9. On the demonstrations on 1–5 May 2015, see the reports on the Haaretz web-

site, www.haaretz.co.il/1.2626117 (accessed 3/December/2016); on Walla: http://news.walla.co.il/item/2850507 (accessed 3/December/2016); on NRG: www.nrg.co.il/online/1/ART2/692/587.html (accessed 3/December/2016); YNET: www.ynet.co.il/articles/0,7340,L-4653474,00.html (accessed 3/December/2016).

10. On Or Yehuda's mayor's refusal to absorb more Ethiopian families in the city's school, see the report on the Haaretz website, www.haaretz.co.il/misc/1.1041347 (accessed 3/December/2016).

11. Arie Kizel, *Ha-Narativ ha-mizrahi ha-hadash be-Yisra'el* (Tel Aviv: Resling, 2014).

12. See the Haaretz website, www.haaretz.com/news/national/author-israel-can-claim-the-title-of-the-most-racist-state-in-the-developed-world.premium-1.443908 (accessed 3/December/2016); www.haaretz.com/news/national/sami-michael-the-true-zionist-1.449051 (accessed 3/December/2016).

13. On aspects of this Mizrahi revival, see Smadar Levie's epilogue in the second edition of *Wrapped in the Flag of Israel: Mizrahi Single Mothers, Israeli Ultranationalism, and Bureaucratic Torture*, 2nd ed. (Leicester: PM Press / Kairos, 2016).

14. "Young Mizrahi Israelis' Open Letter to Arab Peers," 24/April/2011: see the 972 website, http://972mag.com/young-mizrahi-israelis-open-letter-to-arab-peers/13695/ (accessed 3/December/2016).

BIBLIOGRAPHY

ARCHIVES

American Jewish Joint Distribution Committee, online and in New York.
Central Zionist Archive (Ha-Archiyon ha-Tzioni ha-Merkazi), Jerusalem.
Israel State Archives (Ginzach ha-Medina), Jerusalem.
Lavon Archive (Ha-Machon le-Heker Tnu'at ha-'Avoda 'al-Shem Pinhas Lavon), Tel Aviv.
Metzudat Ze'ev, Beit Jabotinsky, Tel Aviv.
National Library of Israel, Posters collection, Jerusalem.
Yad Tabenkin, ha-Merkaz ha-Mehkari, ha-Ra'yoni ve-ha-Ti'udi Shel ha-Tnu'a ha-Kibbutizit, Ramat Ef'al, Israel.
Yad Ya'ari, Kibbutz Giv'at Haviva, Israel.

NEWSPAPERS AND JOURNALS

Hebrew
'Al ha-Mishmar.
Ha-Aretz (Haaretz).
Ha-Boker.
Ha-Dor.
Davar.
Hed ha-Mizrah.
Herut.
Kol ha-'Am.
Kol Yotz'ey 'Iraq be-Yisra'el.
Ma'ariv (Maariv).
Ha-Tzofeh.
Yedi'ot Ahronot.
Ha-Yom.

Arabic
Al-Huriya.
Ila al-Amam.
Al-Ittihad.
Al-Jadid.
Al-Mirsad.
Sarkhat al-Ma'abir.
Sawt al-Ma'abir.

BOOKS AND ARTICLES

'Abbasi, Mahmud, and Shmu'el Moreh. *Tarajum wa-athar fi'l adab al-'arabi fi Isra'il, 1948–1987*. Shifa' 'Amr, Israel: Dar al-Mashriq li'l tarjama wa'l Tiba'a, 1987.

Abutbul, Guy, Lev Grinberg, and Pninah Motsafi-Haler, eds. *Kolot mizrahiyim: Likrat siah mizrahi hadash 'al ha-hevrah ve-ha-tarbut ha-Yisra'elit*. Tel Aviv: Masada, 2005.
Agasi, Tikva. *Mi-Baghdad le-Yisra'el*. Ramat Gan: Kolgraph, 2004.
'Akirav, Tzvi. "Hug Bavli bi-shnat 1953." *Neharde'a—Bit'on Merkaz Moreshet Yahadut Bavel* 31 (Fall 2010): 48–49.
Alcalay, Ammiel. *After Jews and Arabs: Remaking Levantine Culture*. Minneapolis: University of Minnesota Press, 1993.
———. *Keys to the Garden: New Israeli Writing*. San Francisco: City Lights Books, 1996.
Altug, Seda. "Sectarianism in the Syrian Jazira: Community, Land, and Violence in the Memories of World War I and the French Mandate (1915–1939)." Ph.D. diss., Utrecht University, 2011.
Amir, Elie. *Tarnegol kapparot*. Tel Aviv: 'Am 'Oved, 2015.
al-'Ani, Ge'ula Sehayyek. *Ganevet ha-tarnegol: Yomana shel yaldat ma'abara*. Kiryat Ono: Safra, 2011.
Arbeli Almozlino, Shoshanna. *Me-ha-Mahteret be-Bavel le-memshelt Yisra'el*. Tel Aviv: Ha-Kibbutz ha-Me'uhad, 1998.
Avisur, Yitzhak, ed. *Mehkarim be-toldot yehudey 'Iraq u-betarbutam*. Or Yehuda: Merkaz Moreshet Yahadut Bavel, 1991.
Ballas, Shim'on. *Be-guf rishon*. Tel Aviv: Ha-Kibbutz ha-Me'uhad, 2009.
Bareli, Avi. *Authority and Participation in a New Democracy: Political Struggles in Mapai, Israel's Ruling Party, 1948–1953*. Brighton, Mass.: Academic Studies Press, 2014.
Bar-Yosef, Eitan. *Villa ba-jungel: Africa ba-tarbut ha-Yisra'elit*. Jerusalem: Machon Van-Leer and ha-Kibbutz ha-Me'uhad, 2013.
Barzel, Na'ima. "Ha-Kavod, ha-sin'a, ve-ha-zikaron ba-diyunim be-she'elat ha-pitzuyim ve-ha-shilumim me-germania bi-shnot ha-hamishim." *Yad va-Shem, Kovetz Mehkarim* 25 (1994): 203–25.
Bar Zohar, Michael, and Nissim Mish'al, *Ha-Mosad: Ha-Mivtza'im ha-gdolim*. Tel Aviv: Hemed, 2010.
Bashkin, Orit. "An Autobiographical Perspective: Schools, Jails, and Cemeteries in Shoshana Levy's Life Story." In *Gender in Judaism and Islam: Common Lives, Uncommon Heritage*, ed. Firoozeh Kashani-Sabet and Beth S. Wenger, 268–310. New York: New York University Press, 2015.
———. "The Barbarism from Within: Discourses About Fascism Amongst Iraqi and Iraqi-Jewish Communists, 1942–1955." *Die Welt des Islams* 52 (2012): 400–429.
———. "The Middle Eastern Shift and Provincializing Zionism." *International Journal of Middle East Studies* 46:3 (2014): 577–80.
———. *New Babylonians: A History of Jews in Modern Iraq*. Stanford, Calif.: Stanford University Press, 2012.
———. *The Other Iraq: Pluralism and Culture in Hashemite Iraq, 1921–1958*. Stanford, Calif.: Stanford University Press, 2009.
———. "A Patriotic Uprising: Baghdadi Jews and the Wathba." In *Violence and the City in the Modern Middle East*, ed. Nelida Fuccaro, 151–68. Stanford, Calif.: Stanford University Press, 2016.

———. "Salmān Shīna." *Encyclopedia of Jews in the Islamic World*. Ed. Norman A. Stillman. Brill Online Reference Works, http://referenceworks.brillonline.com/entries/encyclopedia-of-jews-in-the-islamic-world/shina-salman-SIM_0020160 (accessed 29/October/2016).

———. "Unholy Pilgrims in a New Diaspora: Iraqi Jewish Protest in Israel, 1950–1959." *Middle East Journal* 70:4 (2016): 609–22.

Begin, Menachem. *Basic Outlines of Our World View and Our National Uutlook*. Trans. Yonatan Silverman and Ilana Brown. Ed. Israel Medad. Jerusalem: Menachem Begin Center, 2007.

Beinin, Joel. *Was the Red Flag Flying There? Marxist Politics and the Arab-Israeli Conflict in Egypt and Israel, 1948–1965*. Berkeley: University of California Press, 1990.

Ben Baruch, David. *Bi-Svach kurey ha-klita: 'Al ha-murkavut bi-klitat havarot 'iraqiyot ba-tnu'a ha-kibbutzit ha-hilonit ba-shanim 1950–1952*. N.p.: n.p., 2006.

———. *Ha-Sippurim me-ha-megira ha-emtza'it*. N.p.: n.p., 2010.

Ben Or, Y. L. "Ha-Hinuch ha-'aravi be-Yisra'el." *Ha-Mizrah ha-Hadash* (1950): 1–8.

Berg, Nancy E. *Exile from Exile: Israeli Writers from Iraq*. Albany: State University of New York Press, 1996.

———. *More and More Equal: The Literary Works of Sami Michael*. Lanham, Md.: Lexington Books, 2005.

Bernstein, Deborah S. "Ha-Ma'barot bi-shnot ha-hamishim." *Mahbarot le-Mehkar u-le-Bikoret* 5 (1980): 5–47.

Bibi, Mordechai. *Ha-Mahteret ha-tziyonit ha-haluzit be-Iraq*. 4 vols. Jerusalem: Yad Ben Tzvi, 1988.

Campos, Michelle. *Ottoman Brothers, Muslims, Christians, and Jews in Early Twentieth-Century Palestine*. Stanford, Calif.: Stanford University Press, 2011.

Carey, Roane, and Jonathan Shainin, eds. *The Other Israel: Voices of Refusal and Dissent*. New York: New Press, 2002.

Chetrit, Sami Shalom. *Intra Jewish Conflict in Israel: White Jews, Black Jews*. London: Routledge, 2010.

Cohen, Eric. *Kehila Ktana be-Merhav metropolin: Mehkar khilati 'al Or Yehuda be-ezor Tel-Aviv*. Jerusalem: Eliezer Kaplan School of Economics and Social Sciences, Hebrew University, 1966.

Cohen, Haim. *Ha-Pe'ilut ha-tzionit be-'Iraq*. Jerusalem: Ha-Sifriya ha-Tzionit, 1969.

Cohen, Hillel. *'Aravim tovim, ha-modi'in ha-Yisra'eli ve-'aravim be-Yisra'el: Sokhnim u-maf'ilim, mashtampim u-mordim, matarot ve-shitot*. Jerusalem: Keter-'Ivrit, 2006.

Cohen, Ran. *Sa'id*. Tel Aviv: Ha-Kibbutz ha-Me'uhad, 2016

Darvish, Tikva, *Yehudey 'Iraq ba-kalkala*. Ramat Gan: Bar Ilan University, 1987.

Darwish, Nuzhat Qassab. *Snuniyot ha-Shalom, 'im ha-nashim ha-'araviyot va-ha-druziyot be-Yisra'el*. Or Yehuda: Ma'ariv, 1998.

Diskin, Avraham, ed. *Bhirot u boharim be-Yisra'el*. Tel Aviv: 'Am 'Oved, 1988.

———, ed. *Me-Altalena 'ad hena: Gilguleha shel ten'ua, me-Herut le-Likud*. Jerusalem: Carmel, 2011.

Dory, Latif. "Hamishim ve-hamesh shana la-teveh bi-Kfar Qasim." Defeatist Diary,

Joseph Algazy, October 24, 2011. www.defeatist-diary.com/index.asp?p=articles_new 10737&period=4/10/2011-28/11/2011 (accessed 29/October/2016).

Dvir, Dani. *Tzuf ha-Dvora*. Tel Aviv: Dani Dvir, 2014.

Dagon, Tzila. *Sippura shel Ma'abara be-Ramat ha-Sharon*. Ramat ha-Sharon, Israel: Ha-Merkazim ha-Khilatiyyim Ramat ha-Sharon, 2007.

Eisenstadt, S. N. *The Absorption of Immigrants*. London: Routledge and Kegan Paul, 1954.

———. *Essays on Sociological Aspects of Political and Economic Development*. The Hague: Mouton Press, 1961.

Eldar Akiva, and 'Irit Zartal. *Adoney ha-aretz: Ha-Mitnahalim u-medinat Yisra'el*. Or Yehuda: Dvir/Zemorah-Bitan, 2004.

Gabbai, Nili. *Ha-Isha ha-yehudit be-Baghdad*. Jerusalem: *Agudat ha-akadema'im yoze'y 'Iraq*. Jerusalem: Agudat ha-Akadema'im Yoze'y 'Iraq, 2006.

Gat, Moshe. *The Jewish Exodus from Iraq, 1948–1951*. London: Frank Cass, 1997.

Ghanem, As'ad. *Ethnic Politics in Israel: The Margins and the Ashkenazi Center*. London: Routledge, 2010.

Gil'adi, Jada'. *Isra'il nahw al-infijar al-dakhili: Al-Taqattub bayna al-mustawtinin al-urubiyyin wa-abna' dar al-Islam*. Cairo: Dar al-Bayadir L'i'l Nashr Wa'l Tawzi', 1988.

Goldstein, Amir. "Shki'at ha-tziyonim ha-klalim ve-kishlona shel ha-alternativa ha-liberalit." *'Iyunim bi-tkumat Yisra'el* 16 (2006): 343–93.

Greenberg, Yitzhak. "Ha-Kalkala ha-marhiva shel meshek ha-'ovdim, 1948–1988." In *Hevra ve-kalkala be-Yisra'el-mabat histori ve-achshavi*, ed. Avi Bareli, Daniel Gutwein, and Tuvia Friling, http://in.bgu.ac.il/bgi/iyunim/2005/13.PDF (accessed 29/November/2016). Jerusalem: Yad Ben Tzvi / Machon Ben Gurion le-Heker Yisra'el ve-ha-Tzionut, Ben Gurion University, 2005.

———. "Hevrat ha-'Ovdim u-klitat ha-'aliyah ha-gdola bi-shnot ha-hamishim." *'Iyunim bitkumat Yisra'el* 2 (1992): 94–115.

Gross, Nahum. *Bank ha-Po'alim: Hamishim ha-shanim ha-rishonot*. Tel Aviv: 'Am 'Oved, 1994.

Gutwien, Daniel. "From Melting Pot to Multiculturalism; or, The Privatization of Israeli Identity." In *Israeli Identity in Transition*, ed. Anita Shapira, 215–33. Westport, Conn.: Praeger, 2004.

Haddad, 'Ezra. *Avney Derech: Le-toldot ha-yehudim be-'Iraq me hurban ha-bayt ha-rishon ve-'ad la-thiya ha-le'umit*. Tel Aviv: Irgun Yotz'ey Iraq be-Yisra'el, 1969.

Haddad, Sha'ul. "Mishma'at barzel be-bet sefer Shahmon." *Neharde'a, Bit'on Merkaz Moreshet Yahadut Bavel* 31 (Fall 2010).

ha-Kohen, Dvora. *'Olim bi-s'ara: Ha-'Aliyah ha-gdola u-klitata be-Yisra'el, 1948–1953*. Jerusalem: Ben Tzvi, 1994.

Halamish, Aviva. "Loyalties in Conflict: Mapam's Vacillating Stance on the Military Government, 1955–1966; Historical and Political Analysis." *Israel Studies Forum* 25:2 (2010): 26–53.

———. *Meir Ya'ari*. Tel Aviv: 'Am 'Oved, 2013.

Halperin, Liora. *Babel in Zion: Jews, Nationalism, and Language Diversity in Palestine, 1920–1948*. New Haven, Conn.: Yale University Press, 2014.

Heathcott, Joseph. "Black Archipelago: Politics and Civic Life in the Jim Crow City." *Journal of Social History* 38:3 (2005): 705–36.
Herzl, Theodor. *Der Judenstaat: Versuch einer modernen Lösung der Judenfrage*. Leipzig: Breitenstein, 1896.
Hever, Hanan, Yehouda Shenhav, and Pnina Motzafi-Haller, eds. *Mizrahiyim be-Yisra'el: 'Iyun bikorti mehudash*. Jerusalem: Van Leer, 2002.
Holt, Thomas C. "Marking Race, Race-Making, and the Writing of History." *American Historical Review* 100:1 (1995): 1–20.
———. "The Political Uses of Alienation: W. E. B. Du Bois on Politics, Race, and Culture, 1903–1940." *American Quarterly* 42:2 (June 1990): 301–23.
Hillel, Shlomo. *Ruh qadim*. Jerusalem: 'Idanim, 1985.
Ilan, Naham. "Tivuch Tarbuti: Avraham Sharoni, min ha-modi'in ha-tzva'i el ha-milon ha-'aravi-'ivri." *Pe'amim* (2010): 193–211.
Jacobson, Abigail. *From Empire to Empire: Jerusalem between Ottoman and British Rule*. Syracuse, N.Y.: Syracuse University Press, 2011.
Kabha, Mustafa. "Yehudim mizrahim ba-'itonut ha-'aravit be-Yisra'el, 1948–1967." *'Iyunim bi-tkumat Yisra'el* 16 (2006): 445–61.
Kattav, Shalom. *Likuey me'orot, mi-shirey eretz Yisra'el ha-ahat*. Ramat Gan: Zoharim, 1978.
Kaufman, Ilana. *Arab National Communism in the Jewish State*. Gainesville: University Press of Florida, 1997.
Kazzaz, David. *Min ha-hidekel ve-hal'a: Zichronot me-heyehem ve-korotehem shel yehudey 'Iraq*. Tel Aviv: Ma'ariv, 2006.
Kazzaz, Nissim. *He-Yehudim be-'Iraq ba-ma'a he-'esrim*. Jerusalem: Yad Ben Tzvi, 1991.
Kemp, Adriana. "Medabrim Gvulot: Havnayat teritoriya politit be-Yisra'el, 1949–1957." Ph.D. diss., Tel Aviv University, 1997.
Keydar, Nir. *Mamlakhtiyut, ha-tfisa ha-ezrahit shel David Ben Gurion*. Jerusalem: Yad Ben Tzvi and Ben Gurion University Press, 2009.
Khazzoom, Aziza. "The Great Chain of Orientalism: Jewish Identity, Stigma Management, and Ethnic Exclusion in Israel." *American Sociological Review* 68:4 (2003): 481–510.
———. *Shifting Ethnic Boundaries and Inequality in Israel; or, How the Polish Peddler Became a German Intellectual*. Stanford, Calif.: Stanford University Press, 2008.
Kizel, Arie, *Ha-Narativ ha-mizrahi ha-hadash be-Yisra'el*. Tel Aviv: Resling, 2014.
Kobrin, Rebecca. "The Shtetl by the Highway: The East European City in New York's Landsmanshaft Press, 1921–39." *Prooftexts* 26:1–2 (2006): 107–37.
Lavie, Smadar. *Wrapped in the Flag of Israel: Mizrahi Single Mothers, Israeli Ultranationalism, and Bureaucratic Torture*. 2nd ed. Leicester: PM Press / Kairos, 2016.
Levin, Michael, et al. "Diyun: Ha-Tzmiha ve-ha-hitgabsuht shel tarbut 'ivrit mekomit u-yelidit be-eretz Yisra'el, 1882–1948." *Katedra* 16 (July 1980): 161–233.
Levy, Lital. *Poetic Trespass: Writing Between Hebrew and Arabic in Israel/Palestine*. Princeton, N.J.: Princeton University Press, 2014.
Levy, Shoshana. *'Al Em ha-derekh*. Tel Aviv: Shoshana Levy, 2001.

Lissak, Moshe. *Ha-'Aliyah ha-gdola bi-shnot ha-hamishim, kishlono shel kur ha-hituch.* Jerusalem: Mosad Bialik, 1999.

Luffben, Hezzi. *Ish yotz'e el ehav.* Tel Aviv: 'Am 'Oved, 1967.

Magal, Aryeh. "Al-Mirsad: Mapam's Voice in Arabic, Arab Voice in Mapam." *Israel Studies* 15:1 (2010): 115–46.

Makdisi, Ussama. "Pensée 4: Moving Beyond Orientalist Fantasy, Sectarian Polemic, and Nationalist Denial." *International Journal of Middle East Studies* 40:4 (2008): 559–60.

Man, Rafi. "Mi Shome'a et kol Yisra'el?" *Et-Mol* 237, www.ybz.org.il/_Uploads/dbsArticles/etmol_237-man.pdf (accessed 29/October/2016).

McKeown, Adam. "Global Migration, 1846–1940." *Journal of World History* 15:2 (2004): 155–89.

Meir-Glitzenstein, Esther. *Ben Bagdad le-Ramat Gan: Yots'ey 'Iraq be-Yisra'el.* Jerusalem: Yad Ben-Tzvi, 2008.

———. "Operation Magic Carpet: Constructing the Myth of the Magical Immigration of Yemenite Jews to Israel." *Israel Studies* 16:3 (2011): 149–73.

———. *Zionism in an Arab Country: Jews in Iraq in the 1940s.* London: Routledge, 2004.

Melman, Yossi, and Dan Raviv. *Meraglim lo mushlamim: Sippuro shel ha-modi'in ha-Yisra'eli.* Tel Aviv: Ma'ariv, 1990.

Michael, Sami. *Gvulot ha-ruah: Sihot 'im Ruvik Rosenthal.* Tel Aviv: Ha-Kibbutz ha-Me'uhad, 2008.

ha-Miflaga ha-Komunistit ha-Yisra'elit. *Kfar Kasem: 1956–2006.* Tel Aviv: Ha-Miflagah ha-Komunistit ha-Yisra'elit, 2006.

Mooreville, Anat. "Eyeing Africa: The Politics of Israeli Ocular Expertise and International Aid, 1959–1973." *Jewish Social Studies* 21:3 (2016): 31–71.

Moreh, Shmu'el. *Al-qissa al-qasira 'inda yahud al-'Iraq, 1924–1978.* Jerusalem: Hebrew University Press, 1981.

Moreh-Cohen, Esperance. *Mi-Gdot ha-Hidekel le-gdot ha-Yarkon: Sippurim ve zichoronot.* Jerusalem: Agudat ha-Akadema'im Yotz'ey Iraq, 2006.

Moria, Cherka. "Ma'avakam shel nifga'ey ha-tippul be-gazezet: ha-omnam ma'avak she-nichshal?" *Ma'asey Mishpat* 6 (2014): 135–36.

Mu'allim Dror, Victor. *'Avar lo rahok: Sippurim ve-eru'im she-lo nash leham.* Tel Aviv: n.p., 1985.

———. *Bi-Ntivey Haaim zichronot ve-eru'im she-einam nischahim.* Or Yehuda: n.p., 2000.

Murad, 'Ezra. *Ohalim-Shirim.* Tel Aviv: Alef, 1980.

Nahon, Ya'aqov. *Dfusey Hitrahvut ha-haskala u-mivneh hizdamnuyot ha-ta'asukra.* Jerusalem: Machon Yerushalayim le-heker Israel, 1987.

———. *Megamot ba-ta'asuka, ha-meymad ha-'adati.* Jerusalem: Machon Yerushalayim le-Heker Israel, 1984.

Nakdimon, Shlomo. *Tikva she-karsa, ha-kesher ha-Yisra'eli-Kurddi, 1963–1975.* Tel Aviv: Yedi'ot, 1996.

Na'or, Mordechai, ed. *'Olim u ma'abarot, 1948–1952.* Jerusalem: Yad Ben Tzvi, 1986.

Naqash, Samir. *Yawm habalat wa-ajhadat al-duniya*. Jerusalem: Al-Matba'a al-Sharqiyya, 1980.
Nassar, Maha Tawfik. "Affirmation and Resistance: Press, Poetry, and the Formation of National Identity Among Palestinian Citizens of Israel, 1948–1967." Ph.D. diss., University of Chicago, 2006.
Navot, Nahik. *Sippuro shel ish Mossad*. Or Yehuda: Kineret, 2015.
Nelson, Nancy Jo. "The Zionist Organizational Structure." *Journal of Palestine Studies* 10:1 (1980): 80–93.
Ofer, Dalia, ed. *Ben 'olim le-vatikim, Yisra'el ba-'Aliyah ha-gdola, 1948–1953*. Jerusalem: Yad Ben Zvi, 1996.
Oppenheimer, Yochai. "'Od Hozer ha-niggun be-orkechem: Muzika ve-zehut Yehudit-'aravit." *Pe'amin* 125–27 (2010): 337–408.
Osazki Lazar, Sara. "Me-Histadrut 'ivrit le-Histadrut Yisra'elit: Hishtalvutam shel 'aravim ba-irgun, 1946–1966." *'Iyunim bi-tkumat Israel* 10 (2000): 381–419.
Pe'er, Memi, ed. *Ramat-Gan: City of Gardens*. Ramat Gan: Municipality, Publicity Department, 1998.
Peled, Yoav, ed. *Shas: Etgar ha-Yisra'eliyut*. Tel Aviv: Yedi'ot Ahronot / Sifrey Hemed, 2001.
Perlson, Inbal, and Eytal Dotan. *Simha gdola ha-layla: Muzika Yehudit-'aravit ve-zehut mizrahit*. Tel Aviv: Resling, 2006.
Picard, Avi. *'Olim bi-msura: Mediniyut Yisra'el klapey 'aliyatam shel yehudey tzfon Africa, 1951–1956*. Jerusalem: Mosad Bialik, 2013.
Raz-Krakotzkin, Amnon. "History, Exile and Counter-History: Jewish Perspectives." In *A Companion to Global Historical Thought*, ed. Prasenjit Duara, Viren Murthy, and Andrew Sartori, 126–35. Chichester: Wiley Blackwell, 2014.
Rejwan, Nissim. *The Jews of Iraq: 3000 Years of History and Culture*. London: Weidenfeld and Nicolson, 1985.
Rejwan, Rahamim. *'Al Gehalim: Kovetz sippurim*. Tel Aviv: ZHL/IDF, Mifkedet Hinuch Rashi, Misrad ha-Bitahon-Hotza'a la-Or, 1985.
Robinson, Shira. *Citizen Strangers: Palestinians and the Birth of Israel's Liberal Settler State*. Stanford, Calif.: Stanford University Press, 2013.
———. "Iraqi Teachers in Israel's Palestinian Arab Schools, 1948-1966." Unpublished paper, Stanford University, November 2003.
———. "Local Struggle, National Struggle: Palestinian Responses to the Kafr Qasim Massacre and Its Aftermath, 1956–66." *International Journal of Middle East Studies* 35:3 (2003): 393–416.
Roby, Bryan K. "The Beginning of Oriental Jewish Protests in Israel and the Use of Israeli Police in the Suppression of a 'Mizrahi' Struggle, 1948–1966." Ph.D. diss., University of Manchester, 2012.
———. *The Mizrahi Era of Rebellion: Israel's Forgotten Civil Rights Struggle, 1948–1966*. Syracuse, N.Y.: Syracuse University Press, 2015.
Rokem, Na'ama, and Amir Eshel. "German and Hebrew: Histories of a Conversation." *Prooftext* 33:1 (2010): 1–8.

Rosenberg, Ethel, and Julius Rosenberg. *Michtavim mi-bet ha-mavet*. Tel Aviv: Ha-Kibbutz ha-Me'uhad, 1953.

Rot, Ya'aqov. "Tahalichey hakamat si'at techelet lavan bi-tnu'at ha-Herut." In *Me-Hevrat 'avoda le-irgun 'Ovdim: Leket ma'amarim 'al Histadrut ha-'ovdim bi-yemey ha-yishuv ve-ha-medina*, ed. Avi Bareli, Yosef Gorni, and Yitzhak Greenberg. Kiryat Sdeh Boker: Merkaz le-Moreshet Ben Gurion, 2000.

Rozen, Dov, ed. *Ma'abarot ve yeshuvey 'olim be-aspaklariya shel misrad ha-pnim*. Tel Aviv: Misrad Ha-Pnim, 1985.

Rozin, Orit. *Hovat ha-Ahava ha-qasha: Yahid ve-kolektiv be-Yisra'el bi-shnot ha-hamishim*. Tel Aviv: 'Am 'Oved, 2008.

——. "Negotiating the Right to Exit the Country in 1950s Israel: Voice, Loyalty, and Citizenship." *Journal of Israeli History: Politics, Society, Culture* 30:1 (2011): 1–22.

Safran, Nesia. *Shalom lekha Comonism*. Tel Aviv: Ha-Kibbutz ha-Me'uhad, 1983.

Sanjero, Boaz. "Be-Ein hashad ein hakira amitit: Duah va'adat ha-hakira be-'inayan parashat he'almutam shel yeladim mi-ben 'oley Teyman." *Teoriya u-bikoret* 21 (2002): 47–76.

Schwartz, Meyer. *Or-Yehuda: A New Immigrant Development "Satellite Town" in the Conurbation of Tel-Aviv-Yafo*. Jerusalem: N.p., 1968.

Segev, Tom. "If the Eye Is Not Blind nor the Heart Closed." Haaretz.com, www.haaretz.com/if-the-eye-is-not-blind-nor-the-heart-closed-1.203445 (accessed 29/October/2016).

——. *The Seventh Million: The Israelis and the Holocaust*. Trans. Haim Watzman. New York: Hill and Wang, 1991, 1993.

Semah, David. *Hatta yaji' al-rabi'*. Tel Aviv: Al-Matba'a al-Haditha, 1959.

Shalgi, Phyllis, and Miriam Goldwasser. "Hafra'at ishiyut tipusit li-kvutzat nashim 'iraqiyot le'or ha-reka' ha-tarbuti shel 'adatan." *Megamot* 6:3 (1955): 236–42.

Shamir, Michal, ed. *The Elections in Israel*. New Brunswick, N.J.: Transaction Publishers, 2015.

Shenhav, Yehouda. *The Arab Jews: A Postcolonial Reading of Nationalism, Religion, and Ethnicity*. Stanford, Calif.: Stanford University Press, 2006.

——. "The Jews of Iraq, Zionist Ideology, and the Property of the Palestinian Refugees of 1948: An Anomaly of National Accounting." *International Journal of Middle East Studies* 31:4 (1999): 605–30.

Shiblak, Abbas. *The Lure of Zion: The Case of Iraqi Jews*. London: Al-Saqi Books, 1986.

Shina, Salman. *Mi-Bavel le-Tzion: Zichronot ve-hashkafot*. Tel Aviv: Ha-Merkaz, 1955.

Shmuelof, Mati. "Ariye be-Baghdad" (an interview with Ariye Elias). *Anashim* 474 (March 2006): 22–29.

Shohat, Ella. "The Invention of the Mizrahim." *Journal of Palestine Studies* 29:1 (1999): 5–20.

——. "The Question of Judeo-Arabic." *Arab Studies Journal* 23:1 (2015): 14–74.

——. "Sephardim in Israel: Zionism from the Standpoint of Its Jewish Victims." *Social Text* 19:20 (1988): 1–35.

——. *Taboo Memories, Diasporic Voices*. Durham, N.C.: Duke University Press, 2006.

Sies, Mary Corbin. "The Everyday Politics and Spatial Logics of Metropolitan Life." *Urban History Review/Revue d'Histoire Urbaine* 32:1 (2003): 28–42.
Siton, Rafi, Yizhak Shushan, and Eli Tavor. *Anshey ha-sod va-ha-seter: Me-'alilot ha-modi'in ha-Yisra'eli me-'ever la-gvulot*. Tel Aviv: 'Idanim, 1990.
Smooha, Sammy. *Israel: Pluralism and Conflict*. London: Routledge and Paul Kegan, 1978.
Snir, Reuven. *'Arviyut, yahdut, tzionut: Ma'avak zehuyot bi-yetziratam shel yehudei 'Iraq*. Jerusalem: Yad Ben Tzvi, 2005.
———. "'Till Spring Comes': Arabic and Hebrew Literary Debates Among Iraqi-Jews in Israel (1950–2000)." *Shofar: An Interdisciplinary Journal of Jewish Studies* 24:2 (2006): 92–123.
Somekh, Sasson. *Life After Baghdad: Memoirs of an Arab-Jew in Israel, 1950–2000*. Trans. Tamar L. Cohen. Brighton, England: Sussex Academic Press, 2012.
———. "Reconciling Two Great Loves: The First Jewish-Arab Literary Encounter in Israel." *Israel Studies* 4:1 (1999): 1–21.
Stoler-Lis, Sahlav, and Shifra Schwartz. "'Nilhamot ba-ba'arut u-be-hergelim nehshalim: Tfisot u praktikot shel ahayot ve-rof'im klapey 'olim ba-'aliyah ha-gdolah shel shnot ha-hamishim." *Israel* 6 (2004): 31–62.
Swirski, Shlomo. *Ha-Hinuch be-Yisra'el: Mahoz ha-maslulim ha-nifradim*. Tel Aviv: Brerot, 1990.
———. *Israel's Oriental Majority*. London: Zed Books, 1989.
Taha, Ibrahim. *The Palestinian Novel: A Communication Study*. London: Routledge/Curzon, 2002.
Tzameret, Tzvi. *Yemey kur ha-hituch: Va'adat hakira 'al hinuch yaledy ha-'olim*. 1950. Repr., Beersheba: Ben Gurion University Press, 1993.
Wasserman, Suzanne. "'Our Alien Neighbors': Coping with the Depression on the Lower East Side." *American Jewish History* 88:2 (2000): 209–32.
Watenpaugh, Keith David. *Bread from Stones: The Middle East and the Making of Modern Humanitarianism*. Berkeley: University of California Press, 2015.
Weiss, Max. "Practicing Sectarianism in Mandate Lebanon: Shi'i Cemeteries, Religious Patrimony and the Everyday Politics of Difference." *Journal of Social History* 43:3 (2010): 707–33.
Weitz, Yahi'am. *Ha-Tza'ad ha-rishon le-kes ha-shilto: Tnu'at ha-Herut, 1949–1955*. Jerusalem: Yad Ben Tzvi, 2007.
White, Thomas. *The Emergence of Minorities in the Middle East: The Politics of Community in French Mandate Syria*. Edinburgh: Edinburgh University Press, 2012.
Yablonka, Hanna. *Survivors of the Holocaust: Israel After the War*. Trans. Ora Cummings. New York: Palgrave Macmillan, 1999.
Ya'qov-Yaron, Avner. *Shalom lakh Baghdad*. Jerusalem: Ha-Machon le-Heker ha-Mahteret ha-Tzionit, 2004.
Yehoshu'a, Ya'aqov. *Reshimotav shel effendi ntul Sachar sofrim*, Tel Aviv: Ha-Kibbutz ha-Me'uhad, 2016.
Yehuda, Tzvi, ed. *Mi-Bavel li-Yerushalim: Kovetz mehakrim u-te'udut 'al ha-tsiyonut ve-ha-'aliyah me-'Iraq*. Tel Aviv: Merkaz Moreshet Yahadut Bavel/Mabat, 1980.

Yeudai, Ori. "Forth from Zion: Jewish Emigration from Palestine and Israel, 1945–1960." Ph.D. diss., University of Chicago, 2013.
Yiftachel, Oren. *Ethnocracy: Land and Identity Politics in Israel/Palestine.* Philadelphia: University of Pennsylvania Press, 2006.
Yiftachel, Oren, and Avinoam Meir, eds. *Ethnic Frontiers and Peripheries: Landscapes of Development and Inequality in Israel.* Boulder: Westview Press, 1998.
Yoseftal, Giora. *Giora Yoseftal: Hayav u-po'alo, Mivhar ktavim, dvarim she-ba'l peh, yomanim, mikhtavim.* Ed. Shalom Warm. Tel Aviv: Mifleget Po'eley Eretz Yisra'el, 1963.
Zimmerman, Moshe. *'Avar germani: Zikaron Yisra'eli.* Tel Aviv: 'Am 'Oved, 2002.
Zolfan, Yossi, and Ogen Goldman. *Va'adat ha-hakira ha-mamlachtit le-'inyan he'almam shel yeladim mi ben 'oley Teyman.* Submitted to the Knesset environment and internal affairs committee, 20/June/2001. Knesset, State of Israel website, www.knesset .gov.il/mmm/data/pdf/m00334.pdf (accessed 29/October/2016).
Zubaida, Sami. "Being an Iraqi and a Jew." In *A Time to Speak Out: Independent Jewish Voices on Israel, and Jewish Identity*, ed. Anne Karpf, Brian Klug, Jacqueline Rose, Barbara Rosenbaum. London: Verso, 2008, 267–77.

INDEX

Note: Page numbers in italic type indicate illustrations.

'Abbas, Avraham, 121, 185, 215
'Abbudi, Aharon, 121
'Abbudi, Ishaq, 40
Acre, 200
'Adas, Shafiq, 24
Adoptions, 53–54, 248n145
Agasi, Eliyahu, 200
Agasi, Tikva, 79–80, 184, 186–87, 193, 194, 200
Age, labor opportunities influenced by, 48
Agriculture: child labor in, 83; communities constructed around, 64–65; employment in, 45–46. *See also* Moshavim
Aharon, Edward, 120
Ahdut ha-'Avoda (Unity of Labor) party, 17, 123–24
Al-Akhbar (The News) [newspaper], 19
'Akrai, Ibrahim (Avraham), 121, 208
Algeria, 198
Aliyah (ascent; pilgrimage to Israel): MAPAI and, 103, 105, 107; meanings of, 5, 65; restrictions on, 137; support for, 105, 123, 124, 133–34, 137, 146
Alliance School, Baghdad, 63
'Amari, Esther, 78
American Jewish Joint Distribution Committee (JDC), 81, 164
Amidar, 60, 61–62, 110, 134
Amir, Elie (Fu'ad), 30, 194; *The Dove Flyer*, 225; *Tarnegol kaparot* (Scapegoat), 99–100
Amisav transit camp, 62, 183
Amutat 'Amram–Hatifat Yaldey Teyman, Mizrah u-Balkan (AMRAM), 53
Al-'Ani, Ge'ula Sehayek, 67, 68, 70–71, 73, 82, 86, 184
Anti-Semitism, 4, 24–25, 175, 189
Arabic language: bilingualism involving, 196; dialects of, 13, 183–84; Iraqi Jews' knowledge and use of, 13, 14–15, 114, 182, 183–84, 193–209; Israeli politicians' use of, 15, 19, 113–14, 117, 197; Israeli state and, 14, 193–209; in kibbutzim, 97; literature in, 206–8, 227; political left and, 204–6; propaganda in, 201; speakers of, 193
Arab-Israeli conflict, 24, 221
Arab-Jewish identity, 193–209, 227
Arbeli Almozlino, Shoshanna, 56–57, 98, 124, 194, 223, 249n162
Arditi, Benjamin, 134
Armenians, 124
Ashkenazi Jews: classification of, 107–8; defined, 237n26; diversity of, 211; Mizrahi Jews' relations with, 11–12, 34–35, 89, 141–42, 145, 181, 211–19; in positions of authority, 22, 31, 34, 97, 111, 116–17, 130, 142, 154, 159, 181, 184–85, 197, 209, 211–13; Sephardi Jews compared to, 5, 209; in transit camps, 159

Association of Aram Naharayim, 171, 188–89, 213
Atrakchi, Shlomo, 160
Avodat dahak (adversity labor), 45–46

Ba'ath party, 199
Babylon, 188–89, 225
Babylonian Talmud, 189
Bader, Yohanan, 134
Badon, 36, 88, 166
Bahr Al-'Ulum, Muhammad Salih, 192
Ballas, Shim'on, 72, 125, 129, 183, 190, 206–7, 216, 227, 229
Bank le-Mashkanta'ot, 106
Bank ha-Po'alim, 106
Bar/bat mitzva, 95–96
Bar Haim, Sha'ul, 201
Bar Moesh, Ishaq, 201
Barzilai, Israel, 35
Basri, 'Ozer, 120
Basri, Yusuf, 25
Bat-Yam, 91
Al-Bayati, 'Abd al-Wahhab, 206
Beds, 54, 69
Be'er Ya'aqov transit camp, 171
Begin, Menachem, 18, 127, 131–32, 134–36, 148, 149, 190, 223
Behar, Almog, 225, 226
Beinin, Joel, 116
Beit Lid transit camp, 61–62, 140, 158
Ben Baruch, David, 96; "Ha-Kombayn asher hushat" (The Ruined Combine), 168
Ben Elisar, Eliyahu, 145
Ben Gurion, David, 16, 21, 26, 39, 68–69, 76, 86, 105, 106, 108, 110, 113–14, 122, 124–25, 126, 133, 140, 148, 154, 164–65, 183, 199
Ben Horin, Shalom, 141
Ben Porat, Mordechai, 63, 114–15
Ben Ya'aqov, Avraham, 140, 189, 213
Ben Yehuda, Y., 94
Ben Yishaq, S., 84
Berman, Avraham, 142, 143

Bernstein, Deborah S., 11
Black Panthers, USA 223
Black Panthers, Israel, 223
Blumberg, Miriam, 76
Bney Brak (city), 168
Bney Brak transit camp, 159
Ha-Boker (newspaper), 137, 171
Border Patrol Brigade, 122, 207
Border settlements, 10, 13, 46, 59, 64, 65, 134, 157
Brotherhood, of all Jews, 100, 124, 162
Bureaucracy: and education, 74; and evacuations of children, 91; and manufacturing, 46, 48; and medical services, 41; and transit camps, 34
Burg, Yosef, 144
Burials, 70

Café Noah, Tel Aviv, 197
Cafés, 51
Cairian Trilogy, 227
Campos, Michelle, 5
Capitalism, 130–31
Care packages, 56
Carmel, Moshe, 28
Carmeli, Eliyahu, 111–12
Center for the Heritage of Babylonian Jewry, 225
Cessariya transit camp, 159
Chetrit, Sami Shalom, 237n23
Childbirth, 52–54, 152
Children, 67–102; adjustment of, to life in Israel, 68; evacuation and sheltering of, 86–94, 152–53; food needs of, 21, 41, 69; hardships of, 68–70; ill, 21, 41–42, 68–69; institutionalization of, 81; Israel's treatment of, 101–2; in kibbutzim, 94–100; kidnapping of, 53–54, 100, 228, 248n145; living conditions of, 10, 21; parents' relations with, 71–73; in transit camps, 68–70, 74–82, 86–94, 88, 210. *See also* Teenagers
Christianity, 72, 200

Citizenship, 7–8, 22, 65, 210–11
Class, 94, 128
Clothing, 69, 96–97
Club of the Friends of Arabic Literature in Israel (later Hebrew-Arabic Literary Club), 206
Clubs, 51
Cohen, Avraham, 190
Cohen, David, 120, 121, 191, 214
Cohen, Eliyahu, 190
Cohen, Esperance, 54, 153, 200, 202
Communication services, in transit camps, 42
Communism: anti-Zionism of, 25; and care of children, 91–92; and common struggle of Palestinians and Iraqi Jews, 204–6; on Israeli discrimination, 216; and literature, 208; MAKI and, 17, 124–30, 190–91; negative attitudes toward, 27, 62, 80, 124
Conga, Mary, 51
Cooking, 54, *88*, *166*
Counselors, 76–77
Crime, 50, 59, 81, 157
Culture, Arab, 196–203, 206–9, 216

Dallal, Naʻim, 175
Dallal, Yaʼir, 225
Dance halls, 82
Darvish, Tikva, 45
Darwish, Mahmud, 206, 227
Darwish, Nuzhat Qassab, 194
Davar (Word) [newspaper], 16, 112–13, 115, 171
Davar li-Yeladim (Davar for Children) [newspaper], 70
David transit camp, 164
Davis, Angela, 223
Dayan, Moshe, 133, 170
DDT, 29–30, 38, 152
Dehumanization, 4, 23, 38
Demonstrations. *See* Protests and riots
Dgania A kibbutz, 95

Dgania B kibbutz, 95
Digital communication, 225–26
Dinur, Ben Zion, 154
Directors, of transit camps, 158, 159, 162
Discrimination: against Arabs, 193–96, 202; class-based, 121, 128–29; denials of, 144–45; against Iraqi Jews, 4, 10–12, 19, 97, 124, 139, 183, 189, 212–19; against Mizrahi Jews, 22, 116–17, 121, 126, 130, 133–34, 138–39, 162, 181, 212–19, 224; against Palestinians, 117, 229; sectarian, 145; against women, 57
Disease and sickness: of children, 41–42, 68–69; in transit camps, 31, 38
Doctors. *See* Medical services
Ha-Dor (The Era) [newspaper], 16, 112
Dori, Latif, 120–23, 204, 210, 211, 214
Drori, Avraham, 134
Druze, 200
Dvir, Danny, 42

Eastern Jews. *See* Mizrahi (Eastern) Jews
Education: of Arab children, 199–200; bureaucracy as factor in, 74; counselors, 76–77; holidays as part of, 77–78; of Iraqi Jews, 116; kibbutzim and, 96; lack of resources for, 74–75, 76; quality of, 45, 73–74, 76, 80–81; resistance related to, 153–54; state investment in, 68; supervisors, 76; teachers, 75–76, 78–80; in transit camps, 73–82, 108, 153–54; of women, 52; Zionism and, 77
Egypt, 223
Egyptian Jews, 193
ʻEini, Shlomo Ben Menachem, 213
Einstein, Albert, 176
Eisenhower, Dwight D., 175
Elias, Arieh, 201, 202
Eliyahu, Elie, 225
Eliyahu, Haim, 175, 177
Eliyahu, Yigal (Naji), 78, 175–77
ʻEmek Hefer transit camp, 173

English language, 96
Eram, Moshe, 118
Eshel, Amir, 15
Eshkol, Levy, 8, 27–28, 33, 107
Espionage, 198–99
Ethiopian Jews, 226
Even Yehuda, 91
Exile, 4
'Ezer, Eliyahu, 125, 153, 190
'Ezer, Latif, 133
'Ezra, Nissim, 189
Ezra, Ovadia, ix
'Ezra, Sadiq, 78

Facebook, 225–26
Factories, 46–47
Family life, 52, 71–73, 95
Faraj, Shlomo, 121
Farewell Baghdad (film), 225
Farhud, 24, 26
Fascism, 136, 190
Fattal, David, 114
Fattal, Salim, 201
Fires, 35, 37, 54, 70
Flags, 67, 78, 211
Food: children's need for, 21, 41, 69; provision of, 42–43, 54; supplies of, 42; in transit camps, 31
Al-Futtuwa (paramilitary organization), 190

Gabai, Shoshanna, 196, 226
Gabbai, 'Ezra, 120, 189
GADNA. *See* Gdudey No'ar
Galilee, 157, 168
Gan Shmu'el kibbutz, 95
Gardens, 50, 54
Gaza, 6
Gdudey No'ar (Youth Brigades; GADNA), 90, 153, 190
Geffen, Y., 80, 176
General Zionist Party. *See* Ha-Tziyonim ha-Klaliyim

German language, 194
Germany, 5, 8, 27, 46
Gil, Y., 90
Ginosar kibbutz, 95
Giva'at Brener kibbutz, 93
Giv'on, Shlomo, 118–19
Goldman, Hannah, 57–58
Goldwasser, Miriam, 57–58
Goods, availability of, 42–44
Govrin, A., 163
Greenberg, Yitzhak, 106
Grinstein, Lea, 98
Grocery stores, 50–51
Growing homes, 61
Al-Gurgi, Filfel, 197
Gurji, Elishava, 78

Haaretz (newspaper), 122, 137, 227
Habibi, Emile, 129, 206
Haddad, 'Ezra, 113
Hadera, 91
Haganna, 153
Haifa, 91, 170, 200
Hakak, Herzl and Balfour, 69–70
Halachic law, 224
Halperin, Liora, 14
Haqiqat al-Amr (Matter of Fact) [newspaper], 200, 239n46
Harosh, Avraham, 217
Hartuv transit camp, 159
Hasbara (propaganda), 8, 108–9, 111–13, 116
Hason, Dan, 140
Havia, Sha'ul, 158
Hayyek, Sha'ul, 163
Hazani, Michael, 166
Health care. *See* Medical services
Hebrew language: Israeli politics and, 14–15, 136, 193–94; in kibbutzim, 97; in school, 79–80, 193–94
Hed ha-Mizrah (The Echo of the East) [newspaper], 140–41
Hektin, Ruth, 83
Herut (Liberty) [newspaper], 131, 136

Herut (Liberty) party: criticisms of, 127, 136, 190; demonstrations organized by, 174; Iraqi Jews and, 131–36, 149; Likud Party derived from, 223; MAPAI's opposition to, 131–33; overview of, 18; publications of, 19; and transit camps, 133–35
Herzfeld, Avraham, 144
Herzl, Theodor, 141
Herzliya, 91
Hesqel, Hesqel, 186
Hesqel, Sasson, 71
Hevrat ha-'Ovdim (Workers Cooperative), 106
Hevre Kadisha, 70
High schools, 80–81
Hillel, Shlomo, 27–28, 114–16, 121, 223
Histadrut: Arab division of, 200; and care of children, 89; criticisms of, 133; defined, 16; goods provided by, 43; Herut and, 135; and housing, 59, 61; Iraqi Jews and, 105–7; labor market controlled by, 47, 106–7, 109, 168–69; and labor regulations, 47; labor training provided by, 45; MAPAI's control of, 105, 109; medical services provided by, 41; teachers union of, 75, 76, 80, 106, 176; and transit camps, 109–10, 114, 167; women's organizations of, 52, 57, 69, 74, 106
Histradrut Workers Councils, 48
Hita'hadut ha-Soharim (Association of Merchants), 43
Hitler, Adolf, 136
Holidays, 44, 77–78, 95–96
Holocaust, 5, 6, 23, 24, 26, 27, 140, 211, 212
Holon (city), 40, 91
Holon transit camp, 70, 90, 120, 169
Holt, Thomas C., 9
Households, gender issues in, 51–59
Housing, 35–37, 59–61, 155–57
Human dust, 23, 140
Human material, 23, 59, 64, 65, 104
Hunger strikes, 153, 171

Huri, Moshe [Musa], 38, 42–43, 125, 129
Al-Huriya (Liberty) [newspaper], 19, 132, 136
Hygiene. *See* Sanitation and hygiene

ICP. *See* Iraqi Communist Party
'Ida, Nuri, 163
Idelson, Bebah, 144
Identity: Arab-Jewish, 193–209, 227; Iraqi-Jewish, 9, 11–13, 181–93, 225–26; Israeli, 77; Mizrahi Jewish, 11, 182, 209–19, 226–29
Ideological seminars, 120
IDF. *See* Israeli Defense Forces
Ijlil transit camp (Herzliya), 120, 164, 167–68
Ila al-Amam (Onward) [newspaper], 19, 117, 191, 214–15
Iltizam theory (social-political engagement of literature), 207
Independence Day, 77–78, 201, 210
Industry, 46–47
Infant and child mortality, 53, 68, 252n4
Intelligence forces, 197–99
Intelligence Service 2, 197–98
Internal Revenue Service, 213
Iran, 198
Iranian Jews, 108
Iraq: emigration from, 23–28; Iraqi Jews' nostalgia for, 12, 181, 186–93, 225–26; Israeli conflicts with, 24, 198–99; Jewish community in, 23–26, 28, 78
Iraqi Communist Party (ICP), 25, 125, 190–91
Iraqi Jews: attitudes toward, 6, 9, 11–12, 14, 22–23, 92–94, 108, 110–12, 129, 183, 212–19; blaming of, 9, 55–56, 85, 93, 110–13, 147, 221; citizenship of, 7–8, 22, 210–11; class status of, 94; experiences of, in Iraq, 13–14; grievances of, 19, 113, 115–16, 117, 121, 126–27, 134, 137–39, 141–48, 160–65; identity of, 9, 11–13, 181–93, 225–26; immigrant experience

of, 4, 7, 9, 13, 23–66; Israeli Palestinians compared to, 7–8, 205–6; Israeli Palestinians' relations with, 15–16, 182, 184–85, 199–200, 203–7, 222; language of, 13, 14–15, 114, 182, 183–84; newspapers serving, 19; nostalgia of, for Iraq, 12, 181, 186–93, 225–26; numbers of, 4, 22; Palestinian refugees compared to, 7–8; patriotism of, 7, 15, 186–87, 210–11; and politics, 11, 14, 16–19, 104–49, 189–93, 212; post-immigration developments concerning, 221–29; primitive character ascribed to, 6, 9, 14, 22, 53, 55, 98, 101, 113, 120, 153, 186, 221; pro-German sentiment in, 24; reasons for migration of, 6; relations of, with other Jews, 183–85; scholarship on, 13; in service of the state, 197–203; state treatment of, 7–8; as teachers, 75–76, 78–80, 199–200; in transit camps, 8–9, 34–35; urban settlement of, 62–63
Irgun (ETZEL, Irgun Tzva'i Le'umi), 18, 131
Irgun Imahot 'Ovdot (Organization of Working Mothers), 52, 69
Israel: discrimination against Jews practiced in, 5, 10, 12, 21–22, 183, 212–19, 227; economic resources of, 5, 8, 23, 27–28; Iraqi war with, 24; languages in, 14–15, 193–209; migration to, 4–6, 10, 19–20, 22–23, 27–32, 65; political parties in, 16–19; resistance by Jews in, 11; sectarianism in, 12; urban settlements in, 62–63
Israeli Civil Rights Association, 227
Israeli Compulsory Education Law, 74
Israeli Defense Forces (IDF): criticisms of, 190; draft for, 75, 85, 153; housing for, 61; literacy training provided by, 81; recruitment by, 32; and sheltering of children, 87, 90–91, 94
Israeli Palestinians. *See* Palestinians in Israel

Al-Istiqlal (Independence) party, 190
Al-Ittihad (The Unity) [newspaper], 19, 125–26, 206, 239n48

Jabotinsky, Eri, 144
Jabotinsky, Ze'ev, 18, 131
Jacobson, Abigail, 5
Al-Jadid (The Innovative) [magazine], 19, 125–26, 191, 206, 239n48
Jaffa, 200, 205
Jerusalem, 5, 34, 48, 64, 65, 146, 170, 200, 223, 224
Jerusalem Post (newspaper), 116
The Jewish Agency for the Land of Israel, 39; and care of children, 81, 87, 89; criticisms of, 133; and education, 74; immigration administered by, 16, 28–29; Iraqi Jews' attitude toward, 114; MAPAI's control of, 105; transit camps administered by, 31–40, 48, 51, 90, 92, 105, 135, 155–58, 161–62, 170–71
Jordan, 6
Jubran, Salim, 200
Juna, Amalia, 55

Kabha, Mustafa, 121
Kafar Qassem, 202
Kafar Qassem massacre, 122–23, 164–65, 207–8
Kafar Yasif, 202
Kahan Commission, 123
Karkur transit camp, 83
Kattav (al-Katib), Shalom, 78, 80, 85–86
Kazablan (film), 77
Kazzaz, David, 183
Keren Kayemet le-Yisra'el (Israeli National Fund; KKL), 61
Ha-Keshet ha-Demokratit ha-Mizrahit (Democratic Mizrahi Rainbow), 226–27
Key money, 60
Kfar 'Ana transit camp, 110, 119, 158, 159, 161, 164–65, 186, 214
Kfar Ata transit camp, 161

INDEX 297

Kfar Gil'adi kibbutz, 95
Kfar Menachem kibbutz, 95
Kfar Nahman transit camp, 83, 169
Kfar Ono transit camp, 90
Kfar Saba transit camp, 62, 83, 173, 195
Kfar-Saba, 91
Khalachi, David, 79
Khalifa, Menashe, 125
Khayriyya transit camp, 35, 51, 74, 75, 82, 83, 90, 91, 92, 110, 118, 119, 122, 123, 154, 158–61, 163, 164, 167, 168, 173
Khazzoom, Aziza, 5
Kibbutzim: annexation of territory by, 33; children and teenagers in, 94–100; dress code in, 96–97; and education, 96; food procured from, 54; holidays in, 95–96; Iraqi Jews refused by, 63; political parties associated with, 258n141; representation of, in Knesset, 259n3; stereotypes and prejudice in, 97–100; vanguard status of, 46, 105
Kidnappings, of babies, 53–54, 100, 228, 248n145
Kitchens, 42–43, 43
Knesset: character of debates in, 144, 148; and children, 69, 82–83, 143–44; and immigration, 3, 142–43; Iraqis in, 115–16; kibbutzim representation in, 259n3; and Mizrahi Jews, 141–48, 223–24; as political forum, 104; political parties in, 17, 135, 137; and public housing, 61; and transit camps, 35, 70, 111, 115, 144, 163, 170
Knesset Plenary, 142, 148
Ha-Kohen, Deborah, 39
Kol ha-'Am (newspaper), 40, 83, 90, 91, 124–27, 170, 175, 191, 205–7, 216
Korean War, 36
Kubba, Muhammad Mahdi, 190
Kubeiba, Yusuf, 121
Kubeiba transit camp, 74
Kupat Holim, 41, 106, 112, 114, 133, 160
Kurdish Jews, 23, 64, 94, 156, 183, 252n196

Kurds, 198–99
Al-Kuwaiti, Da'ud, 196–97, 225
Al-Kuwaiti, Salih, 196–97

Labor: child and teenage, 82–86; demonstrations and strike linked to, 168–69; ideology of, 110; industrial, 46; Iraqi Jews and, 44–51; remuneration for, 46; success/failure in finding, 44–45; in transit camps, 45–48; types of, 45, 245n94; women and, 56–57. *See also* Unemployment
Labor bureaus, 47, 48, 56–57, 72
Labor unions, 106
Labor Zionism, 94–100, 216, 224
La-Merhav (newspaper), 123
Lavie, Shlomo, 144
Lavon, Pinhas, 27, 61, 106
Lavon, Zelig, 61, 111
Lavon Affair, 198
Law of guardianship (*hok ha-hanichut*), 83
Lebanon, 6
Left, political, 116–17, 189, 204–6
Leibovitch, Hannah, 175
Letters. *See* Petitions
Levy, Avraham Salem, 133–34
Levy, Carmela, 78
Levy, Lital, 14
Levy, Shoshana, 184
Libraries, 81
Libyan Jews, 108, 193
Liftshitz, 'Oded, 123
Likud Party, 149, 223, 229
Lissak, Moshe, 44
Literature: about Iraqi Jews, 225; Arabic, 206–8, 227
Local committees, 157–60
Lohamey Herut Yisra'el (Fighters for the Freedom of Israel; LEHI; Stern Gang), 18, 131, 136

Ma'abarot. *See* Transit camps
Maariv (newspaper), 137

Maguri-Cohen, Haim, 134
Mahfuz, Nagib, 187
Ha-Mahlaka le-Ma'abarot u-le-Yishuvey 'Olim (Division of Transit Camps and Settlement of Newcomers), 39
Makdisi, Ussama, 12
MAKI. *See* Miflaga Komunistit Yisra'elit, Al-Hizb al-Shuyu'i al-Isra'ili
Makor Haim transit camp, 52, 65, 69, 146, 160
Mandatory Palestine: administrative structure of, 44, 46; Ashkenazi vs. Sephardi communities in, 5, 209; immigration to, 4, 22–23, 46, 107, 114–15, 138, 222; living conditions in, 5; multilingual nature of, 14–15; politics in, 16, 18
Mani, 'Ezra, 197
Manufacturing, 46–47
MAPAI. *See* Mifleget Po'aley Eretz Yisra'el
MAPAM. *See* Mifleget Po'alim Me'uhedet
Marriage, 52, 57, 145
Ha-Mashbir ha-Merkazi, 43
Ha-Mashbir la-'Oleh, 43–44, 106
Mashiah, Naji, 78
Mas'uda Shemtov Synagogue, Baghdad, 25
Matzliah, Ephraim, 181
Mead, Margaret, 249*n*156
Medical services, 41, 52–53, 244*n*75
Meir, Golda, 8, 26, 90, 103–4, 107, 110, 111, 126, 143–48, 156, 200, 201, 217, 229
Meir, Mina, 27
Meir, Saleh, 136
Meir-Glitzenstein, Esther, 11, 13, 62, 65, 97, 156
Melting pot ideology, 4, 10, 14, 117, 121, 214
Men, social activities of, 51
Mental health, 57–58
Merhavia kibbutz, 96
Mesopotamia, 188
Michael, Sami, 48, 125, 129, 183, 184, 194, 195–96, 198–99, 205, 206, 211, 216–18, 227, 229, 247*n*123, 277*n*88; "Al-Aswad" (The Black), 217; "Hadha abbi" (This Is My Father), 217; "Tabaraka al-rabb" (Praise Be to God), 217; *Trumpet in the Vadi*, 227; *Victoria*, 227

Middle Eastern Jews. *See* Mizrahi (Eastern) Jews

Miflaga Komunistit Yisra'elit, Al-Hizb al-Shuyu'i al-Isra'ili (MAKI): and Arabic language, 204, 206; demonstrations organized by, 169, 174; Iraqi Jews and, 124–30, 189–93; on Israeli discrimination, 189; MAPAI's wiretapping of, 109; newspapers published by, 19; overview of, 17–18; parties criticized by, 125–27, 136; and transit camps, 125

Mifleget ha-Smol Ha Sotzialistit (Socialist Left Party), 17

Mifleget Po'aley Eretz Yisra'el (Party of the Workers of the Land of Israel; MAPAI): background of, 107; criticisms of, 125–26, 137, 142, 216, 223–24, 277*n*88; demonstrations suppressed by, 174; Department for Eastern Communities, 114; electoral campaigns of, 109, 113, 114, 138; employment and housing officials affiliated with, 107; Herut's criticism of, 131–33; and immigration, 103, 105, 185; Iraqi Jews and, 105–16; Jewish Agency and, 39; and labor, 47; overview of, 16; power of, 105–6, 109–10, 116, 131, 167, 177; principles and values of, 117; publications of, 19, 112–14, 116; and transit camps, 50, 62, 105–16, 120, 167

Mifleget Po'alim Me'uhedet (United Workers Party; MAPAM): and Arabic language, 204; and care of children, 92; demonstrations organized by, 169, 174; Department for Eastern Communities, 120; Iraqi Jews and, 117–23, 189–91; on Israeli discrimination, 189, 214; MAKI's criticism of, 126; MAPAI's

wiretapping of, 109; overview of, 17; principles and values of, 117; publications of, 19, 32, 117, 118; and transit camps, 118–20
Migdal-Ashkelon, 91
Migdal Gat, 206
Mikha'il, Murad, 201, 202, 208
Mikunis, Shmu'el, 192
Ministry of Agriculture, 42
Ministry of Education, 69, 74, 75, 76, 116, 176, 194, 202, 228
Ministry of Health, 35, 38, 41, 51, 56, 89, 172
Ministry of Interior, 34, 35, 63, 77–78, 89, 92, 157–58; Absorption Division, 39–40
Ministry of Labor, 40, 47, 52, 89. *See also* Labor bureaus
Ministry of Religious Affairs, 213
Ministry of Trade and Industry, 42
Ministry of Transportation, 89
Ministry of Welfare, 41, 47, 51, 87, 90, 244n76
Al-Mirsad (The Observer) [newspaper], 19, 32, 117, 121, 185, 186, 191, 204, 210, 214, 215, 239n47
Al-Misbah (newspaper), 138
'Al ha-Mishmar (newspaper), 122, 214, 239n47
Mizrahi (Eastern) Jews: Ashkenazi Jews' relations with, 11–12, 34–35, 89, 141–42, 145, 181, 211–19; cultural differences among, 184; dialects of, 183–84; diversity of, 12–13, 209; identity of, 11, 182, 209–19, 226–29; Iraqi Jews' identification with, 11–12, 209–19; Israeli attitude toward, 12–13, 21–22, 27, 97, 108, 118, 121, 122, 209, 212–19, 226–29; labor power of, 44–45; migration experiences of, 13; Palestinians' relations with, 204–5, 229; and politics, 223–25; protests by, 173, 179; resistance of, 237n23; Sephardi Jews in relation to, 237n26. *See also* Sephardi Jews

Moreh, Shmu'el, 202, 208, 225, 227
Moreh-Cohen, Esperance. *See* Cohen, Esperance
Mosadot le-Tipul be-'Olim Nechshalim (Institutions for the Care of Backward Immigrants; MALBEN), 81
Moshavim (cooperative agricultural settlements): annexation of territory by, 33; construction of, for newcomers, 63–65; defined, 33; vanguard status of, 46
Moshavot (townships): annexation of territory by, 33, 59; defined, 33; food procured from, 54; transit camps near, 34, 39, 46–47
Mosheh, Sha'ul, 175
Mossad, 198, 201
Mu'allim, Sami, 79
Mu'allim, Victor, 32, 79, 84, 194–95, 213–14; "Neft be-Ramat Gan" (Oil in Ramat Gan), 84–85
Municipalities: and absorption of transit camps, 63; and administration/service of transit camps, 33, 35, 38–40, 169; attitudes of, toward transit camps, 34, 35; and education, 74
Murad, 'Ezra, 35–37
Murad, Yehezkel (Hesqel), 137
Music, 15, 51, 81, 99, 196–97, 201–2, 225. *See also* Songs, protest
Mussolini, Benito, 136
Mutual help, 30, 50, 55

Nahariyya, 91
Nahlat Yehuda transit camp, 75, 120, 144, 157
Nahon, Ya'aqov, 45
Nahum, Ephraim, 213
Names, 97, 99, 194
Namir, Mordechai, 83, 107, 111, 168–69
Na'or, Lea, 76–77, 89
Naqqash, Samir, 187–88, 193; "Fi Manzil al-khiraq wa'l 'aja'ib" (In the House of

Rags and Wonders), 187–88; "Laylat 'aaraba" (The Night of the Willow), 188
Al-Nashi,' Ibrahim, 185
Nashrat al-Markaz (Central Edition) [newspaper], 137
Nasser, Gamal 'Abd al-, 199, 201
Nathan, David, 135
Nawi, Eliyahu, 201
Negev, 157
Ness Ziona (city), 91
Ness Ziona transit camp, 74, 120
Newcomer camps, 32–33
Newspapers, 19, 112–13, 117, 202
Nicola, Jabra, 206
Al-Nidal (The Struggle) [newspaper], 123–24
1948 War, 5
Nissan, Eliyahu, 213
Ha-No'ar ha-'Oved (youth movement), 76, 96
North African Jews, 13, 100, 108, 129–30, 184, 193, 214, 223, 224
Nuqrat al-Salman prison, 191
Nurses, 55–56, 249n156

'Obadiah, Ibrahim, 208
Olmert, M., 109
Operation Cover for the Winter, 89
Operation Rooftop, 87
Orchestra of the Voice of Israel, 225
Organization of Working Mothers. *See* Irgun Imahot 'Ovdot
Or Yehuda (city), 62–63, 79, 112, 119, 182, 225, 226
Or Yehuda transit camp, 88, 215
Ottoman Palestine: Ashkenazi vs. Sephardi communities in, 5, 209; immigration to, 4, 22–23, 46, 107, 222; politics in, 18; Zionists in, 77

Palestine. *See* Mandatory Palestine; Ottoman Palestine
Palestinian refugees: impact of, on surrounding countries, 6; Iraqi Jews compared to, 7–8; language of, 193, 195–96; property of, 26–27; right of return for, 124
Palestinian national revolt (1936–39), 5
Palestinians in Israel: education of, 199–201; and Histadrut, 200; Iraqi Jews compared to, 7–8, 205–6; Iraqi Jews' relations with, 15–16, 182, 184–85, 199–200, 203–7, 222; language of, 193, 195–96; Mizrahi Jews' relations with, 204–5, 229; strictures on, 179, 182, 199, 229; treatment of, 16
Palestinian villages, Israelization of, 33–34, 64, 200, 222
Pardes Hannah (city), 91
Pardes Hannah newcomers camp, 33, 217
Passover, 95
Passports, 186
Patriotism, 7, 15, 78, 186–87, 210–11, 224
Peck, A., 216
Penn, Alexander, 193
Persitz, Shoshana, 143–44
Petach Tikva (city), 62, 91, 92, 106
Petach Tikva transit camp, 91, 92, 112, 134, 159, 195
Petitions, 160–65, 175–77
Phones, 42
Ha-Po'el ha-Mizrahi party, 39
Police: actions of, 62, 83, 112–13, 140, 155–56, 169, 173; malfeasance and brutality of, 7, 31, 115, 126, 134, 205, 217; in transit camps, 31, 118, 154, 167
Polio, 68, 89
Politics: grievances of Iraqi Jews, 19, 113, 115–16, 117, 121, 126–27, 134, 137–39, 141–48, 160–65; Iraqi Jews and, 11, 14, 16–19, 104–49, 189–93, 212; language as concern of, 14–15; Mizrahi Jews and, 223–25; nature of, 148; opposition parties in, 16–17; parties in, 16–19, 104–41, 148–49; ubiquity of, 104. *See also* Resistance

Preserving the Iraqi Language (Meshamrim et ha-safa ha-'Iraqit), Facebook Group, 226
Professional occupations, 45
Propaganda, Arabic-language, 201. See also *Hasbara*
Prostitution, 59
Protests and riots: breaking up of, 115; over closing of camps, 62; criticisms of, 171; labor-related, 50; over living conditions, 32, 90, 92; locations of, 168–70; MAKI and, 125; by Mizrahi Black Panthers, 223; by non-Iraqis, 173–74; outcomes of, 151–52; over police brutality, 217; political, 114, 178; political party involvement in, 169, 174; as resistance, 165–74; songs accompanying, 154; theatrical character of, 172–73; in Wadi Salib, 129–30, 133, 213; the Wathba, 177–78, 191. See also Resistance
Public housing, 60–61

Al-Qa'ida (newspaper), 191
Al-Qasim, Samih, 206, 227
Qassab, Nuzhat, 200, 201, 211
Qujman, Hesqel, 125
Qujman, Ya'aqub, 32, 190

Rabin, Yitzhak, 8, 94, 224
Race: Iraqi Jews seen through lens of, 6, 121–22; MAKI and, 127–30; MAPAM and, 117, 118, 121–22; Mizrahi Jews seen through lens of, 21–22, 118, 121, 141, 212–14, 226; political left and, 116–17; Sephardim party and, 138–39; sheltering of children affected by, 89–90; in United States, 21–22, 125, 278*n*97
Radio, 201
Rahamum, Eliyahu, 71–72
Ramat Gan, 63, 91–92, 115, 160, 169, 182, 189
Ramat ha-Sharon transit camp, 51, 83, 91, 92, 120, 155, 169, 170, 172, 195

Ramatim, 168
Ramla, 91
Razkan, Uriel, 221
Refael, Sami, 121
Refael, Yitzhak, 145–46
Rehovot transit camp, 74, 78, 92, 136, 156, 171, 172, 173, 179, 216
Rejwan, Nissim, 116, 202
Rejwan, Rahamim, 32; "'Al Gehalim" (On the Burning Coal), 203–4; "On the Road to the Transit Camp," 29–30; *Yeled shovav* (A Naughty Boy), 72–73
Rent, 60
Reparation Agreement, 27
Resistance, 151–79; apathy as, 93; by children and teenagers, 102; education-related, 153–54; forms of, 11, 152, 222; housing-related, 155–57; individual acts of, 152–57; and local committees, 157–60; petitions as tools of, 160–65, 175–77; to political exploitation, 151; public events as form of, 165–74; and Rosenberg executions, 175–77; vandalism as, 167–68. See also Protests and riots
Ringworm disease, 90, 100; radiation treatment against, 100
Riots. See Protests and riots
Rishon le-Zion transit camp, 90, 92, 162–63
Roads, 40, 42, 47
Robeson, Paul, 278*n*97
Robinson, Shira, 7, 78, 200
Roby, Bryan, 11, 121, 151
Rokach, Israel, 126, 145
Rokem, Na'ama, 15
Romanian Jews, 184
Rosenberg, Ethel and Julius, 175–77
Rosh ha-'Ayn transit camp, 159
Rotman, Drora, 1–2
Rozen, Dov, 39–40, 157–58
Rozen, Pinhas, 145
Rozetti, M., 163

Rozin, Orit, 11, 41, 54, 109, 137
Rubin, Hannan, 111, 144, 145, 147, 214
Russian Jews, 226

Sabra and Shatila massacre, 123
Sada al-Ahali (newspaper), 191
Sadiq, Hesqel, 190
Sadiq, Yehudah, 190
Safran, Nesia, 205
Sagi, Kochava, 55
Sahayyek, Edmond, 201
Al-Sa'id, Nuri, 127, 191
Sakiyya transit camp, 74, 83–84, 91, 112, 118, 122, 123, 158–60, 163, 164, 170, 173
Salman, 'Aliza, 163
Salman, Avraham, 175
Salman, David, 121, 167
Salman, Gurjia, 153
Samocha, Shlomo, 143
Sanitation and hygiene, 31, 37–38, 41, 242n53
Sarur, Esther, 121
Sasson, Benjamin Saleh (Salih) Silas, 137–38, 189
Sawt al-'Arab (radio station), 201
Sawt al-Ma'abarot (The Voice of the Transit Camps) [newspaper], 190
Sawt al-Ma'abir (Voice of the Transit Camps) [newspaper], 19, 239n47
Sawt Isra'il bi'l 'Arabiyya (Voice of Israel in Arabic), 201–2
Schwartz, Shifra, 55–56
Sdeh Nahum kibbutz, 95, 98
Second generation Iraqi Jews: educational deficiencies of, 45; employment problems of, 50; identity of, 225; and politics, 223
Second Israel, 32, 118–19, 135, 213
Sectarianism, 12, 115, 145, 214, 229
Secularism, 95, 99
Semah, David, 63, 125, 190, 193, 206–8, 229; "Sawfa ya'udu" (He Shall Return), 207–8; "Al-Wathba al-ula" (The First Wathba), 191–92
Semah, Gurji, 143
Sephardi Federation, 82
Sephardi Jews: Ashkenazi Jews compared to, 5, 209; defined, 237n26; Eastern Jews in relation to, 237n26; and Ha-Sephardim party, 18. *See also* Mizrahi (Eastern) Jews
Ha-Sephardim party: criticisms of, 128; General Zionist party's merger with, 137; Iraqi Jews and, 137–41, 184; overview of, 18; publications of, 140; and race, 138–39
Sex and sexuality, 98–99
Sha'ar ha-'Aliyah, 30–32, 106
Shabat, Reuven, 167
Shabta'i, Gurgi, 142–43
Shabtai, K., 172
Shacks, 36–37, 55, 59–60, 74, 92, 155
Shalgi, Phyllis, 57–58
Shalgi, Re'uven, "The Transit Camps in the Circle of Suffering," 118
Shalom, Saleh (Salih), 25
Shalom, Yona, 155
Shamash, Ibrahim, 215
Shammesh, Eliyahu, 163
Shapira, Moshe, 111, 142–43, 145
Sharoni, Avraham, 197
Sha'shu'a, Salim, 208
Shas Party Hit'ahadut ha-Sfaradim Ha-'Olamit Shomrey Torah (Global Unity of Sephardim Loyal to the Torah), 141, 224–25
Sha'ul, 'Abdallah, 217
Sha'ul, Yosef, 78
Shav, Yitzhak, 142–43
Shawqi, Ahmad, *Majnun Laila*, 202
Sheetrit, Bechor, 59, 115–16, 120–21, 123, 137, 140, 143
Shemesh, Kokhavi, 223
Shenhav, Yehouda, 26, 226–27

Shikun ʿOvdim, 59, 61, 106
Shina, Salman, 138
Shin Bet (General Security Service), 198, 201
Shmuelof, Mati, 225
Shohat, Ella, 11, 154, 227
Shohat, Nir, 201
Ha-Shomer ha-Tzaʿir (MAPAM youth movement), 175
Shva, Shlomo, "The Road of Poverty," 119–20
Shviro, Elihau, 70
Smuggling, 157
Sneh, Moshe, 17, 83, 146, 175–76
Snir, Reuven, 15, 208
Social Aid of the Committee of Iraqi Jews, 159
Social engineering, 8
Socialism: betrayal of ideals of, 100, 110, 119; indoctrination in, 96, 100; Iraqi Jews' unfamiliarity with, 44, 95; in kibbutzim, 95–96; MAPAI and, 16, 110, 116; MAPAM and, 17
Society for Exiled Iraqi-Jewish Academics, 225
Sofer, Yehezkel, 189
Solel Boneh, 59, 77, 106
Somekh, Menashe, 201
Somekh, Sasson, ix-x, 63, 125, 129, 175, 192, 206, 225, 227, 229, 278n97; "Tilka al-qulub" (These Hearts), 207
Songs, protest, 154
Soviet Union, 16, 17
Sprinzak, Yosef, 145, 170
Squatting, 155–56
Stalin, Joseph, 96
Statism, 105
Stoler-Lis, Sahlav, 55–56
Supervisors, educational, 76
Susu, ʿEzra, 3
Swirski, Shlomo, 44
Synagogues, 51

Syria, 6, 223
Syrian Jews, 108

Taʾifiyya (sectarianism), 214
Talpiot transit camp, 47, 52, 55, 65, 69, 70, 112, 118–19, 120, 140, 146, 151, 160
Tamdor, Ora, "In the Transit Camp of Talpiot *Maku* Order," 119
Tasa, Dudu, 225
Teachers, 75–76, 78–80, 199–200
Teʾatron la-Maʿabarot (TELEM), 202
Teenagers: on discrimination, 215–16; education of, 81–82; in kibbutzim, 94–100, 215–16; social activities of, 81–82
Tel Aviv, 35, 48, 63, 81, 87, 168, 170–71, 182, 222, 223, 227
Teneh, David, 107, 165–66
Tents, 35–37, *36*, 155
Teʾoriya u-Bikoret (Theory and Criticism) [journal], 227
Theater, 202
Thugs (biryonim, singular: Biryon), 50, 109, 247n123
Tiberias transit camp, 112, 183
Tira transit camp, 84, 173
Tnuva, 106
Torah, 179
Transit camps (Maʿabarot, singular: Maʿabara): administration of, 16, 38–40, 157–60, 175–77; children in, 68–70, 74–82, 86–94, *88*, 210; closing of, 59, 61–62; components of, 34; concept of, 33; construction of, 32–33, 35; costs of, 33; education in, 73–82, 108, 153–54; ethnic makeup of, 34; labor opportunities in, 45–48; living conditions in, 21, 31, 33, 35–38, 41, 103, 111, 118–19, 143, 144, 159, 161, 186; locations of, 33, 35, 38, 40, 231; market activities in, 51; numbers of residents in, 59; overview of, 8–9; preparation for admittance to, 30–32; quality of state administration

of, 21–22, 103–4, 109–13, 118–20, 134, 161–62; residents leaving, 155–56, *178*; self-rule in, 157–60; women's experience in, 51–59
Transportation, 40–41, 47
Truman, Harry, 125
Tubi, Tawfiq, 122, 127
Tu Bi-Shvat, 77
Turkey, 198
Turkish Jews, 108
Two-state solution, 17
Ha-Tziyonim ha-Klaliyim (General Zionist Party): Iraqi Jews and, 137; MAPAI's wiretapping of, 109; overview of, 18; profit orientation in, 131; Sephardim party's merger with, 137, 138
Ha-Tzofeh (newspaper), 175

Ulysses (intelligence unit), 199
Unemployment, 48, 110, 146–47, 168–69
United States: administrative aid provided by, 42; care packages sent by, 56; economic resources provided by, 8, 46; immigrants from, 60; race relations in, 21–22, 125, 278*n*97

Vandalism, 167–68
Van Leer Institute, 227
Vermin, 38
Vocational schools, 81, 153
Voice of Israel, 181. *See also* Sawt Isra'il bi'l 'Arabiyya

Wadi Salib riots, 129–30, 133, 213
Wages, 48, 135–36
Al-Watan (The Homeland) [newspaper], 19, 113
Water, 37–38, 54, 169–70, 173, 186
Wathba, 177–78, 191
Waya, Salim, 163
Weather, evacuations of children because of, 86–94, 152–53
Weiss, Max, 12

Weizmann, Chaim, 77
Welfare bureaus, 41, 48–49, 71–72, 244*n*76, 247*n*118. *See also* Ministry of Welfare
Wilenska, Esther, 126, 142, 146–47
Wilner, Meir, 122, 128, 148
Women: adolescent and young adult, 57–58; and childbirth, 52–53; criminal activities of, 59; education of, 52; Iraqi education of Arabic, 200–201; in labor market, 56–57; mental health of, 57–58; resistance practiced by, 152; state's blaming of, 55–56; transit camp experience of, 51–59
Workers' councils, 106
Work permits, 46, 47

Ya'ari, Meir, 17
Yad ha-Ma'avir transit camp, 144
Yadin, Yigal, 90
Yad la-Ma'abara (A Hand for the Transit Camp), 41
Yagur kibbutz, 95
Al-Yawm (The Day) [newspaper], 19, 116, 200, 239n46
Yedi'ot Ahronot (newspaper), 137
Yehezkel, Avraham, 195, 215–16
Yehoshu'a, Ya'aqov, 113
Yehuda, Haim, 146
Yemen, 198
Yemenite Jews, 13, 53–54, 100, 108, 144–45, 159, 173, 183–84, 193, 228, 248*n*145
Yiddish, 194, 195
Yishay, Elie, 225
Yishuv (Jews in Palestine before 1948), 5, 6, 93, 113, 118
Yona, Yossi, 226
Yonah, Naji, 143
Yosef, Dov, 110
Yosef, 'Ovadia, 224
Yoseftal, Giora, 39, 89, 90, 92–93, 107, 156, 157, 159, 167

Yosifun, Ze'ev, 202

Zalman, Roger, 158–59
Zamir, Yosef, 136
Zarai, Naji, 142
Zarnuga transit camp, 74, 91, 120, 158, 159
Za'rur, Menashe, 132
Za'rur, Yosef, 41–42

Zilkha, Na'im, 133
Zionism: criticisms of, 190; and early migration to Israel, 4–6, 23, 24–27; and education, 77; indoctrination in, 96, 100, 108–9; Iraqi Jews' relations with, 24–26, 114–15, 161–62; in Israeli state structure, 8; in kibbutzim, 94–100; and labor, 46; liberal, 228–29; and politics, 16

Stanford Studies in Middle Eastern and Islamic Societies and Cultures
Joel Beinin, *editor*
Editorial Board
Asef Bayat, Marilyn Booth, Laurie Brand, Laleh Khalili, Timothy Mitchell, Jillian Schwedler, Rebecca L. Stein, Max Weiss

---

Nahid Siamdoust, *Soundtrack of the Revolution: The Politics of Music in Iran*
2017

Laure Guirguis, *Copts and the Security State: Violence, Coercion, and Sectarianism in Contemporary Egypt*
2016

Michael Farquhar, *Circuits of Faith: Migration, Education, and the Wahhabi Mission*
2016

Gilbert Achcar, *Morbid Symptoms: Relapse in the Arab Uprising*
2016

Jacob Mundy, *Imaginative Geographies of Algerian Violence: Conflict Science, Conflict Management, Antipolitics*
2015

Ilana Feldman, *Police Encounters: Security and Surveillance in Gaza under Egyptian Rule*
2015

Tamir Sorek, *Palestinian Commemoration in Israel: Calendars, Monuments, and Martyrs*
2015

Adi Kuntsman and Rebecca L. Stein, *Digital Militarism: Israel's Occupation in the Social Media Age*
2015

Laurie A. Brand, *Official Stories: Politics and National Narratives in Egypt and Algeria*
2014

Kabir Tambar, *The Reckonings of Pluralism: Citizenship and the Demands of History in Turkey*
2014

Diana Allan, *Refugees of the Revolution: Experiences of Palestinian Exile*
2013

Shira Robinson, *Citizen Strangers: Palestinians and the Birth of Israel's Liberal Settler State*
2013

Joel Beinin and Frédéric Vairel, editors, *Social Movements, Mobilization, and Contestation in the Middle East and North Africa*
2013 (Second Edition), 2011

Ariella Azoulay and Adi Ophir, *The One-State Condition: Occupation and Democracy in Israel/Palestine*
2012

Steven Heydemann and Reinoud Leenders, editors, *Middle East Authoritarianisms: Governance, Contestation, and Regime Resilience in Syria and Iran*
2012

Jonathan Marshall, *The Lebanese Connection: Corruption, Civil War, and the International Drug Traffic*
2012

Joshua Stacher, *Adaptable Autocrats: Regime Power in Egypt and Syria*
2012

Bassam Haddad, *Business Networks in Syria: The Political Economy of Authoritarian Resilience*
2011

Noah Coburn, *Bazaar Politics: Power and Pottery in an Afghan Market Town*
2011

Laura Bier, *Revolutionary Womanhood: Feminisms, Modernity, and the State in Nasser's Egypt*
2011

The authorized representative in the EU for product safety and compliance is:
Mare Nostrum Group
B.V Doelen 72
4831 GR Breda
The Netherlands

www.ingramcontent.com/pod-product-compliance
Lightning Source LLC
Chambersburg PA
CBHW020830160426
43192CB00007B/590